SECOND EDITION	JUNE 2009
EDITOR	MARCIA STEWART
COVER DESIGN	SUSAN PUTNEY
PRODUCTION	MARGARET LIVINGSTON
PROOFREADING	JIM BRUCE
CD-ROM PREPARATION	ELLEN BITTER
AUDIO	RICHARD STIM & ANDREA ROSS
INDEX	BAYSIDE INDEXING
PRINTING	DELTA PRINTING SOLUTIONS, INC.

Portman, Janet.
   Every landlord's guide to finding great tenants / by Janet Portman. -- 2nd ed.
      p. cm.
   Includes bibliographical references and index.
   ISBN-13: 978-1-4133-0864-8 (pbk. : alk. paper)
   ISBN-10: 1-4133-0864-3 (pbk. : alk. paper)
   1. Landlord and tenant--United States--Popular works. 2. Rental housing--United
States--Popular works. I. Title.
   KF590.Z9P667 2009
   346.7304'34--dc22
                              2009011091

Quantity sales: For information on bulk purchases or corporate premium sales, please
contact the Special Sales Department. For academic sales or textbook adoptions, ask
for Academic Sales. 800-955-4775, Nolo, 950 Parker Street, Berkeley, California 94710.

2nd Edition

Every Landlord's Guide to
Finding Great Tenants

By Attorney Janet Portman

Acknowledgments

Talented and generous people at Nolo helped me write this book. Without them, I'd still be toiling away. My thanks go to:

Jake Warner, Nolo's founder, who had the idea for the book and the trust in me that I could write it

Mary Randolph, our Vice President for Editorial, who patiently waited and encouraged me while I did it

Terri Hearsh, book designer *extraordinaire*, who figured out how best to present the material and made countless suggestions for improvements along the way

Rich Stim and Andrea Ross, who directed and produced the audio portions of the CD-ROM; Tamara Traeder, who had the idea in the first place; and Doug Varn for his careful work transferring the forms files to the CD-ROM

Stan Jacobsen, our erstwhile researcher, for helpful materials culled from libraries; Alayna Schroeder, our research editor who took on any request with a smile and did it in lightning speed; and Terry McGinley, our department assistant, who polished off many practical research requests

And by far the greatest thanks go to my editor and friend, Marcia Stewart, who taught me how to be a Nolo editor when I got here many years ago and is still asking the right questions, making the right cuts, moving things around so they make sense, and graciously just fixing it when needed. I still have a lot to learn from you, Marcia.

About the Author

Janet Portman, an attorney and Nolo's Managing Editor, received undergraduate and graduate degrees from Stanford and a law degree from Santa Clara University. She is an expert on landlord-tenant law and the coauthor of *Every Landlord's Legal Guide, Every Tenant's Legal Guide, Renters' Rights, The California Landlord's Law Book: Rights & Responsibilities, California Tenant's Rights, Leases & Rental Agreements,* and *Negotiate the Best Lease for Your Business.* As a practicing attorney, she specialized in criminal defense, conducting trials and preparing and arguing appeals before the Court of Appeal and the California Supreme Court.

Table of Contents

4 How to Advertise Effectively

5 How Should You Show Your Rental?

6 Preparing Your Rental Application and Screening Materials

7 Fielding Initial Questions and Phone Screening

8 Prepare Your Rental for an Open House or Showing

9 Face to Face: Showing the Rental and Negotiating with Prospective Tenants

10 Evaluating Rental Applications

11 Checking Applicants' Credit Reports

12 Checking Landlord, Employer, and Personal References

13 Checking Applicants' Criminal Backgrounds

14 How to Choose and Work With a Tenant-Screening Agency

15 Choosing Your New Tenant

16 How to Reject—What to Say, What to Write

Appendix

How to Use the CD-ROM

Index

Choosing Good Tenants Makes Good Business Sense

Tenants are your most valuable asset, and choosing good ones is the most important decision landlords make. A bad choice can result in damage and lost rent, but even when tenants leave without much fall-out, tenant turnover is expensive: It costs the average landlord two to three times the monthly rent every time tenants change. These costs include lost rental income, advertising and screening costs, and the value of your time to pull together and run the whole tenant selection show.

What separates the properties with stable tenants from those that have revolving residents? Simply put, both sides want the landlord–tenant relationship to continue. The tenants want to stay because the property meets their expectations and needs. And their landlords want to keep them because good tenants pay the rent, take reasonable care of the property, and are considerate neighbors. This book gives you the precise legal, financial, and practical information you need to find and rent to good tenants and keep your rental income steady and safe.

Good tenants do more for your bottom line than minimize your turnover rate. Your business will prosper in other ways, too:

- **You'll avoid costly discrimination complaints and lawsuits.** Discrimination claims are on the rise. You'll need to call your lawyer to reply to even the most-groundless claims— and you know how fast that meter runs.
- **You'll save the time, money, and headaches of terminating a tenancy**

Tenant Turnover Hurts the Bottom Line

Residential renting in the United States is big business—about a third of all housing is rented. How many of these owners are making money? One good indicator is a property's turnover rate. Here are the facts, from the U.S. Census Bureau Property Owners and Managers Survey.

In multifamily properties, only 15% had zero turnover in one year. These landlords are probably making money. A separate 15% had a 20%–49% turnover rate—these owners are struggling, for sure. When it comes to single-family rentals, 23% have tenants who stay more than five years—these owners are certainly enjoying a steady income. On the other hand, a whopping 22% had tenants who stayed one year or less—these owners are having a tough time.

or filing an eviction lawsuit (or fighting a tenant-initiated lawsuit). Nothing can destroy a profitable year more quickly than an eviction lawsuit, even one that you ultimately win. You can narrow the chances of a lawsuit in two ways: by identifying lawsuit-prone and rule-breaking applicants and not renting to them, and by acting within the law yourself, so that you don't invite trouble. Careful tenant selection (and scrupulous adherence to the law) are especially important when you've signed a long-term lease or have rent-controlled property.

- **Other tenants are more likely to stay put.** If you bring a disruptive resident into a multiunit building, you won't be the only one who suffers. Even if you take prompt action against the troublemaker, it will take you a while to get rid of him if he decides to dig in. In the meantime, your good tenants will leave—and your turnover rate will go up. And suppose you live on the rental property yourself? A poor tenant choice will mean that this person is your neighbor, too.

- **You'll have a steady cash flow.** For many landlords, an uninterrupted cash flow is essential to keep up with the mortgage and other operating costs. If you own one or two properties, you can't afford to go without rental income for months at a time.

- **You'll sleep better at night.** It's well known that stress can have negative consequences on your physical and mental health. If you can find and keep residents who don't bother you or cause you worries, you may add years to your life.

What's the law got to do with it?

While common sense and business moxie go a long way towards helping you identify and land good tenants, you can't do it successfully without also knowing the law. Most landlords are aware that they must follow fair housing laws, but few understand that the law permeates every aspect of your tenant selection process. You could read every book on tenant selection on the market and not learn the legal details on issues covered in this book. Here are just a few examples of when the law enters the picture:

- **Showing the place.** The law dictates how you deal with current residents when you want to show their unit (you must follow specific notice requirements) or do a pre-move-out inspection (your entry rights are limited).

- **Renting to illegals.** If you're concerned about this, you need to know how to safely approach illegal resident issues when screening potential tenants.

- **Renting to ex-cons.** Surprisingly, there are legal and practical risks in both running (and not running) a criminal background check, and you may face legal restrictions on using Megan's Law databases.
- **Discrimination you didn't intend.** You may have the purest motives, but if your actions have the effect of discriminating, you're in for trouble (for example, targeted advertising can backfire if you're not careful).
- **Using a credit report.** You can't order a report to go after "skips" unless the original consent form covers this use.
- **Bidding wars for hot rentals.** You need to know how to participate in a bidding war among prospective tenants (but not initiate one).
- **Rejecting applicants.** Depending on the circumstances, you can't just say, "No," or not call back. You must give rejected applicants legally required information—ditto for those you accept with conditions.
- **Responding to disabled applicants.** Federal law is very specific on how you discuss (not negotiate) requests for changes in your policies or rental terms.

Are you surprised by the legal component of what you might have thought were strictly business decisions and actions? You're not alone—the federal government spends millions of dollars catching (and thereby educating) clueless landlords. But you don't have to be one of them.

Is this book for you?

This book is for all landlords who want to run a profitable business, protect their investment, and avoid legal hassles. The millions of landlords who own only a few rentals, and who choose to do most of the work themselves, will find this book especially useful. You'll find advice on off-loading the tasks that are practically difficult to do as an individual (such as performing a multistate criminal background check), but most of the time, each aspect of tenant selection is explained so that you can implement it yourself. Landlords with large rental complexes and leasing agents, or property managers or management companies, will find also useful information in this book, such as how to say and document their decisions in ways that reflect their commitment to following the law.

This book is useful for landlords in all markets, cold or hot. When you're competing for tenants in a cold market, you need to be as aggressive as possible—but you must not be so eager that you cut legal corners or make poor choices. The advice here will keep you safe, while helping you get your place rented as efficiently as possible. The legal edge will also benefit owners in moderate or hot markets, when lots of tenants are vying for your place: Ironically, when faced with a wide choice of applicants, landlords sometimes relax their legal guard and base their choices on factors that are irrelevant or risky.

Finally, two basic assumptions underlie all of the advice in this book:

- **You aren't renting out a dump.** You take care of your property and don't let it get run-down, and you don't tolerate problem tenants. If you conclude that you can't afford basic physical and resident upkeep, or if the property and/or the neighborhood won't support the rent you need, sell the property and invest in something else.
- **You're willing to work hard.** When you invest in stocks, you put the stock certificate in the drawer and monitor the market. That's a lot easier than investing in rental property and holding open houses, checking references, and dealing

with even the best of tenants. If you're uncomfortable interacting with people and dealing with problems, hire a management company to perform every task or sell and invest in something else.

Ten ways to keep your rental business profitable

The blueprint for a profitable rental property business is fairly simple and consists of ten basic principles. This section lays out these principles and other chapters in this book show you how to implement these practices.

① Make a plan

Before you escort a prospect through your rental—and even before writing your ad copy—you need a specific plan

---

Renting to Section 8 Tenants

"Section 8" is a federally run and financed housing assistance program. Private landlords receive two-thirds of the rent from the tenant, but the local housing authority pays the rest. In most states, landlords can choose whether to participate in the program.

If you have property in a low-income area of town, you may find that most of your applicants are Section 8 renters, and you may need to accept them in order to stay in business. Participation in Section 8 has its drawbacks, however. Chapter 2 covers Section 8 in detail.

for getting your place rented. This book provides step-by-step advice on making and following your plan, which has five basic components:

- **Establish the basic terms of the deal.** Decide on the rent, deposit, date available (build in time for repairs and refurbishing), pet policy, number of occupants, length of the rental term (month-to-month or a long-term lease).

- **Set basic requirements for the resident.** Choose a minimum income, number of positive references from employers and current and past landlords, and your criteria for a healthy credit report. Decide whether you'll do criminal background checks on all applicants who make it through earlier, more basic screening. Determine what policies are nonnegotiable and when you're willing to be more flexible.

- **Plan your advertising strategy.** What you'll say in your ad depends heavily on your decisions on your rental terms and resident requirements. Now, *where* will you advertise? To craft a successful strategy, you need to figure out who will be your likely tenant (such as singles, a family, students), as well as the temperature of the market for rentals like yours.

- **Prepare for phone calls and showings by having details of your property at hand (such as the exact size of the bedrooms, neighborhood features) and facts about the competition.** Your preparation should also include getting your place in shape before you show it to prospective tenants, and working around current tenants (if any).

- **Show the unit.** You can do individual tours or hold an open house. This choice will depend heavily on your market and your personal preferences, and will affect how you advertise.

Implementing your plan will put your rental in front of the tenants who are likely to want to live there, and who are the kind of tenants you want. In a word, the plan efficiently moves you from a vacancy to an occupied property. You don't have to spend a ton of money on advertising. You do need to spend some time on planning how and where you'll launch your rental efforts.

② Deal with current tenants fairly and respectfully

Although your mission is to find new tenants, you can't do so without interacting with the set that's still there. You must respect their privacy and follow state laws on showing their home to applicants. This will help you both avoid legal hassles with departing tenants, and show newcomers that you are an upright landlord who follows the law.

③ Comply with fair housing laws

You'll operate at your peril if you don't know and follow federal, state, and local fair housing laws, which should inform your words and deeds at every step of your selection process. Make choices (on where you advertise, what you say, how you screen, and how you choose tenants) based on sound business reasons, devoid of stereotypes or your personal feelings. Unless you can say, "Any reasonable businessperson in this situation would do the same thing," you may be applying preferences or assumptions (about particular races, religions, ethnic origins, and the like) that could get you into legal trouble.

④ Be consistent

Consistently applying your screening and selection criteria is the hallmark of a lawsuit-proof business. Here's why: Suppose you reject an applicant who has insufficient income, but accept another applicant who has the same income. If the rejected applicant is a member of a protected group, he may claim that the rejection was due to his religion, ethnicity, or membership in another legally-protected group. You'll have an upward fight to dispel this claim. The only way to win is to avoid, in the first place, inconsistent application of your tenant-screening and selection criteria and practices. This includes, for

example, showing the unit to all who qualify, accepting applications from every interested applicant, and checking references and credit for all who meet your business-based standards.

⑤ Maintain some flexibility, especially with disabled tenants

Wouldn't you know it—the law tells you to be consistent in one sentence, yet flexible in the next. Yes, it's true—you must be willing to vary your criteria and standards for disabled tenants and applicants when necessary. That will happen when the variation is required in order for the disabled person to live comfortably and safely at your property, and when the change will not be unduly burdensome for you. Chapter 2 explains these rules in detail.

Flexibility is also in order when dealing with first-time renters. There's a lot of them out there—28% of all tenants are younger than 30 years old. (U.S. Census Bureau's American Housing Survey for 2007.) Logically, these people would never be able to rent if the lack of a current or prior landlord reference automatically eliminates them. There's nothing wrong with substituting equivalent criteria for first-timers (such as accepting nonlandlord references), as long as you apply the same approach to *all* first-time renters.

6 Do thorough screening and rank your applicants

Always take the time to do the checking necessary to assure yourself that this person is a good business risk. Nothing will be gained by hastily choosing a tenant. No matter how certain you are that your instincts will not let you down, or that you've learned enough after looking at a credit report (but before talking to references), you cannot afford to take a chance by renting to someone who has a skeleton in a closet that you didn't open. First, it will cost you time, money, and endless aggravation to get that tenant out; and second, if you short-cut your process for this tenant but not for another (who you reject, and who happens to belong to a protected group), that disappointed tenant might have grounds for a fair housing claim.

If an applicant is really as solid as you think, you'll lose nothing by completing our five-step screening process, which is depicted in the visual below. (Chapters 7 through 13 provide details on each step of the screening process.) You can reject an applicant at any stage, as long as your rejection is based on solid business reasons, and is consistently applied. Every time you complete a step, you'll rank the acceptable applications in order of attractiveness. Often, you'll need to rerank when you learn more at the next step.

Understand the Complications of Using a Tenant as Your Manager

Owners of multiunit buildings often hire tenant-managers (some state laws require that a manager live on site for larger properties), and many small property owners who live far away choose a tenant to handle day-to-day issues for them. When screening applicants for the tenant-manager position, understand that you are now an employer as well as a landlord. To avoid legal problems, you must follow employment law basics, understand the tax issues involved, and clarify the role of the tenant-manager. In particular, managers need to be as well-versed in fair housing law as you are, because their mistakes will land at your door.

Five Steps for Successfully Screening New Tenants

To identify the best applicant for your rental, follow these steps. At the end, you'll have your pick.

Step One: Prescreen on the phone, unless you decide to advertise and host an open house for all who want to come.

Step Two: Screen using an applicant's answers on your rental application, by looking for an acceptable number of occupants, minimum income, no eviction history, and the like. Rank your applicants.

Step Three: Screen by evaluating the credit report, and rerank if needed.

Step Four: Screen using third-party information, from current and past landlords and employers, which should corroborate information given by the applicant in the application (if you learn more, rerank).

Step Five: Perform additional screening (such as a criminal background check) on your top applicant(s).

7 Be careful what you say

Protecting your bottom line involves not only what you do (ordering a credit report for every top candidate who has made it past the application review, for example), but what you say along the way—from the first phone call (when tenants inquire about the rental and you do some prescreening) to the last (accepting or rejecting tenants). Ill-chosen words can precipitate a fair housing lawsuit, commit you to promises that you never intended, or sow confusion leading to problems.

Be sure you know how to get the information you need—but avoid fair housing shoals along the way. For example, it's fine to ask how many people will be living in the rental unit to make sure they meet your reasonable occupancy limit, but asking about the ages and sex of the occupants, and whether they are married, may be an invitation to a lawsuit.

Though it's tempting, don't puff or overhype your rental. It's fine to be enthusiastic and extol the benefits of your property, and it's necessary in competitive markets. But promising things that are only remote possibilities (such as that a parking space will open up soon) may only lead to trouble. The bottom line: Deliver what you promise.

Finally, clearly explain to tenants your key terms, policies, and expectations, and do so early in the screening process. You'll avoid wasting time on inappropriate tenants or tenants who want something else (such as a property that allows pets).

Throughout this book, you'll see scripts with typical applicant questions that landlords encounter along the renting way. Matched to the question is a suggested way of answering—one that's accurate and legally safe—and an example of how *not* to say it, along with an explanation of why. On the CD-ROM, you'll find audio clips of exchanges between landlords and applicants illustrating similar common conversations.

8 Put it in writing and keep good records

There's no way you could get through this list, written by a lawyer, without encountering that supremely lawyer-like admonition, "Get it in writing!" Why is this important? A paper trail accomplishes two desired ends:

- **First, by using the worksheets, letters, and checklists in this book, you'll be steered towards the legally safe path.** If you follow the directions, it's unlikely that you'll stray. For example, a letter informing an applicant that he's been rejected due to information on a credit report needs to include specific legal information—and should avoid certain topics. By using the adverse action letter included on the book's CD-ROM, and entering only the

information relevant to the applicant, you're covered.

- **Second, written documents are hard evidence that you followed the law.** If you're ever challenged, you won't need to rely on "he said, I said" evidence. Instead, your filing cabinet full of completed letters and notes of conversations will be admissible evidence in your favor. In particular, the Tenant Information Sheet, a master document for each applicant where you record relevant information you find along the screening path, will show your methodical process and business-like conclusions. Even the files for applicants who dropped out will be helpful evidence, for they will establish that you regularly do business in a legally compliant way.

The chapters in this book that involve step-by-step decision making, and communications with applicants and tenants, have corresponding forms that help you accomplish the tasks. At the start of each chapter, you'll see a sidebar "Landlord's Forms Library," which lists them and gives a brief description of each along with record-keeping advice.

9 Screen all occupants and roommates

When you're renting a unit to more than one tenant, whether it's a husband and wife or a group of unrelated roommates,

Top Ten Good Tenant Criteria

Your rental plan involves developing and applying standards that you can legally and safely use to weed out poor risks. Here's a quick overview of top tenant-screening and selection criteria; you'll find all the details in later chapters, including advice on when it makes business and legal sense to be flexible on some of these issues:

1 Ability to meet your basic rental terms, such as number of occupants, rental term, and pet policy

2 Sufficient income to pay the rent (the industry standard is a monthly gross income that is triple the monthly rent)

3 Satisfactory credit record, in terms of the applicant's debt level and bill-paying history

4 Credit score that reflects a strong likelihood that this applicant will pay the rent on time every month

5 Positive references from other landlords (attesting to the applicant's history of paying rent on time and respect for property and other tenants)

6 Positive reference from the current employer, describing the applicant's ability to get along with coworkers and supervisors

7 Clean rental record (no recent terminations or evictions)

8 History of limited involvement with lawsuits (no history of initiating multiple, groundless lawsuits)

9 Clean criminal record or, at least, one that doesn't lead you to conclude that the applicant is a direct and current threat to persons or property, and

10 Complete and accurate rental application, including addresses of past residences and answers that are corroborated by your independent screening.

you may be tempted to screen only one (or two) of the applicants. Or, when an existing tenant wants to bring in a replacement roommate or add a roommate, you may skip the screening, counting on the steadiness of your existing tenant. Failing to thoroughly screen everyone who will live in your rental is a mistake for two reasons:

- **First, you're potentially depriving yourself of a source of the rent.** Any person who lives on the property can be expected to pay the full rent (how the roommates share the rent is up to them, not you). Practically speaking, you won't often insist that each roommate be able to shoulder the entire rent, since people live together precisely in order to share expenses. But if you don't know anything about a tenant's finances, you're limiting yourself to the residents whom you have screened. Suppose the screened resident falls on hard times, and his unscreened roommate is unemployed and broke? You have no choice but to terminate the tenancy of both of them. Far better to determine at the outset that the second resident is at least as solvent as the original tenant.
- **Second, an unscreened tenant imperils the tenancy in other matters besides the rent.** If the unscreened tenant causes problems and leaves, or is asked to leave by you, that will be the end of the tenancy for everyone (unless existing tenants

can cover the rent or come up with a suitable replacement). Now you've got another vacancy. No matter how earnestly your existing tenants vouch for the newcomer, nothing will be lost by checking him or her out.

⑩ Get professional help or advice when you need it

Though there's a lot you can do yourself, it's the wise person who knows when to call for reinforcements. In particular, you may want the advice of a local landlords' association for help on issues that have practical solutions known by experienced landlords (if you've decided to use a tenant-screening firm, an association may know which outfits deliver the most accurate information, for instance). You may want to consult with a local attorney who's well versed in landlord-tenant law if you're unclear on how to implement a particular state law or local ordinance. And, certainly, if you're sued, you'll want to engage an attorney for all but the most minor small claims court matters.

How to use the Landlord's Forms Library

This book includes over 40 forms— worksheets, letters, and checklists— designed to help you organize your thoughts and actions and record your conclusions (or send communications) in a legally safe manner. Your Rental Kit, for example, includes the forms that you'll give to applicants who want to fill out your rental application. You'll find a handy list at the start of each chapter, with filled-in samples of each form in the text and copies on the CD-ROM included with this book.

Each form appears on the CD-ROM in RTF format, which you can edit and fill in using the word processor on your computer. You can also save each completed form to your hard drive. The RTF file format allows you to adapt the forms to your own situation. You can add or delete language, adjust margins, and print on your own letterhead.

A few tips on using the forms on the CD-ROM:

- Always review the sample form and instructions in the text.
- You can edit the forms according to your specific situation, but if you make major substantive changes, particularly to letters sent to applicants and tenants, it's a good idea to have your lawyer review them.
- When modifying the forms, delete bracketed and italicized prompts next to blank lines (such as "[*tenant*]" at the beginning of a letter), and just type in the information that's called for.
- If you add a lot of material, you will probably have to work with the margins and layout to make the form fit nicely on your sheet.

Be sure to sign and date every letter, and keep copies of each form for your records. (The icon at the end of each Landlord's Forms Library sidebar tells you how.) If you communicate via email, consider printing a hard copy or, if you're averse to using paper, be sure that your hard drive is backed up regularly.

Finally, your careful documentation of rental decisions and communications needs to be organized and stored. Some documents you'll hope never to need to look at again (like letters to rejected applicants), but others will be useful in the future when it's time to re-rent. For example, having asked prospects to note on their applications how they heard about your vacancy, you'll learn what advertising methods reached the most people. When you look at the pool of *qualified* applicants, you'll learn further which methods reached the *most qualified* applicants. This information will guide you the next time this unit becomes vacant—and you'll want to have it at your fingertips. Set up a record-keeping system for filing your papers like that described in the next section, or devise one that works for you.

Why good record keeping is so important—and how to do it

Organize the paperwork generated by your renting efforts by property. For example, if you own one duplex, you'll have two main sets of files, perhaps separated into filing drawers (one for each rental). Follow this sequence every time you re-rent.

Make a new marketing folder every time you begin re-renting efforts

For example, suppose one half of your duplex at 123A First Street becomes vacant and you begin your renting efforts in January 20xx. In your cabinet drawer for that property, you'll start a new hanging file, "January 20xx Tenant Search." You'll put the worksheets, ad copy, and all the other forms you use from this book in that file (using folders as needed) as you advertise and show that rental.

Create a file for applications you receive for this property

Continuing the above example, label another hanging file "January 20xx

Applications." Here, for every applicant, you'll paper clip together the Tenant Information Sheet (a master document where you record contact information for the applicant and make notes of conversations, meetings, and results of each screening step), the rental application, the credit report and your review, and any other papers associated with evaluating this prospect. The final paper will be your acceptance (or conditional acceptance) letter, or a rejection letter (for those to whom you must send written rejections). If you find that this file is getting too big (perhaps you're evaluating several prospects), you can make folders for each, as shown in the illustration below (stagger the file tabs so that when you look at the lineup of files, it's clear that all of them relate to the same renting effort). If you're considering an application from several proposed roommates, clip each roommate's rental application, credit

---

Worksheets and Letters May Affect Current Tenants, Too

Some of the worksheets and forms in this book will be relevant to your current tenants, too. For example, you'll want to inspect occupied units to determine how much work needs to be done before the next batch of tenants moves in—this will affect your start date for the new tenancy. Your inspection request should go into the file for these tenants, as well as any letters announcing a tenant referral program, and your pre- and post-open house checklist, which will document the condition of an occupied unit before and after a property showing. When forms, checklists, and letters affect current tenants, be sure to make copies for their files, as well as for the property's marketing file and applicants' files.

report, and so on together, and put all of these bundles together in one file (labeled "John Anderson et al" or something similar).

Make a file for your chosen tenants

Label this with the names of the tenants and when their tenancy began, such as, "John and Mary Jones, March 20xx." You can move the Jones application materials into this file, so that information they supplied on the Tenant Information Sheet (such as an emergency contact) is easily accessible. Following the application documents, you'll add the lease or rental agreement, a checklist documenting the condition of the property prior to their moving in, and so on. This file will eventually include any letters or notices you've sent each other, amendments to the rental document, and requests for repairs and will end with the end-of-tenancy walk-through that you should do in order to fairly assess any damage or excessive wear and tear (hopefully, it will not end with your termination notice!).

How long should you keep these files? The Landlord's Forms Library at the start of each chapter recommends how long to keep different forms. To defend against a fair housing claim, you'll need them for three years at least, and it's wise to keep them longer. However, you'll need to follow special procedures when it comes to keeping credit reports, as explained in Chapter 11.

Rental Documents Filing System

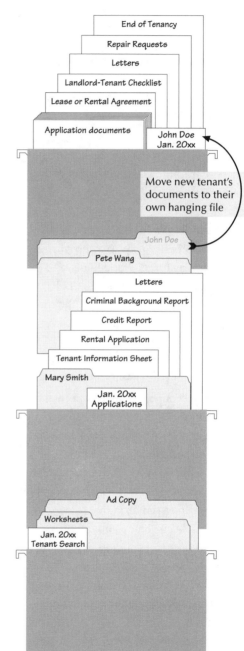

Icons used in this book

Although much of the advice in this book is built around legal rules and safe practices, you're not going to feel like you just entered law school—or the law library. Frankly, the law you need to understand and apply isn't that complicated. Nor is its presentation in this book. Various sidebars and icons set out the basics, making it easy to capture the main ideas with a quick read.

 Landlord's Forms Library. Every chapter begins with a short list of accompanying forms, worksheets, and letters, which you'll find on the CD-ROM. The chapter explains how to use the form and provides filled-in samples.

This icon at the end of the Landlord's Forms Library sidebar suggests where to file your completed paperwork, and how it can be useful in the future.

The Law You Need to Know. Each chapter tells you at the start which laws you need to be aware of. For example, when showing a rental, in most states, you must give current occupants state-mandated notice of your intent to enter.

Before You .... Every chapter begins by highlighting the recommenda-

tions in previous chapters that will prepare you for the tasks at hand. Before advertising, for example, you'll want to make sure current tenants are aware of your plans and as cooperative as you can expect.

 This icon accompanies suggested ways to write, or document, a decision.

 This icon accompanies suggested ways to answer a question or say what you mean or have decided.

This asks you to slow down and consider possible pitfalls and red flags, such as seriously negative information about the applicant.

This icon alerts you to a practical tip or good idea.

 The form discussed in the text is on the forms CD-ROM included with this book.

Take Ten Minutes. Most chapters end with a checklist of things to think about or do that captures what you've learned and done so far. For instance, when wrapping up a current tenancy, you'll be reminded to get a forwarding address for the old tenant and review your state's laws on returning security deposits.

How to Find the Law on Your Own

You may want to read the laws referred to in this book yourself, or you may need to look at local laws, which aren't reproduced here. Here's how to do it.

Federal and state laws. Go to www.nolo.com/legal-research. You'll see several articles that will orient you to the world of legal research, including tips on how to read a statute and how to make sure it's up to date. To access state laws, click the State Laws link, and choose your state. You'll go to the site maintained by your state, with search boxes allowing you to enter the citation of the law you want to read. Clicking "Federal Laws" takes you to federal laws. The Nolo website also has a chart with key landlord-tenant state laws.

Local law. State and Local Government on the Net (www.statelocal government.net) is a great site for finding local law. The Municipal Code Corporation (www.municode.com) is also helpful. You may also be able to go directly to your city or county website. Most use one of the following formats:

- County: www.co.<county name>.<state postal code>.us, as in: www.co.marin.ca.us, or
- City: www.ci.<city name>.<state postal code>.us, as in: www.ci.berkeley.ca.us.

Once you're at the local website, look for links such as city codes, local ordinances, and municipal codes. You'll usually be able to search by keyword or by browsing a table of contents.

Every Landlord's Legal Guide and Other Nolo Resources

Choosing the right tenant is the first step towards a profitable business. Now, you have to keep things moving smoothly and legally. Check out these Nolo products to help you along the way:

- *Every Landlord's Legal Guide*, a 50-state book with CD-ROM, provides all the information and forms you need, from the lease or rental agreement to the documents you'll use at the end of the tenancy.
- California landlords will appreciate *The California Landlord's Law Book: Rights & Responsibilities* and *The California Landlord's Law Book: Evictions*, which provide detailed information and forms for California landlords.
- The Nolo website, www.nolo.com, has lots of free information of interest to landlords. On the home page, choose Property & Money, then Landlords & Property Management.

Complying With Discrimination Laws

No matter the size of your rental operation—whether you live in a duplex and rent out the second unit or operate a multifamily apartment house across town—you need to understand the basic rules prohibiting discrimination in residential renting. If you don't follow the law, you risk expensive lawsuits and crushing penalties. According to the National Fair Housing Alliance, just over 27,000 complaints and lawsuits alleging discrimination were filed in 2007. That's about 75 per day. Here's how you can avoid being one of these statistics.

Who's protected by discrimination laws? Federal, state, and local laws prohibit discrimination against only certain groups of people—known as "protected categories" in legalese. Race and religion are each a protected category—that is, it's illegal to discriminate against someone simply because they are African American or Muslim. But some rules may surprise you—for example, you also can't discriminate based on a person's age, or because someone once (but no longer) used illegal drugs.

You might be tempted to conclude that to avoid discrimination problems, you just need to be extra cautious around members of protected groups—after all, they're the only ones who can successfully sue you. This would be a shortsighted conclusion, however, for at least two reasons:

- **It's not always obvious who's a member of a protected class.** You may have had no idea that someone you rejected was of a certain ethnicity, but if that person decides to sue, you'll be on the defensive.
- **Anyone can file a complaint.** HUD makes it easy—their complaint form is online. All someone needs to do is fill it in and hit "Submit." Dealing with a complaint will be time-consuming, even if it's dismissed.
- **It's not hard to file a lawsuit.** Applicants can bypass the HUD complaint process and go right to court. All it takes is a willing lawyer. Even litigation that you ultimately win will be very expensive and draining.

The lesson is clear: Don't spend your time trying to figure out whether an applicant is in a protected class and can sue you. Assume everyone is protected, then develop business-like criteria for selecting tenants and apply them to everyone in the same way. Make your decisions based on solid business reasons—such as the applicant's ability to pay the rent—not personal preferences. And document your legal reasons for not renting to a prospective tenant. For example, if you regularly reject tenants with poor bill-paying histories, and have records to back this up, you'll be well-positioned to defend yourself against a discrimination claim brought by an applicant who happened to be in a protected category, but who also had poor credit.

Relying on business principles to guide your tenant selection isn't just about lawsuit protection. You'll end up with the best tenant, too, because instead of following hunches or relying on stereotypes, you'll be using multiple tools that are proven winners when it comes to weeding out the bad risks. Your personal preferences or hunches are no match for the total picture of the applicant that will emerge after you've analyzed the rental application, credit report, and reference interviews.

Fair housing complaints are numerous and costly

The National Fair Housing Alliance tracks the number of discrimination complaints filed each year. In 2007, the highest percentage of housing discrimination complaints (cases brought to court or administrative agencies) was filed by persons with disabilities (49%). 23% were based on race; 14% on family status, 9% on the basis of national origin, and 3% each on the basis of sex and religion.

Landlords who violate fair housing laws can be brought to task—in a court of law or before an administrative agency—in one of two ways. An applicant or tenant may complain to a governmental agency, a private fair housing watchdog group, or a private lawyer who may decide to pursue the matter on behalf of the individual.

The Law You Need to Know

Many landlords think that anti-discrimination laws apply only at the point of choosing tenants. This isn't so—they apply throughout the tenancy and prevent you from:

- advertising or making any statement that indicates a preference (or aversion towards) a member of a protected class, whether intentional or not (see Chapter 4 for advice on writing legal ad copy, and Chapter 7 for tips on how to handle phone screening)
- refusing to rent to members of a protected group, falsely denying that a rental unit is available, or setting more restrictive standards or conditions (such as requiring a higher security deposit or a cosigner)
- during the tenancy, providing different services or facilities, and
- terminating the tenancy based on the tenant's membership in a protected class.

An individual who suspects discrimination may file a complaint with HUD or a state or local fair housing agency, or sue you in federal or state court.

Or, a fair housing organization may send "testers" to various rental properties; these people pose as applicants and document the landlords' responses. (See "How Fair Housing Groups Uncover Discrimination," below.) If the organization concludes that the landlord is discriminating, it files a complaint or a lawsuit on behalf of the tester or even the organization itself. Monetary awards against landlords can run to tens of thousands of dollars. As an added insult, landlords can't count on their insurance for defense and coverage

—for all sorts of reasons too lawyerly to recount here, many policies won't apply if you're accused of discrimination. Fortunately, it's possible to avoid the morass of legal liability for discrimination by adopting tenant-screening policies that don't discriminate, and applying them evenhandedly.

⚠ Get expert legal help to defend a housing discrimination claim. Landlords who face discrimination complaints, even frivolous ones, should consult

---

Judges Get Creative

The judges who hear fair housing complaints can impose a host of penalties or negative consequences on losing landlords. Here's a sampling:

- requiring the landlord to spend hundreds of hours in community service
- requiring the use of a professional real estate agency in future rental endeavors
- making the landlord offer the rental to the wronged applicant
- directing the landlord to pay thousands of dollars to cover the cost of fair housing testers' lawyers and lawsuits
- imposing many hours of fair housing training
- requiring the landlord to advertise in particular media
- releasing tenants who lost in court from the court judgment for unpaid rent
- requiring the landlord to establish an escrow account to pay for retrofits for disabled tenants
- insisting on a letter of apology from the landlord to tenants or applicants
- paying tenant moving expenses and giving months of free rent
- ordering thousands of dollars to compensate victorious applicants and tenants for their pain and suffering and humiliation, and
- imposing thousands of dollars as punitive damages (money meant to penalize the landlord).

a lawyer with experience defending against discrimination claims. This book does not cover litigation and cannot guide you through the often fractious and lengthy process.

Legal discrimination: Valid reasons for rejecting applicants

As a landlord, you can have discriminating tastes, as long as your selection criteria are legal ones, based on solid business reasons, not personal preferences. If you turn down an applicant whom any reasonable landlord would say is a poor business risk, you're on safe ground.

Here's an overview of discriminating criteria you may legally and safely use to weed out poor risks. Later chapters explain in detail how to set and apply screening and selection criteria for applicants' income, references, and the like.

How Fair Housing Groups Uncover Discrimination

Landlords who turn away prospective tenants on the basis of race, ethnic background, or other group characteristics obviously never come out and admit what they're doing. Commonly, a landlord falsely tells a person who's a member of a racial minority that no rentals are available, or that the prospective tenant's income and credit history aren't good enough—or, based on "linguistic profiling," the landlord just never returns a call from someone with an accent. From a legal point of view, these can be dangerous—and potentially expensive—tactics. Here's why.

Both HUD and private fair housing groups are adept at uncovering these discriminatory practices by having "testers" apply to landlords for vacant housing. Typically, a tester who is African American or Hispanic will respond to an ad or fill out a rental application, listing certain occupational, income, and credit information. Then, a white tester will call or apply for the same housing, listing information very similar to—or sometimes not as good as—that given by the minority applicant.

A landlord who returns calls to a white tester or offers to rent to a white tester, and ignores or rejects—without valid reason—a minority applicant who has the same (or better) qualifications, is very likely to be found to be guilty of discrimination. Such incidents have resulted in many hefty lawsuit settlements.

Poor credit record

For every person who has passed your first-level screening review, you'll want to pull a credit report. This report will give you valuable information, including the applicant's debt level, bill-paying history, and history of credit collection efforts. It will help you answer the question, "What does this report tell me about whether this applicant is likely to pay the rent on time and otherwise live up to financial obligations?" If you have developed standards against which you measure the applicant's credit history—and importantly, if you apply these standards consistently, to every applicant—you're on solid ground to reject those who fail your test. Chapter 11 explains credit reports in detail.

Insufficient income to pay the rent

You want tenants who can afford the rent. Applying this test is often beside the point after you've looked at the credit report—for example, an applicant with huge debt and poor bill-paying habits may be eliminated on those grounds alone, regardless of how much the person makes. However, there may be other applicants who have excellent debt and payment histories but who have, nevertheless, applied for a rental that would consume half their income. If you have developed a reasonable income requirement (such as a monthly gross income that is triple the monthly rent), and apply it to all applicants, no one will fault you for rejecting applicants who cannot match it.

⚠ **You may want to relax your income requirement if other rent sources are available and stable.** For example, a disabled person who offers a cosigner should not be automatically rejected because you choose not to deal with cosigners. The same lesson applies when renting to students who are supported by their parents, and to applicants who receive public assistance (many states require you to include these amounts when figuring the applicant's income). Chapter 10 explains how to be flexible in these types of situations.

Negative references from prior landlords

An applicant with a history of successful, hassle-free tenancies is probably your dream tenant. Barring any unforeseen developments, such as a job loss, major illness, or a substance abuse problem, you can expect more of the same.

The tricky aspect of evaluating information from former landlords is that it's often anecdotal and, for that reason, hard to reduce to a "thumbs up/thumbs down" form. For example, it's easy to decide that three or more instances of late rent will disqualify an applicant; it's harder to work with a landlord who says, "Well, he was always so difficult to deal with!" Even if you get the details, how do you reduce them to a form that allows you to say, "This applicant is likely to cause too much trouble—this one's out of the running." Chapter 12 helps you devise a system of evaluating and using "soft" information in a consistent way.

Negative references from employers

An employee's behavior is usually consistent with that person's actions as a tenant. Think about it—every quality you look for in a tenant is one that an employer wants; and every negative mark in a personnel file is likely to have its counterpart in your file, too. Tardiness and unfinished projects in the workplace spell late rent for you; inability to get along with coworkers equals difficulty with neighbors; problems with supervisors points towards problems with you or your manager. If an applicant is a problem employee, that person will most likely become a problem tenant. You're on solid ground to reject on this basis. Chapter 12 gives you tips on how to elicit the information you'll need from employers.

Prior evictions

You can legally reject any applicant who has been evicted, and many landlords use this as the make-or-break test for everyone. As unfair as it may seem to many, you can even reject those who won their eviction lawsuit, or those who had the case dismissed (even by the landlord) prior to trial. Successful defendants in eviction lawsuits (let alone those who lose) are not a protected class.

Whether it makes business sense to reject all applicants with an eviction history, however old, is another matter. Many professionals apply a "washout" rule of two or three years. You may also want to think about whether it makes sense to reject applicants who were evicted by banks or other new owners after their landlord allowed the property to go into foreclosure (in Minnesota, records of such evictions are sealed by law). Chapter 10 examines this issue more closely.

History of certain civil lawsuits

An applicant's credit report (or the report from a tenant-screening agency) will often note whether the person has been involved in civil suits, such as those involving child custody, divorce, personal injury suits, and so on. Because litigants in civil suits aren't a protected class, you could theoretically decide to categorically reject these applicants, perhaps on the belief that people who are plaintiffs will be aggressive, demanding tenants, and defendants in lawsuits are likely to be irresponsible residents. But would that be wise? Probably not—if the applicant is truly a poor risk, you'll see evidence of this in other areas, and will be able to reject based on a full picture of the applicant. Chapter 10 gives you more advice on how to evaluate a person's civil lawsuit record.

Criminal record

Most landlords are understandably hesitant to rent to anyone with a criminal record. With one notable exception, explained below, you are legally free to reject, and would be wise to do so when you see recent convictions for crimes involving dishonesty and violent behavior that lead you to conclude that this person currently poses a direct threat to people or property. See Chapter 10 for a detailed discussion of how to evaluate a self-reported criminal record, and Chapter 13 on how to get more information by ordering a criminal background report.

⚠ **You may not categorically reject applicants who have convictions for past drug use.** The Fair Housing Amendments Act, explained below, classifies past drug addiction as a disability, even when that addiction resulted in a criminal conviction. Persons with convictions for drug sale or manufacture (as distinct from convictions for possession of drugs for personal use) are not protected, however, nor are people who currently use illegal substances.

The hot button these days is landlords' use of Megan's Law databases to check for registered sexual offenders. ("Megan's Law" refers to the laws in every state that require states to maintain a database of

convicted sexual offenders who must register with law enforcement where they live.) Though registered offenders are hardly members of a protected class, landlords' use of these databases is not without legal risks. Chapter 13 gives detailed information on Megan's Law searches.

Incomplete or inaccurate rental application

Your rental application should be designed to elicit relevant information that will help you answer the one question you have for everyone: "Is this applicant a good business risk?" You can't make that decision unless you have answers to all (or almost all) of your questions. Moreover, an applicant who can't list a prior employer, or the address of past residences, may well have some skeletons to hide. Don't take a chance with someone who is an unknown.

Inaccurate information is another red flag. If the applicant gives you wrong information concerning an important point, you are justified in rejecting the applicant. For example, suppose you find out that someone has inflated the number of years spent at a prior rental or job, or significantly overstated his monthly income, or mischaracterized the reasons for leaving his latest rental. These are indicators of someone who is dishonest or careless regarding an important matter—you can expect slippery or sloppy dealings with this person in the

Protected Categories: Types of Discrimination Prohibited

The major sources of antidiscrimination laws are the federal Fair Housing Act and Fair Housing Amendments Act (42 U.S. Code §§ 3601–3619, 3631), which are enforced by the U.S. Department of Housing and Urban Development (HUD). States and localities often add more protected categories.

Federal	State
<ul><li>Race or color</li><li>Religion</li><li>National origin</li><li>Familial status—includes families with children under the age of 18 and pregnant women and elderly persons</li><li>Disability</li><li>Sex, including sexual harassment</li></ul>	All of the federal requirements, plus, in some states and cities:<ul><li>Arbitrary discrimination, including occupation and personal characteristics</li><li>Students</li><li>Sexual orientation</li><li>Victims of domestic violence</li><li>Recipients of public assistance</li><li>Criminal record</li></ul>

Federal and state law. For more information about the Fair Housing Act, state fair housing laws, free copies of federal fair housing posters, and technical assistance on accessibility requirements, contact one of HUD's many local offices. You'll find a list of local offices on the HUD website at www.hud.gov/local/index.cfm. You can also call the agency's Housing Discrimination Hotline at 800-669-9777 (or 800-927-9275 TTY).

State and local fair housing agencies. For a list of state and local fair housing agencies, check out www.fairhousing.org, a website maintained by the National Fair Housing Advocate Online.

future. See Chapter 10 for advice on evaluating rental applications.

Inability to meet your rental terms

You can reject applicants who cannot meet your reasonable rental terms. With a few exceptions (such as accepting companion or service animals needed by disabled persons), you make the rules concerning the broad outlines of the rental deal. It's your choice whether to offer a month-to-month rental agreement, or a lease; you determine whether to allow pets (and what kind), and whether you'll include parking; and of course, you set the rent. If an applicant wants a lower rent, a smaller deposit, or a place to park his RV, you can politely reject him.

Rental properties exempt from antidiscrimination laws

Before looking at the types of illegal discrimination you'll want to understand and avoid, consider whether you and your property are covered under the federal laws. The following types of property are exempt from the federal Acts:

- owner-occupied buildings with four or fewer units
- single-family housing rented without the use of discriminatory advertising or without a real estate broker
- certain types of housing operated by religious organizations and private clubs that limit occupancy to their own members, and

---

Display Fair Housing Posters in Your Rental Office

Federal regulations require you to put up special fair housing posters wherever you normally conduct housing-related business. You must display a HUD-approved poster saying that you rent apartments in accordance with federal fair housing law (24 CFR §§ 110 and following). However, if you own and are renting out only one single-family home and are not a real estate broker or agent, the poster requirement doesn't apply to you.

Hang the fair housing posters in a prominent spot in the office or area where you greet prospective tenants and take applications. If you have a model apartment, it's a smart idea to hang a poster there, too. To get free posters, available in English and Spanish, contact the U.S. Department of Housing and Urban Development.

- with respect to age discrimination only, housing reserved exclusively for senior citizens that is intended for, and solely occupied by, persons 62 years of age or older or households with at least one person 55 years of age or older.

Even if you are exempt under federal law, similar state or local anti-discrimination laws may nevertheless cover your rental units. For example, owner-occupied buildings with four or fewer units are exempt under federal law, but not under California law. In any event, it doesn't make ethical or business sense for any landlord to discriminate in the choice of tenants—applicants won't know or care whether you're exempt, and won't hesitate to complain or visit a lawyer if you've discriminated against them. You may ultimately win the battle, but the legal snarling (nasty letters from lawyers, which your lawyer will have to respond to) will be expensive and distracting. Instead, focus on following the law and getting your place rented.

Types of illegal discrimination

Now it's time to look at the kinds of discrimination that are not allowed. If you make decisions based on race, disability, or any of the factors explained below, you're breaking the law and inviting trouble. And, importantly, if your housing decisions have the effect of discriminating against a member of a protected group, it's against the law, even if you didn't directly (or even intentionally) mean to discriminate.

Race and religion

Landlords may not make housing decisions based on an applicant's race or religion—for example, renting only to members of your own religion or race is obviously illegal, as is a policy of rejecting people of a particular race or religion.

As with any legal rule, there are fringes to this one—areas where it's not all that obvious that the law applies. For example, does the law protect self-styled religions, as well as mainstream ones? There's no clear legal answer. What about religions whose manifestos are racist and hate-filled—must you disregard an applicant's adherence to such a creed? There's no clear answer to that one, either. To be on safe ground, do a thorough credit and reference check that will give you enough hard facts to enable you to conclude whether the applicant will be financially responsible and a respectful occupant and neighbor.

National origin

Like discrimination based on race or religion, discrimination based on national origin is illegal, whether it's practiced openly and deliberately or unintentionally.

Even if you are motivated by a valid business concern, but choose tenants in a way that singles out people of a particular nationality, it's still illegal. Say, for instance, that two Hispanic tenants recently skipped out on you, owing you unpaid rent. So you decide to make it a practice to conduct credit checks only on Hispanics. An Hispanic applicant may interpret your actions as sending a negative message to Hispanics in general: Hispanics are not welcome because you assume all of them skip out on debts. A fair housing agency or a court of law would probably agree that this sort of selective policy is illegal discrimination.

On the other hand, if you require all prospective tenants to consent to a credit check (as well as meeting other business criteria as discussed above), you will get the needed information, but in a nondiscriminatory way.

Discrimination in a Post-9/11 World

Until recently, it was not clear whether landlords could inquire as to their applicants' immigration status (however, in New York City and California, landlords are prohibited from asking such questions). HUD has clarified this issue, at least with respect to federal law, pointing out that discrimination based solely on a person's immigration status is not illegal. Therefore, asking applicants to provide documentation of their citizenship or immigration status during the screening process does not violate the federal Fair Housing Act. ("Rights and Responsibilities of Landlords and Residents in Preventing Housing Discrimination Based on Race, Religion, or National Origin in the Wake of the Events of September 11, 2001," posted on the HUD website at www.hud.gov. Use the site's advance search function and type the document title into the query box.)

If you want to confirm legal residency, you can attach the Legal Status in the United States form described in Chapter 6 to your rental application. Chapter 10 shows you how to evaluate the documentation that applicants will supply. (Again, do not do this in New York City or California.)

If you question applicants about their immigration status, be sure to demand proof from all applicants, not just those whom you suspect might come from countries that harbor terrorists. Otherwise, if you single out people of a particular race, religion, or nationality, you may find yourself facing a discrimination charge.

Don't Steer Applicants to Particular Rentals

Even well-meaning suggestions from landlords or managers can be against the law. It's up to your applicants to choose their preferred location, not you.

The applicant	The feature or situation	What *not* to say
Families with kids	Multistory building, pool	"It will be safer for you in the ground-level units, not too close to the pool."
Disabled applicants	Multistory building, pool	"You'll be more comfortable if you don't have to negotiate the steps." "Being away from the hustle and bustle around the pool will be better for you."
Single mom with kids	Kids are home alone after school	"Of course, you'll prefer to have a unit at the back, where the kids' play won't disturb others."
Family with attractive teenage girl who will be alone after school	Multistory building	"It will be a lot safer if you're in one of the upper-floor units."
Family with children	Other families in building	"We have some 'family units' next to other families that I'm sure you'll like."
Applicant is a member of a particular ethnicity	Another unit is occupied by tenants of the same ethnicity	"I'm sure you'll want to be next door to [them]."
Applicant is blind	Applicant applies for an apartment	"Well, I guess we can dispense with the tour, can't we!"

⚠ **Don't discriminate based on how applicants sound over the phone.** Refusing to show your rental unit to an otherwise qualified applicant because you think they sound African American, Middle Eastern, or French is known as linguistic profiling, and it will land you in legal hot water. You'll have a hard time defending yourself in the face of studies that show that more than 80% of listeners can identify a speaker's race before that person has finished counting to 20 (National Public Radio *Morning Edition*, Professor John Baugh, September 5, 2001).

Familial status

Federal law prohibits landlords from discriminating against families or pregnant women. Discrimination in this area includes not only openly refusing to rent to families with children or to pregnant women, but also trying to accomplish the same goal by setting overly restrictive space requirements (limiting the maximum number of people permitted to occupy a rental unit), thereby preventing families with children from occupying smaller units. (For example, insisting that no more than three people occupy a two-bedroom rental has the effect of discriminating against a family of four.) Placing families in certain areas of multifamily complexes (known as "steering"), even if landlords think the location is best for families, is also against the law.

We discuss how to establish reasonable occupancy standards below. The fact that you can legally adopt occupancy standards, however, doesn't mean you can use "overcrowding" as a euphemism for refusing to rent to tenants with children, if you would rent to the same number of adults. A few landlords have adopted criteria that for all practical purposes forbid children under the guise of preventing overcrowding—for example, allowing only one person per bedroom, with a couple counting as one person. Under these criteria, a landlord would rent a two-bedroom unit to a husband and wife and their one child, but would not rent the same unit to a mother with two children. This practice, which has the effect of keeping all (or most) children out of a landlord's property, would surely be found illegal in court and would result in monetary penalties.

It is essential to maintain a consistent occupancy policy. If you allow three adults to live in a two-bedroom apartment, you had better let a couple with a child (or a single mother with two children) live in the same type of unit, or you leave yourself open to charges that you are illegally discriminating.

Finally, do not inquire as to the age and sex of any children who will be sharing the same bedroom. This is their parents' business, not yours.

Disability

Federal law protects tenants who are physically or mentally disabled. A disabled person is someone who has:

- a mental disability that substantially limits one or more major life activities—including, but not limited to, hearing, mobility and visual impairments, chronic alcoholism (but only if it is being addressed through a recovery program), mental illness, HIV positive, AIDS, AIDS-Related Complex, and mental retardation,
- has a history or record of such a disability, or
- is regarded by others as though they have such a disability. The law also protects those who are "associated with" someone who is disabled, such as a family member, cotenant, or caregiver who lives with the tenant or makes house visits.

If you make housing decisions based on these characteristics, you're breaking the law.

It's important to remember that an applicant in this protected group is not automatically going to become your tenant, either. An alcoholic or ex-drug addict who does not have sufficient income or who has poor references can be rejected—though not because of alcoholism or drug addiction, but because you reject all applicants with insufficient income or poor references. If the basis

for your decision is a sound business reason, the applicant's membership in a protected class will not resurrect his application (or cause you legal grief).

Service and companion animals

An applicant who comes with a pet can be rejected on that basis—with one big exception: You must permit a service or companion animal used by a disabled person. (Fair Housing Amendments Act, 42 U.S. Code § 3604(f)(3)(B).) A service animal is described by law as "any guide dog, service dog, or any other animal individually trained to do work or perform tasks for the benefit of an individual with a disability." (28 C.F.R. § 36.104 (2001).) Don't put too much emphasis on the word "trained." The animal must be more than a pet, but you won't get very far with a fair housing judge if you demand a training certificate. You are, however, within your rights to insist that the animal be capable of living on the premises without disturbing the peace of mind of other tenants.

Accommodations and modifications for disabled tenants

Applicants who are disabled are entitled to "reasonable accommodations" from you. You are expected to adjust your rules, procedures, or services in order to give a person with a disability an equal opportunity to use and enjoy a dwelling unit or a common space. This means that you'll need to change your screening procedures if doing so will not unreasonably burden your operations. For example, if you have a policy of not accepting cosigners, you must relax it and at least evaluate a disabled applicant's proposed cosigner if that applicant intends to rely on the cosigner for monetary assistance.

Landlords must also allow disabled tenants to modify their living unit (at the tenant's expense, unless the building is federally financed or is in Massachusetts), if that's what's needed to enable the person to safely and enjoyably live on the property. Landlords may require that the rental be returned to its original condition at the end of the term, unless the modifications are minimal and won't negatively affect the next occupant. You can insist that the tenant place funds in an escrow account that will cover the cost.

Examples of modifications undertaken by a disabled tenant include:

- lowering countertops for a wheelchair-bound tenant
- installing special faucets or door handles for persons with limited hand use
- modifying kitchen appliances to accommodate a blind tenant, and
- installing a ramp to allow a wheelchair-using tenant to negotiate two steps up to a raised lobby or corridor.

Disabled applicants who mention that modifications will be needed can't be turned down on that account. You'll need to evaluate their suitability for your property irrespective of any eventual modifications.

Verification of disabled status

When a tenant or applicant asks for a modification or accommodation, it may be obvious that the person falls within the legal definition of a disabled person, and that the request addresses that disability. In those cases—think of a blind applicant who asks to keep a seeing-eye dog—it would be pointless for you to demand proof that the person is disabled and needs the accommodation. (Indeed, doing so might result in a harassment lawsuit.) However, many times the claimed disability, and the appropriateness of the request, are not so clear. You're entitled to ask for verification, but you must do so carefully.

For years, landlords asked for a doctor's letter. Now, according to a HUD and Department of Justice guidance memo, you must be willing to listen to less formal sources. (*Reasonable Accommodations Under the Fair Housing Act,* Joint Statement of the Department of Housing and Urban Development and the Department of Justice, May 17, 2004.) Sources of reliable information include:

- **The individual himself.** A person can prove that he is disabled (and that a modification or accommodation addresses that disability) by giving you a "credible statement." Unfortunately, the guidance memo does not define this term.
- **Documents.** A person who is under 65 years of age and receives Supplemental Security Income or Social Security Disability Insurance Benefits

is legally disabled. Someone could establish disability by showing you relevant identification cards. Likewise, license plates showing the universal accessibility logo, or a driver's license reflecting the existence of a disability, are sufficient proof.

- **Doctors or other medical professionals, peer support groups, nonmedical service agencies.** Information from these sources might come through letters, phone calls, or personal visits.

- **Reliable third parties.** This wide-open source of information could include friends, associates, and roommates, though some fair housing experts interpret this phrase as meaning any "third-party professional who is familiar with the disability." It's not known whether this definition will become the standard used by courts.

Sex and sexual harassment

You may not refuse an applicant because of that person's sex. For example, a policy against single women (or men) is illegal, as is a practice of offering certain units (such as those on upper floors) to women. No matter what your motivation (you may honestly believe that these units are safer), you must allow the applicant to decide which of your available units suits her or his needs.

Sexual harassment is included within the prohibition against discrimination on the basis of sex. Harassment is a pattern of persistent, unwanted attention of a sexual nature (though a single, particularly egregious incident will also qualify). Harassment can also take the form of conditioning a tenant's rights on the acceptance of sexual attentions. In an application context, for example, it would be illegal for a landlord or manager to condition the offer of a rental on the applicant's willingness to date management.

Age

The federal Fair Housing Act does not explicitly prohibit discrimination on the basis of age, but courts consider age discrimination to be part of familial discrimination. Many states specifically add age to their list of protected groups. It pays for every landlord to assume that age is a protected class. In practice, this means that you cannot reject elderly applicants simply on account of their age (you can offer seniors-only multihousing if you follow federal guidelines, as explained below in "Seniors' Housing").

Once again, however, understand that an elderly applicant is not automatically *entitled* to your rental, either. Elderly applicants, like everyone else, must pass your good-tenant criteria. If an older applicant has insufficient income or has a demonstrated inability to safely live alone, you can reject on those grounds, apart from the applicant's age. You must have evidence to back you up—an assumption on your part that this person's advanced age will result in stoves left on, keys lost, or apartment doors left open will not do. But if you learn from prior landlords that these events in fact happened, you're on solid ground.

Elderly applicants may be disabled, too—and deserving of an accommodation. For example, if an older tenant who is legally disabled also has problems remembering when the rent is due, you may need to adjust your collection practices to provide for a monthly "tickler" for that tenant.

Renting to Minors

You may wonder whether the prohibition against age discrimination applies to minors (in most states, people under age 18). A minor applicant who is legally "emancipated"—is married, has a court order of emancipation, or is in the military—has the same status as an adult. This means you will need to treat the applicant like any other adult. In short, if the applicant satisfies the rental criteria that you apply to everyone, a refusal to rent to a minor could form the basis of a fair housing complaint. On the other hand, minor applicants who are not emancipated lack the legal capacity to enter into a legally binding rental agreement with you.

Seniors' Housing

If you have a multifamily property and decide you'd like to rent exclusively to seniors, you can do so as long as you follow federal guidelines. You have two options:

- **Housing for tenants 55 and older.** 80% of your residents must be 55 or older. You must make it known to the public, through your advertising, that you offer senior housing, and must verify applicants' ages. Once you've reached the 80% mark, you can set any other age restriction as long as it does not violate any state or local bans on age discrimination. For example, you could require the remaining 20% to be over 18 years of age, as long as no state or local law forbids such a policy.
- **Housing for tenants 62 and older.** All of your residents must be 62 or older. This includes spouses and adult children, but excludes caregivers and on-site employees.

Marital status

Federal law does not prohibit discrimination on the basis of marital status (oddly, being married isn't included within the federal concept of familial status). Consequently, in most states you may legally refuse to rent to applicants on the grounds that they are (or are not) married. The issue comes up when a landlord chooses a married couple over a single applicant, or when an unmarried couple applies for a rental (or a current tenant wants to move in a special friend).

Some states have addressed these situations. About 20 states ban discrimination on the basis of marital status, but most of these extend protection to married couples only. In these states, landlords cannot legally prefer single, platonic roommates (or one-person tenancies) over married couples. What about the reverse—preferring married couples over single roommates or a single tenant? Not every one of these states have addressed the issue, but of those that have (Maryland, Minnesota, New York, and Wisconsin), the term "marital status" only protects married people from being treated differently from single people. Single people are not protected.

Now then, what about the remaining possibility—an unmarried couple? In only a few states—California, Massachusetts, Michigan, and New Jersey—does the term "marital status" include unmarried couples. If you own rental property in these four states, you cannot reject applicants solely because they are living together but not married.

Some landlords resist renting to unmarried couples on the grounds that cohabitation violates their religious beliefs. Courts in Alaska, California, Massachusetts, and New Jersey have refused to allow landlords to deny housing on that basis.

Unmarried tenants may be protected by a city or county ordinance prohibiting discrimination on the basis of sexual orientation. Although usually passed to protect the housing rights of gay and lesbian tenants, most local laws forbidding discrimination based on sexual orientation protect unmarried heterosexual couples as well. In addition, unmarried people may be able to challenge a landlord's refusal to rent to them on the basis of sex discrimination, which is covered by the federal Acts.

Sexual orientation

Federal law doesn't specifically prohibit housing discrimination based on sexual orientation, but several states have such laws, including California, Connecticut, the District of Columbia, Hawaii, Maryland, Massachusetts, Minnesota, New Hampshire, New Jersey, New Mexico, New York, Rhode Island, Vermont, and Wisconsin. (California, Connecticut, Minnesota, New Mexico, and Rhode Island also protect transgendered persons, as does New York City.) In addition, many cities prohibit discrimination against gays and lesbians, including Atlanta, Chicago, Detroit, Miami, New York, Pittsburgh, St. Louis, and Seattle. For more information, contact Lambda Legal at 212-809-8585 or check its website at www.lambdalegal.org.

Source of income

In several states, including California, Connecticut, the District of Columbia, Maine, Maryland, Massachusetts, Minnesota, New Jersey, North Dakota, Oklahoma, Oregon, Utah, Vermont, and Wisconsin, you may not refuse to rent to a person simply because he or she is receiving public assistance. You may, however, refuse to rent to persons whose available incomes fall below a certain level, as long as you apply that standard across the board.

Arbitrary discrimination

After reading the above material outlining the types of illegal discrimination, you may be tempted to assume that it is legal to discriminate for any reason not

Section 8 and Low-Income Housing Programs

Many tenants with low incomes qualify for federally subsidized housing assistance, the most common being the tenant-based Section 8 program of the federal Department of Housing and Urban Development (HUD). ("Section 8" refers to Section 8 of the United States Housing Act of 1937, 42 U.S. Code § 1437f.) That program pays part of the rent directly to you. The local public housing agency, you, and the tenants enter into a one-year agreement, which includes a written lease supplied by the local public housing agency. The tenants pay a percentage of their monthly income to you, and the housing agency pays you the difference between the tenants' contribution and what it determines is the market rent each month.

Section 8 is a mixed bag for landlords. First, the advantages:

- The housing agency pays the larger part of the rent on time every month, and the tenant's portion is low enough that he shouldn't have too much trouble paying on time, either.
- If the tenant doesn't pay the rent and you have to evict, the housing agency guarantees the tenant's unpaid portion, and also guarantees payment for damage to the property by the tenant, up to a certain limit.
- You'll have a full house if your neighborhood or area is populated by lower-income tenants.

Section 8 and Low-Income Housing Programs (cont'd)

On the other hand, Section 8's disadvantages are legion:

- The housing agency's determination of what is market rent is often low, and the program caps the security deposit (which may be lower than your state maximum).
- You are locked into a tenancy agreement for one year, and can't terminate the tenancy except for nonpayment of rent or other serious breach of the lease. (Evictions based on grounds other than nonpayment of rent or other serious breaches are difficult.)
- When HUD experiences a budget crunch, it cuts the public housing agencies' budgets. As a result, the housing agencies are likely to lower the landlords' allotments. Though this practice is legally iffy, it's done anyway.
- New Section 8 landlords must often wait up to a month or longer for a qualifying, mandatory inspection—during which they see no rent. These inspections often reveal picky, minor violations that state inspectors wouldn't cite for.

Landlords have traditionally been able to choose not to participate in the Section 8 program without fear of violating the federal fair housing laws. However, as the federal government's ability to provide sufficient low-income housing diminishes, legislators are looking to the private sector to fill the void— and one way to do this is to require landlords to accept Section 8. In New Jersey, if an existing tenant becomes eligible for Section 8 assistance, you may not refuse to accept the vouchers—you must participate in the program as to this tenant, at least. (*Franklin Tower One v. N.M.*, 157 N.J. 602; 725 A.2d 1104 (1999).) In Connecticut, landlords may not refuse to rent to existing or new tenants who will be paying with Section 8 vouchers. (*Commission on Human Rights and Opportunities v. Sullivan Associates*, 250 Conn. 763; 739 A.2d 238 (1999).)

If you do not participate in the Section 8 program and don't wish to do so, and live anywhere except New Jersey and Connecticut, be prepared to get some legal advice if you're asked by current tenants to accept their newly acquired Section 8 vouchers, or if applicants make the same request.

Call your local public housing agency if you wish to participate in the Section 8 program. They will refer eligible applicants to you, arrange for an inspection, and prepare the necessary documents (including the lease addendum) if you decide to rent to an eligible applicant. Be sure to get a copy from HUD of the Section 8 rules and procedures that all participating landlords must use. Often, they vary significantly from your state or local law.

mentioned by name in a state or federal law. For example, because none of the civil rights laws specifically prohibits discrimination against men with beards or long hair, you might conclude that such discrimination is permissible. This is not always true.

For example, even though California's Unruh Civil Rights Act (Cal. Civ. Code §§ 51–53, 54.1–54.8) contains only the words "sex, race, color, religion, ancestry, or national origin" to describe types of discrimination that are illegal, the courts have ruled that these categories are just examples of illegal discrimination. The courts in California have construed the Unruh Act to forbid all discrimination on the basis of one's personal characteristic or trait.

Although no other state specifically outlaws arbitrary discrimination (local ordinances may, however), there is a very strong practical reason why you should not engage in arbitrary discrimination— for example, based an obesity, occupation, or style of dress. Because fair housing

Make Your Commitment to Fair Housing Known

One way to alert your tenants and prospective tenants to your commitment to the fair housing laws is to write all ads, applications, and other material given to prospective tenants to include a section containing your antidiscrimination stance. Prepare a written policy statement as to the law and your intention to abide by it. See the sample statement, below, and don't forget to show fair housing posters, if needed, as explained in "Display Fair Housing Posters in Your Rental Office," above.

FROM: Shady Dell Apartments

TO: All Tenants and Applicants

It is the policy of the owner and manager of Shady Dell Apartments to rent our units without regard to a tenant's race, ethnic background, sex, age, religion, marital or family status, physical disability, or sexual orientation. As part of our commitment to provide equal opportunity in housing, we comply with all federal, state, and local laws prohibiting discrimination. If you have any questions or complaints regarding our rental policy, call the owner at 555-1234.

law includes numerous protected categories—race, sex, religion, and so on—chances are that a disappointed applicant can fit himself or herself into at least one of the protected categories and file a discrimination claim. Even if the applicant does not ultimately win his or her claim, the time, aggravation, and expense caused by the attempt will be costly to the landlord.

Occupancy standards: How many tenants are too many?

Two kinds of laws affect the number of people who may live in a rental unit. State and local health and safety codes typically set *maximum* limits on the number of tenants, based on the size of the unit and the number of bedrooms and bathrooms. Even more important, the federal government has taken the lead in establishing *minimum* limits on the number of tenants, through passage of the Fair Housing Act (42 U.S.C. §§ 3601–3619, 3631) and by means of regulations from the Department of Housing and Urban Development (HUD).

HUD generally considers a limit of two persons per bedroom a reasonable occupancy standard. Because the number of bedrooms is not the only factor—the size of the bedrooms and configuration of the rental unit are also considered—the federal test has become known as the "two per bedroom plus"

standard. States and localities can set their own occupancy standards as long as they are more generous than the federal government's—that is, by allowing more people per rental unit.

The Fair Housing Act is designed primarily to disallow illegal discrimination against families with children, but it also allows you to establish your own "reasonable" restrictions on the number of people per rental unit, as long as your policy is truly tied to health and safety needs. In addition, you can adopt standards that are driven by a legitimate business reason or necessity, such as the capacities of the plumbing or electrical systems. Your personal preferences (such as a desire to reduce wear and tear by limiting the number of occupants or to ensure a quiet, uncrowded environment for upscale tenants), however, do not constitute a legitimate business reason.

To avoid legal problems, you should adopt an occupancy policy that is at least as generous as the federal minimum occupancy standard (two per bedroom), unless your state or locality has adopted more generous standards, in which case, follow them. If your occupancy policy is more restrictive than the legal standard you must follow—that is, you want to allow fewer occupants—you're in for an uphill battle if you're challenged. You'll have to convince a judge that you need a more restrictive policy because of health or safety limitations of the property, or due to legitimate business needs.

⚠ **New York landlords should check out the state's "roommate law."** New York landlords must comply with the "Unlawful Restrictions on Occupancy" law, commonly known as the roommate law. (N.Y. RPL § 235-f.) The roommate law prohibits New York landlords from limiting occupancy of a rental unit to just the tenant named on the lease or rental agreement. It permits tenants to share their rental units with their immediate family members, and, in many cases, with unrelated, non-tenant occupants, too, so long as a tenant (or tenant's spouse) occupies the unit as a primary residence. The number of total occupants is still restricted, however, by local laws governing overcrowding.

Managers and discrimination

If you employ a manager who selects tenants, make certain that the manager fully understands and abides by laws against housing discrimination. On the other hand, if you use an independent management company, the possibility that you will be liable for their discriminatory acts is greatly decreased. If you decide to use a tenant-screening company (see Chapter 14), you'll find that a "term and condition" of working with them is that you agree to hold them harmless for any mistakes that they make. In other words, if they apply discriminatory criteria to their evaluations and you get sued, you won't be able to sue them as the true source of the problem.

You should always let applicants know that you, as well as your manager, intend to abide by the law, and that during the tenancy you want to know about and will address any fair housing problems that may arise. While this will not shield you from liability if you are sued due to your manager's conduct, it might (if you are lucky) result in the tenant's initial complaint being made to you, not a fair housing agency. If you hear about a manager's discriminatory act and can resolve a complaint before it gets into official channels, you will have saved yourself a lot of time, trouble, and money.

Where to Find Information on Legal Occupancy Limits

Figuring out whether your occupancy policy is legal is not always a simple matter. Furthermore, laws on occupancy limits often change. For more information, call HUD's Housing Discrimination Hotline at 800-669-9777, or check the HUD website at www.hud.gov. Check your local and state housing authority for other occupancy standards that may affect your rental property. Ask HUD for a referral if you're unsure what state or local agency to call.

Take Ten Minutes

To safely run your business, you don't have to be a "Philadelphia lawyer" who's an expert in discrimination law. You simply need to follow this practice: For every decision you make, ask yourself if the reason behind it has everything to do with the business issues it involves and nothing to do with the personal characteristics of the applicant or tenant. Take ten minutes now to apply that test to the following scenarios. The lawsuit-free answers are at the end of this sidebar.

Scenario 1: You're reviewing two applications for the same rental, one from a family with three children, another from five adult roommates. You increase the security deposit for the family on the grounds that kids cause more wear and tear than adults. Are you risking a discrimination lawsuit?

Scenario 2: You're considering an application from an elderly woman who strikes you as a bit scattered and forgetful. Worried that she will become a problem (forgetting her keys, her rent due date, and so on), you question her about her memory and whether she's locked herself out recently. Are you risking a discrimination lawsuit?

Scenario 3: Though you have a no-pets policy, an applicant asks you to accept his cat, whom he describes as a much-needed "comfort animal." The applicant looks perfectly normal to you, and you say no. Are you risking a discrimination lawsuit?

Answers

Scenario 1: Yes. You can safely increase the deposit based on the *number of occupants*, but you cannot increase it because they are children.

Scenario 2: Yes. You may question her former landlords and other references about whether she has been able to live safely and competently on her own, but you may not subject her to such questions.

Scenario 3: Yes. Some disabilities are not obvious, and an animal may qualify as a service animal if the applicant can provide verification. You need to point out to this applicant that if he would like you to accommodate him under the Americans with Disabilities Act, you will need to see documentation of his status and a description of how the animal is needed to enable him to live safely and comfortably on your property.

⚠️ **Never give managers or rental agents the authority to offer their own rent concessions or deals to selected tenants or applicants.** If you want to offer inducements—a discount for signing an extended lease or one free month for tenants who begin renting in the month of March—do so on a consistent basis. Make sure offers are available to all tenants who meet the requirements of the special deal. Otherwise, a tenant who gets a worse deal from your manager than his identically situated neighbor is sure to complain—and if he is a member of a group protected by fair housing laws, he's got the makings of a case against you.

If, despite your best efforts, you even suspect your manager may use unlawful discriminatory practices to select or deal with tenants—whether on purpose or inadvertently—you should immediately resume control of the situation yourself. Alternatively, this may be the time to shield yourself from potential liability and engage the services of an independent management company, which in most cases will be responsible for its employees' actions.

■

How to Deal With Current Tenants—
Before You Look for New Ones

It's a rare landlord who will begin looking for tenants with an empty rental property. Most of the time, you'll start your search while existing tenants are still living in the unit. This chapter gives you practical steps to minimize the amount of time between the end of one tenancy and the start of another, enlist your current residents in your marketing efforts to find new tenants, and smoothly usher the current tenants out the door.

The first part of this chapter covers tenants who are easiest to deal with—those whose lease is up or who have decided to move on, for reasons of their own and not because you've told them to leave. Tenants who are moving voluntarily have probably lined up their next living situation, be it another rental or a purchased home, and have every reason to leave your rental in a timely fashion. If you're lucky, current residents will cooperate with your efforts to find new tenants and will leave as planned, giving you ample time for cleaning and refurbishing before the next batch moves in.

Unfortunately, tenants who are not leaving voluntarily—whose tenancy you've terminated—are another matter. You may even have to evict them. Others may not leave as scheduled (perhaps their plans for their next rental fell through), or a unit may need cleaning and repairs that take weeks, with no rent checks coming in. The last thing you want is to spend time and money

advertising, screening, and leasing to new tenants, only to find that you can't deliver the premises as promised. The second part of this chapter explains how to avoid the frustrating and expensive scenario of dealing with problem tenants, and what to do if you can't deliver the rental on time to the next tenant.

The Law You Need to Know

As you prepare to say good-bye to current tenants, be sure to abide by state laws that bear on this point in the tenancy, including:

- the amount of notice you must give month-to-month tenants when terminating their residency
- the procedure you must follow when entering tenants' homes (see "State Laws on Notice to Inspect or Show Rental Property" at the end of this chapter)
- state laws on inspections prior to move-out, to enable tenants to learn of intended deductions from their deposits and to minimize those deductions, and
- state laws on returning security deposits (see "State Laws on Returning Security Deposits" at the end of this chapter).

Landlord's Forms Library

To help you usher out the current tenants and prepare the way for the new, use the following forms, which are explained in this chapter and included on the CD-ROM.

- **Move-Out Letter.** Reminds departing tenants of the move-out date, explains your cleaning requirements, and covers final inspection procedures and details on the return of security deposits.
- **Pre-Move-Out Inspection Request.** Asks the tenant for a preliminary walk-through inspection to determine work that may be necessary before re-renting, and notes potential deposit deductions.
- **Pre-Move-Out Inspection Request, California.** Informs California tenants of their right to a move-out inspection and includes required information on landlord's right to deduct from deposit.
- **Pre-Move-Out Inspection Report.** Provides a room-by-room inventory of the condition of rental property and the estimated cost of repairing or replacing any item.
- **Landlord's Plans to Advertise and Show Rental.** Tells departing tenants of your plans to show the rental and asks for their cooperation in doing so.
- **Letter of Recommendation.** A perk for cooperating departing tenants, this memo recommends them to their next landlord.
- **Departing Tenant's Questionnaire.** Gives outgoing tenants the opportunity to critique what it's been like to rent from you.

Store copies of these forms in the departing tenants' file, and keep them for two years at least. If the tenants claim that they didn't know your cleaning expectations, dispute your deposit retention, or weren't warned of intended deductions, you'll have contrary proof. If, for some reason, the tenants don't leave as expected, a Move-Out Letter provides proof that you informed them of the move-out date, which could come in handy if you have to evict. When you receive the Departing Tenant's Questionnaire, take a good hard look—you may learn something that will influence how you advertise the unit. If so, place it in the advertising and showing folder for this property.

✓ Before You Usher Out the Current Tenants

Take a moment to reflect on your experience with the current tenants. Is there something you can learn from it, that will enlighten your marketing campaign for the next batch? For example:

Experience with current tenant	What to do next time
Tenants had a dog that barked and was often off leash.	Specify no pets, or screen the pet more thoroughly (emphasize in ads).
Tenant often paid rent a few days late.	Impose a late-fee policy.
Many noise complaints from neighbors.	Ask applicants' current and prior landlords about any noise problems.
Lots of requests for cosmetic improvements (good ideas, but a hassle).	Consider taking a week to thoroughly spiff-up rental, maybe demand higher rent.
Tenant complained about streetcar noise at night.	Make sure applicants know about this before deciding to live here.
Always paid rent on time, model tenant.	Remember to thank and acknowledge good tenants (holiday gift basket?).

⚠ Put the brakes on if you have any doubts about the cooperation of tenants who are moving out.

Wait until the tenant is completely out. And *never* advertise a unit that's the subject of a termination notice until it is vacant, period. Though you may lose a month or two in rent, you'll avoid the complicated problems that come with not being able to deliver the rental on time.

Send departing tenants a move-out letter

When the end is voluntary, remind leaseholding tenants that their lease is about up. Your need to remind tenants who've given you notice to end a rental agreement is less pressing. Still, a polite reminder won't hurt, especially since some tenants—particularly those who have lived in the unit a long time—may forget that the lease is about to expire. A gentle nudge will serve the added purpose of reminding tenants of exactly when you expect them to be totally out of the unit (surprisingly, many tenants assume they have the right to come back and clean and pack up, even after the rental term is over).

A Move-Out Letter will give you the opportunity to review how you expect the rental to be left, including specific cleaning requirements, details on your final inspection procedures, and where and how you will send any deposit refund that is due. Refer to the chart at the end of this chapter, "State Laws on Returning Security Deposits," which lists return deadlines. If you and the tenant documented the condition of the rental at the start of the tenancy in a walk-through checklist, you may want to refer to it, attach a copy, and explain that it may help the tenant remember the original condition of the unit (generally, tenants are responsible for post-move-in damage and excessive wear and tear).

You'll find a Move-Out Letter form that you can adapt to your particular situation and move-out process on the forms CD-ROM that accompanies this book. A sample is shown below.

Do a pre-move-out inspection of the rental

The amount of time you'll need to spend cleaning and fixing the rental will affect the available date you list in your advertising. It may take just a day or two, or it may take a few weeks. To avoid unpleasant surprises (who knew that dry rot riddled the bathroom sub-floor?) or needless downtime, get some information about the condition of the rental before you place your ads and actively begin courting new tenants. Here's how to do it.

At least a week before you advertise a vacancy, try to get into the unit and check it out. You'll want to know how much cleaning it's likely to need

(admittedly, this involves guessing how much the tenants will do, but you can make a good estimate based on the quality of the current housekeeping); whether you'll need to replace items, such as carpeting and drapes, that are damaged or have succumbed to normal wear and tear; and whether you want to take advantage of this turnover time to refurbish the unit. See Chapter 8 for tips on efficiently using this time to improve your rentals.

In many states, you have no right to enter a tenant's home to inspect or show it to prospective tenants unless you have given residents a specified amount of notice (two to 24 hours is common, as is "reasonable notice"). Refer to the chart at the end of this chapter, "State Laws on Notice to Inspect or Show Rental Property," for your state's rule. But even in states that are very restrictive, you can always ask tenants to enter on less notice, as long as you aren't coercive. If the tenant gives permission, you can enter without having given the required notice. Be sure to specify a day and time, and follow that schedule.

To help persuade tenants to let you have an advance peek, explain that the purpose of your visit is twofold: Not only do you want to assess the unit for needed repairs and refurbishing, but you want to give the tenants a preview of what, if any, problems you see that may require deductions from their security deposit. This gives tenants an opportunity to do needed cleaning or repairs and to avoid

Move-Out Letter

April 6, 20xx

Mary Rollins
1706 Parker Court
Anytown, CA 12345

Dear Ms. Rollins,

We hope you have enjoyed living here, and are on track to vacate on or before May 1, 20xx. In order that we may mutually end our relationship on a positive note, this move-out letter describes how we expect your unit to be left and what our procedures are for returning your security deposit.

Basically, we expect you to leave your rental unit in the same condition it was when you moved in, except for normal wear and tear. To refresh your memory on the condition of the unit when you moved in, I've attached a copy of the Landlord/Tenant Checklist you signed at the beginning of your tenancy. I'll be using this same form to inspect your unit when you leave.

Specifically, here's a list of items you should thoroughly clean before vacating:

- ☑ Floors
    - ☑ sweep wood floors
    - ☑ vacuum carpets and rugs (shampoo, if necessary)
    - ☑ mop kitchen and bathroom floors
- ☑ Walls, baseboards, ceilings, and built-in shelves
- ☑ Kitchen cabinets, countertops and sink, stove, and oven—inside and out
- ☑ Refrigerator—clean inside and out, empty it of food, and turn it off, with the door left open
- ☑ Bathtubs, showers, toilets, and plumbing fixtures
- ☑ Doors, windows, and window coverings
- ☑ Other: wash the deck

If you have any questions as to the type of cleaning we expect, please let me know.

Please don't leave anything behind—that includes bags of garbage, clothes, food, newspapers, furniture, appliances, dishes, plants, cleaning supplies, or other items that belong to you.

Please be sure you have disconnected phone and utility services, canceled all newspaper subscriptions, and sent the post office a change of address form.

Once you have cleaned your unit and removed all your belongings, please call me to arrange for a walk-through inspection and to return all keys. Please be prepared to give me your forwarding address where we may mail your security deposit.

It's our policy to return all deposits either in person or at an address you provide within 21 days after you move out. If any deductions are made—for past due rent or because the unit is damaged or not sufficiently clean—they will be explained in writing.

Sincerely,

Sally Robinson

Sally Robinson

Landlord

555-123-4567

sallyrobinson@coldmail.com

deposit deductions. In several states, this preinspection is required by law, so it pays to check your security deposit statutes (see the chart at the end of this chapter). Once tenants know that they can take steps to protect their deposit, even hesitant ones may be motivated to work with you.

The CD-ROM that accompanies this book includes a Pre-Move-Out Inspection Request form that you can use when requesting permission to conduct a pre-move-out inspection. You'll see a sample below. California landlords should use the form specifically for their state, Pre-Move-Out Inspection Request, California.

If you've successfully convinced your residents to allow you in for an inspection, record what you find on an inspection report. This document will form the basis for any security deposit deductions, and it may be the first thing you show your cleaning service or contractor. Use the form in this book, adapting it if you wish to include rooms, furnishings, or unique features of this rental. You may instead want to use an inventory you conducted when the tenancy began, adding columns for this inspection and estimated repair or cleaning costs, as explained below.

You'll find the Pre-Move-Out Inspection Report on this book's CD-ROM, and a filled-out sample below.

To begin using the form, fill in (by hand or on the computer) the street address of the unit, the name of the person who is doing the pre-move-out inspection (probably you), and the date of the inspection. Use the "Condition at Pre-Move-Out Inspection" column when you inspect the unit. Mark "OK" next to the items that are in satisfactory condition—basically clean, safe, sanitary, and in good working order. You will fill in the Estimated Cost of Repair/Replacement column later if you can't give a realistic estimate now. When the tenant leaves, you'll inspect again and can deduct these costs from the security deposit if the tenant has not addressed the problems to your reasonable satisfaction. Many states require you to accompany any deposit return with an itemized statement of costs (again, check your state statutes). This form will come in handy there, too.

Although you may have some difficulty getting a full picture of the condition of the rental, due to residents' belongings and furniture, an early inspection will give you a pretty good idea of what you may have to do to ready this home for the next occupants. Be sure to give your current tenants a copy of this form showing what you've found—after all, one of the reasons they agreed to the inspection was your promise that they'd get a preview of what you might deduct for when doing a final inspection.

Keep this form handy, so that you can refer to it when evaluating the condition

Pre-Move-Out Inspection Request

April 6, 20xx

Mary Rollins
1706 Parker Court
Anytown, CA 12345

Dear Ms. Rollins,

As your tenancy ends its last days, I'm sure you're busy planning for your move and packing up. I hope that your leave-taking will be smooth and that I'll be able to return as much as I can of your security deposit. As you know, the deposit can be used for unpaid rent and to remedy damage beyond normal wear and tear.

I'll be inspecting your home when you leave, in keeping with our state's law that covers the return of a tenant's security deposit. Before that time, however, I'd like to do a preliminary walk-through to identify possible areas of concern. This will give you a chance to accomplish needed cleaning or certain repairs, which may help protect your security deposit. And I'll have a chance to assess the condition of the unit for purposes of re-renting. For example, if I decide to do some work, I'll take that into consideration when I advertise the date that the unit will be available.

Please contact me using the information listed below if you're interested in an informal walk-through of your rental.

Sincerely,

Sally Robinson
Sally Robinson
Landlord
555-123-4567
sallyrobinson@coldmail.com

Pre-Move-Out Inspection Report

54 Anderson Way _____   14B _____   Belleview, Il 12345 _____
Street Address   Unit Number   City, State, Zip

Inspection done by ___ Marc Nathanson _____   Date ___ Sept 13, 20xx ___

	Condition at Pre-Move-Out Inspection	Estimated Cost of Repair/Replacement
LIVING ROOM		
Floors & Floor Coverings	water stain, 6", front door	$200
Drapes & Window Coverings	windows need washing	window service 2 hours @ $40/hr
Walls & Ceilings	OK	
Light Fixtures	OK	
Windows, Screens, & Doors	torn screen, south window	$45
Front Door & Locks	OK	
Smoke Detector	needs batteries	$5.00
Fireplace	needs sweeping	
Other		
KITCHEN		

of the property before you set a "date available" in your ads. As described in Chapter 8, Prepare Your Rental for an Open House or Showing, you'll want to thoroughly assess the condition of the rental and the need for refurbishing. You may want to consider whether you can command an increased rent if you make upgrades.

Inform tenants of your plans to advertise and show the rental

Your re-rental strategy should go beyond making sure that the current residents are aware of (and intend to honor) their move-out date, and you should be thinking of more than just the cleanliness of the kitchen floor. For maximum convenience to you and your applicants, you want the current residents' willing cooperation, and even participation, in your marketing efforts. Begin your efforts long before you stop by with prospective tenants. Start by informing current tenants of your re-rental plans, asking for their cooperation, and inviting them to discuss their plans with you. You can use our letter, Landlord's Plans to Advertise and Show Rental, shown below. Here's how to complete it.

Start by filling in the date, the tenant's name, and the rental property address. In the paragraph introducing your advertising plans, list them. Unless you know now

where you'll advertise, read Chapter 4 before making your choice.

In the paragraph describing how you'll show the unit, describe your plans for individual tours or an open house. Read Chapter 5 for guidance on which method to choose.

In the sentence describing notice, refer to your state's laws in "State Laws on Notice to Inspect or Show Rental Property," at the end of this chapter, and include the citation to your state statute. Follow the notice rule; if your state laws provide for reasonable notice, you'll be on safe ground if you give at least 48 hours' notice. As for the days and times of day that you expect to show the rental, you should abide by normal business hours (this may include Saturday). You may, however, be able to arrange for different hours if your tenants will cooperate (see the section below on winning your tenants' cooperation).

The CD-ROM that accompanies this book includes a letter to current residents, Landlord's Plans to Advertise and Show Rental.

Offer tenants a reward for working with you

State law restrictions on days and times for showings are designed to minimize the intrusion experienced by residents. But these rules can be highly inconvenient

Landlord's Plans to Advertise and Show Rental

February 5, 20xx

Robert Small
77 4th Street
Nicely, WA 12345

Dear Mr. Small,

I hope you have enjoyed living here, and will soon be settled in a new home.

I have begun thinking about how I'll prepare and show this property to interested tenants. I want to assure you that I respect your privacy and legitimate need for security, and will do all that I can to accommodate you. I know that this is a busy time for you and I understand that intrusions can be very inconvenient. I hope we can work together.

First, let me share with you my plans for advertising and showing this rental. I expect to advertise it by placing an ad in the Daily Gazette and putting a For Rent sign on the lawn that specifies "Do not disturb occupants."

My plans for showing the rental include scheduling an open house for a weekend day at the end of the month. If I don't get enough visitors, I'll show it individually, too.

Of course, I will give you proper notice before bringing anyone here. In particular, in keeping with state law (Or. Rev. Stat. § 90.322) I will give you 24 hours' advance notice of any showing, giving you a specific day and time, and hold a showing on the following days/times weekdays from 9 a.m. to 5 p.m. and Saturdays from 10 a.m. to noon.

I will not place a "lock box" on your door. I will do all I can to monitor visitors' actions while in your home.

Please don't hesitate to call me if you'd like to discuss any aspect of my plans.

Sincerely,

Jake Madison
Jake Madison
Manager
555-123-4567
jakemmadison@coldmail.com

for applicants, many of whom conduct their searches after work and on the weekends. If you can offer a selection of evening and weekend hours, you'll have a better chance of showing the unit to all qualified applicants.

To show the unit on days or times other than normal business hours, you'll need the consent of current tenants (do not pressure them if they are not willing). Be prepared to compensate residents who are willing to give you flexible showing times or who will agree to evenings or weekends. You might offer a complimentary dinner at a local restaurant, movie tickets, or a promise that you'll accelerate the return of the security deposit. Never *condition* the return of the security deposit on your resident's cooperation. You must use and return the deposit according to your state's rules, irrespective of the tenant's willingness to work with you on flexible or extended show times. As long as your request for cooperation is not coercive, there's nothing wrong with it.

Chapter 9 provides details on seeking tenants' cooperation when you're actually showing the rental unit. It discusses the value of having the tenant away during the individual tour or open house, how to develop safety and security plans for showing an occupied unit, and how to do a last-minute walk-through of the property.

Offer departing tenants a take-away letter of recommendation

Another way to encourage current residents to work with you in your re-rental efforts is to offer a letter on your letterhead that they can take away with them to show prospective landlords, attesting to their good qualities. Of course, this assumes that the departing tenants were, in fact, good residents and that you trust them to follow through with their promise to clean and work with you. A resident who burns you but still uses the letter would be taking the risk that the next landlord would contact you to confirm the letter and learn the truth—so accepting the letter may itself induce cooperation.

Condition the letter on residents' willingness to clean early, accommodate your showings of their rental, give you copies of their utility bills, or complete your exit interview (explained below). Use our form, Letter of Recommendation. When landlords see it, they'll probably call you anyway, but tenants will appreciate having the letter on hand to show immediately.

You'll find the Letter of Recommendation on the CD-ROM that accompanies this book.

Letter of Recommendation for <u>Daniel Sanchez</u>

To: <u>Rental Property Owner or Manager</u>

From: <u>Marion Chu</u>

Regarding: <u>Daniel Sanchez</u>

<u>June 10, 20xx</u>

This is a letter of recommendation for <u>Daniel Sanchez</u>, who has lived at the above address, which I <u>own</u>, since <u>May 1, 20xx</u>. Throughout that time, <u>Mr. Sanchez</u> paid the rent on time and conscientiously took care of the property. When <u>Mr. Sanchez</u> left, there was no damage beyond normal wear and tear, and <u>Mr. Sanchez</u> owed no back rent. I would happily rent to <u>Mr. Sanchez</u> again.

I hope you will find this letter helpful in evaluating <u>Mr. Sanchez</u>. Please feel free to contact me to confirm the details of this letter.

Sincerely,

Marion Chu

<u>Marion Chu</u>
<u>Landlord</u>
<u>555-123-4567</u>
<u>marionchu@coldmail.com</u>

Make a copy of the letter you've given to your residents, and place it in their tenancy file. You'll find it handy when you get a call from a subsequent landlord.

Ask departing tenants to complete an exit questionnaire

Take a lesson from savvy employers and ask your departing tenants to give you a critique of what it's been like to rent from you. You can use the Departing Tenant's Questionnaire for this purpose.

When you review the completed questionnaire, evaluate it realistically. Problem tenants may use it as an opportunity to vent—many of their gripes are probably not justified. Even good tenants may hesitate to criticize you, fearing that you'll not give a good recommendation to future landlords. But you'll be surprised at the willingness of many tenants to be candid.

You have a lot to learn from tenants who will take the time to give honest feedback. The questions on the form are designed to give you information that will help with your marketing and overall management. For example, a tenant may appreciate an aspect of your rental that you were unaware of, thus prompting you to emphasize it when you advertise. Or, you may learn that you need to spend more time supervising your manager, or checking up on the janitorial service that cleans common areas.

The final question asks tenants if they would be willing to serve as a reference for *you*, by speaking with prospective renters or sending comments via email. Of course, you'll want to take them up on this offer only if their review is positive and you've had smooth sailing. If you're in a cold market and need every advantage you can get, securing the help of ex-residents this way can be very worthwhile.

When you give the form to the tenants, let them know that they can mail it back to you after the security deposit is settled. Include a stamped, self-addressed envelope, or attach it to an email and ask the tenant to return it that way. When you get the questionnaire back, note when you reviewed it and what, if anything, you plan to do with what you've learned.

You'll find the Departing Tenant's Questionnaire on the CD-ROM that accompanies this book. A sample is shown below.

Departing Tenant's Questionnaire

Tenant's name: ___Mavis Kelley___

Rental unit address: ___107 Bayview Street, #5, Sandler, ME___

Dates of occupancy: ___May 1, 20xx to April 30, 20xx___

Today's date: ___March 1, 20xx___

Thank you for taking a few minutes to complete this questionnaire. We value your suggestions and criticism and will use them constructively to improve our property and service.

1. Your rented home: What are the most important improvements we could make to the physical aspects of your rental that would make it more attractive to the next tenant? ___It would be great to have new windows (save on heat, less noise).___

2. Our common areas: What could we do to make these areas more usable or attractive? ___Better lights in all common areas, especially the laundry room.___

3. Our service: What suggestions do you have regarding our business practices and the way we interact with our residents? ___You should pay more attention to the little details—lights, cleaning.___

4. The rent: Do you feel that the rent you paid as of the end of your tenancy was fair? ___Yes___

5. (For multifamily rentals) Your neighbors: Do you feel that we have appropriately screened and chosen the other tenants who live at this property? ___Yes___

6. (For properties with a manager or other employees) Our employees: Were your interactions with our employees professional and satisfactory? _____
   _The manager is very gruff and it's not pleasant to deal with him._____

7. Our pitch: If you were writing an ad for this rental, what aspects would you emphasize? What aspects would you omit? _Good location, large rooms,_____
   _close to good shops. But it's noisy._____

8. The bottom line: Would you live here again? Why or why not? _Yes, though if_____
   _I had more $, I'd look for a quieter location._____

9. Other comments or suggestions: _Your cleaning service isn't doing a good job.__

10. Would you be willing to serve as a reference for this property, by speaking with interested renters over the phone or communicating via email? If so, please provide the best way to reach you: _____Yes—I'd prefer email:_____
    _maviskelley@coldmail.com_____

Office use

Reviewed by: _____   Date: _____

Notes: _____
_____
_____

How to work with tenants who are not leaving voluntarily

Unfortunately, not everyone who leaves your rental property will do so of their own accord, with a friendly handshake and a wave as they drive off. In fact, you may be planning on filling a vacancy because you're about to create one, by asking a troublesome tenant to leave. Chances are that this person does not have another living situation lined up, so the likelihood goes up that this departure will not be easy and on time. Your goal is to keep your focus on the bottom line, not on your emotional response to having to deal with someone whom you feel has not held up his end of the bargain. You want this occupant out as quickly as possible, with as little fallout as you can manage, so that you can confidently advertise, show the unit, and soon resume the rent stream with new occupants. Here's how to support that approach.

Ask Residents for Copies of Current Utility Bills

Everyone these days is concerned about the cost of gas, electricity, water, and other services. It's important that prospective occupants have an accurate idea of what they can expect to pay, since this may be a factor in their decision making. At the worst, unexpectedly high utility bills may make it hard for the tenant to afford the rent, resulting in their leaving or your need to terminate or even evict for nonpayment of rent. What a waste of your time if this happens!

To make sure applicants proceed with their eyes open, give them the facts. Ask current tenants to copy their bills or tell you how much they typically spent (in winter and summer months, if possible). You'll have this information on hand when asked (either during your phone interview or later at an open house or individual tour). As an incentive for current residents, tie the production of utility bills to your offer of a letter of recommendation, covered above (assuming you would otherwise give a recommendation).

Having utility bills also gives you a chance to compare your property's total utility cost against competing rentals. With an accurate figure on what it costs to live in your unit, you can say something like this: "When you add the utility costs to the rent, you can see that this unit is still less than the one-bedrooms down the street at Tan Apartments." Later, in Chapter 7, you'll see how to prepare a Rental Property Comparison Sheet, which can be a powerful marketing tool in a competitive market.

Properly terminate the tenancy

Landlords have wide latitude when it comes to terminating month-to-month tenancies—as long as you are not ending a tenancy for a discriminatory reason (a topic discussed in Chapter 2), or (in most states) a retaliatory reason, such as terminating because the tenant reported unfit living conditions to a health inspector. You can legally terminate a month-to-month tenancy by simply giving the requisite amount of written notice (the notice period in most states is 30 days).

You can also terminate "for cause" when the tenant has failed to pay the rent, violated another important lease term, or engaged in serious misbehavior, such as intentional damage, drug dealing, or interference with other tenants' peace and quiet. In some situations, you must give the tenant an opportunity to stop the offending behavior (such as by paying the rent or getting rid of the pet), but other times, you can demand that the tenant move out, period. The notice periods when the termination is for cause vary from one day to ten or so days.

State laws are very specific as to how you must notify a tenant whom you're asking to leave, in either a 30-day notice or in a termination for cause. The rules tell you what the notice must say and how to say it (including, in some states, the font size and style!). Your first step must be to carefully read and apply these laws—if you are unsure, hire an attorney to handle the matter.

The consequences of launching a termination with an improper notice are apt to be very annoying. A tenant who realizes that the notice is defective may ignore it. Then, when you go to the next step—an eviction lawsuit—the judge may toss your case and you'll have to start over. Meanwhile, a new set of occupants won't be able to move in, and your old tenants will be living rent free (at least for the moment).

Conduct damage control

Dealing with tenants whom you've told to leave will be awkward at best and downright unpleasant at worst. After all, the decision to move wasn't theirs. If they're feeling angry and resentful, it's partly because they've lost control of a very important aspect of their own lives—where to live. The key to getting tenants off your property with minimal delay and damage is to return to them some measure of control, by rewarding them in exchange for their cooperation.

Compensating tenants who have stiffed you for the rent, damaged your property, or made life miserable for neighbors may be the last thing you'll feel like doing. But here is where you must stop reacting emotionally and keep your focus as a businessperson. Remember, you need to minimize your monetary losses by ending this unfortunate tenancy as soon as possible and bringing in fresh, qualified tenants. Of course, you won't want to send signals to other tenants that you're a pushover—but this approach needn't result in that, either.

Start by talking with the tenants. Some may be so mad or irrational that any attempt to talk will be futile. But if you can have a frank discussion, explain that your decision to terminate is final and that you will follow through with an eviction lawsuit, if needed. Try to see if there is anything you can do to facilitate the tenant's move. If the door is slammed in your face, so be it. But some tenants will see the writing on the wall and jump at the chance to soften the blow of the termination. Following are some of the ways landlords can smooth the transition. It goes without saying that you must offer these incentives to all departing tenants whose cooperation you need, without regard to their ethnicity, age, sex, race, and so on. If you make such offers only to those of a certain race or ethnicity, you're discriminating:

- Offer a few hours of your handyman (and your pickup) to help the tenant move belongings to another location.
- Offer to forgive a portion of the tenant's overdue rent in exchange for vacating by a certain date. Put the offer in writing and agree that a neutral third party will be the judge as to whether the tenant left on time. That way, tenants have the assurance that if they comply, you'll have a hard time successfully suing them for the entire amount of unpaid rent.
- Agree that you will not report the tenant's rent arrearage to credit

reporting agencies if he or she leaves as scheduled (this will not prevent you from suing to get paid).

- Agree that if contacted by future landlords, you will reveal only the dates in which the tenant lived on your property (disclosing the reason for the tenant's departure is legally risky anyway). Savvy landlords who hear this on the phone will read between the lines.

Reconsider your timetable if you must evict

Some tenants can't and won't believe that they have to move. No amount of straight talk or cajoling with incentives will result in their packing up. These folks have to be evicted, and even after the judgment comes down, they have to be physically moved out by the sheriff.

If you expect that you'll have to go to court to get the current resident out, don't advertise the unit. Here's why:

- **Timing.** Even if you've followed your state's termination procedures scrupulously, you can't be 100% sure that a detail didn't escape you. Starting over will add weeks to the time the unit will be vacant. Most applicants want units that are ready or soon will be.
- **Curve balls.** Complying with termination requirements won't assure a win. You never know what defenses the tenant will offer—and you can never assume that you will

win. If you lose, you won't have a vacancy to fill.

- **Appearance.** When showing the unit to prospective residents, you want the cooperation of a willing current occupant. The tenant who's leaving involuntarily has no reason to accommodate you. This translates into a hostile reception, a messy unit, and even bad-mouthing you to your visitors.

Allow for extra turnover time

Let's suppose now that you've terminated a tenancy and the residents have left, either on their own or after an eviction lawsuit. Unless you have reason to think differently, you should assume that this unit will need extra cleaning and refurbishing, particularly if the tenants have vacated after a short notice period—for example, after receiving a three-day notice to pay the rent or quit.

This translates into added downtime while you clean and refurbish. Chapter 8 discusses preparing the unit for the next rental, including how much time you should allow for when the tenancy has not ended on a positive note.

What happens when you can't deliver the rental on time?

The consequences of not being able to turn over a rental on time range from the embarrassing to the very expensive:

- **An unfortunate start to your relationship with the new tenants.** Assuming your tenants do eventually move in, they'll undoubtedly be mad and feel that you definitely owe them for the inconvenience. These feelings may easily translate into lack of consideration for you or your property.

What Happens When Leaseholding Tenants Stay On?

It's not unusual for leaseholding tenants to stay in their rental past the end of their lease. In most states, if the landlord accepts their rent, these tenants become month-to-month tenants. But what if you don't want them?

In most situations, you can file an eviction lawsuit right away to get rid of these "holdover" tenants. You don't have to first serve them with a termination notice, since their tenancy ended when the lease expired. But be careful: If you accept rent or in any way indicate that you're okay with their staying on, a judge might conclude that you implicitly agreed to their remaining as month-to-month tenants. Then, you'd have to terminate with proper notice (30 days in most states).

- **Bad press.** Other tenants will learn of the snafu and will think less of your ability to smoothly run your business.

- **Shoddy work.** To minimize the time your next tenants are cooling their heels elsewhere, you'll be tempted to clean or repair hurriedly. Rushed jobs are often botched jobs—you'll pay the price later, when a quickie repair doesn't hold up, for example.

- **Added expense to finish work on time.** If you have less time than expected to clean or refurbish, you may need to pay overtime or hire extra workers to ensure the unit will be ready for the next tenants.

- **Missed opportunities.** Cutting corners to get the next occupants moved in deprives you of the opportunity to not only do needed cleaning and repairs, but to renovate (and command a higher rent).

- **Temporary housing costs.** Frustrated tenants who have to find temporary housing and pay storage costs could sue you for the expense. Unless your lease or rental agreement includes a clause that protects you from such suits, you could face a hefty bill.

- **The value of the tenant's canceled lease.** Suppose the disappointed tenant cancels the lease and decides to look elsewhere, but cannot find a comparable rental for the same rent that you were offering? That tenant has a valid claim against you for the difference between the new, higher rent and the rent the tenant expected to pay under your lease.

Take Ten Minutes

Getting ready to re-rent involves some time and effort. But extra attention can yield valuable information and results.

- Review the Departing Tenant's Questionnaire if you receive it back in time. Try not to be defensive when you encounter criticisms.

- Update the Rental Property Fact Sheet when you're done preparing this unit for re-rental. Chapter 7 shows you how to fill in a Fact Sheet for every rental, which lists vital information that applicants are likely to ask about when responding to your ad. If you rely on an old version, you're likely to forget that you replaced the dishwasher or repainted the master bedroom, information that might tip the balance in favor of your property.

- Make sure you have a departing tenant's new address and contact information.

- Find out your state's rules for returning security deposits and comply with them.

State Laws on Returning Security Deposits

Here are citations for statutes pertaining to security deposits in each state. Some states exempt landlords from following security deposit rules when renting to a person who is under contract to purchase the property; when the occupant is an employee of the landlord, who must live on the property; and when the landlord owns fewer than a specified number of rental units (check your statutes to see if any exemptions apply).

State	Statute	Deadline for Landlord to Itemize and Return Deposit
Alabama	Ala. Code § 35-9A-201	35 days after termination of tenancy and delivery of possession
Alaska	Alaska Stat. § 34.03.070	14 days if the tenant gives proper notice to terminate tenancy; 30 days if the tenant does not give proper notice
Arizona	Ariz. Rev. Stat. Ann. § 33-1321	14 days
Arkansas	Ark. Code Ann. §§ 18-16-303 to 18-16-306	30 days
California	Cal. Civ. Code §§ 1950.5, 1940.5(g)	21 days
Colorado	Colo. Rev. Stat. §§ 38-12-102 to 38-12-104	One month, unless lease agreement specifies longer period of time (which may be no more than 60 days); 72 hours (not counting weekends or holidays) if a hazardous condition involving gas equipment requires tenant to vacate
Connecticut	Conn. Gen. Stat. Ann. §§ 47a-21	30 days, or within 15 days of receiving tenant's forwarding address, whichever is later
Delaware	Del. Code Ann. tit. 25, § 5514	20 days
District of Columbia	D.C. Code Ann § 42-3502.17; D.C. Mun. Regs. tit. 14, §§ 308 to 310	45 days

State Laws on Returning Security Deposits (cont'd)

State	Statute	Deadline for Landlord to Itemize and Return Deposit
Florida	Fla. Stat. Ann. §§ 83.49, 83.43(12)	15 to 60 days, depending on whether tenant disputes deductions
Georgia	Ga. Code Ann. §§ 44-7-30 to 44-7-37	One month
Hawaii	Haw. Rev. Stat. §§ 521-42, 521-44	14 days
Idaho	Idaho Code § 6-321	21 days or up to 30 days if landlord and tenant agree
Illinois	765 Ill. Comp. Stat. §§ 710/0.01 to 715/3	For properties with 5 or more units, 30 to 45 days, depending on whether tenant disputes deductions or if statement and receipts are furnished
Indiana	Ind. Code Ann. §§ 32-31-3-9 to 32-31-3-19	45 days
Iowa	Iowa Code Ann. § 562A.12	30 days
Kansas	Kan. Stat. Ann. §§ 58-2550, 58-2548	30 days
Kentucky	Ky. Rev. Stat. Ann. § 383.580	30 to 60 days, depending on whether tenant disputes deductions
Louisiana	La. Rev. Stat. Ann. §§ 9:3251	One month
Maine	Me. Rev. Stat. Ann. tit. 14, §§ 6031 to 6038	30 days (if written rental agreement) or 21 days (if tenancy at will)
Maryland	Md. Code Ann. [Real Prop.] §§ 8-203, 8-203.1	45 days
Massachusetts	Mass. Gen. Laws Ann. ch. 186, § 15B	30 days
Michigan	Mich. Comp. Laws §§ 554.602 to 554.616	30 days

State Laws on Returning Security Deposits (cont'd)

State	Statute	Deadline for Landlord to Itemize and Return Deposit
Minnesota	Minn. Stat. Ann. §§ 504B.175 to 504B.178	Three weeks after tenant leaves and landlord receives forwarding address; five days if tenant must leave due to building condemnation
Mississippi	Miss. Code Ann. § 89-8-21	45 days
Missouri	Mo. Ann. Stat. § 535.300	30 days
Montana	Mont. Code Ann. §§ 70-25-101 to 70-25-206	30 days 10 days if no deductions
Nebraska	Neb. Rev. Stat. § 76-1416	14 days
Nevada	Nev. Rev. Stat. Ann. §§ 118A.240 to 118A.250	30 days
New Hampshire	N.H. Rev. Stat. Ann §§ 540-A:5 to 540-A:8; 540-B:10	30 days. For shared facilities, if the deposit is more than 30 days' rent, landlord must provide written agreement acknowledging receipt and specifying when deposit will be returned—if no written agreement, 20 days after tenant vacates
New Jersey	N.J. Stat. Ann. §§ 46:8-19, 46:8-21, 46:8-26	30 days; five days in case of fire, flood, condemnation, or evacuation. Does not apply to owner-occupied building with two or fewer units where tenant fails to provide 30 days' written notice to landlord invoking provisions of act
New Mexico	N.M. Stat. Ann. § 47-8-18	30 days
New York	N.Y. Gen. Oblig. Law §§ 7-103 to 7-108	Reasonable time
North Carolina	N.C. Gen. Stat. §§ 42-50 to 42-56	30 days
North Dakota	N.D. Cent. Code §§ 47-16-07.1	30 days

State Laws on Returning Security Deposits (cont'd)

State	Statute	Deadline for Landlord to Itemize and Return Deposit
Ohio	Ohio Rev. Code Ann. § 5321.16	30 days
Oklahoma	Okla. Stat. Ann. tit. 41, § 115	30 days
Oregon	Or. Rev. Stat. § 90.300	31 days
Pennsylvania	68 Pa. Cons. Stat. Ann. §§ 250.511a to 250.512	30 days
Rhode Island	R.I. Gen. Laws § 34-18-19	20 days
South Carolina	S.C. Code Ann. § 27-40-410	30 days
South Dakota	S.D. Codified Laws Ann. §§ 43.32-6.1, 43-32-24	Two weeks to return entire deposit or a portion, and supply reasons for withholding; 45 days for a written, itemized accounting, if tenant requests it
Tennessee	Tenn. Code Ann. § 66-28-301	No statutory deadline to return; 10 days to itemize
Texas	Tex. Prop. Code Ann. §§ 92.101 to 92.109	30 days
Utah	Utah Code Ann. §§ 57-17-1 to 57-17-5	30 days, or within 15 days of receiving tenant's forwarding address, whichever is later, but if there is damage to the premises, 30 days
Vermont	Vt. Stat. Ann. tit. 9, § 4461	14 days
Virginia	Va. Code Ann. §§ 55-248.15:1	45 days
Washington	Wash. Rev. Code Ann. §§ 59.18.260 to 59.18.285	14 days
W. Virginia	No statute	
Wisconsin	Wis. Admin. Code ATCP 134.06	21 days
Wyoming	Wyo. Stat. §§ 1-21-1207, 1-21-1208	30 days, or within 15 days of receiving tenant's forwarding address, which-ever is later; 60 days if there is damage

State Laws on Notice to Inspect or Show Rental Property

This is a synopsis of state laws on the amount of notice required before landlords may enter a rental.

State	Statute	Notice Required
Alabama	Ala. Code § 35-9A-303	2 days
Alaska	Alaska Stat. § 34.03.140	24 hours
Arizona	Ariz. Rev. Stat. Ann. § 33-1343	Two days
Arkansas	Ark. Code Ann. § 18-17-602	No notice specified
California	Cal. Civ. Code § 1954	24 hours (48 hours for initial move-out inspection)
Colorado	No statute	
Connecticut	Conn. Gen. Stat. Ann. §§ 47a-16 to 47a-16a	Reasonable notice
Delaware	Del. Code Ann. tit. 25, §§ 5509, 5510	Two days
DC	No statute	
Florida	Fla. Stat. Ann. § 83.53	12 hours
Georgia	No statute	
Hawaii	Haw. Rev. Stat. §§ 521-53, 521-70(b)	Two days
Idaho	No statute	
Illinois	No statute	
Indiana	Ind. Code Ann. § 32-31-5-6	Reasonable notice
Iowa	Iowa Code Ann. §§ 562A.19, 562A.28, 562A.29	24 hours
Kansas	Kan. Stat. Ann. §§ 58-2557, 58-2565	Reasonable notice
Kentucky	Ky. Rev. Stat. Ann. § 383.615, 383.670	Two days
Louisiana	La. Civ. Code art. 2693	No notice specified
Maine	Me. Rev. Stat. Ann. tit. 14, § 6025	24 hours
Maryland	No statute	
Massachusetts	Mass. Gen. Laws Ann. ch. 186, § 15B(1)(a)	No notice specified
Michigan	No statute	
Minnesota	Minn. Stat. Ann. § 504B.211	Reasonable notice

State Laws on Notice to Inspect or Show Rental Property (cont'd)

State	Statute	Notice Required
Mississippi	No statute	
Missouri	No statute	
Montana	Mont. Code Ann. § 70-24-312	24 hours
Nebraska	Neb. Rev. Stat. § 76-1423	One day
Nevada	Nev. Rev. Stat. Ann. § 118A.330; 76-1432	24 hours
New Hampshire	N.H. Rev. Stat. Ann. § 540-A:3	Notice that is adequate under the circumstances
New Jersey	No statute	
New Mexico	N.M. Stat. Ann. § 47-8-24; 47-8-34	24 hours
New York	No statute	
North Carolina	No statute	
North Dakota	N.D. Cent. Code § 47-16-07.3	Reasonable notice
Ohio	Ohio Rev. Code Ann. §§ 5321.04(A)(8), 5321.05(B)	24 hours
Oklahoma	Okla. Stat. Ann. tit. 41, § 128	One day
Oregon	Or. Rev. Stat. § 90.322	24 hours
Pennsylvania	No statute	
Rhode Island	R.I. Gen. Laws § 34-18-26	Two days
South Carolina	S.C. Code Ann. § 27-40-530	24 hours
South Dakota	No statute	
Tennessee	Tenn. Code Ann. § 66-28-403, 66-28-507	No notice specified
Texas	No statute	
Utah	Utah Code Ann. § 57-22-5(2)(c)	No notice specified
Vermont	Vt. Stat. Ann. tit. 9, § 4460	48 hours
Virginia	Va. Code Ann. § 55-248.18	24 hours
Washington	Wash. Rev. Code Ann. § 59.18.150	Two days
West Virginia	No statute	
Wisconsin	Wis. Stat. Ann. § 704.05(2)	Advance notice
Wyoming	No statute	

How to Advertise Effectively

The first step to finding good tenants is to let people know your rental is available. There are lots of ways to get the word out about your rental, from the old-fashioned sign in the window to newspaper or online ads to participation in an employer referral program. Where and how you advertise will depend on many factors, including:

- the temperature of the market for rentals like yours—you'll need to be more aggressive if the market is awash with similar vacancies
- the type of renter who will likely be your tenant—advertise where they will see your ad
- the size of your rental property (single-family home or multiunit building)—large landlords may be able to secure "bulk" rates that make some advertising avenues more affordable
- how much time you'll give yourself to fill the vacancy—you might have a month if tenants give notice and are cooperative, or only a few days if a tenant has just moved out, leaving unpaid rent
- where you live in relation to the rental—some ad methods, such as posting signs, require hands-on work
- your budget—you'll need to make sure that higher ad costs will be justified by a quicker rental, and
- your own preferences for doing business.

✓ Before You Advertise

Before investigating your options and designing your advertising campaign, check that you've taken care of the essential preliminaries:

☑ Make sure you have the cooperation of current tenants (if any), or wait until the unit is vacant (Chapter 3).

☑ Know what you're seeking in a tenant (your screening plans and rental priorities) and make sure your lease or rental agreement is consistent on key terms, such as rent and deposits (Chapter 6).

☑ Decide how you will show the rental (individual tour or open house) and how you plan to pre-screen prospects (Chapter 5).

☑ Get advertising recommendations from landlords with similar local properties.

☑ If a local real estate office or property management firm is handling all your advertising, be sure to ask what their advertising plans are, including any special costs. Chapter 1 discusses how to find and work with a local real estate office.

Your advertising efforts need to be cost-effective, but not so miserly that you end up with months of vacant time. Sometimes it pays to spend a bit more in order to quickly generate a group of suitable applicants. For example, suppose your rental is $1,500 per month, which means that each day of vacancy costs you $50. It may be worth it to spend a few hundred dollars to fill this vacancy faster than you would using a low-cost approach that won't reach as many potential residents, particularly if you have a cash flow problem (you need the rent to pay the mortgage). If you rent the unit fast, that extra advertising expense will pay for itself. The key is to design and place ads that will generate at least a minimum number of qualified applicants.

Identify your market

Your advertising strategy may be as simple as placing a "For Rent" sign in front of your building plus an online ad on craigslist, or it may consist of a range of paid advertising, including newspaper ads. This chapter reviews the options and explains what works best in different situations. Your first step towards designing your advertising strategy is to ask yourself, "Who is likely to want to live here, and where are they likely to look when seeking a rental?"

Consider the neighborhood

The attributes (and drawbacks) of the neighborhood will shape the range of people who will want to live there. Most

Landlord's Forms Library

This chapter includes the following forms, which will help you organize and implement your advertising approach:

- **Marketing Worksheet.** Lists the details about the rental, such as size, rent, amenities, and terms that will help drive your advertising efforts.
- **Tenant Referral Program.** A handout for current tenants that describes who can participate in your tenant referral program, what's the prize for a successful referral, and other rules.
- **Employer Referral Amendment.** For landlords who work with a local employer as a source of applicants, this lease amendment spells out the incentives, such as a reduced security deposit, that you've offered tenants of participating employers.

Make an advertising file for your rental property with these forms, plus copies of your ads and flyers. Include your Marketing Worksheet and note the results of the different types of ads (you'll complete this portion when you start getting calls from tenants or holding open houses). Use what you learn the next time you advertise.

of the time, after analyzing your location, you'll end up with a fairly defined set of potential renters. Now and then, you'll conclude that the area will appeal to a widely mixed group of renters, but that's the exception. After considering the following points, you'll probably be able to describe your potential residents with some detail:

- **What's the current mix of residents?** By looking at who lives in the neighborhood already, you'll get a sense of the type of people who are attracted to this area. If your rental is in a multiunit building, or you've owned the property for quite a while, you should have a good idea of who's likely to rent it. You can also talk to shop owners who service the area about who lives in the neighborhood. You may learn that most tenants work at a nearby company, or that they commute long hours to distant jobs. Perhaps they're mostly young families who eventually buy their own homes, or maybe they're a mix of students and singles.

- **Are there large employers or colleges nearby?** Though we don't find many formal "company towns" these days, it's not uncommon for whole sections of town to comprise employees of large manufacturers or other businesses. In cities with large colleges or universities, there are almost always student neighborhoods, either near the schools or in adjacent (often more affordable) neighborhoods. Universities and large employers have housing assistance offices, which may be fertile sources of tenants.

- **Is the rental in an outstanding school district?** Renters may choose your neighborhood in order to take advantage of the excellent local school district.

- **Is there a major medical or military facility close by?** Hospital workers often work long and unusual hours, which makes living nearby a real plus. Military personnel are likewise apt to live near their bases (and the military is providing less and less on-base housing). Medical and military installations can be a huge source of applicants for you.

- **Is the rental conveniently close to good interurban public transportation?** If so, you may be able to appeal to renters who not only work locally but at a distance, too.

- **Is there a well-rounded array of shops, movies, and restaurants nearby?** You may be able to capture one of the growing numbers of "renting by choice" ex-homeowners, who have given up punishing mortgages and remote locations for the convenience of close-in living.

- **How safe is the neighborhood?** If it's relatively crime-free, you may attract singles and families; if it's iffy, you may be looking at adults without children.

The Law You Need to Know

Your advertising plan needs to be targeted and cost-efficient—and within legal bounds. Be safe by remembering these legal rules:

- Antidiscrimination laws, explained in Chapter 2, affect the wording and placement of your ads.
- For landlords who develop a tenant referral program, your state laws may regulate how you run it.
- For landlords who offer rent incentives in rent control areas, the rent control ordinance may impose restrictions on your program.

Consider the rental

By taking a careful and honest look at the size, amenities, and rent of the unit you're trying to fill, you can further describe the pool of applicants you'd like to attract. A modest one-bedroom in a blue-collar neighborhood won't attract executive types, so you can forget about advertising in a glitzy rental magazine. On the other hand, an ad in a local newspaper might be quite effective. So, consider the following aspects of your unit:

- **Size.** This factor is very important. A three-bedroom unit will primarily attract families, but will also appeal to roommates who live together as friends or couples. An ad in a local parent or school magazine might be a good bet for reaching families, but you wouldn't bother if your rental is a studio. To reach couples and roommates, list in a local alternative newspaper that appeals to young people.
- **Rent.** The monthly rent will further define the pool of likely applicants. If you apply the industry's rule of thumb that the rent should not be more than one-third of the tenant's income, you can figure the minimum income and project how you'll reach those folks. For example, someone who brings home $4,000 a month can afford your $1,000 rent, but is not likely to see your ad on the bulletin board at the yacht club. A $2,500 rent is something else again, since the person who can afford that may well be able to afford the expense of a boat.
- **Pets.** If you're willing to accept pets, you'll open a whole avenue of advertising that petless landlords won't use. Some local SPCA websites offer landlords a place to list their vacancies (check out www.sfspca. org).
- **Amenities.** Your rental offers more than just a roof over the tenants' heads. It may have parking, play areas, a high-speed Internet connection, furnishings, a gourmet

kitchen, a security system, a pool, or a gym. Perhaps the unit is already accessible to someone using a wheelchair. These attributes will appeal to particular types of tenants.

Create a Marketing Worksheet

You'll find it convenient to list in one place the various details about your rental (rent, size of unit, terms, and so on) that you'll need for your advertising efforts, no matter what avenue you choose. This is the one piece of paper you'll take to the neighborhood newspaper office and show the classified ad desk clerk, or use when you compose an ad online or design a flyer to post on neighborhood bulletin boards. You'll use this sheet personally, too, when you start taking phone calls from interested applicants or prepare a Rental Property Fact Sheet to hand out at open houses, as explained in Chapter 6. Finally, a Marketing Worksheet gives you a place to record what advertising method you chose, what worked, and what didn't—valuable information for the next time you market this rental.

The Marketing Worksheet form is simple to fill out. Below is a sample filled out by a hypothetical landlord Ann, a retired schoolteacher who kept her first house when she remarried after her first husband passed away. The house is a charming, single-family residence in a

college town near the state capitol. Ann defined her pool of likely applicants—her market for this house—by thinking about the neighborhood and her specific rental. The sample doesn't reflect Ann's showing method or whether she will prescreen—we'll address those issues in Chapters 5 and 7, and show you her conclusions there.

You'll find the Marketing Worksheet on the CD-ROM that accompanies this book.

Use a digital camera for quick, inexpensive photos. If your place is good-looking, these can add a lot of value to online ads and bulletin board ads, and you can email them to prospects who call in response to your ads.

Use word-of-mouth

Many experienced landlords will tell you that word-of-mouth is the best method, hands down, for finding good tenants. For starters, word-of-mouth is cheap. It has the potential to yield the best tenants because they are effectively prescreened by your friends and acquaintances before they get to you. Word-of-mouth is likely to work best when:

- **You provide a clear description of the property and its basic terms.** You can use a flyer, like you would post on a neighborhood bulletin board, discussed below.

Marketing Worksheet (excerpt)

Marketing Worksheet

Last updated: _April 3, 20xx_   By: _Ann_

Rental Property

Address _37 "D" Street, Collegetown, CA_

Location

Neighborhood residents	Professionals, students, not too many families
Employers/colleges/universities	State college w/in biking distance. Train (30 min. ride to capitol (10 min. walk to station). 8 blocks to elementary school, 6 blocks to middle school, 2 miles to high school
Hospitals/military bases	Dental and medical buildings downtown, hosp. at west end (5 miles away)
School districts Elementary	Baywood District (scores in top 1/3 of state)
Secondary	Collegetown Unified, scores in top half

Rental

Size	3 bedroom, 2.5 bath, sep. dining room, 2-car garage, fenced yard, storage shed
Rent	$2,000/month, $4,000 security deposit
Terms	One year lease, one dog & one cat OK
Amenities	Hardwood floors, new Meile dishwasher, washer & dryer, freezer in garage, established rose garden, gardener twice a month included, farmers' market 2x/week, 5 blocks away.

Describe the pool of likely applicants

Retired couples, students, government workers commuting to capitol, families

- **The referring person knows you well.** A friend, relative, work colleague, or even a local businessperson with whom you have a good relationship (such as your doctor, dentist, or lawyer) all may provide good referrals. Someone who knows that you have high business standards will send you appropriate candidates.
- **The referring person has good judgment.** Someone whose values and business expectations are similar to yours should give you good leads.
- **The referring person is one of your good tenants.** A tenant who has lived on your property and knows how you conduct business is likely to refer someone who will be comfortable with your style. (Offering a tenant referral program, described below, is a more formal way to enlist residents' help in finding tenants.)

- **The referring person really knows the person being referred.** This is crucial. For example, suppose your tenant Jim tells you about a friend of his Aunt Sally—the friend wants to rent your place. Jim may know nothing about Aunt Sally's friend, and is probably passing on the reference out of a sense of obligation to Aunt Sally. You are really getting *Aunt Sally's* recommendation, and since you don't know Aunt Sally, her friend has not been prescreened by someone whose filters you trust.

If you get a referral by word-of-mouth, resist the temptation to offer a lease right away, no matter how great the person sounds. Never shortcut your normal screening processes—always give a referral a rental application and follow through to confirm it. You may discover that the applicant isn't as solid as you were led to believe. And you must never forget the fair housing giant in the

---

Word-of-Mouth: Will It Work for You?

Word-of-mouth works best when:
- You have a wide network of friends and acquaintances who know how you do business and are familiar with your standards.
- You trust the judgment of the referring person.
- The referring person is one of your good tenants and knows how you conduct business.
- The referring person knows the one being referred (rather than a friend of a friend of a friend).

corner—don't let it appear that you have lower standards for some people (other people may be members of a protected group, and may complain).

Set up a tenant referral program

If you're seriously interested in filling vacancies by word-of-mouth, consider setting up a tenant referral program. The time and effort you put into the program will pay off as qualified applicants come to you courtesy of your current good tenants. Don't decide to forego this avenue because you have only one or two rentals—though your army of referring tenants is smaller, you still may get a good lead. Use a tenant referral program to tell current tenants how your program works (a filled-out sample appears below). Here are the details:

- **Who can participate.** Open the program to current tenants who are paid up in their rent, and who have signed off on your program rules (see below). Don't overlook your departing tenants, who may be especially fertile sources since their friends and acquaintances know they're moving and the subject has undoubtedly been discussed. ("You're moving next month? Wow, I wish I could find another place, too … this one is so noisy.")
- **What's a successful referral?** You'll want any new resident to have paid

all deposits and rent, and to have lived in the rental for at least one month (you may want to specify a longer time). The new tenant must have listed the referring resident when applying for the vacancy. Put this information on the "Where did you learn of this vacancy?" question at the end of the rental application (included in Chapter 6).

- **Add some legal protections.** Describe referring residents as independent contractors, not employees (this keeps you free of entanglements such as income tax withholding that an employment relationship would involve). Specify that the person making the referral must abide by fair housing laws (you wouldn't want a tenant telling prospects that you want only childless tenants, for example), and will be disqualified if they do not. Give yourself the option of changing or ending the program at any time.
- **What's the prize?** Make the reward attractive enough to generate some interest. You can give cash awards, gift certificates, or rent reductions—anything worth $100 or more will do the trick. But be careful: In some states, such as Texas, referral programs are illegal (only licensed brokers can fill this role) and others, including Florida, limit the value of the award. Check with your state department of real estate for the rules. You should find

yours by searching on your state government's home page, or check out the website State and Local Government on the Net (www. statelocalgov.net/index.cfm), which includes a comprehensive directory of state and local government websites.

- **Give tenants a flyer with details on your property and a sheet on your referral program.** Prepare a flyer similar to the one you'd post on a neighborhood bulletin board, discussed in the next section. Use the Tenant Referral Program form, on this book's CD-ROM, for all participating tenants to sign, acknowledging that they've read the rules and agree to abide by them. Distribute the information to all residents, even those whose

judgment you don't trust. If their leads are no good, you'll find out by evaluating the rental applications of the people they've referred.

You'll find the Tenant Referral Program form on the CD-ROM that accompanies this book. Use it to inform your residents of the way your program works.

Post "For Rent" signs

"For Rent" signs in the window or the front yard are economical ways to advertise if you can count on some traffic past your property and a sign can be easily seen from the street. They're also highly effective in hot markets, when seekers are trolling the neighborhoods for

---

Tenant Referral Program: Will It Work for You?

A tenant referral program works best when:

- Your state does not restrict such programs.
- You own a multiunit building or several rental houses in the area.
- Your current residents are mostly good tenants (it takes one to know one). If you have a bunch of marginal residents, you're likely to get references to the same.
- Your incentives are attractive enough to generate interest among your tenants.
- You are willing to take the time to set your program up right, by communicating rules that protect you and clarify how the program works.
- You're in a soft market and need an edge to set your property apart (the edge is your tenants' personal recommendations).

Tenant Referral Program

Dear Tenant,

The rental property at <u>37 "D" Street, Collegetown, CA</u> will soon be vacant and on the market. I'd like to offer you the chance to help me fill it with good, qualified tenants—like you! If you can refer an applicant to me who passes my good-tenant criteria and who rents the property from me, I'll reward you with <u>$100</u>. Here's how the program works:

1. At the time you make the referral and until the end of your tenancy, you must be fully paid up in your rent and any deposits, and not be subject to a termination notice.

2. The referred applicant must tell me the first time we meet (at an open house, for example) or speak (in a phone conversation) that he or she was referred to me by you. Your name must also appear on the "Where did you learn of this vacancy?" question in my Rental Application.

3. Before you may collect the reward, the new tenant must have paid all deposits and rent, and must have lived in the rental for at least <u>2 months</u>.

4. You understand that your participation in this program does not make you my agent or employee (you are an independent contractor). You also agree to abide by all federal, state, and local fair housing laws.

5. Your signature at the end of this form indicates that you have read it, understand it, and agree to abide by its terms.

Thank you for your interest in my referral program!

<u>Pat Malley</u>
Landlord

<u>March 3, 20xx</u>
Date

_____
Current tenant

_____
Date

available rentals. If the rental is occupied, discuss the sign with your tenant first, and include a request not to disturb the occupants.

⚠️ **Think twice about using a sign when the unit is vacant and it's easy to figure this out from the street.** You don't want to invite a burglary (vacant homes are easy targets for thieves who want to steal appliances), or make the unit a haven for drug dealers who want a private place to do their business.

If you're using a sign that you'll place on the ground, put it at right angles to the street, so that drivers coming from both directions can see it. If your rental is on a cul de sac or lightly used street, consider using a sandwich board on a nearby corner with more traffic. Be sure to check with local police regarding permissible use of the sidewalks or curbs and with the local zoning department for any regulations regarding signs.

Use a clean, well-made sign that is easy to read. You can buy these at a hardware store or sign shop, or order them from a place like Peachtree Business Products, which sells all kinds of signs and property management supplies. (You can check out Peachtree's catalog online at www.pbp1.com, or request a copy by calling 800-241-4623.)

Your sign should include only the basic information: number of bedrooms, available date, and your phone number. Mention the rent if you think that the rent is consistent with the property's curb appeal and other rents in the neighborhood. In other words, include the rent if people seeing the sign won't be surprised that a unit in your building or neighborhood rents for the stated amount. But if the building or area are not as nice as the rental itself—perhaps

---

"For Rent" Sign: Will It Work for You?

Property signs work best when:

- There's lots of car or foot traffic past your rental property.
- It's easy to see the rental unit yard or windows from the street.
- The rental is in a building that's well maintained, not a hidden gem in an otherwise unattractive setting.
- You're in a hot market or area where seekers are trolling the neighborhood.
- Your signs are neat and clear with sufficient information to pique interest. If your sign is shabby, it sends a message that the rental may be, too.

the unit is in the back, next to a quiet garden, or you've completely redone it—leave the rent out. After someone sees the unit, the rent won't appear to be out of line.

Advertise in the newspapers

After word-of-mouth and "For Rent" signs, ads in the local newspaper are the most popular and effective means of reaching potential renters. If your rental is in or near a large metropolitan area serviced by a major paper, your ad will probably also run in the online version of the paper, which will greatly expand your audience.

Here are the issues to consider before placing a newspaper ad.

Which newspaper should you use?

If your property is in a small town or a rural area serviced by one nearby paper, place your ad in that one paper. But many times, a local paper overlaps with a larger regional paper. For example, readers of the California *Long Beach Sentinel* are quite likely to also read the *Los Angeles Times*. Should you place your ad in both? Consider the following factors:

- **Where do tenants come from?** If you're pretty sure that your applicants will be locals, stick with the local paper. On the other hand, if your rental is in a bedroom community, a growing city, or a college town, your applicants may be searching from out of the area. Those folks may not have even heard of the local paper—but chances are they know about the large paper that covers your town and will figure out how to get a copy or will see the ad online.

- **What's worked in the past?** Consult other landlords in the area and ask them what newspaper worked best for them. Consider your own experience, too—if you've found that local advertising may take longer but tends to yield a higher number of qualified applicants, it may be the best avenue.

- **Check the papers themselves for rentals like yours.** Tenants will look in papers that have a decent volume of ads. You may be served well with an ad that's one among many because these listings are going to be read by a sizable number of people. Lone ads in papers that don't have any other properties like yours are just that—alone and without many readers.

- **Cost.** As with any advertising, you'll want to measure the cost against the amount of lost rent for every week that the rental remains vacant. If your response rate of qualified applicants increases dramatically with a pricier but more widely read newspaper, it's worth the added expense.

- **Online component.** An online listing, whether in the paper's own website or through an affiliation with an online service, will greatly extend your exposure. This feature will benefit applicants from beyond the physical reach of the newspaper—and if they're your applicant pool, this is how to get to them.
- **Foreign language versions.** If there are large numbers of foreign speakers in your applicant pool or town, you'll want to reach these folks in their own language. If the group is big enough, the local paper may offer an online translation (for example, the *San Jose Mercury News* will list your ad in its Spanish and Vietnamese online versions).
- **Ability to handle the details online.** Placing your ad from your computer, rather than in person or on the phone, will be convenient, especially if you don't live locally or can't easily appear at the newspaper office in person.

Besides local newspapers, consider any neighborhood papers that may circulate in your area. These publications are less dedicated to overall news coverage than their larger cousins, and tend to concentrate on truly local issues and politics. Some are quite well established and have a dedicated readership. You may find that neighborhood papers are fruitful sources of tenants if your rental is the kind of place its readers would choose. For example, suppose you have a studio apartment within walking distance of good shops, restaurants, movies, and medical and dental offices. If the neighborhood weekly features these types of local small businesses, it must mean that it's read by local residents who patronize these establishments (otherwise, the businesses wouldn't continue to advertise there).

When should your ad run?

Be sure your ad runs for at least one Sunday, because many tenants consider the Sunday paper as the definitive place to begin a search. Whether to run the ad during the week will depend on your assessment of the market and the chances of a quick rental. Obviously, you don't want to pay for ad space that you think you won't need; on the other hand, taking out a second ad may be more expensive than choosing a longer run time at the outset. For guidance, consult with others in the neighborhood with similar properties—if neighboring landlords needed only one Sunday placement, you might try that; but if it generally takes a week or more to land acceptable tenants, heed the advice. You may also be able to take advantage of special rates for consecutive day placement, and you should find out if the paper designates a particular day to showcase home rentals.

If you need to list a property for more than a week, refresh your ad by changing the look and the wording (you don't want applicants to conclude that a rental is still available because it's a dog). Be sure to check the paper to confirm that the ad runs as you wrote it—ask for a tear sheet (the newspaper's rough draft) if you don't live nearby and can't easily get a copy of the paper, or if the ad doesn't run online. You should get your money back and a fresh, correct ad if the paper has published incorrect text.

What should your ad say?

An effective ad will catch the reader's attention and convey enough information to accurately describe the unit. Since most ads are priced by the line, you won't want to go overboard with unnecessary descriptions, however. Your goal is to generate responses only from those who want—and can afford—what you're offering and can meet your terms. The last thing you want is to field dozens of calls that end with, "I'm sorry, it doesn't sound like this rental will meet your needs." And should you decide to dispense with prescreening phone calls, you certainly don't want an open house full of people whom you would never rent to. On the other hand, you wouldn't want an empty house because your ad was too boring to generate any interest.

All ads should include basic information, such as:

- **Location.** Some newspapers and websites will group ads according to their neighborhoods—if yours does this, it's less important to describe the area. You may decide to omit mentioning the neighborhood if it has negative connotations (hopefully, your unit is part of a renaissance). Mention the street address only if that's a plus (for example, your building is noticeably better looking than its neighbors); include cross streets if precise location is critical (in some neighborhoods, a block or two either way makes a big difference).

- **Number of bedrooms and bathrooms.** Be creative here—you may want to describe one of the bedrooms as a den in order to capture the home office crowd.

- **Major amenities.** Include decks, gardens, garages, dishwashers, fireplaces, security services, high-speed Internet access, recent renovations (especially involving the kitchen), and whether the unit is furnished.

- **Rent.** Most readers of your ad will be looking for rents at or below a specified amount. If you omit the rent, you're likely to get calls or visits from people who can't afford the rental. If you're tempted to leave the rent out, it's probably because you've overpriced the unit—if you've set a market rent, you should have no hesitation in stating it.

- **Incentives.** Mention any incentives that you've decided to offer, such as a month's free rent—but heed the cautionary advice, below.

- **Utilities.** Include who pays for water, gas, electricity, and heat. In some areas and at some times of the year, these are hefty amounts that will make a difference to the tenant's monthly expenses.

- **Pets.** Applicants usually know whether they need a rental that is dog or cat friendly. Including your policy in the ad ensures that you'll get applicants that fit your preferences—and you won't waste time with others. Don't assume that allowing pets will set you up for damage—interestingly, expanding the market to pet-owning tenants may actually result in more applicants who are extra conscientious (because they know

that there are fewer pet-friendly rentals than no-pet rentals, they may try extra hard to be attractive applicants and good tenants).

- **Attention grabber.** Finally, use a word or a phrase early in the ad that will grab the reader's attention. Focus on the main selling point of your rental. If it's within a well-known school district, headline your ad with, "First-Rate Schools!" If proximity to convenient downtown areas is its main asset, point that out ("walking distance to Solano Avenue restaurants and shops"), and so on, whether it's the rent ("Affordable!"), the views ("Ocean View!"), the neighborhood charm

Use Incentives With Caution

When competition is fierce, many landlords will offer incentives (such as one month's free rent, or a promise of a new appliance to incoming tenants) to entice applicants. To make up for the lost revenue, they'll often raise the rent a little bit or charge some other fee. Savvy tenants are wary of these deals, figuring that if the landlord has to go to these extremes, there must be something wrong (there often is), or it's a gimmick (landlords will figure out how to make up for the perk in the long run).

Incentives are a risky way to attract residents—you want someone who will choose your property because they want to live there, not because they *think* they will save a bit of money or get something for free. The person who chooses your rental because of the incentive is like the shopper who makes a purchase because it's on sale—many of those garments languish in the closet because the shopper never really liked them in the first place. This tenant is not likely to be happy and will move on soon.

Abbreviations in Your Ads

Here's a list of some typical abbreviations used in advertising

A/C	air conditioner	micro	microwave
AEK	all electric kitchen	pkg.	parking
ba	bathroom	renov.	renovated
bldg.	building	remod.	remodeled
BR	bedroom	RM	room
DA	dining area	S/S	side by side
disp.	disposal	sf	square foot
DR	dining room	trans.	transportation
DW	dishwasher	Util. incl.	utilities included
FP	fireplace	W/D	washer/dryer
HW	hardwood floors	W/in clst.	walk-in closet
incl.	includes	w/w	wall to wall carpet
sh/shr	shared, to share	eff	efficiency (a studio or one-room apartment)
LR	living room	cable ready	electrical structure ready for Cable TV

Be careful that you do not go overboard with these handy shortcuts—weary readers are likely to give up if they have to decipher every other word. You're better off using a few commonly known abbreviations, and either trimming the information you provide or paying a bit more for an extra line or two. If you post online, you'll find that the provider will automatically select some abbreviations, and you'll have to live with that. But when composing your own ads, consider these factors before peppering them with abbreviations:

- **Who is your reader or applicant?** Ads for high-end rentals that may attract older applicants should not include more than the basic shorthand. These readers may be unfamiliar with these advertising shortcuts.

- **Which abbreviations do other ads in this paper use?** Take a look at the other rental ads and note which abbreviations are commonly used, and whether the paper provides a "key" at the start of the Classified section. Avoid terms that do not appear on the list.

- **Can you summarize using whole words?** Sometimes it's better to be general than specific, if you can get your point over. For example, instead of listing the new stove, refrigerator, and dishwasher, you can say, "new kitchen appliances."

Classic Neighborhood!"), or the renovations ("Redone Beauty!").

- **Date available.** Most housing seekers will assume that a listing is either available now or on the upcoming first of the month. If your rental won't be available until after that, say so.

- **Contact and viewing information.** You'll need to decide how you're going to show the rental—in a public open house or individually by appointment. Chapter 5 guides you through this decision. If you're doing individual tours or private open houses, you will probably do some prescreening over the phone, so you'll need to list a phone number in your ad, and maybe specify the best hours to call (Chapter 7 explains phone screening in detail). If you are cutting right to the chase —holding a public open house— just list the date and time and street address, with a cross-street if it's hard to find (or if the intersection highlights its desirable location).

- **Fair housing commitment.** All landlords should know and follow fair housing laws, described in detail in Chapter 2. If you can afford to add to your ad, it's a good idea to recite your commitment to abiding by these rules. Something as short and simple as, "We abide by fair housing laws" will do. (Some landlords must post fair housing posters, as described in Chapter 2.)

⚠ Be enthusiastic, but don't over-hype your rental. It's a mistake to mischaracterize your rental. You'll end up wasting your time when disappointed applicants turn away in dismay, and you may even be held to your misrepresentations should someone rent from you in reliance on your promises or descriptions and then withholds rent, breaks a lease, or sues in small claims when you don't deliver. If you have a small bungalow in a so-so part of town, don't make it sound like a designer showcase in a great neighborhood.

Design your ad

Now it's time to design your ad—choosing its words and look. Fortunately, you don't need a degree in design or marketing to pull this off. Instead, you can take a lesson from the professionals who do have these degrees and experience—and then use your knowledge to craft your own copy. Here's how.

The website of the *Los Angeles Times* (www.latimes.com) has a particularly thoughtful and complete system for creating a print classified ad (its online ads are handled by apartments.com). It takes you step-by-step through the information a good rental ad should include, with suggested wording, drop-down lists, and even formatting options. The website is as good as a worksheet, allowing you to craft and change the ad as you wish (the site even gives you a mock-up that shows just how your ad will look in a newspaper). Visit the site to see how it works (from the *Times* home page, choose Rentals, then Place an Ad), and use the samples there as a model against which to gauge other sites or plain print advertisers. If the local papers don't offer the same service, use the *L.A. Times* as a model for doing your own ad.

Here's what you should consider when choosing a newspaper to run your ad:

- **Region.** If you're placing an ad in a large paper, check to see if it publishes different versions for different areas of its circulation area (for example, the *L.A. Times* lists several regions within its circulation). You should be able to choose the region where you want your ad to run.

- **Ad style.** You should be able to choose between small print or large, and a headline or not. If you

design your ad online, you should get previews of how each choice will look.

- **Elements of the ad.** The newspaper should prompt you through the basic information it deems necessary for your ad, such as the number of bedrooms, bathrooms, length of rental term (month-to-month or a fixed-term lease) and the rent.

- **Your personalized message.** Most papers give you space to tout your rental, where you can include information about proximity to schools, new appliances, parking, pets, and so on.

- **Email contact for photos, directions, or other details.** If you have digital photos of your property, or want to give interested readers directions from common landmarks or

---

Newspaper Advertising: Will It Work for You?

Advertising in a large regional paper works best when:

- You're interested in reaching a wide audience (typically in a soft market).
- That's the traditional way landlords in your area find tenants.
- Your pool of interested tenants is likely to look there (especially so when tenants come from out of town).
- Interested renters are likely to also look online and the paper has an online component.

Advertising in a local or neighborhood paper works best when:

- The paper is widely read and your pool of tenants is likely to be local.
- It's a paper with a theme, such as one devoted to family issues, or a particular readership, such as residents who work in high tech, and certain aspects of your rental will attract this group.

additional details, consider setting up an email account dedicated to this tenant search only. You don't even need a digital camera—see "Use Free Internet Services to Provide Pictures, Maps, and Directions," below, for advice.

Avoid ads that unintentionally discriminate

Never advertise properties with a stated preference as to the age, color, race, ethnicity, sex, handicap, familial status, or religion of the tenant. This is clearly illegal. (See Chapter 2 for details on fair housing laws and protected groups.) But even if you don't overtly discriminate in your ad, you could be accused of discrimination if your advertising ends up indirectly discriminating against certain groups, by giving the impression that you have certain preferences. This could happen in two ways.

Your ad uses language that sends discriminatory signals. Landlords need to be careful that they do not unwittingly write discriminatory ads. For a while in the early 1990s, the issue of discriminatory ads became quite fraught, with owners wondering whether "master bedroom"

Use Free Internet Services to Provide Pictures, Maps, and Directions

As handy and ubiquitous as digital cameras have become, there is an even easier way to show prospective renters what your property and neighborhood look like. And you don't even need any hardware.

Free services provided by Google (Google Earth), Amazon, and Microsoft provide street-level pictures, detailed maps, and driving directions for any address in most major cities from anywhere in the country (more-populous areas have received the websites' first attention and will give you more-sophisticated and detailed information). You can save the maps and directions, and email them to interested viewers. This is a great way to boost the information you provide to interested housing seekers.

But beware: Tenants looking for housing are just as apt to use these websites to get more information or to confirm your representations. By typing in your rental's address, they can have a look at the surrounding neighborhood (including restaurants, shops, and so on). If you've exaggerated ("handsome park nearby!"), they'll easily discover the truth if said park is really a mile away on the other side of the tracks.

or "close to Trinity Catholic Church" signaled a preference for (or against) certain protected classes. HUD addressed the issue in a 1995 memo that identified certain words and phrases and clarified whether they were evidence of a discriminatory intent. *Assuming no other evidence of discrimination in your ad,* you should be on safe ground if you:

- use these phrases to describe the property: "master bedroom," "rare find," "desirable neighborhood," "mother-in-law suite," "bachelor apartment," "two-bedroom," "cozy," "family room," "great view," "third-floor walk-up," "walk-in closets," "jogging trails," "walk to bus stop," "nonsmoking," "sober"
- provide a description of your amenities or policies: "apartment complex with chapel," "kosher meals available," "no bicycles," "quiet streets"
- use secularized phrases or symbols that refer to religious holidays ("Easter special," "St. Valentine's bonus"), or
- use the legal name of an entity that includes a religious reference ("close to Trinity Catholic Church"), as long as you include a disclaimer that you do not discriminate on the basis of religion, sex, and so on.

Where you advertise is exclusionary. Fair housing laws don't prevent you from sending ads *toward* anyone or any group, but if the ad placements have the effect of shutting out a protected group, you're breaking the law. Put slightly differently, you can narrow your market—and pitch your ad efforts accordingly—only to the extent that this doesn't result in steering your rental away from a protected group. This might happen if your advertising excludes particular groups of people from even learning that your rental is available —for example if you advertise only in places where people of a particular group (religious or ethnic) are likely to see it. Protect yourself from possible charges of discriminatory intent by placing an ad online or in a newspaper of general circulation in your area, as well as the more targeted publications such as a single foreign language paper. For example, if you feel that Chinese American renters might be particularly interested in your rental because it's in a neighborhood populated by Chinese Americans, advertise in the major city newspaper as well as the Chinese-language paper.

To read HUD's complete memo, go to www.hud.gov, choose the Search/ Index link on the home page, and type "Guidance Regarding Advertisements" in the search box. Look for the January 9, 1995, Memorandum in the results list.

Check out rental magazines

For Rent and *Apartment Guide* are newsprint-like publications that tenants can pick up for free from sidewalk racks or grocery stores. Both publications have website counterparts (see below). *For Rent* covers about 30 states and comes out twice a week. *Apartment Guide* publishes monthly and covers 40 states. Several regional and local publications serve other areas, such as *Homes & Land* (print magazines for selected regions), *Just Rentals* (a print and online magazine for the Boston area), and *Rental Guide* (a weekly Bay Area, California, magazine and website).

Most small landlords will not want to pay the fairly high advertising costs set by national publications, which seem to be geared to volume operations (their marketing copy is full of references to "your communities"). Regional magazines charge less. Don't dismiss any of them without taking stock of whether one appears to be working well in your area. For example, if you are near a large employer or military base and have seen that a particular publication is prominently featured on the street, in housing offices, and in grocery stores, you may want to consider placing an ad there. Check with other landlords to find out whether they've used the publication and found that it generated qualified applicants. Look at the magazine's listings yourself and compare them with what you see in the local and regional paper, and online. If there are lots of listings (even if they're repeated elsewhere), it may be worth your while—but if there are only a few ads in a town that has many vacancies, you probably won't want to use this type of rental magazine.

Rental Magazine: Will It Work for You?

Advertising in a print rental magazine works best when:
- The magazine is available at numerous popular places around town.
- There are lots of listings already for your area.
- You want to take advantage of the online component too (see below).
- You don't have a good print alternative, such as a local paper.
- You have multiple vacancies and can advertise them in one listing, minimizing the cost per unit.
- You need to rent your place quickly, which will help justify the cost.

Post flyers on neighborhood bulletin boards and online

"Apartment for Rent" or "House for Rent" flyers placed on bulletin boards or other public places where casual advertising is accepted, such as grocery stores, self-operated laundries, or coffee houses can be an effective and inexpensive way to reach local folks looking for rentals. Many websites dedicated to specific concerns, such as a local parents' website, also have pages set aside for information on related issues, including housing. You may also be able to get into a military or college housing office or onto their websites (or try a more formal referral policy, as described below in "List with local employers"). With local, small employers, find out whether you can post on an internal, nonwork-related bulletin board, be it real or virtual.

When designing a flyer, describe the rental and provide some way for readers to take away the phone number (put the number on tear-off strips of paper or index cards). You can design a simple ad with the bare minimum of information (type of housing, such as apartment or detached house, number of bedrooms and bathrooms, rent, and date available) or use a digital camera to add photos of the outside and interior rooms (or use the free mapping service offered by Google and others, described above). Consider the following issues before committing the time it will take to place and monitor your posting (online postings are obviously easier to handle than physical ones).

- **Is this where your applicants hang out?** You'll want to post your ads where your market will see them. If you are renting a pricey single-family home, chances are that

Bulletin Board Flyer: Will It Work for You?

Community bulletin boards, physical or online, work best when:
- Your rental is in a small town or close-knit neighborhood where people congregate at places that have bulletin boards.
- You've learned from other landlords that this method works.
- The type of person who will look at these bulletin boards is also your ideal renter.
- The website you've chosen caters to people who would be attracted to a particular aspect of your rental or its location.

your applicants aren't washing their clothes at a laundromat. On the other hand, if you have an apartment near a college, the bulletin board at the local bagel shop might be just the ticket. Think creatively. If you allow pets, post a note in vet offices or pet food stores.

- **Does your rental have an amenity that ties in with where you'll post the ad?** For example, if your rental has a big yard that's perfect for kids and is a block from the elementary school, find out whether local preschools or your city's parks and recreation department have bulletin boards. If your property has a great garden, put up a notice at a local nursery.

- **Is there a direct connection between the purpose of the website and the highlights of your rental?** Don't bother with online postings unless the readers who need housing are going to be particularly attracted to your rental—or, put another way, unless people coming to this website are going to expect rentals that complement the website. For instance, a runners' club site will attract viewers who put proximity to parks, trails, and bike paths high on their list of priorities. If your property meets these needs, you're likely to get a response.

Use an online rental service

Online advertising services have proliferated in recent years, with national firms and many regional companies. Five companies dominate the scene on the national side, with three offering online placement and one adding placement in a national magazine. The services offered by regional firms vary widely, with the most sophisticated located in large metropolitan areas. "Online Advertising," below, gives you a snapshot of the major players.

Listing with one of the big national services is likely to cost more than using newspapers and regional firms, and for this reason, this is most suitable to large operations with several rental properties. However, you may want to explore online advertising if you're interested in maximum exposure for your rental. The big players give you the ability to track results, which can be important when assessing whether you should use this service next time.

Regional online services are too numerous to list. They're apt to be less expensive, since they cover only a part of the country, and may offer more targeted services than national firms. For example, MetroRent, which covers the San Francisco Bay Area, offers a market survey service that will give you statistics on rents and vacancies for properties like yours. Practically every large metropolitan area has similar offerings.

Online Advertising

The following five companies offer online advertising for the entire country. Check their websites for current information.

Company name	Services	Cost
Rentals.com	Gives you statistics on number of visitors, how many went to more detailed pages. Distributes your web address to search engines, so that searches of your town will put your property on the results list.	Basic ads start at around $30.
Move.com	Online ads only, no print magazine. Renters find listings by specifying maximum rent, number of bedrooms. Owners can post pictures, floor plans, and describe the neighborhood. Viewers can email owner directly from the site.	Call to obtain a quote.
ForRent.com	Online ad plus placement in *For Rent* magazine.	Listings start at $100.
Apartments.com	Online ad only, photos.	Prices start at $69.
Rent.com	Online ad only.	Listing is free; landlord pays $15 every time a renter contacts you.

Before signing up with any online service, go to the site and pretend you're a renter who's using it to search for a rental like yours. Look for these qualities in an online ad site:

- **Ease of use.** Can you cut through the associated ads and glitz to begin your search? Is it clear how to search?

- **Cost to the renter.** The service should be free to searchers. Rent.com offers a $100 reward to tenants who rent through their service—and by requiring registration, the site captures a nice market for associated advertising (for moving services and the like).

- **Narrow focus.** Can a user specify aspects of a rental (such as size, location, and price) that will narrow the results to the appropriate ones?

- **Results.** When you are done specifying your requirements, do you get a list of rentals that really match what you've asked for?

- **Number of results.** How many rentals come up on the list? Are they similar to yours in basic features? A large number of well-described hits indicates that the site has a lot of traffic and sorts the properties well. A few results, or ones that are misplaced, indicate that the site is not used that often or run that well.

- **Check the refund policy, if any.** If no one rents through your ad, check to see whether you'll get a full or partial refund. Can you cancel within a certain time of placing the ad?

Choose a site that is easy to use, clearly describes a rental's key features and selling points, and appears to be well used.

Online Rental Service: Will It Work for You?

Online rental services work best when:

- You've discovered that many comparable rentals are listed online.
- You expect that a significant number of prospects may be coming from out of town, with no access to your window signs or ads in the local paper.
- You're willing to pay the fees, which may be high in comparison with print alternatives.
- You want to provide a lot more detail on the property, including photos, than you can in a regular newspaper ad.
- It's a widely used regional service or is paired with the local newspaper (like apartments.com).

Make your own website

It's pretty easy and inexpensive to design your own website or pay someone else to do it. A website used in conjunction with other modes of advertising can be a real boon. For example, in your newspaper ads, bulletin board flyers, or listings with employers, you can go beyond your initial description of the rental by referring people to the site for photos and a floor plan.

Most of the time, you won't want to use a website as your primary method of advertising because renters will have a hard time finding it. Suppose a searcher types "single-family home in Denver" into a search engine. The "hits" that result will be dominated by the big publications, which have clever ways to ensure that they show up high on the results list. Your site will appear way down the list, if at all—and few searchers will go beyond the initial page of results.

Take advantage of free listings on craigslist.org

No discussion of advertising methods would be complete without mentioning craigslist.org, described as a "rummage sale with only the things you want." (*PC Magazine,* October 14, 2003.) Started in 1995 by San Francisco software engineer Craig Newmark, the site provides local community classifieds and forums in a relatively noncommercial environment (no banner ads). Craigslist provides listings in all states, receives millions of postings each month, and has over 50 million users per month in the United States (housing receives the second-highest number of page views, after jobs). The site is free to both landlords and tenants.

Craigslist has proved to be enormously popular with both landlords and tenants, and not just because it's free. Its policies and layout are simple and easy to use.

Personal Website: Will It Work for You?

Advertising with your own website works best when:
- You're using it in conjunction with other methods, such as postings on bulletin boards, newspaper ads, and word-of-mouth.
- You've designed your site with key words that are likely to be picked up by a search engine and placed high on the results list.
- Your pool of renters will easily look to your website if they learn of it from another source—for example, if you list in the local community college bulletin board, you can be sure that these viewers won't hesitate to have a look on their computer or PDA.

Craigslist: Will It Work for You?

Using craigslist as your only or primary method of advertising works best when:
- Your rental is within a metropolitan area served by craigslist.
- You've checked listings for rentals like yours and there are a lot.
- Your market of probable renters will think to use craigslist.
- You use craigslist in conjunction with another method—why not, since it's free?

Local papers where craigslist is strong have felt the pinch (as if "their lunch money has been taken," says the founder). To find out whether a craigslist site covers your town, go to craigslist.org and look for your city on the home page. Then pretend you're a renter looking for a vacancy like yours. Do you find comparable listings? If so, you can conclude that the service is well known, and can expect decent traffic. Traffic—or page views—is what you want. In some cities, craigslist is the only place where landlords list a vacancy. You can't beat that.

List with local employers

If your property is near an employer with at least 100 employees, check to see if it has an employee assistance program that helps employees find housing. Companies that actively recruit employees offer such programs as enticements. Here's how it works: The landlord offers housing at a discount (or offers some other unusual perk, such as a month's free rent) and the company lists the rental on its employee website or in other materials. Both sides win: The employer helps employees get settled, and the landlord gets free marketing.

An employer-to-landlord housing referral program will do more for you than just deliver a prospective tenant. If the company you deal with investigates its new hires carefully (as all cautious employers do these days), you'll be getting a stream of applicants whose backgrounds have already been scrutinized—in other words, they've been prescreened on many of the same issues that interest you. Good employees and good tenants share many of the same characteristics, and if you're dealing with a picky employer, chances are you'll get qualified applicants. And, of course, you'll know that the applicant has a job!

Work with a reputable employer

Because the value of an employer referral program lies in its ability to deliver a stream of qualified applicants, you'll want to work with employers who hire quality folk. This doesn't mean that you should shun all but the most sophisticated companies. It does mean that you want established companies with good reputations. Ironically, companies with the least turnover (who are likely to generate fewer referrals than those with revolving doors) are your best bet, since the low turnover rate bespeaks a careful hiring approach. What you lose in volume of referrals, however, you'll make up in quality.

The reputation of a local employer isn't the only factor you'll need to consider. Evaluate any potential partner on the following grounds:

- **Location.** Referrals will want to be within reasonable commuting distance to their workplace. If there's direct and convenient transportation, your rental will look even more attractive.
- **Salary and rent.** Try to learn the salary range of the employees who are likely to be interested in your property. If your rent is one-third or less than the prevalent salary, you won't be out of the employees' price range.
- **Employer size.** Companies with large numbers of employees are not only more likely than small companies to have referral programs, but they probably run more careful pre-employment screening. The reason lies more with sad experience than know-how—large companies, with a large workforce, are statistically

more likely to learn the hard lessons of poor screening (employee lawsuits and high turnover) than their smaller counterparts.

Choose a rental incentive

Your next step is to choose the incentive, or hook, that will send applicants your way. Your giveaway depends on the market—if it's tight, you might not need to offer much. Begin by calling the HR department or housing office and ask about a typical incentive—if it's something that will work for you, you can stop there.

Ideally, your incentive should be tied directly to a term or condition of the rental itself. For example, you could offer reduced rent for the first year, a lower security deposit, or special terms on breaking a lease when tenants relocate for work. Varying the terms of the rental adds one more reason why an applicant should visit, and then rent, from you. These are the only come-ons that will really work.

Rent control ordinances may limit your ability to offer reduced rent. By offering reduced rent, you're giving some tenants a special deal on a rent-controlled unit. Other tenants who rent the same type of unit but at a higher rent may argue that you're breaking the rent control law. Though it may seem far-fetched, don't assume a creative lawyer won't make this argument. If you live in a rent-controlled city, check with the agency that administers the law, the local tenants' union, or your lawyer.

Employer Referral Incentives

There are pluses and minuses to any incentive you offer in an employer referral program.

Incentive	Pluses	Minuses
Reduced rent	Lost rent may be less than costs of alternative advertising.	You can't make up the rent; other tenants may be resentful.
Reduced security deposit	Big boon to tenants who haven't received their last deposit back yet. If tenants leave with no unpaid rent and no damage, you won't need the deposit anyway.	If tenants leave with unpaid rent and damage, you may not have enough to cover it.
Lease-breaking allowances (allowing termination with 30 days' notice)	Assures employer and employee that your lease won't be a problem if employee is transferred.	Works only for lease-holding, not month-to-month, tenants.

Sell your idea

Having called around and identified the employer you'd like to work with and the incentive you'll offer, it's time to make your pitch. A large company probably has its own protocol; dealing with a small one may involve not much more than a phone call.

Be prepared to sell your idea as though you were hoping to rent to the HR person you speak to. Why would someone want to live in your property? Why would this company want to associate with you—will their employees be happy that they live in your rental? Have photos available and be prepared to explain (for multifamily properties) how your low turnover rate indicates a group of satisfied tenants. Bring transit maps and schedules that show the ease and speed with which employees can travel from home to work; include statistics on the local schools, showing their high marks for academic achievement. Mention how long you've been in the business and what you've done to make sure you're on top of things (memberships in landlord associations, attendance at seminars, purchases of books like this!). Point out that you've never had to evict a tenant or sue one for back rent or damage—this spells good management to any corporate type. If at all possible, invite the HR person to your property, where you can give a proper tour.

When you and the employer have reached an agreement as to how the employer will present your offer to employees, it's a good idea to follow up with a letter, restating the understanding you reached and thanking the employer for the opportunity. You won't want to write a contract or a formal agreement. Why? Because neither one of you would go to court to enforce this arrangement. If the employer stops referring applicants to you, so be it; and if you decide to no longer offer the incentives to these employees, you can cancel the program with a call to the employer. (Keep in mind, however, that once you accept a tenant through the program, you are legally bound to follow through with the incentives that got that tenant to your leasing office in the first place.)

Modify your rental agreement or lease

The incentive you choose will almost always affect one or more terms of your rental document—for example, if you offer reduced rent for a period of time, the rent clause needs to be modified. If you have your lease or rental agreement on your computer, you can redo the clauses as needed.

Instead of redoing your lease or rental agreement, you can also write an amendment to your standard form. An amendment is an agreement that changes only specified parts of the original document. An amendment has the added

---

Employee Referral Program: Will It Work for You?

An employee referral program works best when:
- A large, reputable employer is within reasonable commuting distance of your property.
- The employer has a fair amount of turnover.
- You're in a tight market and need this edge to attract qualified tenants.
- You have multiple rentals and would like to develop a regular, steady source of tenants.
- You're willing to offer a perk that will benefit the employer as well as the tenant (such as an early termination right, which benefits the employee who may be transferred and the employer, who will more readily transfer someone if it knows that the worker can get out of a lease without negative consequences).

advantage of spelling out the terms and conditions of the incentive program itself. For example, you wouldn't want to offer a rent reduction to a tenant who is behind in the rent, so your amendment should specify that this perk applies only when tenants are paid up.

You can use the "Employer Referral Amendment" to clip to your rental agreement or lease. Be sure to clearly spellout the incentives that you have offered. The form includes the common perks discussed here (reduced rent, lower security deposit, early termination right). For perks that are yet to come, such as a period of reduced rent or an early termination right, the form specifies the prerequisites (the tenant must not be in violation of any lease term or condition). A sample appears below.

You'll find the Employer Referral Amendment on the CD-ROM that accompanies this book.

Use a real estate office to advertise for and screen tenants

Out-of-town owners or others who want to avoid the initial on-the-ground work to find tenants may decide to use a local real estate agency to advertise and perform at least initial screening. You'll pay handsomely for this service (typically one month's worth of rent), but it may make sense if you don't want to get involved

from afar. Choosing this method removes you from the hands-on approach that most of this book is built around, since you are not responsible for the early tasks (such as composing and placing the ad, fielding inquiries, and showing the rental) that the book covers, nor will you have to make the phone calls to references that some owners dread. And if the agent or broker chooses the tenant for you, too, then your next how to book should be on landlording in general.

This book will still be useful, however, if you set the acceptance criteria that you want the agent to apply. For example, the chapters that cover credit reports, background screening, and questioning references might help you as you and your agent set minimum qualifications. Similarly, if you will be making the final pick, you'll want to know how to interpret reference comments and credit history; and you may need to know how to legally reject the runners up.

Finally, no matter how much work you off-load onto a real estate agent, you must understand that this person is your representative when it comes to dealing with the public and potential renters. Having read this book as if you were going to perform all of the tasks yourself—and learning the legally safe ways to do them—you'll be in a position to know whether your agent is following good practices. If you have doubts, you must find someone else. At best, risky ways of doing business will reflect badly on you; at worst, you could become legally entangled in any serious misdeeds of your agent.

Employer Referral Amendment

This is an amendment to the lease or rental agreement dated _____
(the Agreement) between _____ (Landlord)
and _____ (Tenant)
regarding property located at _____
_____ (the Premises).

Tenant rented Premises from Landlord after being referred to Landlord by Tenant's
employer, _____ (Employer). As an incentive to
rent the Premises, Landlord offered Tenant the following incentives (Incentives):

☐ 1. Reduced security deposit. The security deposit for the Premises will be
     $_____, instead of the normal $_____. Tenant understands that if
     Landlord uses any portion of the deposit during the tenancy to cover unpaid
     rent or pay for damage beyond normal wear and tear, Tenant will replenish
     the deposit up to its normal level of $_____.

☐ 2. Reduced rent. The rent for the Premises will be $_____ for the months
     of _____.

☐ 3. Early termination for leaseholding tenants. In the event that tenant
     ☐ is permanently transferred by Employer to a location more than _____
       miles from Premises
     ☐ leaves Employer's employ for any reason
     Landlord will terminate the lease 30 days after the following conditions are met:
     ☐ Landlord receives a notarized letter signed by Tenant and Employer,
       on Employer's letterhead, stating that Tenant is being permanently
       transferred to another Employer location that is _____ miles or more
       from Premises
     ☐ Landlord receives a notice of intent to terminate the lease signed by Tenant.
     ☐ Fifteen days before the termination date, Tenant has fully paid all rent
       due and any other charges incurred by Tenant.

☐ 4. Tenant understands that in order to take advantage of any Incentive, Tenant
     must fully perform all lease or rental agreement obligations throughout the
     rental term.

_____   _____
Landlord   Date

_____   _____
Tenant   Date

_____   _____
Tenant   Date

To find a real estate agent or broker willing to perform advertising, showing, and some screening, follow these tips:

- Get in touch with other landlords in the area (contact a landlord association) and find out whether certain real estate offices offer these services. Hire someone who regularly performs advertising and screening for rentals.

- If you're a new owner, ask the real estate agent or broker who sold you the property or your own agent if they know of someone suitable—or use one of them, if you were favorably impressed.

- If you know people in the town where your property is located, ask them for recommendations of good real estate offices.

- Understand that most real estate offices that offer these services do so in order to become known to renters whom they hope will be home buyers on their next move. Look for real estate offices that have high-volume, active residential property sales. Or, check out fledgling offices that are looking for creative ways to attract clients.

- Always investigate the reputation of the person and office you engage. Check their state's real estate licensing website to confirm that their licensing is current and without a negative history. Ask the broker or agent for references, and contact them.

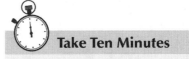

Take Ten Minutes

Figuring out where to list your rental can be a challenge if you have a lot of options—a regional paper, a local one, a place where window signs will be seen, and more. Which method will work? Find out what has worked for properties like yours:

- Ask your current tenants how they learned of the rental availability.

- Talk to other landlords in the neighborhood and find out what's worked for them.

- Pretend you're looking for a place just like yours. Check out the newspapers, rental magazines, bulletin boards, "For Rent" signs in the area. Where do you find the most listings? That's where applicants will look, too.

- Remember to take down flyers, delete online listings, and so on when your vacancy's filled, to cut down calls.

- Remind yourself to note on the Marketing Worksheet where people heard about your rental (the Tenant Information sheet, Visitor Log for Open House, and Rental Application included on the CD-ROM all have places to note this).

How Should You Show Your Rental?

As you decide how to advertise your vacancy, you'll need to choose how you will show the rental to interested tenants. You'll choose from among three basic methods:

- individual tours, in which you meet an interested renter at the property and conduct a tour just for that person (or persons)
- private open houses, attended by multiple prospects who have been invited by you, or
- public open houses, where anyone who has seen your ad or knows of the vacancy can show up.

You can, of course, use more than one way to show your rental—for example, you can hold individual showings in conjunction with an open house for maximum exposure, but be prepared to spend a lot of time doing so.

Each approach has its advantages and drawbacks, and what works for you and your rental might not necessarily work for the owner of the rental next door or even for your second property across town.

We'll look at each type of showing, starting with the most labor intensive (individual tours), then moving to private open houses and, finally, public open houses. For each showing method, we'll ask the following "Six Questions," which you should pose for your own situation. (You already asked yourself many of these questions when you planned your advertising campaign.) The answers will guide you toward the right showing method. You can record your answers on the How to Show This Rental worksheet, included in this chapter.

- What's the temperature of the market? Is it hot or cold?
- How attractive is the rental?
- Who is the market for this rental?
- Is the unit vacant or occupied?
- How much time do you have to devote to showing this rental, and what's your comfort level?
- Should you prescreen?

Landlord's Forms Library

How to Show This Rental Worksheet. Use this worksheet for recording your conclusions to the questions you should consider when deciding whether to hold private showings, a private open house, or a public open house. When you've filled it out, you'll be able to make a thoughtful choice.

The next time you need to fill this (or a similar) vacancy, you may want to consult the worksheet. Were your conclusions about the market correct? Did you get the volume of visitors you expected, and did you later learn that a different method might have produced better attendance? File the worksheet in the folder along with your Marketing Worksheet and the other papers you've prepared for this vacancy.

The Law You Need to Know

Most of the considerations that go into deciding how to show your rental are practical, not legal. But the law isn't totally out of the picture, for example:

- Showing an occupied rental, no matter which method you choose, involves residents. You must abide by your state's notice and entry rules (see "State Laws on Notice to Inspect or Show Rental Property" in Chapter 3).

- Less-attractive rentals may need to be spiffed-up ("staged"), which you'll want to do only once or twice (for open houses). Be careful that your plans don't cross the line into misrepresentation—if you bring over a new appliance, ceiling fans, or plants, visitors may reasonably conclude that they come with the rental.

- In a hot market, you may choose an open house and sit back while qualified visitors vie for the rental. You may even get offers of more rent. Be sure that the offer comes from the visitor, not you, lest you be accused of a bait-and-switch operation.

Before You Decide How to Show Your Property

Before tackling the question of how to present your rental to interested renters, check that you've:

- ☑ looked at a few days' or weeks' worth of rental ads for properties like yours. Are open houses held on a typical day or are rentals shown mainly by appointment?

- ☑ consulted your calendar to see how much time you'll have to accomplish this task. If work or family obligations are heavy, you may have to plan your showing mode accordingly.

- ☑ considered whether you'll do some refurbishing before the next batch of tenants moves in. Such work will delay the start of the next tenancy, which means you may need to choose the most efficient way to show the unit—and you may need to use more than one way (a public open house plus private showings for prescreened applicants who can't get to the open house). Chapter 8 gives some tips on readying your rental.

Individual property tours

A private property tour is just that—a one-on-one showing. To prevent a property tour from becoming a time sink that can involve completely unqualified prospects, you should prescreen and invite only those who pass your preliminary questions.

An individual tour gives you and your visitors a good chance to size each other (and the property) up. Prospective tenants have your uninterrupted attention and you, too, can ask questions and get a sense of what they would be like as tenants. It's harder to have this kind of experience in an open house setting. So for maximum face time and inspection time for both of you, the tour is it. But is this method the best way to efficiently show your rental? Answer that question by seeing how an individual showing stacks up when measured against the Six Questions.

1 What is the temperature of the market?

Your first question requires a frank analysis of the market—no surprise, since the market is the main factor that drives most of your renting decisions. If the market is soft for rentals like yours, you already know that you're going to have to work harder, and spend more time and money, to get your place rented. You've probably already decided that you'll need

to advertise as widely as possible, and now you're contemplating the next step: accommodating the responses you get by giving your phone number in your ad and scheduling tours for those who have called.

In a soft market, you'll need to schedule appointments at the prospective tenant's convenience. You can, of course, try to schedule serial showings on one day, but your ability to successfully do even that will depend on how many choices your callers have. If tenants don't want to meet you on a Saturday afternoon, you may lose them to another more flexible property owner of a comparable unit who will meet their request. If Friday evening's the only time the prospective tenants are available, so be it.

If you are lucky enough to be operating in a hot market, you'll feel less pressured to accommodate the schedules of interested visitors. You can set the terms of the showing by holding serial tours on a particular day or an open house. Of course, even though you can confidently hold an open house that doesn't mean you'll want to—as Question 5 will show you, your personal style may lead you to conclude that you don't want to deal with hordes of home seekers. But for now, understand that if the market is in your favor, you won't need to spend time schlepping to the rental property every time you hear from an interested seeker, but can schedule showings that are convenient to you.

2 How attractive is the rental?

Property tours are, by definition, repeat performances. If your rental looks good now and you can count on its continued good looks, you shouldn't hesitate about bringing visitors through several times. On the other hand, if your property needs work, even simple cosmetic touch-ups, you may want to try to spiff it up and show it only once, at an open house. This issue is closely related to whether the unit is occupied, but even unoccupied rentals may need attention that you won't want to do repeatedly. Chapter 8 provides tips on getting your property ready for showing.

An individual tour may suit a landlord who has a diamond in the rough. If you know you'll need to explain certain features, minimize others, and direct attention to the unit's positive aspects, you'll have an easier time doing it when you're dealing solely with one or two prospects during a tour. For instance, suppose you have a property that, however nice and competitively priced, is simply hard to rent, either because of its features (an odd assortment of rooms, for example) or its location (facing a major interstate freeway). If that's the case, consider individual showings.

3 Who is the market for this rental?

Take a look back at the Marketing Worksheet that you developed when thinking about where to advertise, in Chapter 4 (you'll find this form on the CD at the back of this book, in case you haven't completed it yet). Given your pool of potential renters, what can you conclude about the effectiveness of doing individual tours? The answer lies in the degree of flexibility you can expect from these folks, and their comfort level when it comes to dealing with landlords. If you're dealing with hard-charging professionals or people with long commutes, you know they have little free time and you'll need to accommodate them with an individual tour. Retired people generally have more available time and could more easily meet your set time for an open house, as can students. Choose to do individual tours if you expect you'll be renting to a family who may be heavily involved with their children's school and play activities. And if your pool of likely renters includes a large number of immigrants who may have limited English skills, understand that they may be more comfortable appearing at an open house instead of having to call to schedule a tour.

4 Is the unit vacant or occupied?

If you're showing an occupied unit, multiple individual tours will be disruptive to current residents. It may also be cumbersome for you to set them up if your state has detailed laws regarding how much notice you must give residents before showing their home to prospective tenants. Your current residents' housekeeping style may also influence your decisions. If your tenants are on the sloppy side, you don't want to spend time cleaning up every time you bring by one or two prospective renters. It's more efficient to do one clean sweep in preparation for an open house. And if you have a small unit, it will look bigger when residents' belongings aren't thrown about and cluttering the place up.

But don't automatically conclude that an occupied unit spells no individual showings. Tenants who are leaving for reasons of their own—and not because you've terminated their tenancy or begun eviction proceedings—may be willing

to work with you if their tenancy has had smooth sailing. Chapters 3 and 9 give you some ideas on how to work with current tenants when showing the unit. For now, think about the level of cooperation you're likely to encounter, and if you decide that an occupied unit with cooperative residents actually looks better than an empty one, you may want to opt for individual tours.

Don't plan to show a rental occupied by tenants you've asked to leave. As advised in Chapter 3, careful landlords don't show such rentals at all until these tenants are gone. But if you're determined to rerent fast, at least minimize the opportunity for angry tenants to wreak revenge by sabo-

---

The Challenge of a Vacant Rental

Showing a vacant unit lets you skip the messy problems of dealing with current tenants, even those who are cooperative. With a vacant rental, you don't have to worry about a window or lawn sign disturbing the occupants, and you're free to choose the times for showings, whether by individual appointment or open house.

You might conclude that it really doesn't matter, then, whether you schedule an open house or individual showings when the unit is empty. Think again—what impression will the empty unit make on an interested tenant? Some vacant rentals look better when occupied. This is especially true if the unit isn't that spiffy. If this describes your unit, you'll want to mimic the warm effect of a lived-in home by adding a few touches, such as a vase of fresh flowers, some art work for the walls, towels for the bathroom, and potted plants. (You'll find tips on doing this in Chapter 8.) You won't want to do these things every time you bring over one or two interested applicants to take a look. In short, consider an open house when you can stage the place just once.

taging you with nasty comments. In short, do an open house instead of multiple individual showings—but heed our advice in Chapter 3 for maximizing your chances for a good impression.

5 How much time do you have and what's your comfort level?

Individual tours have the distinct disadvantage of taking a lot of time. Since you are devoting a showing to every prospect, you stand to spend hours with people who won't end up renting from you. You can lessen the wasted time by accurately describing your property in rental ads and prescreening these visitors, as described in Chapter 7. But you still may end up making several trips to the property at inconvenient times. If you have only one unit and a lot of time to devote to painstakingly choosing your tenant, you can afford to do a one-on-one showing (and maybe even an open house, too). But if you have several rentals, or if you have a day job and must take care of rental business in the evenings and weekends, one open house may be the only practical way to show the rental.

Individual tours also put you in the rental with people you don't know. It's a good idea to bring a buddy, as explained in the Chapter 8 discussion of security precautions, but especially if you're a one-person operation, you may not be able to manage that. If you're nervous at the prospect of individual tours, you may not want to do them. Your anxiety may increase depending on the area of town you'll be in and the time of day that the showing is likely to take place. Do you want to travel to a mostly deserted downtown area to show your financial district condo at night, when the professionals who are your market are going to want to see it?

On the other hand, if you have a lot of time, a flexible schedule, and don't mind trekking to the rental's neighborhood on multiple occasions, you will more kindly consider the individual tour option.

Only you will know how important this factor of your available time and your working style will be. One thing is for sure: Do not commit to a course of action that you cannot keep up or that will have negative consequences on your working or personal life.

6 Should you prescreen?

Prescreening visitors before you invite them on an individual tour will involve asking prospective tenants a few questions designed to determine two things: Is this rental what they're looking for, and are they the type of renter you would rent to? Some landlords would never hold a tour, or even an open house, without prescreening, figuring that this is the only way to avoid wasting time with people who will never live in the rental. Others view the practice as off-putting and a way to discourage interested applicants, and point out that if your ad is sufficiently complete, you should have given enough information to enable visitors to effectively prescreen themselves (they won't bother calling if you state the terms clearly).

In the context of individual property tours, the need to prescreen goes up, for two important reasons:

- **Time.** Individual tours are already time-consuming. If you don't eliminate the obviously unsuited (or give people enough information to eliminate themselves), you're going to spend even more time showing the place.
- **Safety.** Doing a tour with a stranger presents some risks. If you've pre-screened, you'll have information that you can confirm at the time of the showing. People who are up to no good are more likely to present you with different information when you meet them than those on the up and up, and you can bail if needed.

How to prescreen prospects in a phone conversation is covered in detail in Chapter 7. After reading it, you may decide that you'll take your chances and do your interviewing and screening in person, where you'll have a better chance of avoiding the put off that prescreening questions can cause. Or, you may conclude that there's no way you'll do tours with people who may turn out to be wholly uninterested in your property or unsuitable as renters.

Individual Property Tour: Will It Work for You?

Individual property tours work best when:

- The market is soft and you're willing to work hard to fill your vacancy.
- Your rental looks good now and will probably continue to look fine when you bring people through.
- Your probable applicants are very busy or have inflexible schedules that won't mesh with one announced open house date.
- The rental is vacant and looks fine in its empty state.
- The rental is occupied by cooperative tenants, and your state law on showing occupied units is not too restrictive.
- You have the time and flexibility to conduct multiple showings, and are not worried about safety issues.
- You are willing to take the time to prescreen before making an appointment.

Private open houses

A private open house enables you to efficiently show the rental to more than one prospect. It's more efficient than multiple individual showings, yet may not capture as many visitors as a public open house. To hold a private open house, you have to give your phone number in your ad, then talk to the callers and inform them of the open house day and time. You can prescreen at that time or not. Whether it will work for you depends on how you answer the Six Questions.

① What is the temperature of the market?

If you're in a soft market, a private open house is likely to be a forlorn affair. By choosing a set day and time, you're possibly excluding some visitors (those who might come by if you were willing to do individual tours at times of their choosing). And since it's not open to the public (people have to call you to find out when you'll show the rental), you've further narrowed your guest list.

You can mitigate the narrowing effect of a private open house by offering the option of an individual tour to callers who can't attend, or you can offer a few different dates and times for tours—assuming you have prospects who seem to be genuinely interested and qualified. Be careful that you offer this

variation fairly and without breaking antidiscrimination laws. For example, don't offer the option of an individual tour only to working singles, however justified you may be in thinking that their schedules are less flexible. You may be hit with a claim that you're discriminating against families if you don't offer the same convenience to everyone who appears qualified.

In a tight market, of course, the advantage is with you. You can minimize the time you spend on showing the rental, and further shorten it by prescreening those who call (see below). An open house in a tight market gives you the added edge of letting the would-be tenants see each other, heightening the sense of competition for the rental. You may even see renters offering more rent.

② How attractive is the rental?

Apart from the state of the market, the individual features of your rental may also affect whether it lends itself to an open house. For example, if your unit has obvious advantages and features, with no additional explanation necessary, your need to personally extol these virtues to every visitor goes down. You may as well hold an open house, which doesn't lend itself to individual sell jobs anyway (just patrol the situation, answering questions and supplying information as needed, as explained in Chapter 9).

You may also have a unit that needs some work, either cosmetic or more substantial. Most of the time, you'll want to address the issues once, in preparation for an open house, instead of multiple times for tours. When the unit is occupied, in particular, you won't want to be your residents' housekeeper over and over. Chapter 8 explains how to get your rental ready for showing.

3   Who is the market for this rental?

Only those who have the flexibility to meet your schedule will attend your private open house. And, since it requires them to call you to get the showing date and time, they must be willing to take that step. In sum, this group is composed of those with relatively large amounts of free (or flexible) time, and who aren't cowed by picking up the phone and making a cold call to a landlord.

Now, consider the market you identified in your Marketing Worksheet in Chapter 4. Are your probable tenants likely to show up when you've set the date, and will they call first? If they have a very full schedule, your property may be eliminated right away when your announced date doesn't work with their schedule. Or, if your likely tenant is someone with poor English skills, you won't get the call if that person is reticent about using the phone. On the other hand, a private showing might be fine for property

that appeals to university students or retirees used to doing business on the phone.

4   Is the unit vacant or occupied?

Planning an open house around current residents involves many of the same considerations you have when thinking about running individual tours (see the discussion above). On the plus side, with one open house, you're disturbing the residents only once, and if you need to do a bit of staging, you'll be doing that once, too (readying an occupied unit for an open house is covered in detail in Chapter 8).

There's one hurdle, however, that you should take care to consider. Suppose your current tenants are cooperative but nervous at the prospect of opening their home to the curious eyes of a group of strangers (they may be less concerned during individual tours, when you'll be right at the elbow of any visitor). Residents may also be worried about theft or vandalism during an open house. If you hear strong opposition from current residents, be sure you can reassure them that you'll take adequate steps to monitor your invitees during the open house. The last thing you want is a claim that an item of irreplaceable value disappeared during an open house. Chapter 9 discusses how to develop security plans for showing an occupied rental.

In some situations, an open house might be the best way to show an occupied rental. When you have cooperative residents who are not overly concerned about security, and who have made a nice home of the rental, you'll find that they've staged the place already for you. In that event, take advantage of their positive attitude and arrange for an open house. You may hear visitors say, "We could set it up like this, too."

⑤ How much time do you have and what's your comfort level?

An open house puts you and your rental center stage—for one performance (well, maybe two, if you need to). It's highly efficient, because you capture all interested prospects at once. But it may still involve some planning. And if you're in a hot market, you may be inundated. If you're going to have a private open house, think about these issues:

- If your time is tight, a private open house is a good choice in a busy market. You can further optimize the time you spend by prescreening (see below).
- For owners who have more time to spend, consider a blend—hold a private open house and, for those who can't make it to your open house, offer a private showing.
- If the prospect of showing a rental on your own to multiple sets of strangers makes you nervous, a private open house at least gets the job done quickly.

Private Open House: Will It Work for You?

Private open houses work best when:

- The market is at least moderately hot.
- You are willing to offer individual tours if callers are interested and qualified, but can't attend.
- The rental needs some work to show well (do it once).
- Potential renters are likely to be flexible enough to make your day and time.
- For occupied units, there's reason to disturb the residents just once.
- For vacant rentals, you need to do some work to make them homey.
- You have limited time to devote to showings.
- You are willing to ask a few prescreening questions to steer qualified visitors to the open house.

6 Should you prescreen?

Almost by definition, holding a private open house involves some prescreening unless you simply announce the date and time via a prerecorded message on your answering machine. When people call, you're bound to have a conversation. The question is, do you simply invite your caller to the open house, or do you take the opportunity to determine whether this caller is really a potential tenant?

Passing up a chance to refine your guest list is almost always a mistake. You'd be surprised how many callers think that your rental will go for a lower rent, or have more bedrooms, parking, or a smaller security deposit—despite the clarity of your ad. Why waste time greeting these visitors at an open house and reviewing their application, if only to discard it when you learn that they earn one-tenth of the rent or hope you'll accept them with their pet mastiff? A few well-phrased questions on the phone can settle basic issues and leave you with visitors who stand a chance at securing the rental. Even in a soft market, your time is valuable.

Public open houses

A public open house is a showing that's announced in your ad or your window or lawn signs, or even on a sandwich board on the curb. You announce the day and time of the open house, and essential details on the rental. It's at the other end of the spectrum from individual tours of prescreened callers. At a public open house, you never know who will show up. Obviously, you don't prescreen visitors to a public open house, so you won't have this consideration to weigh if you're considering this option. You should, however, think about the remaining five questions before deciding whether this avenue is right for you.

Details on Your Open House

Choose an open house day and time that corresponds to when potential renters are likely to be available. The days and times of open houses for homes that are for sale might work for you, too (such as two to three hours on the weekend). Make sure your ad gives enough information to attract the kind of applicant you want—someone who understands from your copy that the unit has only one bedroom and is suitable for three residents, max.

1 What is the temperature of the market?

Ironically, a public open house works well in both hot and cold markets. In a hot market, you may decide to hold an open house because you are confident that lots of people will attend—and surely there will be enough qualified applicants to choose from. In a hot market, why bother with individual showings, which require phone calls and time-devouring trips to the rental? For that matter, why do a private open house, which requires you to take phone calls from interested renters? In fact, competition for your place may result in a bidding war, with qualified renters offering to pay more than the advertised rent.

Conversely, in a cold market, you may choose a public open house because, having announced it in your ad, you know that a large number of people have read that the unit is being shown. You're not apt to get as large a turnout when you rely on the renter to call you first, either for a showing or a private open house. And in a cold market, tenants may feel that they shouldn't have to work hard to see a vacancy. Being able to see a rental without calling first will appeal to some folks.

So, what's the impact of the temperature of the market on your thoughts of holding a public open house? Frankly, it's a toss-up. Look to the other factors before making your decision.

2 How attractive is the rental?

The condition of your property is a factor in a public open house as well as a private one. As with private open houses, explained above, if you have to stage the property, it will be easier to do it once rather than multiple times for individual showings.

3 Who is the market for this rental?

A public open house is, in some respects, the easiest form of showing as far as renters are concerned. True, they have to abide by your date and time, but they don't have to call first. And if someone just happens to see your sign while out looking for vacancies, the ability to just waltz in and have a look is very appealing.

Now, think about your market. Are these renters the type who would hesitate (or not bother) to call you first to make an appointment for a showing or get details on a private open house? If so, a public showing is for you. For example, an open house in an immigrant community might generate a lot of interest if there are no barriers (like making a preliminary phone call) to seeing it. An open house on a Saturday afternoon in a college town might also get a lot of traffic from students who don't want to commit themselves in advance to showing up. Or, are your future tenants likely to be families? If so, you might choose a Sunday afternoon, figuring that this is the best time to avoid colliding with Saturday sports and Sunday morning religious services. It all boils down to trying to figure out your prospective applicants' preferences for the best times to see your property.

4 Is the unit vacant or occupied?

The wisdom of holding a public showing, as with a private open house, will depend on whether the rental is occupied and, if so, on the attitude of your residents (see the discussion on private open houses, above). Besides the considerations mentioned there, one more pops out: In a public setting, you have no control over who will attend, and how many people will show up. If the market is hot and your rental attractive, a big turnout spells more safety and security concerns than you'd face with a pre-selected group at a private open house or individual showing. You may even face wear and tear issues. (Do you really want to steam clean the carpets again?)

Public Open House: Will It Work for You?

Public open houses work best when:

- You have either a very hot or cold market.
- Your ad includes rental terms that are specific and important to you (such as maximum occupants, pets policy, security deposit), so that visitors know what to expect and will attend your open house knowing what your terms are.
- The rental needs to be prepared for showing.
- You've figured out your market and concluded that prospects are likely to respond positively to your set date and time.
- Your current residents should be disturbed only once with one showing.
- Your vacant rental needs to be warmed up for showings.
- You don't want to bother with prescreening prospects or even taking calls and giving directions.
- You don't mind getting some applications from applicants who won't be in the running.
- You've picked a convenient time for your open house, such as a weekend afternoon (not the same day as the Super Bowl!).

5 How much time do you have and what's your comfort level?

Unlike a private open house, which requires at least minimal contact with those whom you'll invite, a public open house gets you off the invitations hook. But the amount of work involved in actually holding the open house may differ greatly. If lots of people show up, you could be overwhelmed, and if you're not prepared, the success of the showing could be compromised. The answer is to be prepared for the number of visitors your market sense tells you may appear—this translates into enough helpers to assist visitors and monitor their actions. Are you willing to prepare for this possibility? If not—if you want a more controlled scene—the uncertainty of a public open house may not be your cup of tea.

A public open house will also involve more work for you down the line. Since you won't be able to prescreen visitors, and may not be able to conduct meaningful interviews during the open house itself, you may find that people whom you've hardly talked to are asking you for applications. Are they qualified to be your next tenants? Though you can weed some of them out by distributing an informational sheet about your rental (your Rental Property Fact Sheet, described in Chapter 6), there's no guarantee that visitors will read it and take it to heart. You're bound to discover that some applicants exceed your occupancy level, have insufficient income, or list a pet in spite of your no-pets specification. Sure, you can reject the application then, but you will have spent some time in reviewing it before you do so. When you're reviewing a lot of applications, that's a chunk of time.

You'll find the How to Show This Rental worksheet on the CD-ROM that accompanies this book.

Below, you'll see how our hypothetical landlord Ann thought about and answered the questions we've put to each showing method examined in this chapter. She used the How to Show This Rental worksheet, and at the end of each question, she chose the method that the answer suggested. You'll see that she didn't get uniform answers to each question. In the end, she had to put it all together and decide which questions, or factors, were most important to her (for example, she decided that she definitely did not want to hold individual tours, even though the market wasn't very hot). There's no scientific formula for the right conclusion, but there is a way to organize the issues so that you make an educated decision.

How to Show This Rental Worksheet

What's the temperature of the market?

Market is good but not tight—many apartments, single fam. homes available as school starts. Lower interest rates show home sales going up. University has not finished married fam. housing, might be a plus for me.

Conclusion:

☑ Individual tour   ☑ Private open house   ☐ Public open house

How attractive is the rental?

Looks great now with current residents. Garden in bloom, lots of good light for the interior; obviously a nice house, no issues to explain.

Conclusion:

☐ Individual tour   ☑ Private open house   ☑ Public open house

Who is the market for this rental?

Students (school begins Sept. 20), families, commuters to state capitol, university workers.

Conclusion:

☐ Individual tour   ☑ Private open house   ☑ Public open house

Is the unit vacant or occupied?

Residents are cooperative, won't mind tours. Would prefer one open house. Insist on being home when place is shown, shouldn't be a problem.

Conclusion:

☑ Individual tour   ☑ Private open house   ☐ Public open house

How much time do I have to devote to showing this rental, and what's my comfort level?

Can show on weekdays and on weekends, but busy this month with other plans. Do not want to make many trips to house in evenings. Do not want to show to strangers.

Conclusion:

☑ Individual tour   ☑ Private open house   ☐ Public open house

Will I prescreen for individual tours or private open house?

Will definitely prescreen for private open house.

How will I show this rental?

Use a private open house at _____ unless I get too few calls or people can't make it (then offer individual tours). Prescreen for safety. Rental looks good and won't need prepping.

Take Ten Minutes

This chapter guides you through the many considerations that bear on how to show your rental to prospective tenants. Having made up your mind, you're ready to make a plan:

- Consult your calendar and figure out some good slots of time to show the unit to qualified applicants.
- Check other rental ads for nearby properties to see when landlords are showing their rentals—if there's a common day and time, you'd be wise to go along, since most tenants will be out and about at that time.
- If you have current tenants, make sure they're aware of and comfortable with your showing plans.

Preparing Your Rental Application and Screening Materials

You're getting very close to being ready to field the first questions from interested renters. During a phone call, or later at a property showing, you'll identify qualified applicants who will receive your rental application. After you review the application, contact references, and review a credit report, you'll make an offer. With marketing copy at the ready, it's time to place that ad and get started. Well, almost.

What's missing? You need to be very sure how you'll respond when interested renters present you—on the phone, on the sidewalk in front of the property, or in the rental entryway—with questions or statements like these:

- "There are five of us who want to share the apartment."
- "I have a Golden Retriever and a puppy—the puppy is just adorable."
- "I'm a full-time student, but my parents are willing to be cosigners. Can I have an application?"
- "I'm a musician and supplement my income by giving lessons at home. I hope that's not a problem."
- "I've got a credit report that I ordered for myself recently—I'll bring it along when I see the place."

These questions and remarks concern important rental policies that you must nail down before you advertise or talk with prospective tenants. They are "Top Level" questions, because your response need only be a statement of your policy. For instance, you should be able to say how many people you will allow in the rental and your stand on pets, cosigners, home businesses, and applicant-supplied credit reports.

Now, what about questions or statements that ask you, directly or indirectly, to *vary* your rental policies? These are "Second Level" conversations because you're being asked to negotiate the very policies you would like to apply firmly. Depending on the market and the makeup of your applicant pool, you may need to do just that. Here are some examples of Second Level conversations:

- "Can we start the lease two weeks later than what's in your ad?"
- "Would you consider lowering the security deposit if I pay $10 more in rent each month?"
- "I'd rather have a month-to-month arrangement instead of a lease, okay?"
- "I'd like to install a dishwasher and mount some track lighting—not a problem, right?"
- "I declared bankruptcy a few years ago, but have been steadily employed since then—that won't put me out of the running, will it?"
- "My boyfriend lives out of state and visits every weekend. That won't be an issue, will it?"

Heading into rental showings or even initial phone conversations without a firm idea of how you'll handle Top and Second Level questions is a real mistake, for two reasons. First, if you're caught off guard you may answer unwisely, and live to regret it. Second, you may answer inconsistently, conceding to some applicants, not to others. If the disappointed prospects are members of a protected group, you might be courting a fair housing claim.

This chapter suggests rental policies that you can adopt that will be your reference point for answering Top Level questions. Your policies will cover common issues, such as tenancy start dates, number of occupants, pets, and so on. If you get Top Level questions like those above—

and it's inevitable that you will—you'll be prepared. In Chapter 9, we'll cover Second Level questions, with advice on when to negotiate and when to stand firm.

You'll put your policies in a document— your Rental Policies sheet—that you can give to visitors who come to an open house or showing. It will be part of your "Rental Kit," which will also include your Rental Application, authorizations to perform a credit and background check, and other needed forms.

✔ Before You Decide on Your Rental Policies

This is the time to settle on your rental terms and your policies. Once you communicate them, they take on a life of their own, creating expectations in the minds of applicants, and headaches in *your* mind if you've formulated them carelessly. So take a moment to:

☑ Look again at your advertisement for this rental. Your policies should be consistent with the rental terms in the ad, especially the amount of rent.

☑ Make sure you are set up to keep track of credit check fees. You may want to establish a separate account for them or in some way separate these fees from your other rental income. Keeping them separate will simplify your bookkeeping, since you'll be returning the fees from applicants who don't make it to that screening step.

☑ Get ready to process credit card payments, if that's how you'll accept credit report fees (it's by far the easiest, though you'll pay a bit for the service). Your bank will get you started.

☑ Reconsider the market. Have conditions changed since you posted your ad? Has a large employer closed, has school started, have there been significant changes in the economy? Any of these events may affect housing seekers, in ways that require you to rethink basic terms, such as deposit amount.

Landlord's Forms Library

This chapter is packed with forms for you and for your applicants. They comprise your Rental Kit, and will enable applicants to learn of your standards (and opt out if they don't qualify), and give you the information you need to make a smart pick.

- **Rental Policies.** This handout explains your evaluation approach, acceptance criteria, and timeline.
- **Rental Application.** The key document for screening tenants, it collects information on a tenant's rental and employment history, references, income, and credit background.
- **Rental Application Instructions.** This handout tells prospective tenants how to complete the application.
- **Consent to Contact References and Perform Credit Check.** This form gives you explicit permission to call references and pull a credit report. The same permission is on the application, but this form will be useful should you need to fax proof of consent to any reference (you won't have to fax the entire application).
- **Credit Check Payment.** Here, applicants authorize you to use their credit card to pay for a credit check.
- **Receipt for Credit Check Fee.** Use this if applicants give you cash, checks, or money orders to cover the credit check fee.
- **Consent to Criminal and Background Check.** This is a tenant's written permission to conduct a check of criminal conviction records, which you'll need should you decide to perform such a search. It will also cover your use of a tenant-screening firm, should you decide to use one to investigate criminal background, and Megan's Law database checks that you do yourself.
- **Legal Status in the United States.** This form is for landlords who want to confirm that their residents are legally in the United States. It asks applicants to supply proof, such as a U.S. passport or documentation from the Bureau of Citizenship and Immigration Services. California landlords should not use this form.

Your rental application and screening documents are very important. File the Rental Policies and Application Instructions sheets with the property's main file, and create subfiles for prospects' completed submissions (you'll get to these subfiles in Chapter 7). When applicants return the signed and completed forms, you will have the tools you need to determine whether you have a match. If you're ever the target of a fair housing claim, these papers will be important evidence that you follow legally safe, nondiscriminatory procedures.

The Law You Need to Know

Good rental policies are a combination of the practical ("What will work at this property?") and the legal ("May I legally say, require, or forbid this?"). The policies suggested in this chapter are general enough to protect you without crossing the legal limits. Should you decide to be more specific in what you will and won't allow on your property (such as home businesses), you'll need to do a little legal digging on your own. Specifically, you may want to investigate:

- discrimination protections created by state or local law that go beyond the federal rules (see Chapter 2)
- local zoning laws. Contact your zoning department.
- home day care protections. Go to your state's website (www.[state postal code].gov) and look for links to consumer pages. In a search box, type "home day care" and "landlord," and
- state or local restrictions on your ability to use criminal conviction databases and reject on the basis of what you find (see Chapter 13 for a full discussion).

If you will do phone screening (a topic covered in Chapter 7), this chapter gets you ready for the conversations you'll have before you show the property. After the call, you may even want to email your Rental Policies to callers, who may want more information about your criteria before they spend time in person checking out the rental. You will eventually show the unit, and will need this information at that time, at least.

When it's time to show the unit, print several copies of these documents and assemble several Rental Kits, ready to hand out at an open house or individual tour. You may also want to email these files to applicants, who can fill them in electronically and send back the completed files.

Your rental policies

Applicants will need to know what you look for in a tenant so that they can opt out if they won't qualify, and so that they know you're consistently applying fair and legal selection criteria. Your policies will also clue them in on where you're willing to accept alternative evidence of good-tenant qualities. For example, when you say that you need references from prior landlords, but add that you'll accept similar references from teachers and schools for first-time renters, you've let first-timers know how they can stay in the running.

Giving applicants a copy of your Rental Policies (and answering questions consistent with those policies) may also lessen the sting of rejection—and hopefully diminish the chance that a disappointed applicant will sue you over imagined discriminatory motives. Here's how: Having explained that overextended credit cards, for example, may form the basis of a denial, you have signaled to the applicant that this issue is important to you. If the applicant does indeed have too much debt, your eventual rejection should come as no surprise. Sure, it's debatable what "too extended" means. But most of the time, when you look at the big picture, it will be clear. Experience shows that if you lay your cards on the table—with a specific description of what you're looking for in a tenant—you will fare better when you have to break the bad news to unsuccessful applicants.

As you read through the Rental Policies, you'll see that the rental criteria are phrased mainly in positive terms. Rather than specify what will disqualify an applicant, each policy notes what qualities you are looking for. This convention is deliberate—you want to present a positive approach, and you want to leave yourself the option to reject for reasons that you haven't specified (you can't list them all). Also, you won't see numeric requirements, such as "at least two years at your present job,"

"a total of three positive references from past landlords and employers," or "a credit score of at least 700." There are good reasons for avoiding numeric or hard-and-fast policies when evaluating applications, including:

- **They won't always result in the best applicant getting the rental.** Consider a "two years at present job" requirement. What if you have an excellent applicant who has changed jobs recently by getting a better job? This shouldn't count against him or her.

- **Because a rigid system doesn't always work, you'll be tempted to cook the results—but could get nabbed in a fair housing claim if you do.** If you relax your "standards" when you find they don't work (as described above), and give the nod to someone who has fewer years on a job, say, than someone else, the rejected applicant will have ammunition against you (your failure to follow your own system) if he or she decides to file a fair housing claim.

Understand that this doesn't mean that you should apply anything but sound business standards when evaluating applicants. It simply means that you don't want to announce a rigid scheme that could prevent you from applying those standards reasonably. Chapter 10 provides detailed advice on how to develop flexible, yet legally safe, alternatives to standard good-tenant criteria. For example, self-employed persons may not have an employment history, but that should not count against them (as it would if you excluded those without positive references from employers). The key is to substitute equally valid sources of information when you need to (in this case, try a reference from a long-standing business partner of your self-employed applicant, a vendor or client, or a commercial landlord).

Below, you'll see several suggested rental policies (all of them comprise the Rental Policies sheet that you'll give to interested applicants). The text sets each one out, and follows it with a brief description of what it means (including a reference to other chapters in this book that describe the issue more thoroughly). As with every form in this book, you are free to vary the policies—and indeed will need to do so when you fill in the number of occupants your rental will accommodate—when you consider optional statements or clauses on issues such as pets, home businesses, and the like. It's a good idea to run your variations past your lawyer if you change the "plain vanilla" policies very much.

You'll find a file for Rental Policies on the CD-ROM that accompanies this book. You can modify it to fit your situation, including adding the optional clauses you wish. A sample appears below.

Our Rental Policies

Greeting

Thank you for giving us your Rental Application. Here are the guidelines we apply to every application we receive. If you have any questions, please feel free to contact us.

This greeting introduces the applicants to the document, and invites them to contact you if they have questions (there's a place at the end for your phone number and email address).

Meeting basic rental terms. Applicants must be able to meet our basic rental terms, which include the rent and security deposit, the tenancy start date, and the maximum number of residents for this rental.

Here, you signal to applicants your basic requirements regarding the rent and security deposit, start date, and maximum number of occupants. Does this mean that you should never vary these terms, for example, by agreeing to a later start date in order to rent to a superior applicant? No, but you should realize that every time you stray from your announced policies, you create the possibility that a disappointed member of a protected class will accuse you of discrimination. As long as there's a valid business reason behind your flexibility, you'll have a good defense. Chapter 2 covers discrimination in detail, and Chapter 9 suggests ways to negotiate and still protect yourself.

We follow fair housing laws. We will fully comply with the federal fair housing laws and will not discriminate on the basis of race, color, national origin, familial status (including age), disability, or sex. We will also follow any state and local laws that forbid additional types of discrimination.

This statement announces your pledge to abide by fair housing laws. The categories listed are the federal ones, which apply to every landlord, but as Chapter 2 explains, many states and localities have created additional protected classes. You must learn whether your state and city have expanded upon the federal protections.

Complete and truthful applications from all adults. We require a separate application from every adult who will live in the rental. We will reject applications that contain information that we cannot verify or that are incomplete (if a particular item does not apply to you, be sure to write "n/a" on the line so we know that you did not skip it). We will reject applications that list false information, and will terminate the tenancy of anyone who has made a materially false statement on the application that we discover after accepting the applicant.

To underscore your commitment to abide by fair housing laws, consider adding the "fair housing and equal opportunity" logo from the Department of Housing and Urban Development (HUD). Go to www.hud.gov and at the bottom of the home page, click the logo. You'll get a page with graphics you can download.

Here, you're advising applicants that every resident must meet your good-tenant criteria, and that you will check to make sure answers are truthful. This includes the critical statement that you will terminate the tenancy of anyone who has falsified "material" (important) information. You may need to call on this provision if you learn (after accepting an applicant) that, for example, the tenant really makes much less than his or her claimed income. But understand that "material" will not include inadvertent mistakes or even misinformation that does not bear directly on the question: "Does this tenant pose a current business risk or threat to property or persons?"

Additional occupants. Only those who have submitted a rental application, and any listed minor dependents, may live in the rental. Any proposed additional residents (other than minor children) must go through our application process. Assuming the addition of another resident will not result in overcrowding, we will evaluate proposed additional residents as we do any applicant.

This clause advises applicants that they may not move in additional occupants after their tenancy has begun, unless the newcomer goes through and passes your application process. (Minor children are an exception to the application rule, as are roommates in certain situations in New York, under the New York "Roommate Law." (New York RPL § 235-f.) Your lease or rental agreement should cover a related topic—your guest policy—so that residents can't get around your additional occupant policy by hosting long-term guests.

Occupancy policy. In order to prevent over-crowding, we will determine the maximum number of residents who may live in a rental, in keeping with our state's fair housing laws and taking into consideration any limiting factors inherent in the building or property. The maximum number of residents for this rental is _____ persons.

You'll need to follow your state's standards for the maximum number of occupants in a rental dwelling. As explained in Chapter 2, the rule of thumb is two persons per bedroom, though some states, such as California, will allow one more. Importantly, many localities have set their own policies that allow more occupants. You must find out what standard applies to your rental unit and apply it firmly.

Applicants' identification. We will need a current photo ID from each adult applicant, such as a driver's license, passport, or military or state identification card. We will need a Social Security number or individual taxpayer's ID number (ITIN) in order to run a credit check. We will handle this information with care and destroy it when it's no longer needed.

This policy advises applicants that you'll need a current photo ID, as well as a Social Security number or a taxpayer's ID number. You're also assuring the applicant that you will do your reasonable best to protect them from identity theft. Indeed, you're legally bound to keep this information carefully and dispose of it when you're done (see "Handle credit reports, criminal background reports, and tenant-screening reports carefully" in Chapter 11).

By asking for a Social Security number or ITIN, you're *not* signaling that only legal residents will satisfy your rental criteria. Illegal immigrants cannot obtain an SSN, but they can get an ITIN. A tenant-screening company can use an ITIN to pull a credit report. If you want to exclude illegal residents (questioning about legal status is not an option in California), you must say so explicitly (see the optional clause for this purpose, below).

This policy does not advise prospects that you'll be asking for their date of birth (DOB). Fair housing experts counsel against collecting this data, pointing to evidence that landlords who keep such information are more vulnerable to charges of age discrimination than those who do not. However, you may find it difficult to get a credit report if you cannot supply the applicant's DOB. If you decide to ask for it, you can change this rental policy to suit your practice.

We contact references and credit sources and run a credit check. We will speak with current and prior landlords, current employers, and run a credit check on all applicants who advance to that stage of our application-screening process. Applicants who are first-time renters, or who are self-employed, may supply alternate types of references (see the instructions to our Rental Application). We will conduct the screening ourselves or hire an independent tenant-screening firm. If you have placed a "freeze" on your credit file, it is your responsibility to lift the freeze to enable us to order your credit report. We strongly urge you to access your credit report (you may get a free report once a year) and check for and correct any inaccuracies, before applying for this rental. Each applicant for whom we run a credit check must pay for this check, in advance.

This clause tells applicants that you will contact the references they'll be asked to supply. Applicants who pick up your full rental kit will get a payment form for the credit check.

In some states, consumers may restrict access to their credit reports by placing a freeze on their file. Credit-reporting agencies will not release a report unless the consumer has specifically given permission. The procedures for placement and lifting of the freeze vary from state to state. Your applicant must contact the credit-reporting agencies, learn the procedure for lifting the freeze, and do so to enable you to pull the report.

Your policy also advises applicants to obtain their credit report before submitting a rental application, to check for inaccuracies and completeness (consumers can get one free copy per year). Errors in credit reports are very common, and consumers can correct them (or, failing that, place statements in the file claiming that certain information is wrong). You don't want to waste time confronting an applicant with a report that, for the first time, the applicant claims is wrong.

Now and then, you'll encounter an applicant who has identification but who will have no credit history—such as a recently arrived immigrant, foreign student, or young, first-time renter. The credit report will essentially be empty. Assuming the person qualifies in other respects, you should not let this factor automatically disqualify him. You can get assurances of financial ability in other ways, such as requiring a cosigner.

Financial responsibility. We rent to applicants who have a history of financial responsibility. Our primary means of evaluating an applicant's financial history is the credit report. If you have a history of delinquent payments or accounts, unpaid debts, or charge-offs (in which a retailer gives up on collection attempts), we may deny your application.

This policy underscores your requirement that an applicant be financially responsible. No matter how high a person's income, if they spend more than they make, they're a poor risk. On the other hand, a modest income, managed wisely, presents a better risk.

Rental history. We rent to applicants who have a history of being good tenants, which includes paying rent on time, being considerate of rental property and neighbors, and leaving rental property in good shape when vacating. We require satisfactory references from at least two prior landlords or the equivalent from first-time renters (such as recommendations from teachers, school transcripts, or letters from neighbors).

Not only are you looking for financially stable renters, you're looking for socially responsible ones, too. This paragraph explains the kinds of positive reports you'll need from past landlords or the equivalent for first-timers.

Criminal history. We will ask applicants to list any criminal convictions. We will strive to rent to applicants who demonstrate a history of honest, nonviolent behavior, and will not, to the best of our ability, rent to anyone whom we reasonably conclude poses a current, direct threat to persons or property.

This paragraph amplifies the theme presented above—your tenants must be free of a criminal past that spells trouble for you, your property, or the neighbors. The paragraph includes the legal standard you must use when evaluating a criminal history—only if you can reasonably conclude that someone poses a current, direct threat, can you safely reject on this basis (Chapter 13 covers criminal histories and rejections on that basis). With any luck, someone with a recent, violent crime will see this policy and not bother submitting an application.

You may have noticed that this policy announces that you will "strive" to rent to peaceful people, and will not, "to the best of [your] ability," rent to those who aren't. These qualifiers signal to everyone that your ability to weed out dangerous folk is not absolute. This may protect you should a dangerous applicant slip through your system and harm another tenant—the victim may not be able to successfully claim that you are somehow at fault by representing to all tenants that your property would be completely free of dangerous people.

If you decide to run criminal back-ground checks on all applicants who advance to that stage, add an optional clause on this (see below).

Minimum income. The combined gross monthly income (before deductions) from all applicants ages 18 and over must be three times the monthly rent. We will verify each applicant's income by asking for pay stubs or tax returns for self-employed applicants. Students or others without an income must supply an acceptable cosigner.

This policy explains the minimum income required for all applicants, and advises self-employed applicants on how they can supply the necessary information. Students will need a cosigner. If you do not want to deal with cosigners, in most places you are free to reject students as having insufficient income—but depending on the market, you may be significantly narrowing your applicant pool by doing so.

Cosigners or guarantors. If the gross monthly income of an applicant is not three times the monthly rent, we may, at our option, require a guarantor who lives within the state. The guarantor must submit a separate rental application and authorize us to use the screening tools we use for any applicant who intends to live here. We will deduct the guarantor's own housing costs from his or her gross monthly income before we consider the income's sufficiency.

This clause signals your willingness to consider an in-state cosigner if an applicant's income is not triple the monthly rent. It explains that the cosigner must pass your financial tests, namely, the cosigner must have enough disposable income to cover the rent if needed. In practical terms, you'll look for a stable cosigner who lives not only in your state but preferably near your rental property (which will make it easy to serve this person with legal papers should you need to sue for back rent).

Optional Clauses

You may want to add more clauses that fit your situation. Below are some common ones, and you may want to write your own.

Holding deposit. If your application is accepted, we will ask you for a holding deposit of $_____ , which we will apply in full to the first month's rent when you move in. If you fail to move in after orally accepting our offer or signing a lease or rental agreement, the deposit will be applied to any damages, including lost rent and costs of re-renting, that we may suffer.

Typically, landlords require holding deposits at the time of application, or after you've accepted the prospect but before you've received the first month's rent and deposit. It's often financially difficult for prospects to pay holding deposits with every application, since they may be considering multiple properties. For this reason, the clause in this book is designed for deposits that you collect after making an offer. Choose an amount that will cause the applicant to hesitate before walking away from it, but not so high as to be punishing. Chapter 15 provides more advice on the subject and includes a receipt and holding-deposit form.

Criminal background check. We will check available databases, including Megan's Law databases, to determine whether applicants have been convicted of a crime. We may hire a criminal-background-screening firm to perform this search. This screening will be done subject to restrictions on available data. We do not guarantee that the screening will reflect all criminal history or an applicant's current criminal status. We require your written consent for this check. More information will be provided to you upon request.

Use this clause if you intend to perform (or hire a firm to perform) a criminal background check or Megan's Law database check. (California landlords, however, may not consult their Megan's Law database for the purpose of denying housing.) You'll see that the clause advises everyone that your search will be constrained by any restrictions on available data—meaning that if a court hasn't posted information on a database, you won't see it. The clause also advises

applicants that you're not guaranteeing that the results of the search will be 100% correct either (you may miss some convictions or find a false match). These disclaimers may protect you from lawsuits if you mistakenly rent to someone with a relevant criminal past, or if you reject someone on the basis of a false match. (You may want to skip ahead now to Chapter 13, which discusses the pros and cons of doing such checks.)

Tenant-screening firm. We may contract with a tenant-screening firm, which may report on your credit history, character, reputation, personal characteristics, and personal history (including evictions and criminal convictions). This check may involve any state's Megan's Law database. We require your written consent for this check. More information will be provided to you upon request.

Use this clause if you wish to use a tenant-screening firm to analyze applicants' suitability for your rental. These firms check credit history and much more, and most will give you either a score or an approved-or-not conclusion. See Chapter 14 for more information.

Pets. We allow the following pets under the following conditions: _____

_____.

If your pet causes a serious disruption or damages the property, your tenancy may be terminated.

If you were to ask a random sampling of landlords whether it makes good business sense to allow cats and dogs, you'd be in for a lively debate. Some will tell you that animals are destructive and disruptive, and drive away good tenants. Others will point out that because pet owners are not welcome in many rentals, they tend to be super-conscientious and stable when they find a rental that will take pets, and that you can effectively screen out unsuitable pets. This is not the place to explore who's right—the bottom line is that if you want to prohibit pets, it's your choice.

Landlords who have decided to allow pets, particularly dogs, should take this opportunity to spell out their expectations regarding tenants' pets. For example, you may want to specify the number, size, and breed of dog that you will accept. Savvy landlords—many of whom have learned the hard way—require references from a veterinarian and prior landlord regarding the pet's behavior and the degree of responsibility demonstrated by the owner. For good examples of a pet policy and for a list of questions to ask that will give you the information you need, visit the San Francisco SPCA's website at www.sfspca.org. Choose the "open door/pet-friendly housing" link and explore the material specifically for landlords. If you wish, you can print their very sensible pet policy and attach it to your Rental Policies sheet, or copy the text and add it to your policies as an additional section labeled "Pet Policy."

! **You must allow a service or companion animal that is needed by a disabled tenant.** Chapter 2 explains the rules.

Smoking. This property is smoke free in all areas, including tenants' rented spaces. Tenants and their guests must refrain from smoking on or near the rental property.

It's becoming increasingly popular for owners to ban smoking in rental properties, especially in common areas of multi-family rentals. You can even decide that tenants' units will be smoke free, as this policy provides. Cities, too, are passing ordinances forbidding smoking in multi-family rentals, including individual units. There are multiple driving forces behind this trend: The chances of a fire will diminish; your maintenance and refurbishing costs will go down when you don't have to remove smoke fumes from walls, carpets, and draperies; and a smoke-free property may even be a marketing plus as residents insist more and more on smoke-free environments. In a few states, residents have successfully sued their landlord for allowing other tenants to smoke, arguing that the smoke wafting into their homes constituted a legal "nuisance" that the landlord was required to eliminate (by evicting the smoker). Landlords in California should take particular note: The state's Air Resources Board has added second-hand smoke to their list of "Toxic Air Contaminants."

Residential use only. This rental is for residential use only, subject to any state or local laws that apply.

With the increased availability of high-speed Internet connections, more and more people are working from home. You shouldn't be worried if your tenant sits at a computer all day and works—in fact, there's a plus to having people home during the day (less chance of a burglary, and a greater chance that you'll be notified right away of a problem, such as a burst pipe). It's another matter, however, when residents set up a car repair business in the driveway or give tuba lessons all day and evening. Home day care centers are a hot button—some states, such as California and New York, do not let landlords prohibit them (though they are regulated). Zoning may also be an issue for you—some communities forbid certain businesses in specified zones. Because home businesses are so varied (and your ability to control them may depend on state law or local ordinances), the rental policy presented here goes no further than to say that the property is to be used for residential purposes only, but the policy does say that you will abide by any laws that protect certain businesses (such as home day care).

If business activities in your rental are of concern to you, contact your local zoning department and ask if there are any restrictions (which you'll want to incorporate in your policy) and any allowances (such as for home day care, which you must follow).

Legal status in the United States (non-California rentals only). We will ask every applicant for proof that they are legally in the United States, which may be supplied by showing us a current passport, birth certificate, or valid documentation from United States Citizenship and Immigration Services. We will not rent to people who cannot supply such proof.

It's not against the law to rent to someone who is in the United States illegally—but it might not make good business sense to do so (you may feel that this person will be more likely to break a lease, and be harder to track down and sue for unpaid rent or damages, than a legal resident). You may also want to make sure that a legal immigrant has the right to remain in the country until the end of the lease term (you'll check the expiration date on his or her documents, most likely on Form I-94. For example, some international exchange visitors, on J-1 visas, may stay only up to one year). California landlords may not use this policy, because it is illegal in California to inquire about immigration status.

If you want to rent to legal residents only, you'll need to advise people that *all* applicants must supply proof of legal status (asking only some to supply that proof will open you up to charges of discrimination, as explained in Chapter 2). You'll want to use an additional form that you can attach to the Rental Application, which is described below.

Think carefully before you decide to require applicants to prove their legal right to be in the United States. First, as a quick glance at the legal status form will show you, the documentation you'll be shown may be one of many confusing forms issued by United States Citizenship and Immigration Services (USCIS). Second, there's no practical way you can confirm that the document presented is the real thing (false papers are legion). Finally, your policy may rule

Should You Automatically Reject for Prior Bankruptcies or Evictions?

This book doesn't include policies advising applicants that a past bankruptcy or an eviction will automatically disqualify them. Many landlords and their advisors will argue that you *should* view either event as the kiss of death, period. That's a short-sighted and dangerous approach—treating an eviction or a bankruptcy as per se disqualifiers ties your hands and opens you to charges of discrimination. Here's how.

You're bound to encounter an applicant who has a bankruptcy or eviction in his past, but is otherwise qualified and would be a good risk—perhaps the best applicant you have. Maybe the eviction was long ago, and the tenant has recovered from his bankruptcy. You'll want to make an exception to your rule and rent to this person, and when you do, you might find yourself challenged by a runner-up who is a member of a protected class and will accuse you of discrimination. This person will shove your failure to follow your "no bankruptcies" rule in your face, as roundabout proof that you had a sinister, discriminatory motive in not renting to him.

The sensible answer is to consider the bankruptcy or the eviction in the context of the entire picture: If this person is truly a poor risk, other factors (such as employment history, other landlord references or the equivalent, credit score, and so on) will combine with the eviction or bankruptcy to give you a defensible decision. Should you decide to follow this route, you'll want to look carefully at the line allowing applicants to explain any "yes" answers they made on this part of the application.

Chapter 10 offers more advice on the subject of evaluating bankruptcies and evictions.

out some applicants who are citizens but do not have a passport (only 25% of all Americans have one) and have no idea where their birth certificate is (or how to get one). Though employers must confirm legal status each time they hire an employee (by examining documents that enable them to complete the IRS form I-9), many employers don't bother and, of course, self-employed persons never encounter an I-9. In a soft market especially, you may regret having to eliminate those applicants. If your screening methods are thorough and deep, as recommended in this book, chances are you'll uncover the risky applicants by other means.

Our Selection Process

We will review applications in the order in whitch we receive them. We will date- and time-stamp each application and begin the review process as soon as possible. We will also note when we have completed our review process.

Here you're telling applicants that you'll follow a first-come, first-served policy when reviewing applications. If you're in a tight market and have several qualified applicants, they will know that time is of the essence, and they may be motivated to contact their references and ask that they be available.

We will evaluate your application as soon as we can. Usually, the evaluation process takes a few days. We will offer the rental to the most qualified applicant, and if applicants are equally qualified, we will make an offer to the applicant whose application was received first. We will send written or email notifications to applicants whom we cannot accept.

This advises prospects that you will use a neutral tie-breaker, and will let people know by email that they did not get the place. Chapter 16 gives specific advice on how to handle rejections.

Your rental application

Your rental application is your most important screening document, because it asks for information that will help you determine whether an applicant is likely to be a stable, rent-paying, and conscientious tenant. You should give an application to every person over 18 who wants to live in your rental property.

The rental application form asks for a wide variety of information, including the prospective tenant's Social Security number or other identifying information that you'll need to request the individual's credit report. It also includes information on applicants' rental and employment history, income, credit background, personal background (including any eviction and bankruptcy history), and

Rental Policies for <u>456 Magnolia, Larksdale, CO</u>

Thank you for giving us your Rental Application. Here are the guidelines we apply to every application we receive. If you have any questions, please feel free to contact us.

Meeting basic rental terms. Applicants must be able to meet our basic rental terms, which include the rent and security deposit, the tenancy start date, and the maximum number of residents for this rental.

We follow fair housing laws. We will fully comply with the federal fair housing laws and will not discriminate on the basis of race, color, national origin, familial status (including age), disability, or sex. We will also follow any state and local laws that forbid additional types of discrimination.

Complete and truthful applications from all adults. We require a separate application from every adult who will live in the rental. We will reject applications that contain information that we cannot verify or that are incomplete (if a particular item does not apply to you, be sure to write "n/a" on the line so we know that you did not skip it). We will reject applications that list false information, and will terminate the tenancy of anyone who has made a materially false statement on the application that we discover after accepting the applicant.

Additional occupants. Only those who have submitted a Rental Application, and any listed minor dependents, may live in the rental. Any proposed additional residents (other than minor children) must go through our application process. Assuming the addition of another resident will not result in overcrowding, we will evaluate proposed additional residents as we do any applicant.

Occupancy policy. In order to prevent overcrowding, we will determine the maximum number of residents who may live in a rental, in keeping with our state's fair housing laws and taking into consideration any limiting factors inherent in the building or property. The maximum number of residents for this rental is <u>four</u> persons.

Applicants' identification. We will need a current photo ID from each adult applicant, such as a driver's license, passport, or military or state identification card. We will need a Social Security number or Individual Taxpayer's ID number

(ITIN) in order to run a credit check. We will handle this information with care and destroy it when it's no longer needed.

We contact references and credit sources and run a credit check. We will speak with current and prior landlords, current employers, and run a credit check on all applicants who advance to that stage of our application-screening process. Applicants who are first-time renters, or who are self-employed, may supply alternate types of references (see the instructions to our Rental Application). We will conduct the screening ourselves or hire an independent tenant-screening firm. If you have placed a "freeze" on your credit file, it is your responsibility to lift the freeze to enable us to order your credit report. We strongly urge you to access your credit report (you may get a free report once a year) and check for and correct any inaccuracies, before applying for this rental. Each applicant for whom we run a credit check must pay for this check, in advance.

Financial responsibility. We rent to applicants who have a history of financial responsibility. Our primary means of evaluating an applicant's financial history is the credit report. If you have a history of delinquent payments or accounts, unpaid debts, or charge-offs (in which a retailer gives up on collection attempts), we may deny your application.

Rental history. We rent to applicants who have a history of being good tenants, which includes paying rent on time, being considerate of rental property and neighbors, and leaving rental property in good shape when vacating. We require satisfactory references from at least two prior landlords or the equivalent from first-time renters (such as recommendations from teachers, school transcripts, or letters from neighbors).

Criminal history. We will ask applicants to list any criminal convictions. We will strive to rent to applicants who demonstrate a history of honest, nonviolent behavior, and will not, to the best of our ability, rent to anyone whom we reasonably conclude poses a current, direct threat to persons or property.

Minimum income. The combined gross monthly income (before deductions) from all applicants ages 18 and over must be three times the monthly rent. We will verify each applicant's income by asking for pay stubs or tax returns for self-employed applicants. Students or others without an income must supply an acceptable cosigner.

Cosigners or guarantors. If the gross monthly income of an applicant is not three times the monthly rent, we may, at our option, require a guarantor who lives within the state. The guarantor must submit a separate Rental Application and authorize us to use the screening tools we use for any applicant who intends to live here. We will deduct the guarantor's own housing costs from his or her gross monthly income before we consider the income's sufficiency.

OPTIONAL CLAUSES

Holding deposit. If your application is accepted, we will ask you for a holding deposit of $100, which we will apply in full to the first month's rent when you move in. If you fail to move in after orally accepting our offer or signing a lease or rental agreement, the deposit will be applied to any damages, including lost rent and costs of re-renting, that we may suffer.

Criminal background check. We will check available databases, including Megan's Law databases, to determine whether applicants have been convicted of a crime. We may hire a criminal-background-screening firm to perform this search. This screening will be done subject to restrictions on available data. We do not guarantee that the screening will reflect all criminal history or an applicant's current criminal status. We require your written consent for this check. More information will be provided to you upon request.

Tenant-screening firm. We may contract with a tenant-screening firm, which may report on your credit history, character, reputation, personal characteristics, and personal history (including evictions and criminal convictions). This check may involve any state's Megan's Law database. We require your written consent for this check. More information will be provided to you upon request.

Pets. We allow the following pets under the following conditions: one cat. If your pet causes a serious disruption or damages the property, your tenancy may be terminated.

Smoking. This property is smoke free in all areas, including tenants' rented spaces. Tenants and their guests must refrain from smoking on or near the rental property.

Residential use only. This rental is for residential use only, subject to any state or local laws that apply.

Legal status in the United States. We will ask every applicant for proof that they are legally in the United States, which may be supplied by showing us a current passport, birth certificate, or valid documentation from United States Citizenship and Immigration Services. We will not rent to people who cannot supply such proof.

Our Selection Process

We will review applications in the order in which we receive them. We will date- and time-stamp each application and begin the review process as soon as possible. We will also note when we have completed our review process.

We will evaluate your application as soon as we can. Usually, the evaluation process takes a few days. We will offer the rental to the most qualified applicant, and if applicants are equally qualified, we will make an offer to the applicant whose application was received first. We will send written or email notifications to applicants whom we cannot accept.

references. It ends with a paragraph that gives you permission to contact the applicant's employer, prior and current landlords, and references, and to run a credit check. The same permission is repeated in a final page, Consent to Contact References and Perform Credit Check. This stand-alone permission will be handy if a landlord or employer asks for proof that the applicant has consented to a conversation—you won't have to fax the entire application.

You'll find the Rental Application on the CD-ROM that accompanies this book, and a sample appears below. The CD-ROM also includes a stand-alone consent form (Consent to Contact References and Perform Credit Check).

The Rental Application is legal as written. If you add questions, make sure you don't introduce even a hint of a discriminatory motive. Consult an attorney if you have any doubt.

Landlord instructions for completing the Rental Application

Before giving prospective tenants a Rental Application, fill in the following information on the top of the form. Later, in Chapter 10, you'll find instructions on how to evaluate the answers.

Date and time received by landlord

Leave this line blank—you'll enter the information when the applicant returns the completed application.

Credit check fee

We recommend you check prospective tenants' credit history with at least one credit-reporting agency, to see whether they have credit problems or a history of paying bills late. It's legal to charge prospective tenants a nonrefundable fee for the cost of the credit check as long as the amount is reasonably related to the cost to you of the credit check, plus a little for your time ($20 to $35 is common). Some states specifically limit fees, such as California, but you'll be safe if you don't stray above $35.

Using a Rental Service?

You may have hired a real estate agent or broker, or used an online service, that has their own rental applications. If you're evaluating their completed forms, skim this section to get an idea of what a good form should ask for. If the application you're using omits critical questions, you may be seeing less than a full picture of the applicant.

It makes sense to run a credit check only on applicants whom you are seriously considering. But if you wait to collect the fee until you've actually reviewed the application and contacted references, you may lose time while trying to contact the applicant and collecting the fee. On the other hand, if you collect credit check fees when you receive applications, but decide (after reviewing applications) that some applicants aren't suitable, you'll have the hassle of returning the fees.

The only truly satisfactory way to approach this problem is to obtain permission to charge an applicant's credit card in the event you decide to run a credit check. You won't waste time contacting the applicant, and you won't have to send a check or money order back to applicants who didn't make it to this stage. For this reason, your Rental Kit will contain a form that applicants complete, giving credit card information and authorizing you to run a charge if you order a report (the Credit Check Payment form is described just below). But if applicants don't have a credit card or balk at your request for their card information, you'll have to make do with collecting the cash, check, or money order now, and diligently returning it if you don't use it. Use the Receipt for Credit Check Fee, described below, if you collect any of these forms of payment.

Never keep a credit check fee if you don't actually run the check. Some states have specific penalties for this type of fraud.

Property address, rental term, and deposits and other monies paid up-front

Include the complete street address, city, state, and zip code. If you're offering a month-to-month rental, simply fill in the starting date; if you're using a lease, enter the starting and ending dates.

Applicants Who Bring Their Own Credit Reports

At the time you hand out your application, you may hear an applicant say, "I have a copy of my credit report right here, so you can use it and not charge me for another one!" In every state but Wisconsin, you can say no, thereby ensuring that you'll get a fresh, undoctored report. (In Wisconsin, you must accept a report that's less than 30 days old if the applicant gives it to you before you ask for it. (Wis. Adm. Code ATCP 134.05(4)(b).) Be careful to stick to your policy here—if you accept applicants' copies from some, but not all, you're inviting a charge of discrimination if spurned applicants are members of a protected group.

Rental Application

Separate application required from each applicant age 18 or older.

Date and time received by landlord _____

Credit check fee _____ Date received _____ Form of payment _____

THIS SECTION TO BE COMPLETED BY LANDLORD

Address of property to be rented: _____

Rental term: ☐ month-to-month ☐ lease from _____ to _____

Amounts Due Prior to Occupancy

First month's rent .... $_____

Security deposit .... $_____

Other (specify): _____ $_____

TOTAL .... $_____

Applicant

Full Name—include all names you use(d): _____

Home phone: (___)_____ Work phone: (___)_____

Social Security number: _____ Driver's license number/state: _____

Other identifying information: _____

Vehicle make: _____ Model: _____ Color: _____ Year: _____

License plate number/state: _____

Additional Occupants

List everyone, including children, who will live with you:

Full name   Relationship to applicant

_____   _____

_____   _____

_____   _____

_____   _____

Rental History

FIRST-TIME RENTERS: ATTACH A DESCRIPTION OF YOUR HOUSING SITUATION FOR THE PAST FIVE YEARS, WITH CONTACT INFORMATION FOR SCHOOL RESIDENT ASSISTANTS IF APPLICABLE.

Current address: _____

Dates lived at address: _____ Rent: _____ Security deposit: _____

Landlord/manager: _____ Landlord/manager's phone: (___)_____

Reason for leaving: _____

Previous address: _____

Dates lived at address: _____ Rent: _____ Security deposit: _____

Landlord/manager: _____ Landlord/manager's phone: (___)_____

Reason for Leaving: _____

Previous address: _____

Dates lived at address: _____ Rent: _____ Security deposit: _____

Landlord/manager: _____ Landlord/manager's phone: (___)_____

Reason for Leaving: _____

Employment History

SELF-EMPLOYED APPLICANTS: ATTACH TAX RETURNS FOR THE PAST TWO YEARS

Name and address of current employer: _____

_____ Phone: (___)_____

Name of supervisor: _____ Supervisor's phone: (___)_____

Dates employed at this job: _____ Position or title: _____

Name and address of previous employer: _____

_____ Phone: (___)_____

Name of supervisor: _____ Supervisor's phone: (___)_____

Dates employed at this job: _____ Position or title: _____

ATTACH PAY STUBS FOR THE PAST TWO YEARS, FROM THIS EMPLOYER OR PRIOR EMPLOYERS.

Income

1. Your gross monthly employment income (before deductions): $_____

2. Average monthly amounts of other income (specify sources): $_____

_____ $_____

_____ $_____

_____ $_____

TOTAL: $_____

Bank/Financial Accounts

	Account Number	Bank/Institution, Branch	Amount

Savings account: _____

Checking account: _____

Money market or similar account: _____

_____

Credit Card Accounts

Major credit card: ☐ VISA   ☐ MC   ☐ Discover

☐ Am Ex   ☐ Other: _____

Issuer: _____

Account no.: _____

Balance: $_____   Average monthly payment: $_____

Major credit card: ☐ VISA   ☐ MC   ☐ Discover

☐ Am Ex   ☐ Other: _____

Issuer: _____

Account no.: _____

Balance: $_____   Average monthly payment: $_____

Loans

Type of loan (mortgage, car, student loan, etc.)	Name of Creditor	Account Number	Amount Owed	Monthly Payment
_____	_____	_____	_____	_____
_____	_____	_____	_____	_____
_____	_____	_____	_____	_____
_____	_____	_____	_____	_____

Other Major Obligations

Type	Payee	Amount Owed	Monthly Payment
_____	_____	_____	_____
_____	_____	_____	_____

Personal Information

Bankruptcy. Have you ever filed for bankruptcy?   ☐ yes   ☐ no
If you answered "yes":
How many times? _____ What type(s)? _____ When? _____

Lawsuits. Have you ever been sued?   ☐ yes   ☐ no
If you answered "yes":
How many times? _____ Concerning what? _____ When? _____

Have you sued someone else?   ☐ yes   ☐ no
If you answered "yes":
How many times? _____ Concerning what? _____ When? _____

Eviction History. Have you been evicted or are you now undergoing an eviction?
☐ yes   ☐ no
If you answered "yes":
How many times? _____ When? _____

Criminal Convictions. Have you been convicted of any crimes?   ☐ yes   ☐ no
If you answered "yes":
For what offenses? _____
When? _____ What was the sentence? _____

Registered Sexual Offenders. Are you required to register as a sexual offender pursuant to any state's law? ☐ yes ☐ no

If you answered "yes":

Where are you registered? _____

For what offense, and when was the conviction? _____

Use this space to further explain any "yes" answers:

_____

_____

_____

_____

_____

_____

_____

_____

Pets. Describe the number and type of pets you want to have in the rental property: _____

Water-filled Furniture. Describe water-filled furniture you want to have in the rental property: _____

Smoking. Do you smoke? ☐ yes ☐ no

References and Emergency Contact

Personal reference: _____ Relationship: _____

Address: _____

_____ Phone: (___)_____

Personal reference: _____ Relationship: _____

Address: _____

_____ Phone: (___)_____

Contact in emergency: _____ Relationship: _____

Address: _____

_____ Phone: (___)_____

Source

Where did you learn of this vacancy? _____

_____

Certification

I certify that all the information given above is true and correct and understand that my lease or rental agreement may be terminated if I have made any materially false or incomplete statements in this application. I authorize verification of the information provided in this application from my credit sources, current and previous landlords and employers, and personal references. I give permission for the landlord or its agent to obtain a consumer report about me for the purpose of this application, to ensure that I continue to meet the terms of the tenancy, for the collection and recovery of any financial obligations relating to my tenancy, or for any other permissible purpose.

_____   _____

Applicant   Date

Notes (Landlord/Manager):

_____

_____

_____

_____

_____

_____

_____

_____

_____

_____

_____

_____

Next, complete the lines that specify the first month's rent (this will be the monthly rent, unless you're beginning mid-month), deposit, and any other monies due. State laws typically control the amount you can collect as a security deposit, such as one or two months' rent, with limits sometimes higher for furnished units. You can check your state in the State Security Deposit Rules chart at the end of this chapter. Rent you collect in advance for the first month's rent is not considered part of the security deposit. If you are charging any additional fees, such as a nonrefundable cleaning deposit or pet deposit, note this at the top of the rental application under "Other," but make sure your state law allows this. Some states specifically prohibit these types of nonrefundable fees, and they consider them security deposits, no matter what you call them.

Be sure to add up the money the tenant must pay you before moving in, and note this under Total.

Tenant instructions for completing the Rental Application

Visitors who appear to be qualified renters should get instructions on how to fill out the application and where to return it. Use the Rental Application Instructions, filled out as shown below in the sample. They refer to your Rental Policies, and reiterate the most important policies. Remember that you, too, must be consistent when handling questions or challenges that you've settled upon in your policies.

You may also want to offer applicants an online alternative—as well as giving the application to the visitor personally, offer to email the documents to the applicant, and ask them to email them back to you. If you do this, you'll want applicants to fax (or scan and email) the page on which they give you permission to run a credit check and contact references; alternatively, you could ask that the applicant sign that part of the application when the prospect asks for an application, and complete the balance of the form online.

You'll notice that the instructions, like your rental policies, assure applicants that you will process applications in the order in which you receive them, and that you'll do so in a "timely" manner. These representations are important, and you should stick to them. Reviewing applications as they come in will help prevent claims of discrimination (no one will be able to say that you cherry-picked applications from nonminorities, for example), and reviewing them reasonably quickly may head off applicants who may pester you with, "When will I hear?"

You'll find the Rental Application Instructions on the CD-ROM that accompanies this book.

Rental Application Instructions

Rental property __2754 5th Street, Mayberry, CT__

Applicant __Monica Waverly__

Application given by _Sam Musari_ on __May 27, 20xx__

Dear Applicant,

Thank you for your interest in renting this property. Every person over the age of 18 who wants to live in this rental must complete an application. If you are applying as a group, return all applications together.

Attached please find:

- a Rental Application form

- a copy of our Rental Policies, which explains our rental terms and the qualities we are looking for in a tenant, and our pledge to keep your personal information safe (you do not have to return this)

- a Credit Check Payment form, in which you authorize us to charge the credit check fee to your credit card, and

- a Consent to Contact References and Perform Credit Check form, which gives us explicit permission to call references and pull a credit report (we may need to fax it (or scan and email it) to references).

You'll find it useful to have these items on hand before beginning this application:

- Applicants who are currently tenants: names and contact information for current and two prior landlords

- First-time renters: names and contact information of teachers, dormitory resident assistants, or employers

- Applicants who are employees: names and contact information for current employer, plus pay stubs for the past two years

- Unemployed persons, including students: names of persons who will support you, or information on alternate sources of support, or

- Self-employed persons: the last two years' worth of tax returns.

We will do our best to complete the evaluation process in a timely manner. We will contact references and order a credit report for the best candidates. We will return any credit check fee we have collected if we do not order a credit report (but we will not refund the fee if we order a report but do not offer you the rental). If you find that a particular question does not apply to you, be sure to write "n/a" in the space, so we know you did not skip this item.

In order to allow us to begin evaluating your application, please sign and return the documents to _____Sam Musari_____ (~~landlord~~/manager) at the following address ___2755 5th Street, Mayberry, CT___

Electronic alternative. If you would prefer, you may complete this application and associated documents on your computer and return them as attached files. Please fax (or scan and email) the signed last page of the application, a signed Credit Check Payment form, and a signed Consent to Contact References and Perform Credit Check form (please follow up by mailing the originals). Be sure to give us your email address so that we may send you the files. Return the files to us at the email address below.

We will process applications for this rental in the order in which we receive them, and will choose the best-qualified applicant.

If you have any questions, please do not hesitate to call or email us.

Sam Musari
Manager

_555-123-4567_
Telephone

sammusari@coldmail.com
Email

Consent to contact references and perform credit check

Some of the references you contact will ask for written proof that the applicant has given permission for them to talk to you. The Consent to Contact References and Perform Credit Check form is a one-page document that you can easily fax to anyone who requests it. The applicant will have given you the same permission when signing the last page of the application itself. Filling out this form is simple—just write in your name. When you get it back, you'll check to make sure the applicant has signed and dated it.

You'll find a Consent to Contact References and Perform Credit Check form on the CD-ROM that accompanies this book.

Credit check payment

The instructions ask applicants to enclose your fee for a credit check, and assure them that you will not order a credit report unless they pass your initial review (and that you'll return unused fees). Applicants can attach a check or give you credit card information, using your Credit Check Payment form. On the payment form, fill in the maximum amount the applicant is authorizing you to charge (without this limiting amount, many applicants will not give you their card information), and enter

the date the permission will expire (you should be able to conclude your screening within a couple of weeks).

You'll need to contact your bank to see which cards they will support and if they will process these payments for you as part of the services they offer to small businesses. Find out if the bank offers any accounting support, what the service charges are, and if any event triggers a penalty or extra fee.

Filling out the form at this point won't take much time. The applicant will fill in his or her name, and you will enter the rental property address when you're assembling your Rental Kits. But now, next to "Accepted Cards," check the boxes that correspond to the cards your bank will deal with. When you run the card, you'll fill in the "Transaction run for credit report" section.

You may charge for your actual costs, plus a little more for your time. When ordering single reports, you're safe if you stay within the $35 range (you'll pay less if you're a member of a landlords' association that has negotiated a bulk deal with a credit-reporting service, or if you have signed up on your own with an account). Chapter 11 includes information on why you need to destroy or obliterate the credit card number in order to comply with federal law that protects consumers' personal information.

You'll find the Credit Check Payment form on the CD-ROM that accompanies this book. Be sure to enter the

Consent to Contact References and Perform Credit Check

I authorize _____Sam Musari_____ to obtain information
about me from my credit sources, current and previous landlords, employers, and
personal references to enable ___Sam Musari_____
to evaluate my rental application. I give permission for the landlord or its agent to
obtain a consumer report about me for the purpose of this application, to ensure
that I continue to meet the terms of the tenancy, for the collection and recovery
of any financial obligations relating to my tenancy, or for any other permissible
purpose.

_____

Applicant signature

_____

Printed name

_____

Address

_____

Phone Number

_____

Date

Credit Check Payment

Applicant: _____

Rental: _____

Accepted cards: ☐ VISA   ☐ MC   ☐ American Express
☐ Discover   ☐ Others _____

Cardholder's name: _____

Card number: _____

Expiration date: _____ Security code: _____

I authorize the landlord/manager of the above rental to use the credit card described here to pay for a credit report. This authorization does not cover charges in excess of $_____ and will expire on _____.

_____   _____
Signature   Date

_____
Printed name

_____

OFFICE USE

Application received: _____

No credit check, date decided: _____

Transaction run for credit report

Transaction date: _____

Credit-reporting agency: _____

Run by: _____

Cost: _____

maximum amount the tenant is authorizing you to charge and the expiration date for this permission. A sample form is shown above.

Receipt for credit check fee

Some of your applicants may not want to give you their credit card information to use for the credit check fee. If you accept cash, checks, or money orders, give applicants a receipt (required by law in a few states, this is good business practice for everyone).

Either you or the applicant should fill in this self-explanatory form. After you sign it, be prepared to make a copy for your applicant. Of course, you must follow through and return the money if you do not order a report (but you need not make a refund if the report puts this applicant out of the running). If you order a report, you'll fill in the portion at the bottom ("Office use"), which records how and when you spent the money.

You'll find a Receipt for Credit Check Fee form on the CD-ROM that accompanies this book.

Consent to criminal and background check

If you've decided to do a criminal background check on your applicants by paying an online firm to run a database check, or if you're hiring a resident-screening service, you need to abide by the Fair Credit Reporting Act. Although this law does not require that you obtain advance written permission, it's a good idea to ask for it. If you make any negative decisions based on the information you learn from these reports, you'll need to send applicants written notice including a disclosure of their rights, as explained in Chapter 16.

When you or your employee checks Megan's Law databases, the FCRA does not apply. However, it's prudent to give notice and ask permission anyway, and may, in fact, be required by some states' privacy laws (this form also mentions Megan's Law checks). Remember to apply your policy consistently: If you subject one applicant who has made it to the top of the pile to this level of scrutiny, you must subject all who reach that point to the same level of background checking.

You'll find the Consent to Criminal and Background Check form on the CD-ROM that accompanies this book.

Receipt for Credit Check Fee

_____ [Landlord],

has received a credit check fee of $ _____, to cover the cost of ordering and

reviewing a credit report for _____ [Applicant].

Applicant gave Landlord (check one):

   ☐ cash

   ☐ money order, number _____, dated _____

   ☐ check, number _____, dated _____

Landlord will return the credit check fee to Applicant if Landlord does not order
a credit report. If Landlord orders a credit report and does not rent to Applicant,
Landlord will not refund the fee to Applicant.

_____   _____
Landlord/manager   Date

_____   _____
Applicant   Date

OFFICE USE

Credit report ordered on [_date_] from [_credit-reporting agency_] by [landlord _or_

manager] in the amount of $ [_cost of credit report_].

Consent to Criminal and Background Check

I authorize _____ [Landlord/Manager]
to perform a criminal background check on me or to hire a tenant-screening
firm to investigate my background. These actions may result in a report on my
character, reputation, personal characteristics, and criminal history and will
involve searching any state's "Megan's Law" database for my name. I agree to hold
_____ [Landlord/Manager]
harmless if the results of this search include incorrect information that _____
_____ [Landlord/Manager],
in the exercise of ordinary caution, would not have known about. I understand
that _____ [Landlord/Manager]
will provide more information to me upon my request.

_____   _____
Applicant's signature   Date

_____
Printed name

_____
Address

_____

_____
Phone number

_____   _____
Reauthorized, signature   Date

Legal status in the United States

You may want to confirm that all tenants have the legal right to be in the United States throughout the lease term. (Again, California landlords may not perform this check.) If so, add to your Rental Policies the optional clause described above, which advises applicants that they must supply proof of legal status. You'll need to give applicants an additional form, Legal Status in the United States, which gives applicants an opportunity to describe their legal status.

You'll find the Legal Status in the United States form on the CD-ROM that accompanies this book. A sample appears below.

If you're using this form, fill in the rental property address at the top and attach the form to your Rental Application. Chapter 10 takes you section by section through the completed application, and will help you evaluate the documentation that applicants provide.

Lease or rental agreement

One last task awaits you before you can confidently show your rental or take applications. Take a look at the lease or rental agreement that you intend to use for this unit. Are you wondering why you should worry now about a document that

you'll sign at the end? The short answer is that this is the only time you can easily change the rental document. Once applicants see favorable lease provisions in a lease or rental agreement, they'll resent it if you change the final document to your advantage. And after you and the tenant sign a lease, it's too late.

Chances are that you have a "standard" rental document that you've found works for you, one that perhaps you've taken from a book or software, or have received from a landlords' association. You may have bought a form at a stationery store (a poor option, since these forms are never state law compliant). And if you have multiple rental properties, you probably want all of your rental documents to have the same provisions. Fair enough—but don't let convenience get in the way of smart business practices. Pull out that form and think about the following issues:

- **Are there legal changes that the document doesn't reflect?** Landlord-tenant law changes frequently, on the federal, state, and local levels. You should be keeping up with developments in your field, and must make sure, for example, that your security deposit clause accurately reflects the law, such as whether you must pay interest on the deposit (and how much and when).

- **Does this lease accurately reflect the physical condition of the unit?** For example, if you have renovated and

Legal Status in the United States

Applicant _____

Rental address _____

Please check the boxes that apply and supply information as requested. Bring the required documentation to the landlord/manager when you return the Rental Application, or soon thereafter. We cannot process your application until we have reviewed your documentation.

☐ I have the legal right to be in the United States because I am a U.S. citizen.

    ☐ I am a citizen by birth or through my parents (provide an original birth certificate or a copy certified by the issuing agency, a U.S. passport, a Certificate of U.S. Citizenship, or a Certificate of Birth Abroad).

    ☐ I am a naturalized citizen (provide a U.S. passport or a Naturalization Certificate).

☐ I have the legal right to be in the United States because I have valid documentation from U.S. Citizenship and Immigration Services (USCIS).

    ☐ I am a legal permanent resident (provide Permanent Resident Card or a foreign passport showing an I-151 or I-551 stamp, or an I-94 form, Arrival-Departure Record).

    ☐ I entered the United States on a visa and am on an authorized, temporary stay (provide passport from country of citizenship plus I-94 form, Arrival-Departure Record):

    My permitted stay expires on: _____

    ☐ I am a refugee (provide passport from country of citizenship plus I-94 form, Arrival-Departure Record, stamped "Admitted as a Refugee"; or Refugee Travel Document).

    ☐ I have an application pending with USCIS or other right to stay in the United States (provide work permit or USCIS receipt or other notice indicating right).

☐ I do not have a legal right to be in the United States.

_____   _____
Applicant's signature   Date

can legally certify that the rental is lead free, does your lease say so? Does the lease or rental agreement include the yard or garage that you've recently made available to tenants, and does it specify what parts the tenant may use?

- **Have you learned that certain clauses spell trouble—can you improve on them?** For example, your late fees clause may specify a fee when the rent is more than five days late, and as a result, many tenants regularly pay rent four days late. Maybe it's time to shorten that interval or increase the fee (but check your state laws first).

- **Are there additional terms or clauses that would help avoid problems?** Some leases prohibit unauthorized occupants (residents whom you haven't approved), but don't clearly explain that, as far as you're concerned, a long-term guest is the same as an unauthorized resident. Perhaps it's a good idea to spell that out.

- **Have you learned anything valuable from the questionnaire your last tenant left with you?** If the tenant gave you some thoughtful feedback on the Departing Tenant's Questionnaire (Chapter 3), consider it. For example, your lease may promise only a weak response when tenants alert you to repair problems. If that was an issue for your last resident, maybe it's time to reform your practices (and bring your lease up to snuff).

Use a State Law Compliant Lease!

Any form lease or rental agreement you buy in a stationery store will not comply with your state's laws. Many of them ignore tenants' rights, which will lull you into ignoring them, too—until you are brought up short by a judge. Ironically, some forms will impose greater obligations and restrictions on you than your state's law does! Don't take a chance or needlessly hamper your business with these incomplete or wrong documents. There are better alternatives from Nolo:

- *Every Landlord's Legal Guide*, a comprehensive legal and practical guide for landlords, includes a lease and rental agreement on the book's CD-ROM. Use the 50-state legal charts to prepare a lease or rental agreement specific to your state.

- *Leases & Rental Agreements* is a book with a tear-out lease and rental agreement and 50-state charts with needed state law information.

To order these products and for more information, go to www.nolo.com.

Remember, too, that your ad, your Rental Policies handout, and everything you say about the rental must be consistent with your lease or rental agreement. If you promise something that the lease or agreement doesn't reflect, you'll be hard pressed to argue that you really didn't mean it. In fact, by law you might have to deliver. So it's a good idea to review the lease now and bring it into line with your plans. For example, suppose you've decided to begin charging for parking, but your lease doesn't include this extra monthly charge. Fix the document now. If you mistakenly sign a lease that is silent on the issue of parking fees, few tenants will let you amend it to add the charge.

Take Ten Minutes

Preparing your rental policies caused you to think hard about some issues in your rental business, perhaps uncovering problems or inefficiencies that you'll want to address. Perhaps you now know:

- Your occupancy policy for other rentals you own does not comply with a local standard. Be prepared to comply in the future as to these rentals.
- Setting yourself up to receive credit card payments was easier than you thought, and less expensive—perhaps you should make it possible for tenants to pay rent by credit card, too.
- You'd like to change an important rental term you announced in your ad—such as, "no pets"—because you've learned that the market won't support this exclusionary policy. Fine. Write your policies to accept pets—but understand that it's harder, legally, to go the other way and make terms less friendly to tenants than those you initially announced. You might be accused of a bait and switch operation.

State Security Deposit Rules

Here are citations for statutes pertaining to security deposits in each state. Some states exempt landlords from following security deposit rules when renting to a person who is under contract to purchase the property; when the occupant is an employee of the landlord, who must live on the property; and when the landlord owns fewer than a specified number of rental units (check your statutes to see if any exemptions apply).

State/Statute	Limit	Disclosure or Requirement	Separate Account	Interest
Alabama Ala. Code § 35-9A-201	One month's rent, except for pet deposits, deposits to cover undoing tenant's alterations, deposits to cover tenant activities that pose increased liability risks			
Alaska Alaska Stat. § 34.03.070	Two months' rent, unless rent exceeds $2,000 per month	Orally or in writing, landlord must disclose the conditions under which landlord may withhold all or part of the deposit.	✔	
Arizona Ariz. Rev. Stat. Ann. § 33-1321	One and one-half months' rent	If landlord collects a nonrefundable fee, its purpose must be stated in writing. All fees not designated as nonrefundable are refundable.		
Arkansas Ark. Code Ann. §§ 18-16-303 to 18-16-305	Two months' rent			
California Cal. Civ. Code §§ 1950.5, 1940.5(g)	Two months' rent (unfurnished); 3 months' rent (furnished). Add extra one-half month's rent for waterbed			
Colorado Colo. Rev. Stat. §§ 38-12-102 to 38-12-104	No statutory limit			

State Security Deposit Rules (cont'd)

State/Statute	Limit	Disclosure or Requirement	Separate Account	Interest
Connecticut Conn. Gen. Stat. Ann. §§ 47a-21	Two months' rent (tenant under 62 years of age); one month's rent (tenant 62 years of age or older)		✔	✔[1]
Delaware Del. Code Ann. tit. 25, § 5514	One month's rent on leases for one year or more; no limit for month-to-month rental agreements (may require additional pet deposit of up to one month's rent). No limit for rental of furnished units.		✔[2]	
District of Columbia D.C. Code Ann § 42-3502.17; D.C. Mun. Regs. tit. 14, §§ 308 to 310	One month's rent	In the lease, rental agreement, or receipt, landlord must state the terms and conditions under which the security deposit was collected (to secure tenant's obligations under the lease or rental agreement).	✔	✔[3]

[1] Interest payments must be made annually and at termination of tenancy. The interest rate must be equal to the average rate paid on savings deposits by insured commercial banks, as published by the Federal Reserve Board Bulletin, but not less than 1.5%. (Connecticut)

[2] Orally or in writing, the landlord must disclose to the tenant the location of the security deposit account. (Delaware)

[3] Interest payments at the prevailing statement savings rate must be made at termination of tenancy. (District of Columbia)

State Security Deposit Rules (cont'd)

State/Statute	Limit	Disclosure or Requirement	Separate Account	Interest
Florida Fla. Stat. Ann. §§ 83.49, 83.43(12)	No statutory limit	Within 30 days of receiving the security deposit, the landlord must disclose in writing whether it will be held in an interest- or non-interest bearing account; the name of the account depository; and the rate and time of interest payments. Landlord who collects a deposit must include a copy of Florida Statutes § 83.49(3) in the lease.	✔[4]	✔[5]
Georgia Ga. Code Ann. §§ 44-7-30 to 44-7-37	No statutory limit	Landlord must give tenant a written list of pre-existing damage to the rental before collecting a security deposit.	✔[6]	
Hawaii Haw. Rev. Stat. §§ 521-42, 521-44	One month's rent			
Idaho Idaho Code § 6-321	No statutory limit			
Illinois 765 Ill. Comp. Stat. §§ 710/0.01 to 715/3	No statutory limit			✔[7]

[4] Landlord may post a security bond securing all tenants' deposits instead. (Florida)

[5] Interest payments, if any (account need not be interest bearing) must be made annually and at termination of tenancy. However, no interest is due a tenant who wrongfully terminates the tenancy before the end of the rental term. (Florida)

[6] Landlord must place the deposit in an escrow account in a state- or federally-regulated depository, and must inform the tenant of the location of this account. Landlord may post a security bond securing all tenants' deposits instead. (Georgia)

[7] Landlords who rent 25 or more units in either a single building or a complex located on contiguous properties must pay interest on deposits held for more than six months. The interest rate is the rate paid for minimum deposit savings accounts by the largest commercial bank in the state, as of December 31 of the calendar year immediately preceeding the start of the tenancy. (Illinois)

State Security Deposit Rules (cont'd)

State/Statute	Limit	Disclosure or Requirement	Separate Account	Interest
Indiana Ind. Code Ann. §§ 32-31-3-9 to 32-31-3-19	No statutory limit			
Iowa Iowa Code Ann. § 562A.12	Two months' rent		✔	✔[8]
Kansas Kan. Stat. Ann. §§ 58-2550, 58-2548	One month's rent (unfurnished); one and one-half months' rent (furnished); for pets, add extra one-half month's rent			
Kentucky Ky. Rev. Stat. Ann. § 383.580	No statutory limit	Orally or in writing, landlord must disclose where the security deposit is being held and the account number.	✔	
Louisiana La. Rev. Stat. Ann. §§ 9:3251	No statutory limit			
Maine Me. Rev. Stat. Ann. tit. 14, §§ 6031 to 6038	Two months' rent	Upon request by the tenant, landlord must disclose orally or in writing the name of the institution and the account number where the security deposit is being held.	✔	

[8] Interest payment, if any (account need not be interest-bearing) must be made at termination of tenancy. Interest earned during first five years of tenancy belongs to landlord. (Iowa)

State Security Deposit Rules (cont'd)

State/Statute	Limit	Disclosure or Requirement	Separate Account	Interest
Maryland Md. Code Ann. [Real Prop.] § 8-203, § 8-203.1	Two months' rent	Landlord must provide a receipt that describes tenant's rights to move-in and move-out inspections, and right to receive itemization of deposit deductions and balance, if any; and penalties for landlord's failure to comply. Landlord may include this information in the lease.	✔[9]	✔[10]
Massachusetts Mass. Gen. Laws Ann. ch. 186, § 15B	One month's rent	At the time of receiving a security deposit, landlord must furnish a receipt indicating the amount of the deposit; the name of the person receiving it and, if received by a property manager, the name of the lessor for whom the security deposit is received; the date on which it is received; and a description of the premises leased or rented. The receipt must be signed by the person receiving the security deposit.	✔[11]	✔[12]

[9] Landlord may hold all tenants' deposits in secured certificates of deposit, or in securities issued by the federal government or the State of Maryland. (Maryland)

[10] Within 45 days of termination of tenancy, interest must be paid (at annual rate of 3%, not compounded) only on security deposits of $50 or more. Deposit must be held in a Maryland banking institution. (Maryland)

[11] Within 30 days of receiving security deposit, landlord must disclose the name and location of the bank in which the security deposit has been deposited, and the amount and account number of the deposit. (Massachusetts)

[12] Landlord must pay tenant 5% interest per year or the amount received from the bank (which must be in MA) that holds the deposit. Interest should be paid yearly, and within 30 days of termination date. Interest will not accrue for the last month for which rent was paid in advance. (Massachusetts)

State Security Deposit Rules (cont'd)

State/Statute	Limit	Disclosure or Requirement	Separate Account	Interest
Michigan Mich. Comp. Laws §§ 554.602 to 554.616	One and one-half months' rent	Within 14 days of tenant's taking possession of the rental, landlord must furnish in writing the landlord's name and address for receipt of communications, the name and address of the financial institution or surety where the deposit will be held, and the tenant's obligation to provide in writing a forwarding mailing address to the landlord within 4 days after termination of occupancy. The notice shall include the following statement in 12 point boldface type that is at least 4 points larger than the body of the notice or lease agreement: "You must notify your landlord in writing within 4 days after you move of a forwarding address where you can be reached and where you will receive mail; otherwise your landlord shall be relieved of sending you an itemized list of damages and the penalties adherent to that failure."	✔[13]	

[13] Landlord must place deposits in a regulated financial institution, and may use the deposits as long as the landlord deposits with the secretary of state a cash or surety bond. (Michigan)

State Security Deposit Rules (cont'd)

State/Statute	Limit	Disclosure or Requirement	Separate Account	Interest
Minnesota Minn. Stat. Ann. §§ 504B.175 to 504B.178	No statutory limit	Before collecting rent or a security deposit, landlord must provide a copy of all outstanding inspection orders for which a citation has been issued, pertaining to a rental unit or common area, specifying code violations that threaten the health or safety of the tenant, and all outstanding condemnation orders and declarations that the premises are unfit for human habitation. Citations for violations that do not involve threats to tenant health or safety must be summarized and posted in an obvious place. With some exceptions, landlord who has received notice of a contract for deed cancellation or notice of a mortgage foreclosure sale must so disclose before entering into a lease, accepting rent, or accepting a security deposit; and must furnish the date on which the contract cancellation period or the mortgagor's redemption period ends.		✔[14]
Mississippi Miss. Code Ann. § 89-8-21	No statutory limit			
Missouri Mo. Ann. Stat. § 535.300	Two months' rent			

[14] Landlord must pay 1% simple, noncompounded interest per year. (Deposits collected before 8/1/03 earn interest at 3%, up to 8/1/03, then begin earning at 1%.) Any interest amount less than $1 is excluded. (Minnesota)

State Security Deposit Rules (cont'd)

State/Statute	Limit	Disclosure or Requirement	Separate Account	Interest
Montana Mont. Code Ann. §§ 70-25-101 to 70-25-206	No statutory limit			
Nebraska Neb. Rev. Stat. § 76-1416	One month's rent (no pets); one and one-quarter months' rent (pets)			
Nevada Nev. Rev. Stat. Ann. §§ 118A.240 to 118A.250	Three months' rent	Lease or rental agreement must explain the conditions under which the landlord will refund the deposit.		
New Hampshire N.H. Rev. Stat. Ann §§ 540-A:5 to 540-A:8; 540-B:10	One month's rent or $100, whichever is greater; when landlord and tenant share facilities, no statutory limit	Unless tenant has paid the deposit by personal or bank check, or by a check issued by a government agency, landlord must provide a receipt stating the amount of the deposit and the institution where it will be held. Regardless of whether a receipt is required, landlord must inform tenant that if tenant finds any conditions in the rental in need of repair, tenant may note them on the receipt or other written instrument, and return either within five days.	✔[15]	✔[16]

[15] Upon request, landlord must disclose the account number, the amount on deposit, and the interest rate. Landlord may post a bond covering all deposits instead of putting deposits in a separate account. (New Hampshire)

[16] Landlord who holds a security deposit for a year or longer must pay interest at a rate equal to the rate paid on regular savings accounts in the New Hampshire bank, savings & loan, or credit union where it's deposited. If a landlord mingles security deposits in a single account, the landlord must pay the actual interest earned proportionately to each tenant. A tenant may request the interest accrued every three years, 30 days before that year's tenancy expires. The landlord must comply with the request within 15 days of the expiration of that year's tenancy. (New Hampshire)

State Security Deposit Rules (cont'd)

State/Statute	Limit	Disclosure or Requirement	Separate Account	Interest
New Jersey N.J. Stat. Ann. §§ 46:8-19, 44:8-21, 44:8-26	One and one-half months' rent. Any additional security deposit, collected annually, may be no greater than 10% of the current security deposit.		✔[17]	✔[18]
New Mexico N.M. Stat. Ann. § 47-8-18	One month's rent (for rental agreement of less than one year); no limit for leases of one year or more			✔[19]
New York N.Y. Gen. Oblig. Law §§ 7-103 to 7-108	No statutory limit for nonregulated units	If deposit is placed in a bank, landlord must disclose the name and address of the banking organization where the deposit is being held, and the amount of such deposit.	✔[20]	✔[21]

[17] Within 30 days of receiving the deposit and specified times thereafter, landlord must disclose the name and address of the banking organization where the deposit is being held, the type of account, current rate of interest, and the amount of the deposit. (New Jersey)

[18] Landlord with 10 or more units must invest deposits as specified by statute or place deposit in an insured money market fund account, or in another account that pays quarterly interest at a rate comparable to the money market fund. Landlords with fewer than 10 units may place deposit in an interest-bearing account in any New Jersey financial institution insured by the FDIC. All landlords must pay tenants interest earned on account annually or credit toward payment of rent due. (New Jersey)

[19] Landlord who collects a deposit larger than one month's rent on a year's lease must pay interest, on an annual basis, equal to the passbook interest. (New Mexico)

[20] Statute requires that deposits not be comingled with landlord's personal assets, but does not explicitly require placement in a banking institution (however, deposits collected in buildings of six or more units must be placed in New York bank accounts). (New York)

[21] Landlord who rents out non-regulated units in buildings with five or fewer units need not pay interest. Interest must be paid at the "prevailing rate" on deposits received from tenants who rent units in buildings containing six or more units. The landlord in every rental situation may retain an administrative fee of 1% per year on the sum deposited. Interest can be subtracted from the rent, paid at the end of the year, or paid at the end of the tenancy according to the tenant's choice. (New York)

State Security Deposit Rules (cont'd)

State/Statute	Limit	Disclosure or Requirement	Separate Account	Interest
North Carolina N.C. Gen. Stat. §§ 42-50 to 42-56	One and one-half months' rent for month-to-month rental agreements; two months' rent if term is longer than two months; reasonable, nonrefundable pet deposit	Within 30 days of the beginning of the lease term, landlord must disclose the name and address of the banking institution where the deposit is located.	✔[22]	
North Dakota N.D. Cent. Code §§ 47-16-07.1	One month's rent (or if tenant has a pet, not to exceed the greater of $2,500 or amount equal to two months' rent)		✔	✔[23]
Ohio Ohio Rev. Code Ann. § 5321.16	No statutory limit			✔[24]
Oklahoma Okla. Stat. Ann. tit. 41, § 115	No statutory limit		✔	
Oregon Or. Rev. Stat. § 90.300	No statutory limit			

[22] The landlord may, at his option, furnish a bond from an insurance company licensed to do business in the state. (North Carolina)

[23] Landlord must pay interest if the period of occupancy is at least nine months. Money must be held in a federally insured interest-bearing savings or checking account for benefit of the tenant. Interest must be paid upon termination of the lease. (North Dakota)

[24] Any deposit in excess of $50 or one month's rent, whichever is greater, must bear interest on the excess at the rate of 5% per annum if the tenant stays for six months or more. Interest must be paid annually and upon termination of tenancy. (Ohio)

State Security Deposit Rules (cont'd)

State/Statute	Limit	Disclosure or Requirement	Separate Account	Interest
Pennsylvania 68 Pa. Cons. Stat. Ann. §§ 250.511a to 250.512	Two months' rent for first year of renting; one month's rent during second and subsequent years of renting	For deposits over $100, landlord must deposit them in a federally or state-regulated institution, and give tenant the name and address of the banking institution and the amount of the deposit.	✔[25]	✔[26]
Rhode Island R.I. Gen. Laws § 34-18-19	One month's rent			
South Carolina S.C. Code Ann. § 27-40-410	No statutory limit			
South Dakota S.D. Codified Laws Ann. § 43.32-6.1, § 43-32-24	One month's rent (higher deposit may be charged if special conditions pose a danger to maintenance of the premises)			
Tennessee Tenn. Code Ann. § 66-28-301	No statutory limit		✔[27]	
Texas Tex. Prop. Code Ann. §§ 92.101 to 92.109	No statutory limit			

[25] Instead of placing deposits in a separate account, landlord may purchase a bond issued by a bonding company authorized to do business in the state. (Pennsylvania)

[26] Tenant who occupies rental unit for two or more years is entitled to interest beginning with the 25th month of occupancy. Landlord must pay tenant interest (minus 1% fee) at the end of the third and subsequent years of the tenancy. (Pennsylvania)

[27] Orally or in writing, landlord must disclose the location of the separate account used by landlord for the deposit. (Tennessee)

			Separate Account	Interest
State/Statute	**Limit**	**Disclosure or Requirement**		
Utah Utah Code Ann. §§ 57-17-1 to 57-17-5	No statutory limit	For written leases or rental agreements only, if part of the deposit is non-refundable, landlord must disclose this feature.		
Vermont Vt. Stat. Ann. tit. 9, § 4461	No statutory limit			
Virginia Va. Code Ann. §§ 55-248.15;1	Two months' rent			✔[28]
Washington Wash. Rev. Code Ann. §§ 59.18.260 to 59.18.285	No statutory limit	In the lease, landlord must disclose the circumstances under which all or part of the deposit may be withheld, and must provide a receipt with the name and location of the banking institution where the deposit is being held. No deposit may be collected unless the rental agreement is in writing and a written checklist or statement specifically describing the condition and cleanliness of or existing damages to the premises and furnishings is provided to the tenant at the start of the tenancy.	✔	
W. Virginia No statute				

State Security Deposit Rules (cont'd)

[28] Landlord must accrue interest on all money held as security at annual rate equal to 4% below the Federal Reserve Board discount rate as of January 1 of each year. The deposit must begin earning interest as of the date the rental agreement is signed, but no interest is payable unless the landlord holds the deposit for over 13 months after the date the rental agreement was signed and there has been continuous occupancy of the same unit. Interest must be paid upon termination of the tenancy. (Virginia)

State Security Deposit Rules (cont'd)

State/Statute	Limit	Disclosure or Requirement	Separate Account	Interest
Wisconsin Wis. Admin. Code ATCP 134.06	No statutory limit	Before accepting the deposit, landlord must inform tenant of tenant's inspection rights, disclose all habitability defects and show tenant any outstanding building and housing code violations, inform tenant of the means by which shared utilities will be billed, and inform tenant if utilities are not paid for by landlord.		
Wyoming Wyo. Stat. §§ 1-21-1207 to 1-21-1208	No statutory limit	Lease or rental agreement must state whether any portion of a deposit is nonrefundable, and landlord must give tenant written notice of this fact when collecting the deposit.		

Fielding Initial Questions and Phone Screening

Once your rental ad hits the newspapers, Internet, or even just the front lawn or tenant grapevine, you should be prepared to answer inquiries about the rental. Many of you will take the opportunity to prescreen applicants in an effort to identify qualified tenants. If you will be doing individual tours or a private open house (to which you invite people who have called in response to your ad) you will definitely be handling phone calls from interested applicants. You'll be well served to take whatever time is necessary to ask and answer relevant questions over the phone, in order to avoid showing the rental to people who are not qualified or who decide that the rental is not appropriate.

If you decide to hold a public open house—to which anyone who has seen your ad may show up—you won't be prescreening applicants over the phone, and you may be tempted to skip this chapter. That would be a mistake, because many of the questions a caller will pose will be the same as those you encounter at an open house. For example, the Second Level questions described in Chapter 6—those that ask whether you'll consider varying your basic rental terms—could come just as easily from an in-person open house attendee as a caller with the newspaper on his or her lap. This chapter will give you the tools to answer fairly and legally when you're pressed on your policy on cosigners or pets, or whether you'll consider a lower security deposit in exchange for a slightly higher rent. It will give you some tips on how to get information from the prospect, too—whether you're on the phone or standing in the rental's hallway.

✓ Before You Take the First Phone Call

Your tenant search begins in earnest with phone calls and initial inquiries. Double check the following issues:

- If your unit is occupied, make sure you have the cooperation of current tenants (covered in Chapter 3).
- If current tenants are moving out, make sure they're still on schedule and that the unit will be vacant when you plan to show it.
- Review your screening priorities and adjust them, if necessary (Chapter 6).
- Know the dates, times, and details on how you're going to show the property (Chapter 5).
- Have lists of the places where you advertised and copies of ads and flyers.
- Role play with your spouse or a friend so you feel comfortable dealing with potential callers. You may discover some issues you haven't thought of, and you may be grateful for the chance to practice.

You're about to take the first step of your screening process—one in which you winnow and woo applicants through phone conversations or discussions at property showings. You'll identify those prospects who are likely to meet your basic rental terms, and encourage them to attend a property showing (Chapters 7 and 9).

Before you talk with prospective tenants, make sure you have your Rental Policies sheet in order (Chapter 6 guided you through its preparation) and all the details you need to handle questions about the property and how it stacks up with the competition. This chapter shows you how to develop the materials you need. It also gives you suggestions on how to plan for, field, and follow up with calls in a businesslike and friendly manner. It covers:

- the mechanics of the call—phone numbers, call forwarding, messages, and the like
- preparing for the call, by having on hand a description of the property, a chart comparing how competing properties measure up against yours, and a series of questions to ask the caller
- handling the call—how to get the information you need, and what to say and not to say
- rejecting callers who don't meet your tenant criteria, and
- moving qualified applicants to the next screening step.

The Law You Need to Know

As ever, you must understand and apply fair housing laws when it comes to talking with prospective tenants. Other legal restrictions apply to your conversations, too, in particular:

- Understand that you can't circumvent the rules by, for example, claiming a vacancy is no longer available when you hear a child's voice in the background or a foreign accent on the other end of the phone.
- In case you're tempted to record phone conversations, thinking that you can protect yourself against fake claims of discrimination that way—don't! Many states impose criminal penalties against those who record conversations without the consent of the other party. If you're worried about fair housing claims, learn the law and apply it.
- Don't misunderstand the lawyer's mantra, "Get it in writing!" for the proposition that what you say won't obligate you as well. In fact, if your statements (about the property and your policies) play an important part in the applicant's decision to rent, you'll have to follow through.

Landlord's Forms Library

The forms in this chapter are for both you and your eventual applicants. You'll want to prepare them before you take calls or show the property:

- **Rental Property Fact Sheet.** Lists your rental property's main features and attributes, including rent, deposit, utilities, neighborhood, type and size of rooms, appliances, parking, and laundry. You can refer to this while handling calls and give it to interested visitors.
- **Rental Property Comparison Chart.** Compares your rental to competing properties on issues like rent and parking.
- **Tenant Information Sheet.** The form you'll use to track each prospect's progress through your screening, with questions to help you during the initial conversation and places to record your findings and conclusions at every subsequent step of your evaluation system.

Once you start identifying qualified applicants (and hopefully advance them to a rental showing), you'll need to begin a file for each prospect. (You don't need to bother with those who tell you early on that they're not interested.) The Tenant Information Sheet will be the first item in that person's file, followed by the Rental Application. If you ever have to respond to a discrimination claim, these are the first pieces of evidence examined by your own lawyer and will make a huge difference in your ability to defend yourself. Naturally, they will show that you asked legally safe questions, made decisions based on sound business reasons, and consistently applied your tenant selection criteria.

The forms that pertain to the property itself, such as the Rental Property Fact Sheet and the Rental Property Comparison Chart, should go into this property's file for this vacancy (you've been adding documents to this file all along, with the recent addition of the forms in your Rental Kit (see Chapter 6)).

Make it easy to reach you

When potential tenants call the phone number listed in your ad, they'll have their first experience dealing with you personally. If your ad was clear, complete, and enthusiastic, the caller will expect a similar experience on the phone.

It's imperative that interested tenants can easily reach you. Most housing seekers will have a list of potential rentals and will begin calling the most attractive ones first. If you're not available (or unable to call back soon), you're likely to lose out on these candidates. When market conditions are soft, you can't afford to be passed by. Here's how to ensure that you field these calls in a professional manner.

Use a business line

For even the smallest-scale landlord, it will be worth the time and expense to set up a separate business line for tenant-related calls. Here's why:

- **You know it's business.** A separate line allows you to separate your business and professional life— when the business line rings, you can answer knowing that it's a current tenant or a potential one, not your brother or your kids' friends.
- **You greet the caller professionally.** With a dedicated business line, you can adopt the appropriate tone and leave a businesslike message on your answering machine or voice mail, with details on the rental, which might sound odd to those calling you for personal reasons.
- **You'll get the call.** By not using the home line, you won't have to worry about whether you're getting calls fielded by one of your kids or having the phone tied up by another family member.
- **You can easily document the expense as a deduction.** The cost of your dedicated business line is an ongoing business operation expense that you can deduct on a yearly basis. (For information on how to do so, see *Every Landlord's Tax Deduction Guide*, by Stephen Fishman (Nolo).) If you handle tenant calls on your home phone (or on another business line), you'll have to painstakingly separate the long-distance calls that were landlord related from those that were not, and you won't be able to deduct the basic monthly cost of maintaining the line. By having a dedicated line, you can simply deduct the whole thing without dissecting the phone bill.
- **The caller learns that you're reachable—a good quality in a landlord.** The line you use for interested potential renters should also be the one that current tenants use when they need to reach you. Design your greeting so that this is clear—for example, you might say,

"Hello, this is Sam Jones, owner and manager for Oak Lane Properties. If you're a current tenant and need to reach me, please press one. If you're interested in renting at Oak Lane, please press two...." In this way, interested tenants will learn that you're a conscientious landlord who will be available should they need to reach you about a repair or other problem.

Don't worry about not being in the same physical place as your business line. You can arrange to forward calls from the business line to another number at your convenience. For example, you can have landlord-related calls ring at your office number during the day, but not during the evening or on weekends. Or, knowing that you won't be near the business phone on a Saturday, you can send the calls to your cell phone.

Use a cell phone

If you're seldom in a place with a land line for long (or don't have a land line), you may decide to use your cell phone to take calls. The cell phone has the dubious advantage of always being with you and theoretically always answerable. Its disadvantage, however, is that its reception may be spotty, you may have to turn it off at times, and (unless you're willing to turn it off and not receive personal calls) you may get business calls at very inconvenient times. If interested

callers will be contacting you on your cell, consider these points:

- **Reception.** How good is it? If you are often in out-of-range areas, callers will become frustrated when they are constantly routed to your voice mail.

- **Will you keep it on?** Many landlords have day jobs that require them to silence their cell phones. If that's the case with you, your callers won't get through and may give up if they constantly get your voice mail.

- **Can you have the conversation when the phone rings?** When you answer, you may be too busy to have a conversation with your caller (you may be driving, talking to a customer at your day job, or busy at your desk). Will you answer only to whisper, or conduct a hurried conversation, or promise to call right back? For some callers, such a reception will be more annoying than going right to voice mail. You may as well have a clear message on a land line answering service that you check frequently and answer professionally.

- **Where will you be when this call comes in?** The advantage of a land line is that the phone is indoors where you can sit down, take notes (and use the phone-screening tools explained in this chapter). A cell phone that's on your belt or in your purse may go off while you're in the car, in a shop, or handling other business. In these situations, it will be awkward for you to get the caller's contact information, take notes on the conversation, and consult your selling tools.

If a cell phone is your only means of communicating with interested renters, do your best to minimize problems that might arise. Have your rental property information with you, if possible, along with a stiff legal pad or other notebook you can use while on the phone (and invest in an earpiece if your cell doesn't have a speakerphone). Do not keep the phone on unless you really are prepared to have a conversation. Check your voice mail regularly.

Return calls quickly

Even the most conscientious landlord can't personally take every call. If you're on the line or otherwise not available, your greeting message should assure callers that you'll call back as soon as possible. Make at least two attempts to return these calls.

! **Return even those calls that don't sound promising.** It's worth your while to avoid possible claims of discrimination, which could arise if callers are members of a protected class and their accent tips you off. "Linguistic profiling" is a well-known and illegal practice of some landlords (see Chapter 2).

Use caller ID

You'll find it handy to have your callers' phone numbers securely on your phone. Purchasing this feature with your phone service means that you can confidently follow up with callers who are promising but who have not left a phone number with you (or who have given a number that you've written down incorrectly).

Prepare for the phone call

A call from a prospective tenant is your personal opportunity to weed out the unqualified or uninterested seekers, and to entice those who are truly good candidates for your rental. No matter how confident you are in your phone abilities and your knowledge of your rental property, don't head into this without a clear idea of how you'll accomplish the winnowing and the wooing. Even the pros reach for written cheat sheets when the phone rings. In fact, you'd be wise to reach for three:

- a sheet that describes the attributes of the rental (your Rental Property Fact Sheet)
- a chart that compares your rental to nearby similar rentals (your Rental Property Comparison Chart), and
- a list of questions designed to give you and the caller the information you both need in order to know whether you are a good match (these are on your Tenant Information Sheet).

This following section describes how to prepare and use these materials.

You'll find templates for a Fact Sheet, a Rental Property Comparison Chart, and a Tenant Information Sheet on the CD-ROM that accompanies this book. Filled-out samples appear below.

Prepare a Rental Property Fact Sheet

You'll find it handy—and comforting, if selling over the phone is something you're new at—to have a concise list of your rental's terms and attributes, such as the number and size of bedrooms, details on floor coverings, parking, and access to public transportation, at your fingertips. Not only will it give a note of confidence to your voice, but it will impress your listener with your professionalism and seriousness. And you never know what details are going to be important—you may think that "large, three-bedroom" adequately describes a rental's size, but a caller may want to know the exact room size in order to accommodate furniture. You may not remember the room's dimensions and will fumble unless this information is right in front of you. Your need for a snapshot of a rental's features goes up if you own several properties.

You can add more information as appropriate for this property—for example, on the quality of city services, details about the rental construction, or general information on the neighborhood. If the current tenants are leaving voluntarily (particularly if their tenancy lasted for a long time), you might mention this, too. Nothing will reassure a potential tenant more than saying, "My current tenants, who have been wonderful residents for the past five years, are leaving to take jobs out of state."

You'll use this same Fact Sheet when showing your rental property, as discussed in Chapter 9. Interested applicants will appreciate all the details on this takeaway form, especially if they are looking at lots of similar properties. You may want to omit the section at the end, labeled "Office Use."

The sample Rental Property Fact Sheet, below, shows how the landlord we met earlier in the book, Ann, described her single-family home in preparation for fielding interested callers. Ann consulted her Marketing Worksheet, which she developed when designing her ad. If you've taken that step (discussed in Chapter 4), pull the Worksheet out—and transfer the more general information directly to the Fact Sheet. If you haven't done a Marketing Worksheet, no matter—doing your Fact Sheet now won't take too much time.

Your Fact Sheet will serve you well in years to come. Next time this unit becomes available, you will pull it out, update it, and have it ready for the next rental. So take the time now to enter the information.

Rental Property Fact Sheet

Rental address: 1185 "D" Street, Collegetown, CA

Rent: $2,000   Security deposit: $2,000   Other fees: $ 0

Start date: Aug. 1, 20xx   ☐ Month to month   ☑ Lease, ending date: July 31, 20xx

Pets: 1 dog , if approved   Smoking: no

Parking opportunities: garage   Maximum number of occupants: 7

Total number of bedrooms: 3   Total number of baths: 3

Total square feet: 2,100   Bedroom 1: 70   Bedroom 2: 80

Bedroom 3: 100   Dining Room: 70

Other rooms: large kitchen + dining area

Floor coverings: hardwood throughout (tile in bathrooms)

Paint: painted 1 year ago

Appliances: new as of March 1, 20xx

Common area or outdoor features: great deck, large, fenced yard

Laundry: hookups

Utilities (who pays, usual amount if tenant pays)

Gas: Tenant   Electricity: Tenant

Water: Tenant   Garbage: Tenant   Sewer: Landlord

Telecommunications offerings (cable or satellite and name of provider): _____
cable and DSL

Transportation (bus, rail, underground): local bus, inter-urban tram

Commute time from rental to:

Sacramento	is 20 min.	and costs $10
Oakland	is 2 hours	and costs $14
Berkeley	is 1.5 hours	and costs $12

Schools

    Primary: ___Miller School_____ ; distance from rental, and transportation___0.5 miles, no public transit_____

    Secondary: _Dana Middle_____ ; distance from rental, and transportation__1.2 miles, no public transit_____

    Other: ____Lincoln High_____ ; distance from rental, and transportation__2 miles, no public transit_____

Major medical centers and transportation: _Sacramento Hospital, 30 minutes_ _by train_____
_Collegetown Hospital, 1.5 miles (Bus #5)_____

Major employers and transportation: __University (0.5 miles),_____
_Systis Systems (1 mile)_____

Major shopping areas and transportation: _downtown (0.5 miles, many bus routes)_

Movie theaters: _Several within 1-mile radius_____

Parks, public recreation facilities: _Farmers' Market Plaza (0.5 miles),___
_rec. center (1 mile)_____

Other: __Neighborhood clubhouse/recreation park (1 mile)_____

OFFICE USE

Last updated: _____ by: _____

Used for rentals shown on: _____

Email Your Fact Sheet to Out-of-Towners

Owners who advertise online, including in newspapers that have an online version, may get inquiries from people rather far away who are moving to take a new job, attend school, or just make a fresh start. Indeed, reaching this potentially vast market may be the reason you chose an online marketing campaign.

Now that your ad is out there, don't forget to support your decision. Besides giving these prospects digital photos and Google Earth links (see Chapter 4), you can email them the specifics of this rental that you didn't put into your ad. Attach your Rental Property Fact Sheet to any inquiry and add to it if the prospect asks specific questions that the sheet doesn't answer.

Prepare a Rental Property Comparison Chart

There's one more bit of homework you'll be glad you've done before you begin talking to applicants: Prepare a Rental Property Comparison Chart. This is a place for you to compare your rental to competitors' offerings and record your property's specs on issues such as rent and parking. In a soft market particularly, you can be sure that smart applicants are comparing and contrasting available rentals, looking for the nicest place at the best price. By having comparative information at your fingertips, you'll be able to quickly supply the information people may ask about (and you can even offer it, if you're bold!). If you're in a hot market and can expect to rent your place without needing to better the competition, you can probably skip this step.

Take a look at the Rental Property Comparison Chart that Ann, our erstwhile landlord, prepared for her single-family rental. Ann went to some open houses, checked the ads for listings and details, and asked other landlords she knew about the properties' reputations. You might even go online to a local rental service (such as MetroRent in the San Francisco Bay Area), and get comparables there.

It took Ann a bit of work (and some sleuthing) to get this information, but most of it was easily ascertainable and verifiable; other parts were more subjective. Ann's Comparison Chart gave her confidence when she was asked, "Aren't your rates a bit high?" and "Why aren't you offering one month's free rent?" The section "Phone Scripts," below, provides advice on how to carefully answer these types of questions.

Rental Property Comparison Chart

Last updated: ___August 23, 20xx___ By: ___Ann___

Rental address: ___1185 "D" Street, Collegetown, CA___

Rental Property	My rental	1075 "D" St.	45 10th Ave.	76 "C" St.
Rent & deposit	$2,000/mo.; $2,000 deposit	$1,800/mo.; $3,600 deposit	$2,100/mo.; $1,000 deposit	$1,750/mo.; $800 deposit
Parking	1-car garage, long driveway, street parking	Street only	Street only (very congested)	One space in outdoor lot per unit
Number of bedrooms	3	2	3	3
Utilities	LL pays sewer, water, cable. T pays gas, elec., garbage	Not known	Not known	Tenant pays all utilities
Amenities (laundry, appliances)	Laundry hook-up, cable	Air cond., new heater	No laundry, old kit. appliances	No cable, satellite dish installed
Room size	Older house with large rooms	New construction, so smaller rooms	Older building, large rooms	Brand new, small rooms
Turnover rate	Last 2 tenants stayed 3 + 4 years	Turnover about once a year	Seems to be pretty frequent (lots of ads over the past year)	New
Move-in perks	No	First month's rent free	No	First month's rent free

Add points of comparison as needed—for example, if families will be attracted to your rental, note the distance from schools and the walking route. A competitor may offer a cheaper rent but be located across a busy thoroughfare, making it dangerous to expect children to get to school on their own. That alone could spell the difference for some applicants. Or, if your property is within walking distance of a major transportation access point, note that (and estimate the competitors' distance and quality of travel—no one wants to walk through dangerous neighborhoods before or after work).

You'll find the Rental Property Comparison Chart on the CD-ROM that accompanies this book. Add columns to reflect unique advantages your property has with respect to schools, parks, transportation, and the like. You may want to change the printout to give you a sideways, or landscape, view if you add more columns.

If you're using a comparison chart that you prepared the last time you advertised this rental, be sure you update it now and enter the date you do so at the top. This information will be useless if it's not up to date, and could actually hurt you if information you represent to callers does not square with the facts of your competitors' offerings.

Prepare a Tenant Information Sheet

The person who becomes your tenant will progress through the five steps of your screening process. After Step One (the first phone or in-person conversation and the site visit), you'll have an application to review (Step Two), references (landlords, employers, and personal references) to contact (Step Three), and a credit report to review (Step Four). You may end your screening with criminal background checking (Step Five). At every step along the way, your prospect can either advance to the next step or be rejected (or drop out voluntarily). The Tenant Information Sheet is where you'll track this progress, recording your findings and conclusions. It has these main sections:

- **Summary of Rental Terms.** Here you'll enter the basic key terms and attributes of your rental. It's less detailed than the Rental Property Fact Sheet.
- **Applicant Information.** These questions, which you can ask in a phone call or during an interview on site, capture the applicant's name and contact information, which you will need if the applicant advances. This chapter guides you in how to elicit this information.
- **Interview Questions.** Here you'll record answers to basic, preliminary questions that will establish whether the applicant

meets your basic requirements. You'll learn the answers from a phone screening or an interview you conduct during a property visit. This chapter deals with this conversation.

- **Interview Conclusions.** In this section you'll note the results of your conversation. You will also record the specifics of any intended visit. This chapter explains how to fill this part out, too.

- **Evaluations of additional screening tools.** Succeeding sections are for your findings and decisions following the site visit, rental application review, reference checks, and so on. The rest of the chapters in this book guide you through these events and reviews, and will prompt you to take out this form and note your findings (did the current landlord give the applicant a thumbs up?) and conclusions ("Reject b/c current

landlord has had to serve many 3-day notices to pay rent.").

Using this form as the one place for all of the information you gather on the prospects you screen will make it easier to compare applicants and make the final decision. And using the form (and filling it out wisely) will help you should you be accused of discriminatory motives when rejecting tenants.

How to prescreen over the phone or in person

Now's the time when your thoughtful preparation will begin to bear fruit. You've designed a marketing strategy, implemented it, and have prepared yourself for speaking with applicants by filling out your Rental Property Fact Sheet and your Rental Property Comparison Chart, and you've prepared a Tenant Information Sheet (you'll see a sample filled out below). Your phone is ready

Be a Friendly Businessperson

Callers will form their first impressions based on your phone manner and particularly, your voice and tone. You'll want to aim for just the right balance between friendliness and an appropriate business demeanor. You'll want to sound accommodating, yet not so wishy-washy that callers will wonder if you've figured out what you're doing. And when you ask questions, many of which will concern personal details such as the caller's income, you'll need to do so in a way that doesn't sound intrusive or abrupt. You want to sound interested, but not fawning (applicants can spot that one a mile away).

with a business-like greeting, and you've arranged for call forwarding if needed. With your forms at your side (including your ads, flyers, and list of places where you've advertised), you are all set to answer questions, weed out unsuitable applicants, and advance qualified applicants to the next stage (showing them the rental or, for those you've met on site, giving them a rental application).

Using the Tenant Information Sheet: Summary of Rental Terms

The first section of the sheet, Summary of Rental Terms asks you to enter the essential information for your rental, such as its size, date available, pet policy, rent, and so on. Though you might want to trust your memory as to the details of your rental, you'll find it helpful to have

this information in print in case you get flustered (or if you have multiple rentals). Before you take your first phone call, fill out a few blank sheets to have at the ready.

Using the Tenant Information Sheet: Caller Information

You'll start the conversation by getting some basic information on the prospective tenant, including how they learned of the vacancy and their contact information. Asking for this information at the start of the conversation, rather than at the end, is a debatable tactic. Here are the issues:

- **Pros.** This information may be useful to you even if this caller doesn't progress. First, if you've used multiple advertising methods,

Tenant Information Sheet (excerpt)

Tenant Information Sheet

Summary of Rental Terms

Rental address: _____ 1185 "D" Street _____

Number of bedrooms _____ 3 _____   Maximum number of occupants ___ 7 ___

Rent ____ $2,000 ____   Deposit ____ $2,000 ____   Term ___ Year's Lease ___

Minimum income required __ $6,000/mo. __   Start date __ August 1, 20xx __

Pet policy _____ 1 dog, if approved, cat OK _____

"Does this sound like it will fit your needs? If so, great—let me ask you a few questions, please."

you'll learn which ones generated calls (and later, which avenues generated *qualified* seekers). Second, you may want to contact this caller later if you decide to modify your terms and realize that this caller will qualify. For example, suppose you realize that the asking rent is too high—if you drop it by $100, you'll want to be able to contact the person who declined because your advertised rent was a bit too high.

- **Cons.** Some callers will be put off by questions at the outset. They want information from you, and don't see the need for you to begin the conversation with a quiz. That's why it's important to

introduce these questions carefully, by asking permission to pose them (see the suggestions below). If the caller balks initially but turns into an interested and qualified prospect, you can always go back to this section. Certainly, if you feel uncomfortable launching your conversation with these questions, leave them for later.

Not surprisingly, most professional landlords and leasing agents are trained to get this information first. In big operations particularly, the idea is to generate "phone cards" that capture the caller's basic information. These cards are used by management to determine callers' demographics, which will

Tenant Information Sheet (excerpt)

Applicant Information

Caller's name: _____Brent Campbell_____

Date & time of first call: _Tuesday, Oct. 12, 7:15 p.m._____

How did you learn of this vacancy? ___saw the ad in the local newspaper_____

_____

Rentals with web pages: Have you seen our web page describing this property?

☑Yes   ☐No

Caller's phone number(s): _415-555-4567_____

Caller's email: _____brentcampbell@coldmail.com_____

Caller's current address: _27 Warren Way, Davistown, CA_____

How Do You Feel About a Hard Sell?

Aggressive leasing agents begin their first leasing interview by asking prospects what the caller is looking for in a rental ("So, Mr. Jones, what's the most important thing about an apartment for you? … you say it's covered parking and a fireplace? … okay … and also nice views and a good kitchen? Well, let me tell you, we can provide those….") The idea is to find out what will appeal to the caller, and craft a sales pitch accordingly. Often, the conversation has little to do with basic rental terms, and a lot to do with deliberately hooking the caller on softer aspects. When the agent can't meet the caller's wish list, he or she will try to talk up the next best thing. Ideally, callers will be so convinced that the property meets their needs that the basic rental terms (such as rent and deposits) will take on almost secondary importance.

Professionals swear by this approach, because their studies show it works. Well, maybe. It's never a good idea to talk or trick someone into something they don't want, whether it's a dress or an apartment. A straightforward approach may be your better bet.

influence future marketing efforts. And quite unabashedly, this information will be used as part of an aggressive leasing program if the caller doesn't set up an appointment right away. These leasing agents will call back and persevere to fill their vacancies. If you're not an accomplished salesperson, and don't want to develop the aggressive skills needed to deftly pose these questions at the start of a conversation that you did not initiate, save them for later.

Using the Tenant Information Sheet: Interview Questions

On the Tenant Information Sheet, you'll see that below the questions concerning income, number of expected occupants, and the like, there's a line to enter notes, such as a student's statement that although he doesn't work, his parents will support him; or a couple's statement that the two of them will soon be three. Use the "Qualified" or "Not Qualified" lines to record your conclusions on whether the caller can meet each of your basic rental terms. You're aiming to invite only those callers who have checks on every Qualified row to a property visit.

Remember to keep your rental priorities in mind as you conduct this conversation. With first-time renters and self-employed persons, in particular, you'll need to be flexible and willing to accept evidence that they'll be good tenants even though they don't have a rental history or a steady paycheck.

You may decide to add questions that cover key issues not already set out on the sheet. Add questions only after you've gone through the basics, or include them as one of the terms mentioned in the Summary of Rental Terms section at the top of the Sheet. For example, you may be very concerned about whether a tenant intends to run a home business, having learned from experience that certain businesses cause difficulties at your property. If this issue is a deal breaker, ask it now, before wasting time with a personal visit. (But be careful here—in some states, including California and New York, landlords are restricted from prohibiting family child care businesses.)

The Phone Scripts, below, give some suggestions on how to get the information called for in the Interview Questions (you can adapt these to an in-person situation, too). Be sure that you've developed some rapport first, by going through the features of your rental (prompted by the Summary of Rental Terms section on your form). Use the scripts as a guide to help you develop your own style. Remember, if you've written a clear and accurate ad, your callers already know a lot about your rental—but you know nothing about them.

! Don't get carried away with extra interview questions. The purpose of the phone interview is to identify potential renters based on key qualifications such as income, number of occupants, and desired length of stay, and to convince callers to visit your property (they won't be so inclined if you've subjected them to a cross-examination). If you start discussing peripheral issues, such as how long the caller has lived in the area, you're in for a long chat that will produce information not essential to your main question: Does this caller qualify on the basics?

Address your caller by name. Using the caller's first name will personalize the conversation and may help break the ice. Ask if you can use the caller's first name but use the last name if you sense hesitation or a more formal attitude.

Applicants May Screen Themselves

Don't be automatically put off by close questioning from callers. If a legitimate question and a truthful answer tell you or the caller that this property is not a match, so be it. You wouldn't want to waste time on a site visit, surely. Whether you'll be inclined to begin negotiating at this point, however, is another matter (see the negotiation tips in Chapter 9).

Tenant Information Sheet (excerpt)

Interview Questions

	Qualified	Not Qualified

When would you like to move in? ____Dec. 1____   ☑   ☐

How many people will be living in the rental? ____1____   ☑   ☐

Adults: ____1____   Minor children: ____0____

What is your monthly gross income? ____$7,000____   ☑   ☐

How long would you be living here? ____one year____   ☑   ☐

Pet-friendly rentals: What kinds of pets do you have?

__1 dog, older, "well-trained"__   ☑   ☐

What is your occupation? ____engineer____

Where (or for whom) do you work? ____Data Management____

What is your reason for leaving your current home? __I've been transferred from__
__Jackson.__

Do you have any other questions you'd like to ask me?__Questions re: size of__
__garage, next-door neighbors, garden__

Notes: ____sounds good—businesslike + friendly____

Phone Scripts

Here are some suggestions on how to begin and conduct your call—and some lines to avoid!

Information you want or want to impart	What to say	What *not* to say	What's the difference?
Your greeting	"Hello! Thanks for calling me about this rental. It's still available and I'm happy to answer any questions you may have."	"Yes, this is the landlord."	You're assuring the caller that the rental is still available, and you're making it clear that you're ready to spend some time on this call.
Summarizing the basic rental terms— level of detail will depend on details in your ad and caller's responses	"So, before we get started, I'll summarize the key terms of the rental: This is a one-bedroom, available on the first of next month, at $1,800 per month with a $1,800 deposit. Pets are, okay subject to our pet policy. I use the industry standard of requiring tenants to have a gross monthly income of three times the rent."	"All the information is in the ad. What else do you need to know?"	You're repeating information that may be in your ad, but that's okay, because it reminds everyone of where you're starting from (should you decide to be flexible later).
Introducing the questions you're about to ask	"I hope it's okay if I ask you a few preliminary questions, before we get into details on the rental. Please bear with me—it won't take long."	"First, I have to ask you some questions."	Nobody likes to be quizzed. Acknowledge this and at least promise to be brief.

Phone Scripts (continued)

Information you want or want to impart	What to say	What *not* to say	What's the difference?
Marketing information: How did the caller find out about your rental?	"Can you tell me how you found out about this rental? (I'm wondering if my advertising was effective.) Did you see my web page?"	"How did you know it's available?"	You're basically asking the caller to help you figure out if you're advertising correctly—most people will feel flattered and will answer.
Family with children	"We have several units that will accommodate the size of your family— I'll show you all of them."	"We have some 'family units' next to other families that I'm sure you'll like."	Steering the family to a particular location is illegal— it's their choice as long as the unit is big enough.
Asking for caller's email, phone number, and address	"Can I ask you a few questions on how I might reach you if we decide to go forward?"	What's your email, address, and phone?"	Asking permission to ask these questions may persuade caller to answer. (Caller may defer and want to get right to the point; that's okay, but try to come back to this at the end of the call.)
Asking about reasons the caller is looking for a rental	"May I ask you why you're moving?"	"Why are you looking—have you been evicted or asked to leave?"	By saying, "May I ask you," you're softening an intrusive question and giving the caller an opportunity to defer without sounding belligerent. If he or she is being evicted, you'll find out soon enough if you talk to his or her current landlord.

Phone Scripts (continued)

Information you want or want to impart	What to say	What *not* to say	What's the difference?
Asking about the number of occupants	"How many people, including minor children, will live in the rental?"	"Are you moving in with a roommate or a spouse? Are you an unmarried couple? Do you have kids— how many and what are their ages and sex? How do you intend to allocate the bedrooms?"	To avoid fair housing claims, ask only about the total number of people, without regard to their sex or relationship to one another.
Asking about current income	"As I'm sure you know, landlords often use a rule of thumb that the rent shouldn't be more than one-third the household's gross monthly income. Will you be able to meet this standard? Rest assured that I'll keep this information strictly confidential."	"What's your gross monthly income?"	You're describing this personal question as just routine, asking for a yes/no instead of a dollar amount, and assuring the caller that you won't divulge it.
Asking about the caller's occupation or workplace	"May I ask what type of work you do and where you work?"	"Who's your employer?"	By asking the caller to describe the work he or she does, you're showing interest in the caller (which some will find flattering), and you don't sound pushy. Then, ask for whom the caller works.

Phone Scripts (continued)			
Information you want or want to impart	What to say	What *not* to say	What's the difference?
Scheduling a visit	"It looks like this rental may be suitable for you. I can show the rental on [*name one or two alternate times, or your open house*]. After that, if you are still interested, I'll ask you to fill out an application. I'll need proof of employment, references from current and past landlords and your employer, and a credit report that indicates that you'll be able to handle the rent. If you like, I can email you my Rental Policies, which go into these criteria in a little more detail."	"It's available for showing on Monday morning at ten. If you like it, it's yours."	Be flexible if you can when setting the appointment. Be careful to make it clear that the showing is just another step in the process. The caller must still complete an application and meet your "good tenant" criteria.

Carefully document your conclusions

At the end of the Interview Questions section of the Tenant Information Sheet, you'll see a place for your conclusions. Here you'll sum up the results of your Qualified/Not Qualified determinations, and you'll take into consideration any other relevant information you learned during the conversation. There are three choices:

- **Prospect opts out.** Many callers or visitors will terminate the conversation on their own when they realize they can't meet your income criteria or for some other reason; and qualified callers, too, may opt out when they learn you can't offer a feature they want. Why fill in this information? It's important to have a record should you ever need this document as evidence that, for example, the caller declined to go further because you

couldn't offer covered parking. If this caller later accuses you of a fair housing violation (that you turned him or her down because you suspected he or she was a member of a minority), your notes may be admissible as a business record to support your defense that the real reason had nothing to do with discrimination.

- **Advance.** Check this line for qualified visitors or callers who can meet your basic rental terms (or offered acceptable alternatives) and have told you nothing that would raise red flags concerning their ability to be stable tenants. You'll want to go right away to the next section ("Arrangements to visit property"), which records your plans to show the rental to this prospect.
- **Reject.** Use this line for those who can't meet your basic rental terms. Be sure to look at your line

Tenant Information Sheet (excerpt)

Interview Conclusions

☐ **Caller opts out:** Caller has declined to pursue this rental, reasons: _____

_____

_____

☑ **Advance:** Caller is qualified ____*anxious to see the house*_____

☐ **Reject:** Caller is not qualified, reasons: _____

_____

of check marks on each of the essential rental criteria that you covered during this conversation. Reject those who can't meet them or can't offer you a reasonable alternative (such as a letter from a student's advisor in lieu of an employer's reference). You can also reject based on relevant information you learned during the conversation, such as a tenant's statement that he's moving because the upstairs tenant complained constantly about his rock band's practice sessions. Be sure that the reasons you give (on the phone or in person and on the form) are legally safe. Don't rush to write your conclusions while still on the phone—just be sure to jot them down right after you get off, so your memory is fresh and you don't let this little task slip. See Chapter 16, "How to Reject," for guidance on when to reject and suggested wording.

Dealing with on-the-fence callers

For every qualified caller, you'll want to arrange a site visit. If your caller hesitates, ask why. Use the "Qualified, but no commitment to visit" section of your Tenant Information Sheet to record their hesitations. Many times, you'll hear "I'd like to think it over," or "I'd take the place if...." Jot down what callers say and consider pursuing the conversation.

What you learn when you press an uncommitted caller may make or break the chances for this person—some aspect of this caller's current living situation may pop out and instantly disqualify him or her, or you may learn that the hesitation concerns a minor point that you can get past. "What's the Problem," below, gives some examples of common responses when you propose a site visit. If you're lucky, your caller will simply say, "Yes, I'd like to see it," and you can schedule the visit.

Tenant Information Sheet (excerpt)

☑ **Qualified, but no commitment to visit**

☐ Caller sounds interested, but wants to think it over

☑ Caller is interested if ___rental can be available two weeks earlier (check___

___with handyman + push repair schedule up if necessary)___

What's the Problem?

Even seemingly interested, qualified callers may hesitate at your request that they come by to see your property. Here are some common responses, and what they may tell you about the caller and the chances that you would rent to them.

Response	What it means	Your answer
Yours is the first rental I've called and I'm not sure I'm ready to schedule a visit.	Caller may be too shy to say that he doesn't want the unit for any number of reasons; or he is naïve in thinking that a good unit will be vacant for long.	Okay, but please understand that I process applications on a first come, first-served basis, and I choose tenants the same way. I usually don't have much trouble renting these units, so if you're interested....
I'd like to drive by first and see if I like it from the outside.	Caller is cautious and doesn't want to commit to a visit unless the appearance is pleasing. No problem—if he doesn't like it, you won't waste time with a showing.	That's fine. When do you think you'll be able to do that? Let me give you directions, and I'll give you a call after you've seen it to learn if you'd like to see the interior.
I need to clear up a few things with my landlord first.	The caller may be the subject of a tenancy termination or even an eviction.	Please tell me more about your current living situation—has your landlord asked you to leave?
I'll need to check with my roommates first.	All of the intended occupants aren't in agreement on basic aspects of the rental.	Why don't you check with them again and I'll call you on Thursday to see if we can go forward.
The move-in date is too soon—I haven't given notice yet.	Caller recognizes the need to give proper notice to terminate his or her current tenancy, and doesn't want to pay double rent.	I may be able to work with you here. Assuming your credit history and references meet my criteria, we may be able to delay the move-in date by a couple of weeks.
I don't think I'll come by, but maybe I'll call you in the future.	Caller may be checking out the rental scene in anticipation of a future move or canvassing the market to determine whether the rent increase he or she just got is in line with market rates.	Thanks for your interest.

Schedule a site visit

For qualified, interested callers, set up a site visit right away and record the details in the "Arrangements to visit property" section of the Tenant Information Sheet. If you've planned an open house, share the details; if you expect to do individual showings, choose a convenient time. Be sure to get contact information now if you haven't done so already, and ask for a specific way (email or phone) for you to confirm the site visit. Even those who agree to attend an open house will appreciate your reminder. This call may also save you from waiting at a vacant rental if you are individually showing the place to someone who has changed his or her mind but didn't call to cancel.

Should you negotiate on the first call or conversation?

Your phone conversation may include challenging queries ("Why aren't you offering a month's free rent like the complex down the street?") that become attempts to negotiate over basic rental terms. Phone interviews that move this quickly into brass tacks most often occur in soft markets, when tenants have lots of choices and are anxious to narrow the properties they'll actually visit. Or, you may be dealing with a Looky-Loo who isn't seriously interested in moving but who wants to check out the rental scene (and may be a competing landlord). Then again, perhaps you've got a genuinely interested caller who needs a slight modification to

---

Tenant Information Sheet (excerpt)

Arrangements to visit property

☑ Preset open house: _Saturday, Oct. 18, 10 a.m. – 2 p.m._

   ☑ Caller will attend

When can you come by to have a look? _____

Property tour set up for: _____

Confirm this visit: _____

On-site visit, notes: _____

_____

_____

_____

your terms, such as someone who wants to move in a couple weeks later than your ideal start date, or who wants to bring a pet to your no-pets rental (and the pet sounds pretty innocuous).

Should you begin negotiating at this stage? It depends primarily on how many interested tenants you have spoken to. If this is your first call, it may be a mistake to back down on key terms so early in the game. On the other hand, if you've fielded several calls and have no prospects yet, you may need to rethink your position.

There are many other issues to keep in mind when you decide to negotiate, such as the risk of a discrimination claim from previous prospects with whom you did not negotiate. These considerations apply at any stage in your rental process, from the first phone call to showing the rental, to subsequent conversations. They are covered in Chapter 9—skip ahead now if you need some tips on when and how to negotiate.

Take Ten Minutes

- Review your Tenant Information Sheet and look for the entries that tell you where callers learned about your vacancy. Transfer the information to your Marketing Worksheet. Soon, you'll have useful data on how many qualified callers you got from each marketing piece—information you'll use the next time you advertise.

- Check your calendar to make sure you'll continue to be available for more calls. Change your phone greeting if necessary.

- Continue to monitor the competition by checking advertisements that have appeared alongside yours, and looking for new ones. A special offer at a nearby apartment complex may affect your initial determination that you're renting at market rates.

Prepare Your Rental for an Open House or Showing

Before you open the doors to prospective tenants, you need to make sure the rental is ready for showing. Particularly in competitive markets, you'll want your place to look as good as possible. This chapter explains the prep work involved, including special issues you'll face if the unit is occupied. This chapter will also help you decide whether to delay showing the unit in order to do some repairs and refurbishing.

✔ Before You Prepare Your Rental for Showing

- ☑ Double check that current residents are on track for leaving when planned.
- ☑ Determine how much cooperation you're going to get from current tenants (if the rental is occupied).
- ☑ Do a pre-move-out inspection (Chapter 3) to find out what repairs and cleaning will be necessary.
- ☑ Decide whether to hold an individual showing or public open house (Chapter 5).

Prepare the rental unit for an attractive showing

Basic cleanup doesn't cost much, but it can make all the difference to prospective tenants. Sometimes, a small repair is not just a cosmetic fix, but a legal necessity. For example, proper weatherproofing for roofs, doors, and windows will prevent leaks, which can make a rental unfit, a violation of your legal duty to rent out habitable housing. You'd never intentionally show a place that doesn't meet basic legal requirements, but unless you look around and take action, a problem might slip past you. Here are some tips for detecting deficiencies and sprucing your place up.

Check the outside

First impressions do count, and when interested renters first lay eyes on your property, they will form lots of them. Particularly when you're holding a public open house—when you're counting on curb appeal to reel in rental seekers, and no one has been prepped by you on what to expect—you must make an effort to show everyone that you take care of your property. No amount of, "I'm going to take care of that … and that … in the next few weeks" will dispel the negative impression left by dirty windows, broken mailboxes, or unkempt front yards. Here are the basics:

- In multifamily rentals, make sure the exterior common areas are neat and clean. For all properties, sweep the sidewalk, mow the lawn, prune the shrubs, pull up weeds, and clear papers and debris from the yard, porch, and entryways.

- Check that the doorbell works and that the mail slots are functional and not choked with junk mail.
- Make sure the property is well lit, and the address is visible from the street, particularly if you're showing the rental at night.
- Wash the windows or hire someone to do it for you. Nothing looks worse than grimy windows.
- Add a little greenery. Buy some flowering potted plants that you can place strategically outside.

Neaten the inside

A clean and tidy interior is as important as a ship-shape exterior. Make sure that the bathroom and kitchen are clean, the hallways and counters are clear, and the floors and carpets are vacuumed or swept. If current tenants are still in residence, the best you can do is hope they tidy up before you show it. See Chapter 3 for advice on getting tenants' cooperation in your cleanup efforts.

Keep your eyes on the prize. If you're dealing with an occupied unit and find yourself resentfully thinking, "What, am I the housekeeper and gardener for these folks?"—get over it. It's your property and you need to do all you can to make it attractive for your next set of rent-paying occupants.

Landlord's Forms Library

- **Pre- and Post-Tour Survey with Current Tenants.** Use this form as you walk through an occupied rental, before and after an open house or individual showing. Note on a room-by-room basis any items removed or secured before the showing, and check again when you're done to make sure nothing is amiss.
- **Checklist for Repairs or Refurbishing.** Use this worksheet to list the start and end dates of projects you plan to do before new tenants move in.

File your and Pre- and Post-Tour Survey and Checklist for Repairs or Refurbishing with your other documents relating to this vacancy. You may also want to make copies for the file for the current tenants. You may find them useful, if at the end of their tenancy they dispute damage you've noted or claim that an item went missing during your showings.

The Law You Need to Know

- Most states have strict entry and notice procedures. Be sure you know and follow these rules (see the chart at the end of Chapter 3).
- Virtually every state, and many localities, require landlords to offer and maintain fit and habitable housing. Know those standards and keep them in mind when checking your rental for needed repairs and refurbishing.

Preparing the rental when it's vacant gives you more latitude in what you can do to make it attractive. Bring in a few nice pieces of furniture, including a chair or two that will give people a chance to sit down and imagine what it might be like to live there. Put fresh towels, a new shower curtain, and a new roll of toilet paper in the bathroom. If you've recently bought or sold a house, or have heard the tales of friends who have, you are undoubtedly familiar with the concept of staging, in which the seller hires a designer to arrange the house's furniture to maximum effect. Unless you're in an incredibly tight market, you won't have to go to such extremes. However, you can take a lesson from the concept and apply it appropriately. A coffee table with flowers and a few magazines or books will make the living room appealing. Of

course, make sure that visitors know that any furniture is temporary—that you're not renting a furnished unit.

Get some advice from an experienced decorator or a friend with a good eye. They may be able to tell you how to improve the look of your rental without spending a lot of money. For example, soft lighting in the dining room may enhance its appeal, and that effect could be yours for the $20 it takes to purchase a dimmer switch (they aren't hard to install).

Prepare the rental unit for a safe showing

You'll want to make sure that you and your visitors will not risk injury, particularly if you're showing an occupied rental. Hopefully, you've been a conscientious landlord who has dealt with repair problems promptly and thoroughly, thus minimizing the chances of a problem. And you may have secured an advance look at occupied units as suggested in Chapter 3, enabling you to address any worrisome issues; in addition, your efforts to spruce up the property may also have resulted in important fixes. But as you surely know, accidents can happen even when there's no obvious repair problem—all it takes is a carelessly placed electrical cord to cause a trip-and-fall. Here are a few things to do before you show the rental:

- Put rubber mats over slick areas, such as front steps.
- Coil long electrical or phone cords and get them out of the way.
- Cover open electrical outlets, especially if this unit will accommodate families (people may show up with their small children).
- Block off or child-proof potentially dangerous areas for kids, such as pools, decks, or balconies.
- Remove slippery throw rugs.

Keep pets out of sight. Make sure pets are either absent (pay the neighborhood kid to take Fido for a walk) or securely enclosed in their usual crate or in the yard.

Prepare the rental unit for a secure showing

If your rental is occupied, ask current tenants to remove or secure the following items:

- cleaning supplies and medicines (especially prescription drugs kept in easily accessible places, such as medicine cabinets)
- valuables such as jewelry, china, silver, portable artwork, easily lifted tools, or electronic equipment
- credit cards, ATM-access cards, checkbooks, cash, coin collections, and
- expensive and attractive clothing, such as leather coats and fancy dresses.

You should also take steps to protect your personal safety from the visitors themselves. Think about security issues and be ready, especially if you will be taking strangers through a house that may be empty. These precautions will also benefit the current residents of an occupied rental, who may understandably be worried about their possessions. As a bonus, prospective renters will be impressed by your attention to safety—a good quality in a landlord. Here are some tips:

Privacy Considerations for Occupied Units

If current tenants are still in residence, make sure your efforts to prepare your rental for showing don't collide with your tenants' legal expectations of privacy. States that restrict the reasons that landlords may enter tenants' homes do not include as a permissible reason "to prepare the rental for showing." They allow you access only to *show* the rental. Once again, you'll need your residents' cooperation, so follow our advice in Chapter 3.

- **Don't be alone during individual showings.** The most effective step you can take to protect yourself and any tenant's belongings is to have at least one other person with you. The two of you can divide up the task of monitoring visitors' progress through the rental.

- **If you can't arrange for a partner, at least make sure that someone knows where you are and who you're with.** Carry a cell phone and call when you begin the tour, saying when you'll expect to finish and that you'll check in then. As an added precaution, have your pal call you at a pre-arranged time, with an understanding that you will answer the phone with a set statement that indicates all is well. (For example, "Wednesday will be fine" could be your code.)

- **For busy open houses, consider a team or a security guard.** When holding an open house, particularly one that is crowded or in an occupied unit, consider having two or more helpers present. You will need assistance—there's no way you can monitor visitors' progress through the unit, greet newcomers, and answer questions. The cost of a security guard for a few hours will be money well spent if it gives you peace of mind.

- **Never proceed unless you have been shown one reputable photo ID.** A drivers' license, green card, passport, school ID, or other photo ID from a trustworthy source is the only way you can be sure that the person standing in front of you is the real potential renter. Chapter 9 explains how to check visitors' IDs.

⚠️ **Don't assume that nice properties won't attract iffy visitors.** It's a big mistake to assume that unsavory types will leave your tidy house in a middle-class suburb alone. In fact, just the opposite is likely to happen. Why would thieves or muggers target a modest apartment in the middle of a busy complex, rather than an upscale house that's somewhat isolated from its neighbors? The latter is an easier mark.

Get cooperation and support from current tenants

This section is for landlords who are showing an occupied rental. If your unit is empty, you can skip this section.

Your current residents are an important part of your marketing efforts. In Chapter 3, we advised you to begin working with them long before you stop by with prospective renters, by getting permission to have an advance look at the condition of the rental, and by securing their willing participation in your re-renting efforts. You may have rewarded your tenants with a reduction in rent for the last month, a letter of recommendation for future landlords, a complimentary dinner or other perk, or a promise of an accelerated return of their security deposit. If you've laid the groundwork, now's the time to implement your plan.

Provide proper notice of entry

When it's time to actually show the rental (the focus of Chapter 9), be sure you provide proper notice to current tenants. Review your state's laws (check the chart, "State Laws on Notice to Inspect or Show Rental Property" at the end of Chapter 3, which gives details on days and times you may enter, and methods of notice). Be sure to scrupulously adhere to your state's rules. Not only will this help assure a warm welcome when you and your prospects appear, it will forestall future grief from current tenants and favorably impress your new crop, too, who will see that you respect your tenants' rights and follow the law.

Never use a lockbox. This device, which attaches to the front door handle, holds the door key and can be opened by a combination or another key. Rental agents like lockboxes because they permit easy access, and even landlords have been known to give the combination to interested renters whom they invite to enter and look around. Occupants hate them, of course, because they invite violations of the notice laws most states impose and often result in unsupervised walk-throughs. To avoid problems, handle showings personally.

Assure current tenants that you'll monitor visitors

Residents commonly object to showings and open houses because they are afraid their belongings will be disturbed or taken. You can counter this fear by sharing your safety and security plans with them. Take a quick look at our suggestions above and then consider communicating your plans with current residents like this:

- "Your concern for your belongings is completely understandable. I know just how you feel—I was worried too when we sold our house and had hordes of people tramping through. As a safeguard, I'm bringing my wife and older son with me to keep track of everyone."
- "I know it's uncomfortable to think about strangers looking at your home and your stuff. But most people really won't be interested in your things—they'll be too busy trying to imagine their own belongs in here. You probably remember that yourselves, when you looked at this place before renting it. But I take your point and I'll do everything I can to minimize unnecessary scrutinizing. One thing that would help is if you put away valuable portable items, such as cameras, cell phones, or jewelry." You might even offer to install a locking door handle on

a closet, so that the tenants can place all valuables there.

- "I share your concern about safety and privacy—you've been great tenants, and the last thing I want is to end your tenancy on a sour note. I also want these visitors to see that I respect tenants' privacy rights and will take reasonable steps to protect residents' property. When they realize that I'm "that kind of landlord," they may be all the more disposed to fill out an application. So you see, we are really on the same page here, and here's what I propose: I'll station my husband in the living room, and my friend Jennifer in the kitchen. I'll circulate and keep an eye on things too."

Show the rental while current tenants are away

Most tenants will prefer (or at least may agree) to be absent when you're showing the rental. Some, however, will be worried that strangers will damage or take their property, despite assurances that you will carefully monitor visitors and make sure that belongings are not disturbed. Some tenants may even want to be part of the process by participating and answering questions. Unless you are absolutely certain that current residents will truly be helpful (and positive in their comments), do your best to gently

suggest that they not be home when you show the unit (you cannot insist that they be absent, however). You may mollify annoyed tenants with a little gift, such as an offer of movie tickets, a coupon for a meal, or an out-and-out offer of cash. Don't get hung up on the expense— twenty bucks for a dinner coupon is nothing compared to what you stand to lose in a month's rent if your showing is unsuccessful due to recalcitrant residents. Here are some suggestions on how to phrase your request:

- "I understand that this open house is inconvenient to you. I'd like to give you these coupons for four seats at the Tri-Plex Movie Theater downtown. They're showing several interesting movies on Saturday afternoon—and of course, you can use the coupons anytime."

- "I really appreciate your gracious- ness in working with me as I show the apartment to the next residents. Have you tried the new Thai restaurant in the Oaks shopping center? It's really good—please accept this $30 gift certificate for dinner as my way of saying thanks."

- "I realize that it's been a hassle for you to deal with these visits from future tenants. Please accept this envelope (include a $20 bill and a thank you note) as my thanks— this month hasn't been easy, and I'd like to make it up to you."

Do a walk-through with current occupants before your showing

Current tenants are justifiably concerned that their possessions won't be taken or disturbed, a risk that increases if you do an open house instead of an individual showing. You share that concern—in fact, you want to make sure that any preexisting damage or loss won't be attributed to the acts of your visitors. The only way to establish the condition of the unit is to take stock immediately before and after you hold an open house or conduct a showing. It's a bit like doing a tour with a tenant at the start of a tenancy and again at the end, a system that protects both landlords and tenants. Your walk-through will also give you a chance to remind tenants to remove easily lifted items such as jewelry or small electronics.

Use our form, Pre- and Post-Tour Survey with Current Tenants to guide you in what to look for and correct. You'll see that it has a place for you and the occupant to review each room before and after an open house or showing, so that any changes will be noted immediately. This will cut down on later claims that an item was taken by strangers during a showing or open house.

You'll find the Pre- and Post-Tour Survey with Current Tenants on the CD-ROM that accompanies this book. Use your word processor to modify the form to fit the rental—for example, you may want to add a line for a deck, a garage, or a storage area. Print a copy and bring it with you to the open house. Keep this form on hand to use next time you show this unit. A filled-out sample is shown below.

How to plan for and do repairs and refurbishing

If the unit is empty or you've done a pre-move-out inspection in occupied rentals (see Chapter 3), you should have a good idea of what types of repairs or refurbishing are necessary before new tenants move in. For example, you may need to replace worn carpeting, install new lights, or replace the dishwasher. One of the benefits of doing a pre-move-out inspection is that it gives you an opportunity to assess the need for repairs and refurbishing before you advertise the unit. Of course, there may be problems that you can't see and won't discover until the current tenants vacate, but often you'll get a good idea of what needs to be done.

Put all of the information you have about this rental together and ask yourself: How much work will the unit most likely need, and how much refurbishing do I want to do? Organize your thoughts using the Checklist for Repairs or Refurbishing (you'll see a sample below). Then, if necessary, adjust the start date you'll use when

Pre- and Post-Tour Survey with Current Tenants

Date shown ____May 15, 20xx____ Shown by ____Ann_____.

Area	Before showing	After showing
Front door, entry	throw-rug removed	
Living room	CD collection put away in cupboard	
Dining room	china cabinet locked	
Kitchen	knives in drawer	
Hallways	rugs secured	
Master bedroom	closet cleared of expensive items	
Bathroom 1	clear	
Bedroom 1	clear	
Bathroom 2	clear	
Family room	remotes put away	

Before showing

_____   _____   _____
Landlord/Property Manager   Date   Time

_____   _____   _____
Occupant   Date   Time

After showing

_____   _____   _____
Landlord/Property Manager   Date   Time

_____   _____   _____
Occupant   Date   Time

you advertise, or the move-in date you promise prospective tenants.

You'll find the Checklist for Refurbishing or Repairs on the CD-ROM that accompanies this book. A sample appears below.

How much time should you allow for repairs and refurbishing? Take all of the factors into consideration, such as:

- **The leave-taking.** Voluntary departures give you a chance of a clean unit; terminations almost always result in some mess or damage.

- **The former tenant's habits.** You probably have some idea of whether the resident was a decent housekeeper. Don't expect a slob to leave a clean campsite.

- **The length of the prior tenancy.** Longer tenancies spell more wear and tear, which means you may have to take care of basics such as paint, carpeting, and wall hangings.

- **The type of work you need to do.** Some work is relatively quick, other jobs not so. If you need to order special parts, coordinate several tradespeople, or work on a design-heavy job, your project is going to take longer than when one person uses readily available materials in a "plain vanilla" execution.

Since you're understandably eager to resume the rent stream, you may be tempted and even pressured to re-rent with as little downtime as possible. Unless there are no significant repair or refurbishing projects on the horizon for this unit, speed could be a mistake, because:

- **Deferred maintenance costs more.** If you let problems worsen, the repair will get more expensive. And it will take workmen longer to do their job if they have to work around residents and their belongings.

- **You may have to pay relocation costs.** Some jobs can be done while residents are still in the unit, but many cannot. Even seemingly simple tasks such as repainting can require move-outs (to escape the fumes), which will mean that you'll be paying for nights in a hotel.

- **Deferred maintenance inconveniences tenants.** Although many will appreciate the attention their home is receiving, some will resent the intrusion. Avoid creating grumpy tenants whenever possible.

- **Fixing things up gives you an opportunity to increase the rent.** Now's the time to add an amenity or new appliance and adjust the rent accordingly. You'll have a harder time increasing the rent if you replace or add an item midterm—for tenants with leases, you simply can't do it. For month-to-month tenants, you can increase the rent with the proper notice, but you may

Checklist for Repairs or Refurbishing

1185 "D" Street, Collegetown, CA
Rental property address

July 1, 20xx   _August 1, 20xx_
Date vacant   Date advertised as available

Project	Estimated start date	Estimated finish date	Done?
strip entryway floor + refinish	July 10	Aug 14	
replace dining room window	July 5	July 5	
replace master bath toilet	July 10	July 10	
power-wash the driveway	July 15	July 15	
new dishwasher	July 10	July 12	

encounter resistance and may even trigger a departure.

Don't get fancy in a slow market. That new dishwasher will have to pay for itself with increased rent, which you may not be able to command. Take care of basic issues only.

Take Ten Minutes

You're poised to open the door and usher in your first visitors. First, take a few minutes to:

- Hire your teenager or a local cleanup service to do outside cleanup work.
- Stop by your nearest big box hardware store and buy some new towels, a few plants, and "pet gates" if you need them.
- Visit the local movie complex and pick up a bunch of guest certificates or purchase dinner coupons at a popular restaurant. If you don't give them to current tenants, they make nice move-in gifts, too.

Face to Face: Showing the Rental and Negotiating with Prospective Tenants

If you've followed our advice so far, you're about ready to open your doors to prospective tenants. If you've prescreened in phone interviews, you'll be meeting a select group; on the other hand, if you've decided to simply hold an open house for all who may show up, you'll be facing a crowd of unknown composition and size. The showing is an opportunity for you and prospective tenants to learn more about each other and to decide whether you're a good match—that is, the property meets the tenant's needs, and the tenant meets your basic good-tenant criteria. Hopefully, at the end of the showing or open house, qualified tenants will take a Rental Application, complete it promptly, and advance to the next stage.

This chapter takes you step-by-step through open houses and individual showings, from last-minute tasks (putting signs out front and preparing a visitors' log) to answering prospective tenants' questions, negotiating when questions and requests come up, and carefully discouraging unqualified applicants.

How to hold an open house

If you're showing your rental in an open house, this is your big moment. If it's a private open house, your interested visitors have passed your phone interview and this is their chance (and yours) to see if you've got a match. Or, in a tight

---

✔ Before You Show Your Rental to Prospective Tenants

Before you hold an open house or show the rental unit, be sure you have accomplished the following tasks:

- ☑ You've secured cooperation of current tenants (if any) in your marketing efforts and have done a walk-through with them (Chapters 3 and 8).
- ☑ You've prepared your Rental Application and screening materials, and are clear on your deal breakers and how much you're willing to negotiate on key terms (Chapters 6 and 10).
- ☑ You've prescreened applicants over the phone if you're showing the place by appointment (Chapter 7).
- ☑ You've reviewed the Rental Property Comparison Chart, which compares your rental's amenities and features against comparables, and are ready with answers when questioned about how your property stacks up (Chapter 7).
- ☑ The rental is ready (inside and out) for showing and you've taken security precautions (Chapter 8).
- ☑ You've identified weak spots in your property or the neighborhood and have prepared some answers.

market, you are reasonably sure you'll get a good crop of qualified renters, so you're holding a public open house. In this case, you will be meeting people you've never talked with before and your visitors will have very little information about your rental (usually whatever was in your ad or flyer). Unlike individual tours, when an open house is over, it's over—if you don't get a batch of qualified applicants at the end, you'll have to start again, perhaps with new ads and a new round of phone screening—that may mean that the rent stream won't start for another few weeks. So it pays to do this right.

Arrive early and give yourself plenty of time

Being on time is vitally important. It shows potential renters that you have your act together, and it allows you to begin the event on a positive note

Landlord's Forms Library

- **Visitor Log for Open House.** Put this form at the entryway to your open house. Visitors sign in and tell you how they learned of your vacancy and provide contact information. You'll use the former to evaluate the success of your ad placements, and the latter to contact qualified visitors if you need to.
- **Showing Checklist.** This form lists the things you may need to do and the forms you'll need for your open house or individual tour, and gives you a place to check off each item and add notes if needed.
- **Pre- and Post-Tour Survey with Current Tenants.** Use this form to document the before and after condition of an occupied unit, and to minimize the chance that your current residents will claim theft or damage resulted from your tour or open house.
- **Visitor Information.** Use this to record the name and identifying details of any visitors you meet at an individual property tour. Keep the form in a safe place during the tour (not with you).

File these forms in the folder you've made for this vacancy. You may want to make a copy of the survey and place it in the file of your current tenants, too. Information on the visitor log on where visitors heard about your rental will go into your Marketing Worksheet, enabling you to refine future marketing efforts for this property.

("Welcome! I'm glad to see you ...."), rather than a defensive one ("Oh! I'm so sorry for being late...."). When asked about their experience, the first thing visitors will say, if you're late, is, "He didn't show up on time, but after that ...." Don't create this kind of first impression.

Not only do you want to be on time, you should be at least a half hour early, especially if you're holding an open house in an occupied unit. This gives you time to put out signs to your open house, if you've chosen to do so. And it may give you time to deal with these all-too-familiar scenarios, which can arise in even the best-planned-for event:

- **Your current tenants forgot about the open house and are still in bed or entertaining guests.** You'll need to apply some gentle diplomacy to get the place ready fast. To avoid this problem, call current tenants and remind them of your open house. Put this on your Showing Checklist (discussed below).
- **Current tenants didn't clean up, as promised.** You'll need to pitch in.
- **Current tenants have a sick family member and want to cancel.** If you can't come up with an acceptable solution, work out another date and time as soon as possible. Then, call expected visitors (you'll have phone numbers only if you're holding a private open house) and reschedule. Otherwise, you'll have to wait out front and tell people who show up for the open house.

- **A significant problem has just arisen—a sudden leak, broken window, malfunctioning plumbing—that will create a bad impression on visitors.** Maybe you can think of a temporary fix—but even that will take time. Otherwise, cancel and reschedule as soon as possible.

The Law You Need to Know

- Local ordinances may restrict the placement of A-frames or other signs on sidewalks or medians.
- Bait-and-switch laws make it illegal to advertise one thing but demand another. This doesn't mean that you can't participate in a bidding war—you just can't initiate one.
- Under the Americans with Disabilities Act, disabled applicants may ask for a variation of your rental terms if it's necessary to enable them to live safely and comfortably in your rental. You must at least discuss the matter, and cannot refuse a reasonable request.
- If you promise a feature that's not yet in place ("We're getting satellite service next month!"), a court may hold you to it and make you deliver (or reduce the rent).

Put signs out front

Get these items and have them assembled and ready to go before your visitors arrive:

- **A-frame signs.** Choose those that you can place on the lawn or on a sidewalk median (first, check local rules for placing such items on public property). These signs are particularly appropriate for public open houses in which you have not prescreened applicants or given extra directions, and where you can expect a good number of drop-ins.
- **Lawn and window signs.** Even private (by invitation) open houses will benefit from some signage, if only to help visitors find the place. You can buy signs at a hardware store and fill in the information with a heavy felt-tipped pen, or order custom-made signs from a manufacturer, such as Peachtree Business Products, www.pbp1.com, which offers A-frames and much more.

Prepare and set up a visitors' log

You'll want a record of all visitors to your open house, if only to make sure you can contact people who have given you an application. (Suppose they mistakenly record their phone number on the application—the log probably will have the correct one.) It's useful to have information on even the visitors who look around and leave without talking to you—the fact that they were there, and responded to your question as to how they learned of your rental, will be helpful later as you evaluate your marketing strategy for this rental.

You'll find the Visitor Log for Open House on the CD-ROM that accompanies this book. You'll see that the visitor log includes a column on the right entitled, "Office Use." You'll use this later to record whether this person got an application, and if not, why not.

Position your log at the front door or just inside, and make it convenient for visitors to sign in (don't leave your log on a clipboard on the floor). Make a little sign asking visitors to log in. You may need to bring a card table if the unit is vacant or if the current tenants' furniture won't lend itself to this job (placing a vase of flowers next to the clipboard is a nice touch). Have a few pens on your clipboard and bring some extras.

Organize your Rental Application materials

Assemble copies of your Rental Application Kit (described in Chapter 6) and other relevant materials and bring enough for your expected turnout. Here are the basic forms you'll need and where to put them:

Visitor Log for Open House

Rental   1185 "D" Street, Collegetown, CA

Date and hours of open house   Saturday, June 15, 20xx, 10 a.m. to 2 p.m.

Conducted by   Ann Mayfield

Name	Address	Phone	Email	How did you learn of this rental?	Office Use

- **On the card table at the front door:**
  - **Rental Property Fact Sheet.** This is a takeaway sheet giving visitors a thumbnail description of the property and neighborhood. Make this available next to the visitors' log.
  - **Rental Policies.** This handout explains what you are looking for in your chosen tenant. Visitors who meet your standards will feel encouraged to apply; those who don't will hopefully not waste your time by submitting an application. Put copies of this next to the visitors' log, too.
- **In your briefcase, ready to consult or hand out:**
  - **Pre- and Post-Tour Survey with Current Tenants.** You and current residents used this form to take stock of the rental's interior both before the showing (you'll use again right after the showing is finished).
  - **Tenant Information Sheets.** If you've prescreened visitors, you've already started an information sheet for each visitor, and have entered the prospect's basic information and the answers to the interview questions you posed. This conversation covered issues such as the prospect's income and expected number of occupants. Be ready to confirm these answers and delve more deeply if needed (see

"Prequalifying Visitors to Your Open House" in Chapter 9). You'll enter the results of this visit on the Notes lines for the property visit.

For visitors whom you haven't met yet, you'll want a supply of these sheets so that you can enter relevant information as you learn it during (or soon after) the site visit. Remember, you'll be using the Tenant Information Sheet as you move applicants through the screening steps, so it's important to begin filling them in as soon as you meet or talk to prospects.

  - **Rental Application Kit.** You'll give these materials to visitors who request an application. They include the Rental Application, application instructions, Consent to Contact References and Perform Credit Check, Credit Check Payment (allows you to charge the applicant's credit card for your credit check), and possibly the Consent to Criminal and Background Check (use this if you've decided to run criminal background checks or use a tenant-screening firm). If you've decided to require proof of legal right to be in the United States, include the Legal Status in the United States form (not for use in California).
  - **Receipt for Credit Check Fee.** Have this receipt form handy for

applicants who want to pay for a credit check by check or cash.

To help you make sure you have all of the paraphernalia you need for your open house or tour, use our form, Showing Checklist, shown below. This checklist also includes sections for confirming that you've checked the date and time of the open house with current tenants (if any) and visitors. ("How to conduct an individual showing," below, explains how to confirm details.) You can modify it using your word processor to add specific items that pertain to your property.

You'll find all these forms on the CD-ROM that accompanies this book. Chapters 6, 7, and 8 explain how to prepare all but the last form, the Showing Checklist, which is self-explanatory.

Greet visitors

You or someone with apparent authority (such as your manager) should greet visitors and shake their hands. Let people know who you are and ask their names. Invite them to sign your visitor log (but don't insist if they decline; they can always sign it when they leave and are more at ease). Tell visitors that you will be available to answer any questions, and offer to accompany them through the rental (but don't hover). Give visitors a chance to meander, stop, and talk to their partners or roommates without feeling that you're at their elbow, hearing their every word. Be sure you are accessible but not in the way or superfluous (when in the kitchen, no one needs you to announce, "And this is the kitchen!").

Make the Place Appealing

Chapter 8 provides advice on sprucing the place up and enhancing the attractiveness of a vacant unit. Here are some additional things to do right before an open house or showing:

- Play some pleasant, but unobtrusive, music in the background.
- Pay attention to the light—leave window shades partially up and turn on a few lights, so you have sufficient, but not glaring, light.
- Make sure the house smells good. Scented potpourri in the bathrooms and bedrooms is a nice touch (but if there are any tenants still in the unit, check with them first, in case they have any allergies), or put a pot of spiced apple cider on the stove.

Showing Checklist

Rental property 1185 "D" Street, Collegetown, CA

Date shown Saturday, June 15, 20xx, 10 a.m. to 2 p.m.

Shown by Ann Mayfield

Item or task	Do I have it? Have I done it?	Notes
Signs, A-frames	Pick up on Friday	
Visitor Log for Open House & extra pens		
Rental Policies		
Rental Property Fact Sheet		
Phone Interview Sheets		
Pre- and Post-Tour Survey with Current Tenants (for occupied units)		
Rental Application Kits		
Rental Application Kits — Rental Application		
Rental Application Kits — Rental Application Instructions		
Rental Application Kits — Consent to Contact References and Perform Credit Check		

Item or task	Do I have it? Have I done it?	Notes
Rental Application Kits (cont'd) — Credit Check Payment		
Receipt for Credit Check Fee		
Consent to Criminal and Background Check (optional)		
Legal Status in the United States		
Flowers, plants		
Furniture, tables, lights		
Occupied units: Confirmed day and time of showing		
Individual showings: Confirmed day and time with visitors		

Make sure your helpers are properly informed about their role. Unless your helper is your manager or business partner, every question of substance should be directed to you. The last thing you want is confusion caused by a careless or uninformed answer ("Three teenagers in this bedroom? Sure, no problem!"). If the misinformation stands uncorrected and applicants who become your tenants rely on it ("Oh, I'm sure he wouldn't object to two dogs"), you may even be legally required to follow through, despite your carefully thought-out Rental Policies to the contrary.

Beware the visitor who refuses to sign your log. This person may be just shy, or may be there for nefarious purposes (to case the joint for a future burglary, for example). If you have someone greeting visitors and noticing who signs in and who doesn't, this assistant should alert your other helpers to keep an eye on this person.

Monitor visitors' progress

While you don't want to dog your visitors' footsteps, you do need to monitor their movements to make sure (especially if it's an occupied unit) that no mischief occurs. You can do this yourself if you aren't confronted with a crowd, but if several people show up at once, you'll have a hard time being in many places at the same time. Hopefully, you've anticipated the size of your showing and have arranged for helpers to be stationed, much like museum guards, at critical places. If you're shorthanded and surprised by the turnout, do your best to circulate. It's very important to be available to talk, answer questions, and negotiate, if necessary (see the discussions below on these topics).

How to conduct an individual showing

Many landlords decide to forego a public open house and instead show their rental individually, whether because of market conditions, peculiarities of the rental, or their own schedules or preferences. In these cases, you will have usually done some initial prescreening over the phone and set an appointment for an individual tour.

This section gives some suggestions on how to conduct an individual tour. Many tips from "How to hold an open house," above, apply here as well, so refer back to that section for advice on:

- using a Showing Checklist to make sure you're set on all the final details
- making the place appealing
- arriving early for the showing
- organizing your Rental Application materials, and
- greeting visitors.

Unlike an open house, you won't need to put signs out front or prepare a visitors' log. But you should have your Tenant Information Sheet handy and review it shortly before the event, so the details of your visitors' situation are fresh in your mind (you may even want to have it visible on a clipboard, which will impress your prospects with your organization). For your safety's sake we also recommend checking photo IDs of all visitors to individual tours, as explained below.

Confirm the date

When interviewing prospective tenants on the phone and setting up the appointment, you asked how you could contact them to confirm your tour day and time. Here's how to word your confirming phone or email communication:

"Hello Mr. Smith, this is Jack Phillips, the landlord at 24 First Street. I'd like to confirm our plan to meet at four o'clock tomorrow, Friday the tenth, at the rental property. I'm looking forward to showing you the property. If you need to change the day or time, please give me a call at 123-456-7890 as soon as possible (that's my cell phone). Thanks and, unless I hear from you, I'll see you tomorrow at four."

Line up a partner or off-site contact

Chapter 8 explains why it's never a good idea to show a rental on your own, especially if it's vacant or current occupants are away. Make sure you have a reliable person call you during the showing.

Check visitors' IDs

If you've phone screened your visitors, you should already have their names, addresses, and phone numbers. But is the person who's meeting you on the sidewalk or in your lobby the same person as the one you spoke with—and the real potential renter? The only way to be sure is to ask for a reputable picture ID, such as a drivers' license, green card, passport, or school ID. A photo ID will also give you additional information, such as the driver's license number, which may be essential if you have to track down the individual.

Use the form, "Visitor Information," to record the information, and be sure to obtain it *before* you begin a tour. Check the information on the ID against the responses you got when phone screening this applicant (if there are discrepancies, deal with them, as suggested below). Leave the completed Visitor Information form in your office, with a coworker who isn't accompanying you, or in your locked car. Why is this necessary? The worst case scenario is that you'll be accosted and the culprit will get away. You don't want evidence of who he or she is to be snatched from your purse or briefcase as he or she takes off. Keep that form out of reach. At the end of the showing, attach the Visitor Information sheet to the

Visitor Information

Rental property: _____

Shown by: _____

Date and time: _____

Visitor's name: _____

Visitor's address: _____

Visitor's phone(s): Home: _____ Work: _____

Cell: _____ Email: _____

Visitor's photo ID

Issuing body: _____

Date of issuance: _____

Expiration date: _____

Identifying number: _____

Deal With Discrepancies Between Phone Information and Picture ID

Check photo IDs of all people you've prescreened over the phone, and follow up if the ID includes information that doesn't square with what you've learned already. Answers that aren't persuasive may indicate that you're not talking with the person who furnished the original information.

Issue	What's the problem?	What to ask
The name on the ID is slightly different from the name the caller gave you (different first name).	Your visitor may not be the person who called about the ad, and may not qualify for your rental at all.	My notes from our conversation indicate that it was Edward Jones who called about this rental. The ID is for Sam Jones. Who is Edward?
The street address on the ID doesn't match the address the caller gave you.	The address your visitor gave you over the phone may be phony—perhaps he was asked to leave his real address, or was evicted.	Have you moved since we talked? Or was the address you gave me on the phone a temporary one?
The address doesn't match and is from another state.	Same concern as above, with additional problem that, with distance, it may be harder to confirm information.	I see that your ID is from [another state]. Do you have a more recent one that has the address you gave me over the phone?
The photo, height, and weight information don't match the person in front of you.	You may be dealing with a different person than the one you've prescreened.	I know these drivers' license photos rarely do a person justice—but this photo really doesn't look like you. Can you show me another ID that has a better picture?

Tenant Information Sheet for this visitor, making it part of the growing file for this prospect.

⚠ Always ask for proof of ID from every adult visitor. Selectively checking may invite a fair housing accusation.

You'll find the Visitor Information form on the CD-ROM that accompanies this book. Print copies before leaving to meet your visitors.

Instead of writing down information from an ID, some owners prefer to photo-copy an applicant's ID, leaving the copy locked in their office desk or in their car and returning it at the end of the tour (or tearing it up in the visitor's presence). What's the advantage of this method over transferring the information to a form? Three arguments are typically offered:

- **A better record.** Photocopying the document gives owners an error-free record of its information should they ever need it, and making a copy is quicker than transcribing the information.
- **Visitor peace of mind.** Returning or tearing up the copy of the ID gives the visitor some assurance that since you won't be keeping sensitive information, it's less likely to fall into the hands of an identity thief.
- **Landlord peace of mind.** When the person who makes the leasing

decision is not the same as the person who conducts the tour, there's a possibility that the decision maker will use the copy of the photo ID as a means to discriminate along racial lines. Destroying the ID copy removes this risk.

Whether you should follow this practice depends on the nature of your business. If you're a one-person operation and personally show rentals and make leasing decisions, you've already seen the face of your potential tenant. Lawsuit-proofing your business by returning a copy of a photo ID doesn't make much sense. If you leave the copy at the office where someone is working, returning a photocopy after a property tour is also no guarantee that vital information hasn't already been copied from the copy. On the other hand, visitors may take solace in this practice, and if so, you may want to adhere to it. But keep in mind that if you end up with no drivers' license number or other identifiable information, and learn later that something was missing from the unit you toured, you'll have a hard time finding this visitor.

Talk with your visitors and answer questions

Your performance during an open house or showing will play a major part in whether you come away with several qualified applicants or none at all. If visitors don't like the way you've

How to Get the Ball Rolling

To put visitors at their ease, try these openers. Be sure your questions aren't too intrusive.

What to ask or say	Why to ask it or say it
I hope my directions were okay.	Gives the visitor a chance to show that he mastered the route and it leaves him with a feeling of competence.
Mary and John have been really great about working with me to show their apartment. As you can see from all the boxes, they're getting ready to move—you know how chaotic a time it is!	Acknowledges that someone lives here and brings the issue out in the open, inviting the visitor to identify with the occupants.
The kitchen was recently redone. Is cooking a big part of your life?	Directs attention to an attractive aspect of the rental, allows visitor to say, "Yes, I love to cook," or "No, thank goodness for the microwave." You can follow up appropriately. ("Then you'll love the new cooktop" or "It's a new model and very fast!")
I'm glad you brought the kids along—I'm sure they're important advisors!	Let's you acknowledge the children without being lavish; also gives the parents a chance to lovingly talk about the little darlings.
When you asked about the size of the dining room, I thought I'd mention the oven—it's unusually large. Do you do a lot of entertaining?	Gives you a chance to pump up other aspects of the rental that make entertaining easy, such as its room arrangement (good "party flow") and the ample deck ("great for barbeques").
How 'bout this weather!	If all else fails.

conducted the event or answered their questions, they won't pursue the rental, no matter how well it suits their needs. No one but the most desperate tenant will go into a landlord-tenant relationship with someone they don't like or trust.

The best way to prepare yourself is to see the showing as a role that you can script and practice. This isn't to suggest that you should be fake or disingenuous. Rather, you're acknowledging that the task ahead is a delicate one—a job requiring the right mix of sales moxie, patience, and creativity. Thinking now about how you will conduct yourself will also give you confidence as you head into the open house or tour.

Be friendly, but professional

This one's simple: Everyone can spot an obsequious salesperson, and few like it. Confine your friendly, ice-breaking remarks to neutral subjects ("I'm so glad it didn't rain today, so you can appreciate the deck"). Avoid comments about your visitors, who may not be interested in sharing personal details just yet ("What a great truck you have! How long have you owned it?" or "My, what a bright child. I'll bet she does well in school").

Make the visit about them

Some visitors will feel shy about looking a place over, especially if it's occupied. With these types, you may need to put them at ease and gently draw them out.

Highlight your property's strengths

Take the opportunity to promote the benefits of your rental. Look at some of the ways you can respond to remarks or questions in "Seize the Moment," below.

Respond to visitors' concerns

No matter how hard you've worked with your property, there's going to be some aspect that a visitor doesn't like or wants changed. Be prepared to handle criticisms—for example, few closets or a tiny kitchen. Some landlords' responses are the stuff of stand-up comics ("Small kitchen? Well, at least it won't take you long to mop the floor!") Don't go there— anticipate the negative observations you're likely to hear and have a response that puts the best *reasonable* spin on the issue, and shows that you're interested in the tenant's concerns. Take a look at "How to Say It Positively," below, for some suggestions.

> ⚠ **There's no good explanation for a dirty place.** If the unit is grungy, you've made a mistake—either you didn't adequately clean after the prior tenants left, or you misjudged the ability or willingness of current occupants to prepare their home for the event. The best you can say is, "I know, and I can assure you that I'll have it properly cleaned before anyone moves in."

Seize the Moment

Try to use your visitors' remarks as a springboard for positive descriptions of your property.

Visitors' questions or remarks	What to say
"What lovely color in those trees."	"Yes, aren't the fall colors wonderful? We have a gardener who comes once a week to take care of the grounds."
"There sure was a lot of traffic out on the highway."	"It's a busy area, but you'd be surprised how quiet it gets in the evenings and weekends. On weekdays, there's a crossing guard at the corner for the school kids."
"We were on our way back from a bike ride when we saw your sign."	"There are lots of bike paths in this neighborhood, and one of them goes all the way out to the reservoir. New ones are in the works."
"We passed a little shopping center a mile or so away."	"It's recently been remodeled, and now there's a great coffee shop and bakery. "
"Our little one will be turning five next month."	"The elementary school down the block recently was written up in the paper— their test scores were in the top 10% for the state."
"We left Fido in the car."	"Did you notice the dog park on your way? It's three blocks down the hill and is really popular."
"Gosh, look at that rain!"	"It's really coming down. Our covered carports and walkways will keep you from getting wet when you get home."

How to Say It Positively

Don't be dismayed by your visitors' disparaging words. Aim for an upbeat, but honest, answer.

Negative observation or complaint	What not to say	What to say	What's the difference?
The rent is too high.	It's a fair rent.	I've researched the market, and I think this rent is in keeping with similar rentals.	By tying the rent to an objective measure, such as the market, you've deflected attention away from the fact that you, indeed, have made the decision.
The rooms are small.	That's the way they built apartments back when this place was constructed.	The bedrooms are on the small side, but the living room is standard size.	You'll gain credibility if you acknowledge the obvious and can then point to something positive.
There aren't enough closets.	There's not much I can do about it.	True, but we've added storage facilities downstairs where you can keep a bike and other sports equipment.	You've offered an alternative (be sure it exists!).
There's no dishwasher.	The kitchen doesn't have room.	You might look into buying a portable.	You've suggested an alternative.
The paint is the wrong color.	Well, it's pretty new and won't need repainting for a while.	We found that this shade is very amenable to tenants' decorations, such as their upholstery colors and wall hangings.	You've pointed out that this is not an insurmountable obstacle, and may even be an advantage.
The kitchen is really small.	It's not that bad once you get used to it.	The prior tenant saved space by hanging her pots above the stove—we saved the brackets, and can install the hanger if you wish.	Offering a creative solution to an obvious issue will show the prospect that you have thought about it and are willing to deal with the concern.

Field questions thoughtfully

Most visitors will have questions about the property, such as when it was last painted, types of city services like snow plowing, the age of the building, satellite service, and so on. Your Rental Property Fact Sheet should cover all of these details. People will also have questions about you and your tenants, such as how long the unit's been vacant, how long the last tenants stayed and why they left, how long you've been in business, and if you've ever needed to evict tenants. Questions like these are smart ways for prospects to find out whether you run a tight ship and choose tenants wisely. In a multifamily situation, particularly, callers will want to know that there's a stable population of tenants—a high eviction rate reflects a group of neighbors that may not be so pleasant or a poorly run building that creates problems. You can also expect questions about the safety of the neighborhood, crimes on the property, noise levels, on-street parking, traffic on adjoining streets, whether there's a resident manager, and so on.

It's wise to anticipate these questions by having answers at the ready—and to answer carefully. In soft markets, particularly, callers may have pushed the process by posing these questions in the phone interview, and if so, be sure your answers at any later stage are consistent with what you said earlier. If callers visit the property (and talk to neighbors or current occupants), you can

be sure they will seek to confirm your answers. If you've fudged, they'll find out and will conclude that you're a shifty sort who doesn't tell the truth—this isn't the way to begin your landlord-tenant relationship.

Questions about other tenants

Though you need to be honest, you must also be cautious about what you say about current or even past occupants. For example, don't explain that the current occupant's spouse walked out on her, so she can't afford the rent and had to leave (or you've had to evict her). All that may be true, but it's an invitation to a furious confrontation, if not a charge of slander. Just say, "The current occupant is seeking other housing for personal reasons." Prospects will draw their own conclusions, and one of them may be, "This landlord is professional and doesn't gossip … I like that."

Questions from prospects who may want you to discriminate

Be equally careful when you answer questions that expose a discriminatory bias on the part of your *visitor*. (Remember, fair housing laws apply to you, not to your callers or visitors.) Suppose, for example, you hear, "Are there kids here?" The visitor may be someone who hopes there are other families in the building, with potential playmates for his kids—or he may despise children and be looking for a landlord who avoids renting to families (the worst-case scenario is that he's a "tester" from a fair housing council and is attempting to set you up). Your truthful and legal answer, "Of course, we don't discriminate against residents with children, though at the moment, the other residents in this four plex don't include children" will signal that you speak the truth and follow the law.

Sometimes, it's a good idea to follow up with a second question. In the example above, ask "Why do you ask?" in order to learn whether your adherence to the law is going to prompt this caller to opt out or make him a poor risk for your property. If you hear "I was hoping there might be other families, so the kids could play together," you can relax. But if you hear, "I can't stand the sound of

Don't Rise to the Bait!

You can get into a lot of legal hot water by an ill-advised choice of words. Careful answers are illustrated below.

The question	The careful answer
Are there a lot of kids here?	Our units are one- and two-bedroom, and we do rent to families with children. Why do you ask?
Do you make sure the children don't run wild and make a lot of noise?	Our house rules concerning noise and disturbances apply to everyone, adults and children alike, and we enforce them equally.
Are there a lot of [*ethnic group*] here?	We don't keep track of our residents' national or ethnic backgrounds. We're only interested in whether they are good tenants and neighbors.
Do you rent to [*ethnic group*] with big families?	We have occupancy limits for all of our units, and we apply them to every set of applicants.
Do you control the noise level when [*ethnic group*] have parties?	We have noise standards that we apply to everyone, and any resident who disturbs others with loud parties will hear from management.
Do you let [*ethnic group*] cook outdoors?	Our house rules allow residents to cook on portable BBQs in their yards or balconies. If there's a serious problem with smoke and fumes, we'll address it.

kids' voices," carefully repeat that you follow fair housing laws and *will* rent to families who meet the criteria you apply to everyone. It's important for this person to hear this, because even if there aren't children in your fourplex right now, there might be when a vacancy opens up after he moves in. Hearing your explanation, he'll hopefully reconsider whether he would be happy at your rental.

It's a tricky question whether *you* can reject an applicant who has an aversion to children. You probably can—people who can't stand children are not a protected class, which means they would not have a viable claim of discrimination. And your rejection would be based on a solid business reason anyway (your reasonable fear that this tenant will break a lease when a family moves in, for example). In the "On site visit" section of the Tenant Information Sheet (or in the "Interview questions" section, if you encountered the questions during a phone interview), jot down the gist of conversations like these.

Prepare for questions that invite ill-advised answers. There's nothing other than good manners to stop callers and visitors from asking you explicitly about the ethnic makeup, familial arrangements, religion, age, and so on of your residents. Just be sure that you don't reply in kind! See "Don't Rise to the Bait!" above, for some examples of how to gracefully avoid getting sucked in.

Requests to be shown specific properties

As the section just above illustrates, you cannot join forces with an applicant who wants to know whether you'll discriminate illegally. But suppose an applicant asks you to steer her *toward* a certain living situation, and defines that by reference to legally protected classes? For example, what do you say to the applicant of a particular ethnicity who asks you to show her units near residents of that ethnicity? You might think that, as long as the request comes from the applicant and you do nothing but show what's being requested, you're not violating fair housing laws because you're not denying housing. Indeed, that was the position of HUD for a brief time in 1996 (HUD "Levine" Letter, October 2, 1996). However, HUD quickly withdrew from that position and left the whole matter rather undecided. (HUD "Pennick" Letter, December 3, 1996.) Now, you're better off sticking to the party line, since it could be very difficult to prove, if challenged, that you had nothing to do with initiating or encouraging such requests.

Unfortunately, as you'll see when reading HUD's suggested answer in "Answer Requests Carefully," below, the party line is exceedingly academic. There surely is a way to convey your commitment to fair housing laws without forcibly dragging applicants to rentals that they don't want to see. Depending on the situation, you may be able to strike the right balance between following the law and meeting your applicants' wishes and needs.

Questions about competing properties

If callers ask questions about competing properties, have your Rental Property Comparison Chart (discussed in Chapter 7)

at the ready (but don't distribute it). Take the high road when responding to challenging questions that pit your property or policies against others. Never bad-mouth the competition directly. Instead, highlight what you offer, and leave it to the caller to figure out how your property stacks up. Take a look at "Answering the Competition," below, for examples of how to handle such questions.

Answer Requests Carefully

These requests seem innocuous enough, but you should not accommodate them.

The request	HUD's suggested answer	A more reasonable answer
"We'd like to be near other families with children." "I'd like to be near residents who don't have children." "If you have [_ethnicity_] residents here, I'd like to be near them." "If there are other quiet, older adult residents here, I'd like to live near them." "I'm a practicing [_religion_], and would like to live near other [_practitioners of that religion_]."	"I'm sorry Mr. X and/or Ms. Y, but my business doesn't market, show, or rent on a [_protected category_] basis. We can proceed with a qualifying interview and I can tell you whether this rental meets your other stated needs. You can then ask for a rental application as you see fit. For your information, the Fair Housing Act, passed in 1968, is intended to discourage renting on the basis of race, color, religion, sex, national origin, familial status, and handicap. The choice of where you wish to live is yours, but I cannot facilitate your search if it requires any potentially discriminatory practice or procedure."	"Let me first say that I'm committed to following the fair housing laws. I'd like to show you all of the units we have available that meet your needs; you can be the judge of which one you'd prefer."

Answering the Competition

Here are some examples of how you might respond to questions—even arguments—from prospects who want a better deal based on what the competition is offering.

The challenge	What *not* to say	What to say	What's the difference?
The duplex down the street offers one month free rent. Why don't you?	That's the only way they can get tenants. It's a come-on—they'll make it up by keeping more of your security deposit, which is higher than ours.	I prefer to set a market rent and set a reasonable security deposit amount—have you looked into the deposit amount at that property?	You don't sound like a sour-grapes landlord, and have let it be known that you do business without gimmicks.
The owner I just talked to will accept me without a credit check or talking to my employer—he believes me, why don't you?	I have to check the report from the source, and make sure you're employed and steady.	I make it a policy to run a credit report for every applicant and check references—if I didn't do it for everyone, I'd be breaking the law. If you move in here, you'll know that every neighbor got the same careful screening you did.	You've given a legal reason for your actions, and suggested that your thoroughness will benefit the applicant (his neighbors will have passed your criteria, too).
The other rental I'm considering includes parking, but you charge an extra fee.	Parking is scarce, and it's valuable. I could tack it onto the rent if I wanted to.	Some of our residents don't need a parking space (and others need two). I find it better for everyone if they pay only for what they need. In the long run, it's fairer.	You've suggested that your aim is to be fair to every individual, which will benefit this caller when you apply that approach to another issue (perhaps he doesn't want to pay for cable).
The landlord on First Street will repaint the living room and bedroom for me—but you don't offer that.	The paint's in good shape and if you want a different color, it will cost you.	The paint in those rooms is in good shape and is a neutral color that will go with most decors—still, if you feel strongly, we could talk about it.	You've explained your policy but left open the chance to negotiate. In a cold market, it may be worth your while to spend a bit to land a tenant.

Sell your property, but don't puff

It's a rare salesperson who isn't tempted to sing the praises of the item he or she is selling. There's nothing wrong with this, as long as you don't cross the line from extolling the virtues of what you are offering to promising—even indirectly— that there's more to come. The reason you don't want to cross that line is that if your visitor becomes your tenant and has substantially relied on your promises, you may face some very unexpected consequences, such as:

- **Tenants may legally break the lease.** A tenant may be able to break a lease without responsibility for the balance of the rent if a judge finds that your undelivered promise was a substantial factor in the tenant's decision to rent from you in the first place. For example, suppose you indicate that you'll be installing a security system, but never do so. If your tenant moves out and you keep the security deposit as partial compensation for future lost rent, your tenant may successfully sue for its return (claiming that the promised security system played a substantial part in his or her decision to rent).

- **Tenants may sue you for the reduced value of the rental.** If you promise an amenity but don't follow through, your tenant may be annoyed enough to take you to small claims court, arguing that he's paying for something he's not getting. Sometimes, judges order landlords to deliver, but more often, the judge decreases the rent to correspond to the value of the rental without the amenity. For instance, the tenant in the example above might be able to persuade a judge that a rental without a security system is worth $50 less than the stated rent, based on similar rentals without security systems.

Now then, how might you sing the praises of your rental without dangerous exaggeration? Keep this tip in mind: Every time you're asked about a feature of the rental, try to answer with both "just the facts" and a reference to some special aspect of the rental. You'll be on solid ground if you can say to yourself, "Any reasonable person would agree that my description is accurate." See "Well-Rounded Descriptions," below for some examples.

Well-Rounded Descriptions

With just a little enthusiasm, you can turn an unexciting factual answer into a selling point.

Just the facts	Enhanced, but safe, descriptions
The apartment has two bedrooms.	The apartment has two bedrooms, including a master bedroom that is quite large (12 by 15 feet) and has a walk-in closet.
We're near a bus line.	The Number 10 stops a half-block away, and runs directly downtown (it takes about 15 minutes at rush hour).
We have a play area.	We have a play area that's divided into sections for toddlers and for older children. Of course, it's fenced.
The current tenant is leaving on December 1.	The current tenant is leaving on December 1, having lived here for four years.
The water heater is new.	The water heater is new, and since you'll be paying for utilities, you'll be happy to learn that it's a very efficient model with a Value Star rating.
We have a resident manager.	We have a resident manager who's been with us for ten years. He's a retired contractor and is very quick and handy with repairs.
We allow pets that we have screened and approved.	We allow pets that we've screened and approved and frankly, we've found that responsible pet owners tend to be responsible tenants, too.
The building was built in the 1950s.	The building dates from the 1950s, and has larger rooms, bigger closets, and higher ceilings compared to newer rental properties. We renovated the building a few years ago.
The rent is $1,200 per month.	The rent is $1,200 per month, which is consistent with similar rentals in the area—in fact, in view of its features, it's a good deal. I have a list of comparable rentals and their rents—would you like to hear what they are?
We have a laundry room for tenants to use.	We provide a laundry room with five coin-operated washing machines and five dryers—that's one set for every three apartments. Of course, we pay for the water and electricity to run the machines.

Describe Enthusiastically, But Don't Puff

It's easy to slip into unwise hyperbole when talking to a prospect whom you think has real potential as a tenant. Do your best to resist. Here are some examples of careful—and careless—talk.

Subject	Enthusiastic description	Puffing	What's the problem?
Choice of cable providers	We have a building-wide provider, but I believe that you will be able to choose your own company if you wish. I need to look into this and I'll let you know.	The wires are all in place—all you need to do is choose your cable provider.	The careful landlord has read that cable companies now have to share their wiring—but realizes that she should confirm what she has read.
New appliances in unit	I'll have our maintenance staff check the dishwasher. If I decide it needs to be replaced, I'll do it.	I'll have the staff check the dishwasher—we'll replace it if it doesn't run like new.	The careful landlord will replace the dishwasher only if he decides it is necessary. The careless landlord has essentially promised a new machine (and who decides whether it's running "like new"?).
Additional parking spaces	We often have spots open up. I can put you on the waiting list.	Parking spaces become available all the time—you'll get one soon.	The careless landlord has failed to mention that there's a list, and has promised delivery "soon," which is subjective (does this mean two weeks, or two months?).

Describe Enthusiastically, But Don't Puff (continued)

Subject	Enthusiastic description	Puffing	What's the problem?
New paint inside the unit	The paint is in good shape now, but if your application is the best one, we can talk about it again if you wish.	I never rent units that need a paint job—you'll see that there won't be a problem.	The careful landlord made it clear that whether to paint is his decision. The careless landlord has ceded the outcome to the tenant ("you'll see"), which is a mistake.
Security guards	I understand your concern for safety, and I share it. I'm not sure that a 24-hour security guard is needed on this property, but I'll continue to think it over.	There's nothing more important than our tenants' safety. We'll do whatever it takes to keep you safe.	The careful landlord has acknowledged the applicant's concerns and has promised only to continue to think it over. The careless landlord has practically promised to provide any and all security measures, which is impossible and sets him up for a lawsuit if someone gets past his systems.
A fitness room with equipment	We have a fitness room with seven machines and free weights.	You'll really enjoy our fully-equipped workout room.	The careless landlord has implied that he has an entire gym on the property; the careful landlord has described the facilities accurately.
Lifeguard at the pool	During certain days and times in the summer months, we provide a lifeguard.	We provide lifeguard services.	The careless landlord has suggested that a lifeguard is provided at all times.

How to negotiate with prospective tenants

Whether to negotiate, and when, will depend on the response you get to your advertisement. Assuming you accurately described your rental, that response will depend on the market. When rentals are plentiful, you may get few responses and seekers will push for better terms; when the cards are in your favor, you can stand firm in the face of eager applicants. The one exception concerns discussions with disabled applicants, covered below.

When showing your property at an open house, remember that your conversations with visitors may be overheard. If you're engaging in a spirited discussion of whether to lower the rent, and if so, in exchange for what concessions on the part of the tenant (perhaps the residents will assume the gardening chores that you otherwise would pay for), be prepared to offer the same deal to people who look like they don't know the difference between a rake and a hoe. If you don't—and if these folks are members of a protected group—you may have problems ahead.

Second, even in the hottest market, there are scammer tenants out there, and you need to check them out as you would even if the market were stone cold. Don't be overeager to accommodate. Seasoned landlords will tell you, it takes more money to get rid of a "professional tenant" than you'll make by renting the property quickly.

Hold firm on deal breaker policies

One of the hardest lessons to learn is how to hold the line on matters that are deal breakers for you—these are policies that you have decided you won't negotiate over. Chapter 10 helps you identify what these are for you. Typically, deal breakers include the date the rental is available, maximum number of occupants, the rent, security deposit, pet policy, and sometimes the length of the tenancy (lease or month-to-month). Before talking to prospects, you must be clear in your mind whether these terms are negotiable (if they are, see "Know when to compromise," below).

When you're being challenged or pushed by someone who wants you to modify a deal breaker policy, your natural tendency may be to begin a peacemaking, compromising conversation. You'll hear yourself justifying your reasons (which simply invites more arguments), trying to talk the person out of the demand, or even giving them an opening so they can push further. This can get you into real trouble if you let yourself get talked to the next stage (giving a Rental Application) to someone who can't meet your rental terms. At the very least, you're going to waste a lot of time debating over a rental term that you've already decided is mandatory. The examples in "How to Dig In" give you some idea of the pitfalls of the conciliatory approach.

How to Dig In

Complaints can be openers for unwise compromise—or an opportunity for you to gently restate your position.

The complaint	What *not* to say	What's the problem?	What to say?
I really need a place in two weeks. You said it's vacant now— why can't I have it sooner?	I'm planning on doing some work, and there will be workmen in there, but I guess we could see....	You're giving up on the two-week period you set aside for renovation and needed repairs (which will support the rent you're asking). It's going to take longer (and cost more) if workmen have to work around residents.	I've scheduled work for that time and I'm committed.
But my kids are such great kids— they'll have no trouble sharing the one-bedroom unit with me.	I can't have you and three kids sharing one bedroom!	You're emphasizing the family (and inviting a claim that you're antifamily), instead of sticking to the sheer number of occupants.	Under state law, it's appropriate to rent a one-bedroom to no more than three occupants, no matter who they are.
Paying that rent is going to be a real hardship for me now, since I'm on my own. Can't you lower it a bit?	Yes, I know it's hard to be a single parent, but…	You're about to hear about how tough it is and you'll have a hard time not sympathizing.	I know there are a lot of otherwise qualified renters who also can't afford the rent, but to make ends meet at my end, I have to stick with it.
Your security deposit is so high! That's going to be a problem for me.	Oh, I see. What were you expecting to pay?	You're suggesting that you'll go along with an amount that the caller sets, not you.	I'm sorry, but I'm going to have to stick with that figure, which I use for all my rentals.

		What's the	
The complaint	What *not* to say	problem?	What to say?
Oh, but I have such a well-behaved dog! Won't you at least meet him?	You never know with dogs, and I've had some bad experiences.	You're inviting a debate about how the caller's dog is different, if only you'd meet him.	I'm afraid I can't make an exception, since this is the policy for the entire building.
I'd prefer a lease instead of a month-to-month arrangement. Can't we do it that way?	If you're a good tenant, a month-to-month is practically as good as a lease anyway.	You're leading the caller to believe that she'll get the benefit of a lease (which includes a set rent). What if you want to raise the rent in a few months?	A month-to-month setup gives us both flexibility.

*(table heading: **How to Dig In (continued)**)*

Know when to compromise

As important as knowing how to stick to your guns is knowing when to compromise or negotiate on policies or terms you've decided are not necessarily deal breakers. These issues are practically limitless, from major (lower rent to a shorter term) to minor (requests to repaint). Sometimes it will be wise to negotiate—and sometimes, you'd be foolish to do so. How will you tell the difference? For each request you get, ask yourself these questions:

- **What's the state of the market?** Your willingness to bend your policies will, of course, depend on the temperature of the market. A landlord with a dozen professional couples lined up with checkbooks in hand has little need to change her terms. But someone with a so-so rental in a cool market may need to work with prospects in order to land a tenant. Tenants, of course, understand the market as well as you do, so if you're in a tepid market, don't be surprised if you encounter negotiation feelers right from the start.

- **What will it cost?** Sometimes a prospective tenant's request—for example, storage space for bike or ski equipment or part of the yard to garden—is very important to the tenant but has a negligible impact on you.

- **Can you compromise?** You may be able to get the prospective tenant to agree to shoulder part of the cost of the improvement he's asking for. For instance, if it's a matter of painting the master bedroom, you might agree to buy the paint but have the prospect agree to do the work (or vice versa).

- **With multifamily properties, how will your compromise affect other tenants?** This issue is very important for owners who deal with multiple tenants. If you compromise over an issue that you've held firm on for other tenants, you're going to engender a lot of resentment. Making enemies of the rest of your tenants while pleasing one doesn't make sense and may invite discrimination lawsuits.

- **Do you want to send a message that you can be talked out of your decisions?** Many landlords won't want to negotiate because they fear that tenants will conclude that they're pushovers. Whether to stick to "a deal is a deal" depends on your options. If the market is soft, it won't do you much good to stick to your guns with an empty rental. And agreeing now and then to a reasonable request doesn't mean you have to cave every time.

Know when *not* to answer! If you're not sure what to say when faced with a request or argument, tell the person you understand her point, and that you will need to think about it and get back to her. This is far preferable than a hasty "No" or a poorly thought-out compromise.

Always remember that in the long run, a concession that secures a stable, respectful, solvent tenant is always preferable to a month or two of rent from someone who met your criteria but then became a constant complainer (or whom you had to evict). See "Should You Negotiate?" below, for typical issues landlords are asked to negotiate over, with suggestions on factors that will influence your decisions. Of course, once you see a prospective tenant's completed application and check his or her credit report and references, other factors might influence your willingness to negotiate.

Should You Negotiate?

In all but the hottest markets, you're likely to encounter prospects who want to bargain with you over the rent or another policy. Before you head into an open house or individual showing, give some thought as to where you're prepared to bend. Chapter 10 gives more details on when to negotiate or be flexible on specific terms.

The issue	When to negotiate	When to stand firm
The rent is too high.	The market is soft. You've received few nibbles. You erroneously set the rent too high.	The market is hot. You have lots of prospects. You know that your rent is market based.
I need a one-year lease, not a month-to-month rental agreement.	You're willing to lock yourself into a long-term relationship—which will depend on the attractiveness of the individual prospect.	You've decided that you must have the flexibility of a month-to-month agreement, which lets you terminate with short notice.
I'd like a month-to-month rental agreement, not a one-year lease.	You're fairly sure that, once the tenant has lived there for a while, he'll stay, resulting in a long-term tenant for all intents and purposes.	You aren't willing to accept the possibility that you'll have to re-rent soon.
The security deposit is too high.	You learn from the prospect's former landlord that the tenant paid on time and didn't damage the property—in short, that the deposit wasn't needed.	The prospect didn't get the entire deposit back from his last rental—chances are you might need it, too.
I have a dog and you have a no-pets policy.	You've met the dog and are willing to reconsider.	You have a building full of tenants who have no-dogs clauses that you have enforced—you're sure to have big-time resentment if you begin allowing dogs.
I don't like the color of the paint.	You need to repaint anyway, and the prospect's requests are for a neutral color that can serve the next occupants, too.	You just repainted, or the color requested is odd and will be difficult to undo for the next occupants.

Discussions with disabled applicants

Most of the time, you are legally free to "just say no" to any request that you change your rental terms. You may not get any applicants if your terms are not at market levels, but if you want to be stubborn (or are certain that a better ad next week will yield a better crop of prospects), it's your choice.

The exception to the rule concerns requests from disabled applicants, who may ask you to change your rental terms (known as an "accommodation") or ask permission to perform alterations to their rental unit (known as "modifications"). If the applicant meets the legal definition of being disabled, you must at least consider the issue and engage in a meaningful dialog. This doesn't mean that you must grant the request—it does mean that you need to discuss it and possibly come up with an alternative solution that would meet the disabled person's needs. Only when there's no reasonable solution that will address the issue can you say, "Sorry, I won't be able to meet your request."

Landlords often react in disbelief, thinking that this rule means they're going to face extensive and expensive requests every time a disabled person visits their property. It doesn't quite work that way. You do have to be flexible and creative; you do not have to spend money or make physical changes that would put an unreasonable burden on your business. "Be Flexible with Disabled

Applicants," below, illustrates some ways that you can follow the law. (For more information on dealing with disabled applicants, including verification of disabled status, see Chapter 2.)

Identify prospective tenants

When visitors to an individual tour or open house have come at your invitation—the result of a successful phone screening—you should already have a sense of whether they meet your criteria. On the Tenant Information Sheet, you noted any issues. Now's your chance to continue to prequalify them—that is, to ask questions on important good-tenant criteria and to make sure that other aspects of the rental are acceptable to them.

For people whom you haven't screened at all, such as visitors at a public open house, you really need to use this time to find out if they are suitable. You'll have to work harder than the landlord who escorts a prescreened applicant. This is reason enough to hire helpers who will monitor public open houses, so you can interact with visitors.

The goal in both cases is to end your open house or showing with applications in the hands of people who, as far as you can tell, will qualify for this rental. So, in the course of showing the rental, spend some time asking each visitor questions that will separate the qualified ones from those whom you would not rent to. It's a delicate task—you're asking some

Be Flexible with Disabled Applicants

Here are some common requests landlords get from disabled applicants, and suggested ways of meeting the requests.

Your policy or property	Applicant's request	How to be flexible
You've got a no-pets rule.	Applicant wants to bring a companion animal.	Allow the animal as long as its presence is not unduly disruptive to others.
You don't want to deal with cosigners.	Prospect receives government assistance but needs a cosigner who will help with the rent.	You must consider the cosigner and allow him if his finances are sufficient to cover the rent.
You want a year's lease.	Applicant wants a month-to-month in order to take advantage of treatment opportunities that may open up in another town.	You'd be asking for trouble to say no.
You don't rent to anyone with a criminal record.	Applicant committed the offense when not under treatment for a psychiatric problem; is under treatment now and similar behavior has not recurred.	You must relax your rule unless you can say that the applicant poses a current, direct threat to others.
You have limited parking and tenants must join a waiting list.	Applicant uses a wheelchair and wants a close-in parking spot immediately.	Give this applicant the next available parking spot— explain to others on the list that this is legally necessary.
You don't intend to repaint.	Applicant has a phobia against white walls and asks to paint them another color.	Allow the repainting with assurances that tenant will return walls to original color when vacating.
You give each tenant only one parking spot.	Applicant has daily home visits from a caregiver and asks for an additional space for that person.	If alternate parking is expensive or difficult, you'd be wise to allocate another space to this tenant.

pointed questions (or confirming answers to questions you already asked over the phone), and you have to do it with tact. If you haven't prescreened already, see "How to prescreen over the phone" in Chapter 7 for tips on how to phrase your inquiries and "Prequalifying Visitors to Your Open House," below.

Prequalifying Visitors to Your Open House

Ask these questions before committing yourself to a property visit.

Information you need to prequalify this visitor	How to ask it
Can the visitor afford the rent?	"The rent for this unit is $2,000 a month. The industry rule of thumb is that a tenant's gross monthly income should be at least three times the rent. When we spoke on the phone, you thought that would be fine. Have you had a chance to think it over—will this work for you?"
Can the visitor come up with the security deposit plus the first month's rent?	"The security deposit is two months' rent. So with the first rent payment, that's an initial outlay of $6,000. Will you be able to handle this?"
Does the intended number of occupants meet your occupancy policy?	"This unit has two bedrooms and can accommodate four persons. You mentioned having three roommates—is that still your plan?"
Will the move-in date work?	"The current tenants will move out at the end of the month. I'll need about a week to ready the unit and will begin the lease on the 15th. Does that fit with your plans?"
Does the visitor accept your pet policy?	"As I mentioned in my ad, I accept qualified pets—I'm pretty careful to check out dogs and will be talking with your current landlord and your vet. Is that okay with you?"
Will the lease terms (fixed term or month-to-month) work for this visitor?	"I'm offering a one-year lease—are you comfortable committing to this length of time?"

What's the next step for your visitors?

Visitors who leave your open house or tour will take one of three paths:

- those who are not interested (or are undecided) will depart without taking a Rental Application Kit
- those who are interested but clearly don't qualify will hopefully leave *without* taking a Rental Application, or
- those who are qualified and interested will leave with a Rental Application Kit in hand and a promise to return it right away.

The following sections explain how to encourage and handle each response. In all cases, carefully record the upshot of the visit, by making notes on the Tenant Information Sheet, as shown in the sample from the sheet, below.

Visitors who aren't interested in your rental

You're bound to encounter visitors who conclude, on their own, that your rental isn't for them. These may be emminently qualified prospects who want a concession you won't give (such as a lease, when you are offering a month-to-month deal), or who just don't like something you couldn't change if you wanted to (not close enough to the local school, for example, or the rooms are too small or dark). Always be polite and thank the visitors for their interest, and wish them good luck. You never know who these folks may be talking to (perhaps a friend who's also looking for a place and doesn't care about proximity to the local school). And you can be sure that other people will watch the way you conduct yourself, some of whom you may hope will decide to rent from you.

Be sure to indicate on the "Office Use" section of the Visitor Log for Open House (assuming the visitor signed the log), or the "On-site visit, notes" section of the Tenant Information Sheet, for visitors whom you already talked to, that the visitor declined to pursue the rental further, and why. For example, you might write, "Declined, kitchen too small," or "Declined, too far from bus stop," or "Declined, needs larger storage unit." Why take the trouble to record the reasons? If you're later challenged as to why these visitors did not progress to receive an application, your at-the-time notation of what really happened

Tenant Information Sheet (excerpt)

On-site visit, notes _____

_____

could be valuable evidence in your favor. In addition, if you find that many turn away because of one feature—"rooms too dark"—you may decide to try to do something about this turnoff (such as knocking out a wall between the kitchen and dining room and installing better lighting elsewhere).

Visitors who don't qualify for your rental

Visitors who tell you they can't meet your minimum income requirement, or who insist on a rental term that you won't negotiate over, will not qualify for your rental. Having decided not to negotiate over the issue (or perhaps after futile attempts to reach a compromise), you know now that you aren't going to rent to them. Do your best to avoid giving them an application, for several reasons:

- **It's just not right.** Leading people on isn't a good way to do business. It's unfair to the applicants, who will waste time on the application and vainly hope they'll get the rental. If you collect a fee for doing a credit check, it's really unfair (even if you don't run the check and return the money, you've tied up the tenant's money).
- **You'll waste your own time.** Once you give out an application, you have to deal with it.
- **You're setting the stage for a lawsuit.** Applicants may stop looking for rentals or take other steps based on

their hope that they will rent from you. When you eventually reject them, if they sense that they didn't have a chance from the start, they will be really mad. Don't propel them to a lawyer or a fair housing group, with the story, "I think I was rejected because I'm a minority and he planned to do it all along—the landlord just wanted to hide behind the phone."

So, how can you discourage futile applications with a minimum of stress and hard feelings? As with your rejections at an earlier stage (over the phone, at the end of a phone screening), you'll need to be firm and clear, and identify the reason why there isn't a match. If possible, deflect attention away from the prospect and towards some objective factor that resulted in your decision—in other words, try to make it appear that it isn't the visitor's shortcomings that prompted your rejection. Chapter 16 offers suggestions on how to do it.

Some prospects will insist on taking an application kit even though it's clear that they do not qualify, or want something you aren't offering. In that case, hand one over. True, you will be wasting your time reviewing it, but you're doing so only in order to avoid the outside chance that this person will impute discriminatory motives to your decision and sue you.

As you did with visitors who voluntarily decided not to pursue this rental, make a note in the "Office Use" column of the Visitor Log for Open

House (or in the "On-site visit, notes" section of the Tenant Information Sheet) describing why you did not give the visitor a Rental Application. It is very important to choose your words carefully—they could either support you or come back to haunt you if you're cavalier or just plain inattentive to the legal meaning of your language. Below are some examples of how to do it (and words to avoid).

Make a Record When You Don't Give a Visitor a Rental Application

Certain words and phrases are legal hot buttons. Learn to avoid them.

Reason you're not giving this visitor an application	How to write it	How not to write it
Visitor wants a lower rent.	"States he cannot pay advertised rent."	"Single mom, can't afford it." "Doesn't make enough money." "Looks like he won't pay regularly."
Applicant proposes too many occupants for size of the rental.	"Total occupants exceed occupancy limit."	"Family too large." "Too many kids for number of bedrooms." "Family won't fit." "Too many adults for number of bedrooms."
Visitor demands new paint, appliances.	"Current paint, appliances (as advertised) not acceptable to visitor."	"Lady is demanding, picky."
Visitor wants earlier move-in date.	"Advertised move-in date not acceptable to visitor."	"Divorcing, in a rush to move in." "Student, school starts earlier than rental ready."
Visitor has a pet (no-pets policy).	"Cannot meet no-pets policy."	"Has a dog [cat, bird]."
Visitor doesn't have a job.	"Not currently employed, no other source of steady income."	"Student, no job." "Retired, no job." "Disabled, no job."

Visitors who qualify for your rental

There's bound to be at least one group of visitors who like your rental and want to apply for it. Great—be sure they leave with a Rental Application Kit. Answer any questions that come up, such as "When will I hear?" Be sure to answer truthfully—if you expect to take a few days, don't promise a response tomorrow (and be sure your answers are consistent with anything you said about turnaround time in your Rental Policies).

Now and then you'll encounter a seemingly ideal visitor, whom you may be tempted to rent to on the spot. Don't do it. Most of these folks will indeed turn out to be great applicants, but some of them are practiced scam artists who are very good actors. If you get pressure from someone who wants to shortcut your reasonable screening steps, politely resist and make a note of it—people who

---

Accept Holding Deposits with Care

Eager or anxious visitors may want to give you a holding deposit, particularly if you have a very attractive rental or the market is tight. The applicant who offers a holding deposit is hoping that this "earnest money" will secure a place ahead of others in the applicant queue.

Landlords almost automatically smile at the thought of a holding deposit. On first blush, it seems you can't lose—you have hard proof that your applicant is serious, and you can always apply it to the first month's rent or security deposit if you accept that applicant. There are, however, some drawbacks to accepting a deposit at this stage, including:

- How does this affect your "first-in-time (delivering a completed application) equals first-in-line" policy? Suppose the person who gives you a deposit submits an incomplete application? If this applicant wants the rental, he or she is likely to argue that the omission was insignificant and his or her "money should talk."
- Are you sure you want to hold (and return) deposits from multiple applicants? It may involve a lot of time and trouble.

Unless you're sure that the bookkeeping is worth it, refrain from getting involved in holding deposits at this stage. Later, when you've made an offer, you may want to reconsider (see Chapter 15 for suggestions on how to handle holding deposits).

are in a hurry to rent have often been told to leave their current rental.

Interested tenants are bound to ask how you will handle multiple applications from equally qualified applicants. The only safe and fair way to break a tie is to give the nod to the applicant who gave you a *completed* application first (your Rental Policies sheet includes this policy).

The following chapters take you step by step through the process of evaluating rental applications, running credit reports, and checking references and applicants' background. At each step of the way, you'll reject those who do not qualify and you'll rank the acceptable applicants in order of their attractiveness (and rerank as you learn more in succeeding steps). At the end, you'll have one applicant who has made it to the top, and there's your tenant.

Conduct a wrap-up

When your open house or individual tour is over, be sure to remove any outside signs you've placed on the property or elsewhere. Then take steps to make sure you're leaving the unit safe and secure. Follow these suggestions.

Vacant units

Walk through every room and make sure nothing's amiss—look for spills (did your visitors come with cups of coffee or food?) and dirt or other stains that you'll need to deal with (did your visitors tramp through the parking lot and bring in an oil stain?). Check the condition of any furniture, and remove any props that you brought in. Gather flowers or other perishable items that should be removed.

Close all windows and lock all doors. If you're using motion sensors on outside lights, or timers on inside lights or appliances (such as a radio or TV in an interior room), reset the timers. Return blinds and drapes to the open/closed settings you are using for this unit. Take your unused written materials with you.

Occupied units

It's very important to check over the property before leaving, to make sure that no damage or loss has occurred. Take out your Pre- and Post-Tour Survey with Current Tenants form and, if the current tenant is present, ask him or her to accompany you in a quick tour through the areas visitors entered. The two of you can quickly determine whether anything's been disturbed. If the occupants are gone, ask a friend or someone on your staff to accompany you as you do the review yourself (and ask that person to sign off on the survey form at the place reserved for the occupant).

Take Ten Minutes

- Review your Tenant Information Sheets and Visitor Log for Open House and transfer the information to your Marketing Worksheet. You're collecting data on how many visitors (and qualified visitors) came from each marketing piece. This knowledge will be useful next time you advertise.

- Talk to your open house helpers and find out what worked, what didn't. Did you have too much help, or not enough? Were they prepared to answer questions (and refer most to you)? Did your helpers make any serious gaffes that you should correct right away? You'll need to call that applicant who was incorrectly told by your son that the use of the garage came as part of the rental.

- Reflect on comments you and your helpers heard. Were there consistent murmurings about negative aspects of the rental—and can you improve things next time? Did your hear positive remarks ("It's so light and open!") that you should incorporate into future marketing materials?

- Did you need to negotiate before a visitor would take an application—or were you able to stand fast? If you had to do a lot of negotiating to land some applicants, that tells you that your original terms were not at market rates. On the other hand, if application-receiving visitors were satisfied with your terms, you know that those terms are in line with the market.

At least a few of the people who have visited the rental have made it through your first screening step—that is, a preliminary conversation (on the phone or on site) in which you set out the basic terms of the rental and explored whether you'd had a match. Hopefully, qualified applicants will be interested enough to submit an application, putting themselves into your second screening step—evaluating their rental application. Depending on the attractiveness of your rental and the temperature of the market, you may have dozens of applications to review, or just one or two. This phase of your tenant search involves using the information supplied by applicants to answer these two questions:

- **One:** Is this person likely to be a financially stable tenant who will be considerate of the rental property and neighbors?

- **Two:** Depending on how this applicant measures up to the other applications you have, should you advance this applicant to the third screening step (checking the credit report and contacting references)?

This chapter takes you through the process of evaluating completed rental applications to see if the information

---

Not All Roommates Are Created Equal

If your rental will be occupied by more than one applicant, you'll be evaluating each roommate, as stated in your rental policies. This is important because each occupant must be a considerate resident. It takes only one bad apple in the basket to spoil everything.

Now, suppose you evaluate the applications of three roommates, and one of them clearly flunks an important requirement—having a job, for example. Should you go ahead, banking on the ability of the others to "carry" this person until he finds work? You'll have to assess the ability of the employed tenants to shoulder half the rent instead of one-third, for a few months at least. If you conclude that they won't be able to carry it off, you should reject the applications of all of them.

When it comes to reports from references, be especially careful. Two of your applicants may be highly recommended; the third may be a party animal of the first order. This person is not going to be controlled by his or her roommates—chances are, they'll be miserable and move, or you'll have to evict them when neighbors complain. You can fairly deny the application of this threesome.

supplied meets your standards as expressed in your Rental Policies (this will answer the first question). It also suggests that you rank completed applications in order of attractiveness, so that you can determine which ones to advance (ranking the acceptable applications and seeing how many you have at the top will answer Question Two).

All but the most fortunate landlords (those who have great properties in a tight market) know that they may have to bend their policies in order to fill a vacancy. You've considered this reality already when formulating your policies (though you obviously didn't tip your hand to prospects) and possibly during your property showing. At this application review stage, too, you may need to be flexible. This chapter helps you decide what issues may be negotiable and what issues are clearly deal breakers and reason to reject an applicant outright.

Once an applicant passes the application review and lands high enough on your ranked list, you'll be ready to move on to the third screening step—confirming the information on the rental application by checking credit reports, calling references, and in some cases conducting a criminal background check as discussed in the following chapters.

Before You Evaluate Rental Applications

☑ Obviously, if you've shown your place to a dozen visitors but only one has submitted a Rental Application, you have a problem. Consider lowering the rent, spiffing the place up, or changing your advertising to reach a different or larger demographic.

☑ If you received applications from a single, narrow audience, your advertising may be discriminatory (did your ad use words like "mature atmosphere" or the like that suggest that you would not welcome families?). Chapter 4 explains how to plan an effective— and legal—advertising strategy.

☑ Check to see whether your ad is still running. Pull it if you think you have a good crop of applicants and want to limit the time you spend responding to more calls.

☑ If your ad is still running and you want it to finish, but you realize you've left out critical information (or want to change your terms), contact the publisher, online or not, and see if you can make a change before the ad time runs out.

Some of you may be evaluating applicants who filled out a rental application other than the one in this book. You may have had another form on hand, or may be working with a real estate firm or an online rental service that uses its own forms and turns the evaluation step over to you. That's fine—do your best to match the discussions in the chapter to the line items in the application you're using.

You may decide to skip the Application Review and just mark up the Rental Application as you go along. That's fine, but be sure your notes are clear and nondiscriminatory. When you're done, you can sum things up and enter your decision (proceed or not) on the Tenant Information Sheet.

Landlord's Forms Library

- **Application Review.** This worksheet gives you a place to make notes and indicate "reject" or "proceed" on every important question on the Rental Application.
- **Tenant Information Sheet.** You've been using this form for prospects whom you've talked to on the phone or at the property. If you're evaluating an applicant whom you met for the first time when you gave out the application, prepare a sheet for this person now (see Chapter 7 for instructions on filling it out). The sheet has a place for you to record the results of your Application Review (and subsequent reviews of credit reports, reference conversations, and so on).

Keep each Tenant Information Sheet and Application Review clipped to the Rental Application and file with the applicant's records—even if you've concluded that you won't make an offer to this particular person. The review will be very important evidence should you ever be sued for discrimination, since it will show that you evaluated every application methodically and fairly, giving nondiscriminatory reasons for rejecting applicants. Always keep the Rental Application itself, but obliterate identifying information that could be used by an identity thief, such as all but the last four numbers of the Social Security number (see "Handle credit reports, criminal background reports, and tenant-screening reports carefully," in Chapter 11, for the rules on storing sensitive information). Keep these files in a secure place.

Log in every application

At the top of the Application Review, fill in the following information:

- applicant's name
- the names of other adults who will be living with the applicant (you'll need to make sure that each one of them has completed a rental application)
- the address of the rental
- the date the rental is available
- basic terms, including rent, deposit, occupants, pets, the amount of the credit fee and form of payment, and anything else you think is important
- your name or the name of the person who reviewed the application, and
- the date and time you received the application. If the renter hand-delivers the application, enter the date and time it's given to you. If you get it in the mail, enter the date the application was delivered and the time you opened it. Doing this will help protect you from claims that you unfairly (and perhaps with a discriminatory motive) cherry-picked the applications, looking into only those that appealed to you and discarding the rest. Also, you assured applicants that you would review applications in the order in which they were received, so this honors that promise.

Confirm receipt of credit check fee and consent form

You may be wasting your time if you review an application that you can't advance to the next step—checking the credit report and contacting references—because the applicant has failed to give you explicit permission, the fee, or both. No matter how rosy the picture now, you absolutely should not make an offer without checking credit and references.

Credit check fee

Start by making sure the applicant has attached payment for a credit check (assuming you require this). As explained in Chapter 6, getting the fee up front can save you (and the applicant) time when you decide that this applicant is in the running and merits a credit check. If you have to contact the applicant and ask for the fee, you may waste a day or more. In the meantime, the applicant may choose another rental.

Note on the Application Review that the fee is enclosed and in what form—whether cash, check, or credit card. If you accept payments by credit card, be sure the applicant has given you a Credit Check Payment form (see Chapter 6) with information on the credit card number and cardholder's name, expiration date, and security code. At the bottom of the Credit Check Payment form, enter the date you received the application.

You'll complete the rest only if you decide to run a credit check (after you've reviewed the application and ranked the contenders).

If the applicant gave you a check or cash, be sure you've provided a receipt.

⚠ Protect applicants' credit card information. Applicants will need to have a fair amount of confidence in you to give you their credit card information. Needless to say, if you collect such information, keep it safely and confidentially. When you're done reviewing this application, whether you run the credit check or not, keep the Credit Check Payment form but use a heavy black felt marker pen to obliterate the card number. This will keep you in compliance with the FTC's rule that you dispose of sensitive information when you no longer need it (see Chapter 11 for more information).

Applicants who are applying to several rentals will understandably try to get you to accept a copy of their credit report that they've obtained for free. As explained in Chapter 6, you are entitled to insist on a fresh report that you order yourself in every state but Wisconsin (and even there, the applicants' right to substitute their own copy is limited).

Consent to Contact References and Perform Credit Check form

The bottom of the Rental Application includes a statement that says the applicant certifies that the information is correct and authorizes you to check references and order a credit report. In addition, applicants should submit a separate form, Consent to Contact References and Perform Credit Check, which repeats the consent contained at the end of the application. Note whether the applicant has submitted this form with the application. You may need to fax this consent form to financial institutions, employers, or other people whom you need to talk to. Chapter 11 explains how and when to do this.

How to review Rental Applications

The Rental Application you're about to review is long and contains a lot of information. You might be tempted to read it quickly, get an impression, and leave it at that. That would be shortsighted, for three reasons: First, you could miss an important piece of information. Second, without check marks and notes on the margins or entries on your Application Review, you'll be depriving yourself of the "lawsuit defense" evidence you may need someday. Finally, if you have a lot of applications, reducing the essential information to just one sheet will make it easier to compare and contrast the applicants, which you'll need to do when you rank acceptable applications.

Using the review sheet is a four-step process.

- **Step 1:** Enter short summations of applicants' answers in the Notes column of the sheet.
- **Step 2:** Evaluate the answers, in the Conclusions column, after referring to this chapter's specific advice on how to evaluate each answer. Make a check mark in the far right column, "Red flag," for answers that either disqualify this applicant outright or are seriously troubling.
- **Step 3:** Put aside the applications you will reject outright (Chapter 16 explains how to communicate a rejection). Then, rank the applications that remain, from most promising to least.
- **Step 4:** Decide how many applications you'll advance to the next stage of credit and reference checking. The number you advance will depend on the strength of the ones at the top of your pile and how many applicants you want to consider checking out.

You'll find the Application Review on the CD-ROM that accompanies this book. Print one for every application you receive. You'll see samples below of various sections.

Application Review (excerpt)

Application Review

Applicant: _____Andrew Muhler_____

Other adults who will be living with applicant: __wife and 2 minor children___

_____

Rental: ___1185 "D" Street_____

Date available: ___Aug. 1, 20xx_____ Rental term: _1 year lease_____

Rent: _$2,000_ Deposit: _$2,000_ Occupants: _4_ Pets: _approved dog and cat_

Credit check fee $_35_____ Form of payment: ___Visa_____

Consent to Contact References and Perform Credit Check form received, date:
June 24, 20xx_____

Application reviewed by: __Ann_____

Date and time received: ___June 26, 20xx, 2 p.m._____

Step 1: Summing up the answers

The Application Review form lists each major question on the application, such as rental history and income. For each section, you'll record (under Notes) whether that particular part of the application was completed, and what you learned. For some of the items on the Rental Application, you won't have much to say—for example, with an applicant who proposes three people in a two-bedroom unit, all you need do is write, "three residents, ok." Other answers will call for a more descriptive note, such as an applicant's report that he or she makes a certain salary per month (here, you might say, "makes [$ amount], four times the rent"). And others ask you to sum up what may be a lot of information on the application, such as the applicant's employment history (here, you might boil it down to "receptionist, four jobs in five years" or "bookstore clerk, first post-college job, two years").

Understand that at this point, you're not making a value judgment or decision to reject or proceed—you're simply summing up what the applicant has told you on each question on your application. When you're done with this, you'll go on to Step 2 and apply your good business judgment to your summaries by making a judgment (that's when you'll use the column on the right, "Conclusions"). The sections below cover evaluation approaches that you may need to use in Step 2 when evaluating the applications.

Before you turn a critical eye to the notes on your Application Review form, let's review some principles of smart selection that should be in the back of your mind as you go through each issue. Depending on the market, the attractiveness of your property, and your willingness to sit tight and wait for better applicants, you may find yourself using all or some of these real-world approaches.

Incomplete applications—should you pursue them?

You can put aside the application from someone who does not provide answers to your questions (you can't evaluate an applicant if you don't get the needed information). Your instructions specified that applicants should write "n/a" to questions that did not apply to them, or provide an explanation if they did not answer directly. So you should not see any blank lines.

That's the theory, anyway. Invariably you'll come upon applications that are complete but for a totally skipped item. Should you reject automatically? Perhaps the applicant got distracted and simply missed that item, which he or she could have answered easily. And maybe this applicant looks great but for this missed item. Use some common sense here (leavened with some legal know-how):

Review the rest of the application, following the steps outlined in the balance of this chapter, and determine whether this applicant would progress but for the missed information. If you'd definitely reject on other grounds (income level, for example), the missed item is inconsequential and you can stop here. But if you conclude that this omission is the only thing stopping this applicant from moving into the pile of ranked, acceptable applications, don't be so hasty. You may decide that you have plenty of terrific and complete applications and don't have to bother chasing down missed information, or you may find that this person is worth contacting, because he or she may end up being your pick. It all depends on the competition.

Remember, the point of your instruction to "answer all questions" was to result in finished applications that you did not have to hand back for completion. When applicants don't follow your reasonable rules, they may lose out. When *you* vary your rules (handing back some when you've got a short pile of good applicants, but not bothering when you have lots of great ready-to-proceed submissions), you'll be on safe legal ground if you have a sound business reason underlying your decision. And we've just articulated it—the number and quality of completed applications will dictate whether you take the time and trouble to pursue more answers. Just be sure you don't find yourself giving second chances to people of a certain race, religion, and so on, but not to others—you get the point by now, we trust.

Unclear answers—should you investigate?

Just as you may occasionally see skipped items on the application, you may also want to learn more about an answer that is unclear or needs explanation. For example, short periods spent at a job or at school, or a spotty renting history, may spell trouble (this person may have been asked to leave his earlier rentals or broke his lease himself). Or, it may have an innocent explanation (this person quit his job and school and moved home to help care for an ill parent). Should you take the time to ask for details?

Again, the answer depends on the number and quality of applications that you can rank without having to dig deeper with some. A savvy applicant will anticipate the red flag that such answers will raise, and will supply the explanation without your having to ask for it. A nonsavvy tenant won't have a clue and though he could become a perfectly acceptable tenant, you're under no obligation to coax the favorable details from him. If you've got a big stack of excellent applications ready for a credit report, you won't need to spend the time drawing more information from certain applicants. And if you consistently use this approach with all applications, you should be free of the worry of a fair housing claim.

Applicants who don't fit the norm—should you be flexible?

It's perfectly alright, and good business practice, to be flexible when it comes to the ways applicants can meet your good-tenant criteria. As you've read already, when dealing with first-time renters, students, or self-employed applicants, you should be open to evaluating evidence of financial and personal stability besides the tried-and-true reference from a current landlord and employer. Even in a hot market, you should always be open to receiving assurances that come from alternate, but equally valid sources, such as a letter from a teacher or school transcript (for first-time renters) or a reference from a client or business associate (for self-employed persons).

Applicants who want something else—should you negotiate?

An applicant who wants something other than what you're offering—a lower rent, smaller deposit, right to keep a pet, and so on—presents a challenge. With a pile of acceptable and nondemanding applications waiting for credit reports, you may laugh and say, "In your dreams!" But if the market is cold, or if this applicant is really great, but for this one issue, it's not so simple. In the long run, you may get a better tenant if you bend a little on a point where you can afford to bend. (In fact, savvy superior tenants will know that they are attractive and may

bank on this quality to get you to give them what they want.)

Are you taking a risk if you negotiate with some tenants, but not others? Not if you can point to a sound business reason that prompted the decision to accommodate this one, but not that one. Again, if it appears that you always work with applicants of a certain age, race, ethnicity, and so on, but adopt a "take it or leave it" approach with others, you'll be a sitting duck for a fair housing claim. Be sure that the candidate with whom you negotiate would be attractive (and worth the concessions) to any landlord in your shoes, with your market and your rental.

Use reason, not points, to measure your applicants

When you're ready to rank your applications in Step 3, you'll apply business criteria to place each application in the lineup. That section of this chapter shows you how. You'll use the same know-how when evaluating the credit report and references. But you won't find it based on a point system.

Some landlords suggest using a point system, in which you rate applicants on a numerical scale—for example, ten points for an income that's more than three times the rent, or more points for a lengthy rental history, fewer for a shorter history. They argue that such a system results in a fair and legally defensible result. We don't agree, because of three major flaws in this approach:

- **What looks objective is based on subjective premises.** Proponents of a scoring system like to think it's objective. They argue that once the numbers are added up, the result is clear and puts the decision beyond any claim that a landlord's feelings or motives drove the result. However, behind the numbers are subjective judgments. For example, consider the landlord who gives high marks for an applicant's zero or small debt load, and lower marks for higher debts that were nevertheless paid off over time. There's a value judgment at work here, and the first applicant might not necessarily be a better tenant than the second. Assigning points on this issue doesn't change the fact that the landlord's opinion drove the allocation.

- **It's often meaningless to give high or low points.** It's misleading to assign high points for certain kinds of rental or employment history, and low points for others. For example, giving high marks for two or more positive references from prior landlords will put the first-time renter at a disadvantage. That applicant may, in fact, be just as good a business risk, but if he misses points simply because he's new, he may fall out of the running. Or, you may give high points to someone who has stayed at one job for a long time. True, that spells stability, but someone who has moved around is not necessarily a flake (the worker who is a rising star in the high-tech world may also change jobs frequently but will score lower on your scale).

- **Point systems lock you in.** The whole idea behind a point system

Keep It Confidential

The Rental Application includes some sensitive personal information on your applicants, including their financial details and Social Security numbers. If the application falls into the wrong hands, identity theft would be a breeze. For this reason, you must use utmost care when reviewing and storing these applications (and the credit report or other report, should you order these). See Chapter 11 for a full description of your safekeeping duties under the federal "Disposal Rule," which also covers required destruction of personal information when you no longer need it.

is that it generates a result that you should follow. Trouble is, you may not want to follow it. Interestingly, people who use a point system often find themselves going back and reassigning points in order to get the result they really want.

Below, you'll see a filled-out sample of this Application Review form from Ann, our erstwhile landlord, who received several applications for her single-family rental on "D" street in a college town near the state capitol.

Step 2: Evaluating the application answers

Now it's time to assess the notes you've made on each of the application's queries. This section takes you through the application, item by item, and suggests when you should be flexible, and when you should (or could) reject the applicant. The column to the right of the Notes field, is where you'll record your conclusions. If the answers give you clear reason to reject, put a check mark in the

Application Review (excerpt)

Part	Notes	Conclusions	Red flag
Applicant name and other identifying information			
Additional occupants	wife + 2 minor children		
Rental history	current rental (2 yr) prior (2 yr)		
Employment history	Database Manager, Linkso Systems (3 years)		
Income	$6,500/month		
Credit and			

Red-flag column. When you're done, you should be able to quickly read down the Conclusions and Red-flag columns and either reject an applicant or rank relative to the others you're considering. Then, you'll run credit reports for the top one, two, or three—however many you think you need to pursue in order to maintain a field of qualified applicants.

Applicant name and other identifying information

In the "Applicant" section of the application, a prospective tenant lists his or her full name, phone numbers, and Social Security number, driver's license number, or "Other identifying information." Most people will have a SSN and a driver's license, but foreigners who are here legally may not have either. They may have an Individual Taxpayer's Identification Number (ITIN), which should be sufficient to enable you to get a credit report (but it is not evidence of legal status in the United States).

If you've spoken with this person already (on the phone or in person), you should already have some of the information that's on the application. Make sure the application matches information on your Tenant Information Sheet. For example, if you see more people listed on the application than you were originally told, make a note in the Conclusions column of the Application Review and consider checking it out with a phone call. If the number of occupants

puts this applicant out of the running, note this, too. Or, if it seems that the person you met at an open house had a different story than the application shows, consider investigating with a phone call. You'd be surprised how many people send others to check out a place for them, or to handle a phone interview. If you see that you're dealing with a different person, make a note of it. You'll want to question this applicant at the very least, and quite possibly go no further with the application if you discover that a visitor was deliberately misleading you.

When to be flexible

Determine whether the answer may have been a mistake—for example, your applicant introduced himself as "Randy," but the application lists "Alexander" as his name. You may be dealing with the same person who goes by a nickname. In the Conclusions column, make a note of the discrepancy.

When to reject

Red flag. You must reject if you have no way to order a credit report—that is, no SSN, driver's license number, or ITIN.

You may reject if you conclude that you were deliberately misled during a phone conversation or property visit—such dissembling spells trouble ahead.

Additional occupants

This portion of the application asks for the names of everyone, including minor children, who will be living in the rental, and the relationship of the additional occupants to the applicant. If more than one adult (over the age of 18) will be living in the unit, you should get an application from each one.

Don't get overly concerned about the relationship description. It really shouldn't matter to you whether other adults are spouses, partners, or roommates—what's important is their financial and behavioral stability. In fact, in many states and lots of cities, it's illegal to discriminate against unmarried people (see Chapter 2).

So, you may wonder, why ask about the relationship of your applicants at all? You'll need this information so you can evaluate their credit reports correctly. Most of the time, married people are responsible for housing debts their spouses incur during the marriage. You'll keep this in mind if you advance these applicants to the credit check phase (see Chapter 11).

When to be flexible

Use your judgment when your applicants include a newborn. Babies take up less space than older children and adults. Also, if rooms are unusually large, or if there are lofts or dens that can be used as sleeping quarters, be prepared to think of them as bedrooms.

When to reject

⚠️ **Red flag.** You must reject when the applicant proposes many more residents than would be permitted under the most generous application of the relevant occupancy standard.

You may reject when there are more occupants than a reasonable application of the "two per bedroom" or other relevant occupancy standard will permit. If your occupancy policy is lower than the legal standard and you're confident it's based on solid business needs, you may reject if your applicant proposes too many occupants (and hope you'll survive any fair housing challenge).

Rental history

The application asks for the address of the applicant's current rental and two previous rentals, including the names of the landlords or managers and their contact information, and the reasons for leaving the old residences. Again, check these entries with information you noted following a phone interview. When you call these owners or managers (discussed in Chapter 12), you'll be asking for their version of why the applicant left and double checking other items such as the rent, and you'll want to note any discrepancies there, too.

Be sure to call the landlords or managers of former residences. If the applicant is a troublesome tenant, his current landlord may sing his praises in hopes that he'll move (and become your headache). Former landlords have no such motive. See Chapter 12 for more on the subject of checking landlord references.

When to be flexible

It's usually a good idea to be flexible with applicants who are renting for the first time, either because they are young and just leaving home or school, or because they've sold a home and are renting on a temporary or permanent basis. You may also find applicants who have lost their homes through foreclosure (or sold them when the writing was on the wall) and have reluctantly rejoined the ranks of tenants. Older applicants who have voluntarily become first-time renters (or whose rental history, prior to home ownership, is too old to be of much help) are likewise quite possibly suitable.

Don't automatically eliminate first-time renters from your consideration. If the first-timer's employment history checks out, and the credit report shows nothing alarming, you can probably ignore the absence of a rental history. How should you evaluate these applicants? Focus instead on other measures of trustworthiness and financial stability, which will be revealed by the applicant's gross monthly income and credit report. The same goes for applicants who were unable to keep their home—these folks

may well be able to handle a monthly rental that's possibly way below their former mortgage payment.

Here are some other ways to assess the suitability of first-time renters:

- **Ask for student transcripts.** As suggested in Chapter 6, you can ask a student for school transcripts, which will tell you a lot about this person's ability to stick with a commitment. A string of poor grades, or incomplete courses, may indicate that this applicant doesn't follow through or meet deadlines. He may treat the rent due date with the same casualness that he accords term paper due dates.

- **Ask for references from teachers, counselors, coaches, or Scout leaders.** These people are used to being asked for letters of reference and should be able to tell you how conscientiously the applicant takes his or her studies and deadlines.

- **Consider why first-timers have sold their homes and are moving to rentals.** These applicants have lots of financial history, much of which is relevant to your requirement for financial responsibility and stability. Did they own their home for a reasonable period of time, or were they professional property "flippers?" Did they decide to sell, or were they forced to as a result of overall poor financial planning? Did they regularly make their mortgage payments, or were they frequently late?

When to reject

Red flag. It's important to have a full picture of the applicant's rental (or housing) history. Unexplained gaps may indicate time spent in jail or prison. If that's the case, you may want to investigate further (see Chapter 13 on criminal background checks).

You may also want to reject the applicants who say they were asked to leave the previous rental or were evicted—and don't give you any reason to think that they were unfairly treated.

Employment history

Your applicant's current employment details and history will be very important for you. Primarily, you'll get the name and phone number of the person who can verify that the applicant is indeed employed. You'll call each of these persons and check employer references as explained in Chapter 12.

But there's a secondary benefit to getting employer information. Combined with the previous employer information, you'll see how stable the applicant's job experiences were. Someone who moves frequently from job to job, especially when there's no apparent connection between jobs or a plan that explains the moves, may be someone who won't stay long in your rental. Especially if you learn that an applicant was fired, you'll be able

to conclude that this person might be a bad business risk for you, too.

Don't be too hasty to denigrate applicants who leave jobs—sometimes it's the right thing to do and the mark of someone who realizes they've made a poor choice. There may also be very legitimate professional reasons for frequent job changes, as happened in the early 2000s when dot.com workers, in great demand, moved from place to place. When offering a year's lease, you may want to question your applicant outright, asking about the possibility of continued job changes.

When to be flexible

You may find yourself with an applicant who has no employment history. Self-employed persons can be evaluated in other, equally satisfactory ways. Your Rental Policies handout explained that for self-employed persons, you will need the applicant's tax returns for the last two years. The application repeats this instruction, and a complete application will have these documents clipped to it. As for references, entrepreneurs should be able to produce letters from vendors, commercial landlords, and business associates.

Students also may have no employment history. In these cases, you'll need a cosigner (typically the student's parents or guardian), and with first-time renters who are also first-time employees, you may also want the reassurance of a cosigner. Your Rental Policies handout (Chapter 6) explained this issue, too, so hopefully the applicant has sized up the situation and has presented you with a cosigner's application along with his or her own. (See "What to look for in a cosigner" in Chapter 15 for guidance on how to handle a cosigner's application.)

When to reject

Red flag. You can reject someone who has no current job, no other source of income or support, and no viable cosigner.

Income

Your applicant's income is a vital piece of information. You're asking for the gross monthly income before deductions. The application also asks for other sources of income. These typically include child support (and occasionally alimony), income from stocks and bonds, rental income, and trust fund income. Self-employed applicants' income will be evident from their tax returns. (The rental application asks for two years of tax returns for self-employed applicants.)

Note the total gross monthly income from all sources, and compare it with the rent. It should be at least three times the rent. For example, someone who makes $48,000 a year has a gross monthly income of $4,000, and can afford an apartment that costs $1,000 per month. Someone who grosses $24,000 per year ($2,000 per month) will not qualify for the $1,000 per month apartment.

Net Income Gives a Misleading Picture

You may be wondering why you aren't using an applicant's net income as your "three times the rent" figure. Numerous payroll deductions mean that people's take home pay is far less than their gross income. Because people pay rent from what they actually take home, isn't it more accurate to ask for net income?

Actually, no. Imagine one applicant who has a deduction for health care insurance premiums for a policy that covers all medical costs, while another, without a deduction, pays for every doctor visit or medication. The net income figure for the first applicant may be lower than the second, but in practice, the second applicant may pay more for health care and thus may have less money to spend on rent. Rather than try to make guesses or adjustments when looking at net income, the rental industry decided long ago to stick with gross income. Even the federal government uses this figure when evaluating eligibility for housing assistance.

If an applicant's gross monthly income is not at least three times the rent, you're on solid ground right then to deny the application—*unless* the applicants are married (or domestic partners in states that give such unions the benefits and obligations of married persons). In that event, you must combine the spouses' or partners' incomes and determine whether that combined figure is three times the rent. For all other adults who plan to live together in one rental, you are legally entitled to require that each make three times the rent, though many times this is not practical—that's why people are sharing rentals!

At this point, you're determining whether the self-reported income meets your requirements. Later, if you advance this applicant to the credit and reference check stage, you'll verify the reports and pay stubs by talking with employers or others.

Count government assistance when considering income. Several states require that you put this assistance into the mix (see Chapter 2). While it's true that the assistance may get cut off, that risk is probably no greater than the risk that a tenant will lose a job or have a sudden expense that interferes with the ability to pay the rent.

Insufficient Income—Must You Accept a Cosigner?

Now and then, you'll encounter applicants who know that their financial picture isn't rosy—perhaps they're students or first-time renters with their first job, or they have recently declared bankruptcy. These applicants may approach you at the outset with a request that you consider their cosigner when evaluating their application. Must you do so?

Because of the relatively weak value of a cosigner (especially one who lives in another state), and because evaluating a cosigner is yet another step in a labor-intensive screening process, many landlords refuse to consider them. In a hot market especially, a landlord may not want to bother with this complication. This approach is legal in every situation except one: If a disabled applicant has insufficient income (but is otherwise qualified) and asks you to accept a cosigner, you must relax your policy at least to the extent of investigating the financial ability of the proposed cosigner to cover the tenant's monetary obligations under the lease. If the proposed cosigner is solvent and stable, you must accommodate the disabled applicant by accepting the cosigner. If the cosigner has a poor financial profile, you may reject the applicant on that basis. Dealing with cosigners is covered in Chapter 15.

Cash-Only Workers—How Can You Verify Their Income?

It's well known that a sizable chunk of the working population operates below the radar. Some workers want to be paid in cash in order to avoid taxes, and some who are in this country illegally want to minimize the chance they'll get caught. If you're dealing with an applicant who works this way, consider the effect of a cash-only work life on the following issues:

- **Steady work.** Does the applicant work steadily for one outfit, or for many employers, with jobs picked up haphazardly? If the latter, this applicant may be unemployed for periods of time and unable to pay the rent. On the other hand, this applicant may have a long-held job with one employer, such as a child care worker who has been with one family for years.
- **Verification.** Can you confirm the earnings? Because paying employees by cash is almost always illegal, employers may not be willing to talk to you about their practices.
- **Job security.** Most employees, including those illegally in the United States, work "at will," which means that their employers can fire them at any time, as long as it's not for an illegal reason (such as complaining about safety violations). However, illegal workers often don't understand their rights, and are more vulnerable to illegal dismissals than legal workers (who may have the support of a union). If that happens, this tenant may not be able to pay the rent.

You'll need to make a policy decision about how to handle applicants who get paid in cash, and apply it to every cash-only applicant you encounter. If you want, you can reject everyone who can't show you documented income, and leave it at that. Or you can be flexible, willing to consider cash workers if you can verify their employment and it looks steady (this isn't to say that you'll necessarily rent to them, only that you'll evaluate their income and rank their application with the others).

If you do consider cash-only applicants, be very careful that your conclusions are based on color- and ethnic-blind factors. To be blunt, if you advance the Danish nanny but not the Hispanic gardener, you'd better be able to point to evidence, such as interviews with employers, that made the nanny a better business risk.

When to be flexible

Very few landlords will advocate flexibility on as basic a point as sufficient income. They'll have to be convinced that there's very good evidence that the rent will be paid before they'll bend on this one. Still, you might consider lowering your requirement in rare cases. For example, your applicant may be able to convince you that he lives extremely frugally, and needs less for entertainment, clothing, or travel than most folks. If the rent he was paying at his old place was as high as yours, and he had no history of missed or late payments, you might consider him (after checking with the previous landlord, of course).

When to reject

⚠️ **Red flag.** You should reject if you can discern no legitimate source of income (you may be dealing with a scammer or drug dealer).

You may reject if the combined monthly gross income for all other adults who plan to live together in one rental is less than three times the rent.

Credit and financial information

The entries in this section enable you to determine whether this applicant, even one with a solid work and rental history and an impressive income, is financially healthy enough to take on a monthly rent obligation. Even the best paid applicants will be bad risks if they have a ton of debt.

The applicant should include information on the following:

- **All financial accounts.** This includes checking, savings, money market, and the like, and the balance in each account.
- **Major credit cards and loans, including amount owed and monthly payment for each card and loan.** The amount the applicant currently owes on each card and loan, plus the monthly payment, should square with the information you get from the applicant's credit report if the applicant progresses to that point (see Chapter 11).

This section of the rental application tells you about the person's financial ability to pay the rent each month. If you see two credit cards with large balances and high monthly payments, you'll want to add the monthly payments to the rent and then consider whether this applicant can afford your place. For example, someone who grosses $3,000 a month and applies for a $1,000 a month apartment will have $2,000 left over to pay for everything including credit cards. A monthly card payment totaling $1,500 leaves an unrealistic amount of money for food, gas, clothing, and so on. This applicant should look for a cheaper rental.

Evaluate the current financial situation in light of any differential in rent. If your rent will be considerably higher than the applicant's current rent, your tenant may strain to make the monthly payments, even if his or her income is three times the new rent.

When to be flexible

A person with a mountain of debt presents you with fewer ways to be flexible than one who makes slightly less than three times the rent. Why? Because it's a reasonable business move to consider the latter if he can show you that his finances are tightly managed and he has a cosigner, to boot. The person with large debt has finances that are not in close control and the debt may be growing (with interest). A cosigner isn't likely to cover the consequences of increased debt.

When to reject

Red flag. Reject when you see outstanding debt, leaving unrealistically little left over for rent and other necessities.

Pets

If you advertised your rental as pet free, this section should say "none," unless the pet is needed as a service animal for a disabled tenant. If your rental is pet friendly, you'll see details of current or planned-for pets. Check to see whether the type and number of pets listed corresponds with your policies. For example, if you specified that you'll accept no more than one dog or one cat, you should see a description that fits within your policies. Many landlords go further and specify dog breeds and sizes that they will not allow—the wisdom of doing so is debatable, but if you've chosen this approach, make sure the listed pets conform to your rules.

Owners who will allow pets may have included the optional section in the Rental Policies handout that asked applicants for supporting information and references for their pets. If you included this section and modified it to suit your approach, check to see whether the prospect has included the materials you asked for. Typically, owners ask for proof that the animal is current with needed vaccinations, and may ask for a letter of reference from the current landlord, attesting to the owner's conscientious care of the animal and the pet's non-aggression towards others.

When to be flexible

Depending on the request, you may be willing to modify your no-pets policy. In fact, you may be driven to modify it if you get no better application than this one—will it really make a difference if the tenant has a well-behaved, quiet dog who comes with stellar recommendations from the vet and other landlords? As always, the number and quality of your other applications will affect your approach. For now, note in the Conclusions column of the Application Review whether you're willing to consider it.

Your ability to be flexible on some matters may depend on whether you're renting a single-family property or a unit in a multifamily property. If the latter, understand that it's important to be consistent with a pet policy when many tenants have rented under that understanding (maybe they gave up a pet or chose your property because they don't like pets around). Introducing a pet for one tenant is going to create resentment. In a single-family home, you have more leeway.

When to reject

⚠ **Red flag.** You must reject when other tenants in a multifamily property have rented under the same no-pets rule.

In general, beware the applicant who went through your phone screening, and even your open house, representing that he had no dogs or cats, but lists them in the application. You can say no at this point, for not only has the applicant ignored your policy, he has misrepresented his intentions. No rule requires you to do business with people who are not straightforward—such types are likely to be difficult tenants, too.

Water-filled furniture

Although relatively few tenants have waterbeds these days, you need to know about their plans in advance. The furniture's weight might be more than your structure can withstand, and you may not want the worry that a waterbed will leak and cause damage. A few states, including California, specify what happens when tenants have such furniture (California landlords may not deny the rental on that basis, but they may require an additional half-month security deposit). Check your state laws on water-filled furniture (see Chapter 1 for information on finding the law).

Smoking

Many owners and managers have adopted a no-smoking policy, either in common areas in multitenant buildings or even in individual units. Owners of single-family homes may also decide to rent only to nonsmokers. The pros and cons of having a policy are described in Chapter 6. If you've decided on applying a smoking policy for your rental, you have hopefully made it clear in your ads and reiterated it in your conversations with prospects. Your Rental Property Fact Sheet should also have highlighted your rules. Check to see whether the applicant has answered your question on smoking in a way that's consistent with your policy.

When to be flexible

You have some flexibility when renting a single-family home. You may want to allow someone who smokes only one or two cigarettes per day, and does so outside. Check this representation carefully with the current landlord and employer.

When to reject

⚠️ **Red flag.** If you have a multifamily property and a property wide policy against smoking, you must reject (don't be swayed by someone who says she won't smoke in the apartment). If you allow this smoker, you're bound to be beset by angry tenants, who are counting on a smoke-free environment. You'll lose them—it's not worth it.

Bankruptcy

You may legally reject an applicant who has filed for bankruptcy, and many landlords will automatically do so, even if that filing is several years old. You may reason that people who have filed for bankruptcy were unable to adequately manage their financial affairs, and conclude that such mismanagement spells trouble for the future. Especially when an applicant has declared bankruptcy more than once, you may simply stop reading.

On the other hand, you may be willing to consider applicants who have established good credit practices after their bankruptcy discharge (whose current debts are within a reasonable range of their income) and are gainfully employed. Often, bankruptcy is the only way out and up, and marks the beginning of the return to financial stability. If you've agreed to look at the post-bankruptcy picture, you'll want to look at the explanation line of the rental application to see whether a nonrecurring incident or string of incidents precipitated the bankruptcy.

When to be flexible

You may be willing to look at each case individually if you feel that bankruptcy is not always the result of irresponsible, spendthrift ways, and that, increasingly, very responsible people have been thrown into crushing debt by the sudden loss of a job or large medical costs. You may decide to look beyond the fact of the bankruptcy and consider how long ago it happened, whether the applicant has lived within his or her means since then, what the current amount of debt is, and whether current income appears to be from a stable source. If you decide that this applicant is a good risk based on a complete picture of the person, you may conclude that the bankruptcy will not in itself defeat this candidate. (A look at this person's credit report, should this person advance to that stage, will tell you whether you've made the right call. If you see another growing pile of debt, you can conclude that the applicant hasn't overcome unwise spending patterns and it's reasonable to conclude that another crash is imminent.)

When to reject

⚠️ **Red flag.** You'll want to reject when another bankruptcy seems inevitable—when the spending patterns that caused the first one have reestablished themselves.

You can reject someone with a bankruptcy if you have a firm, no-bankruptcy policy, and aren't interested in looking at the circumstances, then and now.

Lawsuits

You should know whether (and how many times) this applicant has been sued (the nature of the lawsuit should be explained on the application). Unlike an eviction record, however, a lawsuit or two in one's past is not necessarily a red flag—remember, anyone can file a lawsuit, even one based on lies. In fact, many people are sued over ridiculous matters, especially in small claims court, and such lawsuits are routinely dismissed, settled, or won by the defendant. And, someone might be involved in a lawsuit concerning an entirely legitimate dispute, such as a business dispute or child custody battle.

To reject someone simply because the applicant has been sued does not make sense—look to the explanation before reaching a conclusion. If you see large numbers of lawsuits, and especially if they involve neighbor disputes or fights over unpaid bills, the chances that this person will be a poor tenant risk go up, since you can reasonably conclude that the applicant tends not to honor commitments, or cannot get along with neighbors (and at the least, cannot work out problems short of going to court). You won't want to do business with such a person.

The application also asks whether the applicant has sued someone else. Here again, you'll need to look at the explanation to determine whether this applicant's experience makes him or her a poor risk. However, there is a group of litigants—called "vexatious" in legalese—whom you should avoid. These folks have a beef with someone or some company, and figure out (often representing themselves) how to bedevil their opponent with multiple, groundless lawsuits. Closely related are people who frequently sue in small claims court (the problem is so significant that some states limit the number of suits a person can bring per year). These folks can't solve their problems by talking them out and crafting a compromise on their own—or they sue over nonexistent harms or insults. You don't want to do business with a litigation-happy tenant, so if the application reflects multiple small claims cases, think twice.

When to be flexible

Disregard legal disputes that are not likely to reflect on this person's ability to be a good tenant—for example, a custody battle is probably irrelevant.

When to reject

⚠️ **Red flag.** You may reject an applicant who appears to be litigation happy. Especially when you see that an applicant makes multiple trips to the courthouse (look in particular for many small claims court cases, and cases involving past land-lords), you may wonder if you will be the next defendant.

Prior evictions

Most landlords will automatically reject anyone who has been evicted—it's probably a universal rule, right up there with the "three times the monthly rent" standard for income compared to rent. Whether you want to do the same is up to you.

When to be flexible

You may at least want to look at the rest of the application, and particularly at the applicant's explanation of the eviction. Now and then, you'll find someone who explains that he or she was unfairly targeted by a landlord who just wanted him or her out (this happens most often in rent control cities where landlords cannot raise the rent to market rates unless a tenant leaves). Whether you'll want to take the time to confirm this version of events is another matter. If the eviction was justified, you'll probably find that other aspects of this applicant's life (such as employment history) show

similar bumps. Conversely, a person with excellent employment references (and one with another former landlord who speaks highly of the applicant) may well have been the victim of an unscrupulous landlord. If you're worried, ask for more references.

When to reject

⚠️ **Red flag.** Ask what type of termination notice preceded the termination. An "unconditional" termination (when the tenant is told to leave, with no chance to pay the rent or cease the lease violation) tells you that there was probably some pretty bad stuff going on. Most states don't allow landlords to terminate with no chance to save the tenancy unless the tenant has repeatedly broken the rules or not paid the rent, or has been dealing drugs or engaging in other seriously illegal activities.

Convictions for criminal offenses

You'll want to know whether your appli-cant has any criminal convictions. These include felonies and misdemeanors, but do not include infractions or traffic offenses (driving under the influence is not an infraction, but a crime that can be a misdemeanor or a felony, depending on the circumstances and record of the driver).

As explained in Chapter 2, it's clear that you may legally reject an applicant who has a conviction for drug sale or manufacture. People who have drug use convictions, on the other hand, but do not currently use illegal drugs may not be rejected on that basis. What about all the other offenses? Some experts believe you can reject without fear of legal problems, because "convicted persons" aren't specifically protected under fair housing laws; others caution that some offenses are irrelevant and their use exposes landlords to lawsuits by disappointed applicants. Many landlords who see *any* criminal background will stop right there, and move on to the next application.

When to be flexible

If market conditions require you to look more carefully at each application, or if you're willing to look at the individual conviction, its age, and relevance to the applicant's ability to be a good tenant, you may decide that a conviction *per*

se need not rule out an applicant. If this describes your attitude, read on for some tips on what to look for in your applicant's explanation.

How old is the conviction? Before considering even the nature of the conviction, give some thought to its age. If 25 years separate your applicant from a juvenile offense, that tells you something very important about the individual's ability to conform to society's norms. On the other hand, a recent conviction should give you pause.

Are the circumstances that led to the conviction likely to arise again? Many landlords focus on what the conviction was for—assault or forgery, for example—and decide to reject, reasoning that they do not want someone who is violent or writes bad checks as a tenant and neighbor to other tenants. A more thoughtful inquiry would focus instead on the circumstances of the crime and

---

Sealed or Expunged Convictions

All states have laws that allow persons convicted of relatively tame, first-time offenses to "seal" or "expunge" the record if the person successfully completed probation and remained "clean" for a period of time. Under law, a sealed or expunged conviction is the same as if it never happened. This means that a person is entitled to answer "none" if a sealed conviction is the only one in his or her background. You should not penalize this person if you learn of the sealed conviction through other means. Don't worry—records for really bad crimes can't be sealed, and if this applicant is truly not suitable, you'll find out through your normal screening process.

its age, and ask whether it's likely that the same set of circumstances would occur during this applicant's tenancy. Suppose you're looking at a misdemeanor forgery from many years ago, when the applicant was without a job and down on his or her luck? People now and then do turn their lives around, and applicants who have been financially stable for a long period of time may turn out to be acceptable tenants.

Of course, you'll always be taking a chance when you advance an application from someone with a conviction in his or her past. But there's one cross-check you can perform that will usually tell you whether you're being foolish: Chances are that the rest of the information you'll get about this applicant, from prior landlords and employers, will either confirm your optimism or tell you that you're better off to continue your search.

Some landlords will not be content to depend on an applicant to self-report when it comes to convictions. Whether to run a criminal background check—including accessing Megan's Law databases—is covered in Chapter 13.

Is your applicant a registered sexual offender? The rental application asks specifically whether the applicant is required to register under any state's sexual offender registration laws, and if so, where, for what offense, and when. Use the evaluation suggestions above for any "yes" answers, but realize that at least two additional considerations may be relevant:

- Your state or local Megan's Law may prohibit registered offenders from living within a specified radius of a school, playground, or park. If your property is within such a radius, you'll have to reject.
- Statistics on criminal recidivism show that sexual offenders reoffend much more frequently than non-sexual offenders. This means that the interval since the last conviction is very important.

When to reject

⚠️ **Red flag.** If you can conclude that this person poses a current and direct threat to persons or property, you should reject. A registered sexual offender with a recent offense, or one who has many such convictions, is a higher risk than someone with a single, old conviction.

References and emergency contact

This portion of your rental application asks for two personal references and an emergency contact. For now, just make sure these items are filled in, especially the contact information and the Relationship line. If you advance this applicant to the next stage (calling references), you'll need this information, and will record your conversations on the Tenant References section of the Tenant Information Sheet (discussed in Chapter 12).

Application Review (excerpt)

Part	Notes	Conclusions	Red flag
Credit and financial information	3 credit cards w/ $0 bal. 2 credit cards w/ total $3,000 bal.		
Loans	auto loan w/ $5,200 bal.		
Other major obligations	child support $1,000/mo.		
Pets	1 cat OK		
Water-filled furniture	no		
Smoking	no		
Bankruptcy	no		
Lawsuits	1 small claim case against dry cleaner—lost		

Source of information on the vacancy

This section asks applicants to tell you how they learned of your rental. It will be handy if you haven't had a chance to talk with the applicant and haven't captured this information on a Tenant Information Sheet or Visitor Log for Open House. The answers here won't qualify or disqualify the applicant, but may be of interest to you as you evaluate your marketing efforts.

Certification and signatures

The final part of the application includes a certification and a place for applicants to sign and date the application. The certification includes three very important parts:

- **Consequences for false or incomplete statements.** The instructions for your application have already told the applicant that incomplete information may result in your denying the application. Now, you're extending that thought: You're telling applicants that any materially false or incomplete information may be grounds for *terminating their tenancy*. This means, for example, that if you discover after you've rented to this applicant that he or she listed a phony prior landlord

(who succeeded in fooling you), you can terminate the tenancy. Without this provision, you might have difficulty doing so, but even with it, you may have a hard time convincing a judge to evict this tenant unless the tenant has also seriously misbehaved at your property (by not paying rent or disturbing neighbors, for example).

- **Permission to verify applicant's statements.** The certification also gives you permission to contact credit sources (such as lenders and banks), credit bureaus, landlords, employers, and personal references. You may need this permission before these sources will talk to you. You'll also have a separate written form for this purpose.
- **Contact permission extends beyond tenancy's end.** Finally, the certification specifies that the permission to contact the sources mentioned above will survive the expiration of the tenancy. This provision gives you flexibility if you need to collect from a former tenant who has left owing rent or caused damage that's not covered by the security deposit. You may run a credit check or contact the employer to see if the ex-tenant is still employed.

Consult any notes from a visit or phone screening

The last line in your Application Review reminds you to go back to the Tenant Information Sheet and pick up any notes you made during phone calls or a site visit. You may have learned then, for example, that the prospect will require new paint in the bedroom before considering your rental; or you may have heard a request for covered parking, a longer lease, or the like. Enter the relevant details and then, in the Conclusions column, make an evaluation: Maybe the new paint isn't such a big deal, but it will be an expense; perhaps you will have to give up covered parking for your employee in order to meet that request; and maybe you're willing to consider a longer lease but want some rent escalation built in (this will require some negotiation).

On the other hand, pay attention to impressions you received that suggest this applicant may not be a good tenant—did you hear immediate requests for many upgrades and special favors? Complaints about the property or services—even before the applicant has moved in? These signals tell you that the applicant may be high maintenance, and there is nothing illegal about declining to work with a difficult person. Just be sure you've documented your experience and never reach that conclusion based on your assumptions about people of particular races, religions, ethnicities, and so on.

Legal status in the United States

Some of you may have decided to ask all applicants for proof of their right to be in the United States. As described in Chapter 2, you may make this inquiry (except in California) as long as you ask it of all applicants (selectively applying it to only those who "look foreign" is a violation of fair housing law). Chapter 6 explained the additional form, Legal Status in the United States, to attach to your rental application. It asks applicants about their status and advises them of the documentation they need to supply to corroborate their answers. If you took this step, read on; if you didn't, skip ahead to Step 3.

Make sure you get this form back. If you got the form back as an email attachment, you can wait to review the application until you've physically reviewed the documents. Here's how to evaluate the answers and the documentation that the applicant should show you when returning the application.

First, the citizens, who will check the first box on the form. These are the types of documents you should see, depending on which of the next two check boxes the applicant checked.

- U.S. citizens by birth or through parents. A passport (even an expired one) or birth certificate will do. Look for an official stamp or embossed seal on the certificate, which will show that it was issued by a recorder's office. U.S. citizens born in other countries (who

Legal Status in the United States

Applicant _____

Rental address _____

Please check the boxes that apply and supply information as requested. Bring the required documentation to the landlord/manager when you return the Rental Application, or soon thereafter. We cannot process your application until we have reviewed your documentation.

☐ I have the legal right to be in the United States because I am a U.S. citizen.

   ☐ I am a citizen by birth or through my parents (provide an original birth certificate or a copy certified by the issuing agency, a U.S. passport, a Certificate of U.S. Citizenship, or a Certificate of Birth Abroad).

   ☐ I am a naturalized citizen (provide a U.S. passport or a Naturalization Certificate).

☐ I have the legal right to be in the United States because I have valid documentation from U.S. Citizenship and Immigration Services (USCIS).

   ☐ I am a legal permanent resident (provide Permanent Resident Card or a foreign passport showing an I-151 or I-551 stamp, or an I-94 form, Arrival-Departure Record).

   ☐ I entered the United States on a visa and am on an authorized, temporary stay (provide passport from country of citizenship plus I-94 form, Arrival-Departure Record).

   My permitted stay expires on: _____

   ☐ I am a refugee (provide passport from country of citizenship plus I-94 form, Arrival-Departure Record, stamped "Admitted as a Refugee"; or Refugee Travel Document).

   ☐ I have an application pending with USCIS or other right to stay in the United States (provide work permit or USCIS receipt or other notice indicating right).

☐ I do not have a legal right to be in the United States.

_____   _____
Applicant's signature   Date

gained citizenship through their U.S. citizen parents) may have a Certification of Birth Abroad, issued by the State Department (Form FS-545 or DS-1350). Or, they may have a Certificate of Citizenship (Form N-560 or N-561).

- U.S. citizens by naturalization. You should be shown a passport or a Naturalization Certificate (this is a diploma-style document with the person's photo on it).

Next, the legal permanent residents. These are people who aren't citizens but who have the right to live here permanently. They should have a Permanent Resident Card (formerly called an Alien Registration Card), which is popularly known as a green card even though it's no longer green. If their actual green card hasn't arrived yet (it can take months), they should have an I-94 card or stamp in their foreign passport.

Then, the folks who are here temporarily but legally, such as students, tourists, workers, and diplomats. You'll need to see the passport from the applicant's country of citizenship, and a visa. An I-94 form (Arrival-Departure Record) should be attached to the visa or passport. This form will tell you when their permitted stay expires. (Don't go by the date on the visa itself—that's just the last date upon which the person can use it to enter the United States.) If the person is a student, it may say "D/S," for "duration of status," which means the person can stay until completing his or her studies.

You may encounter a refugee, someone who has been admitted to the United States because of the threat of persecution. The passport should be accompanied by an I-94 form, stamped "Admitted as a Refugee." Alternately, the person might show you a Refugee Travel Document, which the United States issues to refugees who have no foreign passport or wish to leave and return to the United States.

Your applicant may fall into numerous other categories of persons allowed to stay in the United States, too many to list here or categorize. For example, many people are allowed to stay while waiting for United States Citizenship and Immigration Service to approve or deny an application they've filed. Or, people with Temporary Protected Status can stay while a civil war or natural disaster is affecting their home country. Many of these people will have work permits, but others will have nothing more than a letter from USCIS. Their lawyer, if they have one, may be able to reassure you and explain the situation.

Finally, your applicant may have checked the box indicating that he or she has no legal right to be in the United States. It's unlikely that too many people will check this box—most of the time, you'll never hear from this applicant.

When to be flexible

By including this legal status form in your rental application, you've already decided that residents' legal status in the United States is important to you. Of course, the reality of the market may force you to reconsider. There's no law against that—but be sure that if you relax your requirement for documentation or for proof of residency for one applicant (from Great Britain, for example), you do the same for the person from Ghana. Otherwise, you're looking at national origin discrimination.

Suppose you discover that your applicant is expected to leave before the end of the rental term? You're on solid footing if your reject, but you may want to reconsider if the remaining time on the lease will be short and particularly if the market is soft. For one thing, many temporary visitors can and will get their permitted stay extended. For another, if this person ends up being your best applicant, you may come out ahead by offering a shorter lease term. Finally, suppose the permitted stay expires and the tenant stays in the United States and at your property, regularly paying rent and causing no problems? You could do worse.

When to reject

You can legally reject any applicant who cannot provide adequate documentation, who is not here with permission of the U.S. government, or whose right to be here will expire before the end of the lease term.

Step 3: Rank your applications

You're now ready to rank the applications based on your evaluations of the Rental Application answers, plus your notes from personal conversations. First, put aside any applications whose Conclusions column has a "definitely reject" note, such as for a recent and relevant criminal conviction, failure to pay the credit check fee, or because the applicant proposes too many occupants. See Chapter 16 for advice on how to communicate the rejections.

The surviving applications represent a range of applicants—some will be better tenants than others. Your job now is to arrange them from most attractive to least. Here's how you do it:

Looking at your Conclusions column, find those who not only meet, but exceed your requirements. Income that's more than three times the rent, low debt load, no relevant convictions—these look most promising. Moving down the line, you'll place less-impressive applications below the best ones, including those with just enough income, a spotty job history without adequate explanation, and so on. All along, you're considering applicants who don't fit the norm, and putting their bids in the mix on the assumption that you'll hear adequate things when you contact these alternate sources for employment or income history (such as a teacher or commercial landlord). And you'll consider the applicant who wants to negotiate, too—the retired applicant with lots of capital but a precious pet may, in the long run, be the best tenant for your one-family bungalow, and it might be worth your while to negotiate the no-pets clause with him or her. And the person asking for fresh paint may be so superior to the next-best applicant that you'll willingly do it. For now, just do your best to arrange the applications from most attractive to least, using your experience as a businessperson to draw stereotype-free conclusions.

Does this all sound rather loosey-goosey? Admittedly, it is a bit. But it's not legally dangerous, or practically foolish, if you bring sound business judgment to the task. As long as you do not apply notions based on discriminatory assumptions and can articulate a business reason for every placement, you'll be alright.

Step 4: Decide how many applications will advance to credit checks and reference checks

The fourth and final step in your application review is to decide how many of your top-to-bottom ranked applications you should advance to the next stage (pulling a credit report and checking references). The number you advance depends on these factors:

- **What's the market?** If you're in a soft market, your best applicants are looking at other properties, too, and have lots of choices. Since you're competing for them, you'll need to advance enough applicants so that at least one will still be looking when you make an offer. In a hot market, where applicants are more desperate, you may not have to keep your pool of advanced applicants so full, since they will be dropping out (renting from other landlords) at a slower rate.

- **What's the curve of your ranked list?** Ideally, your ranked applications will present a steep curve of quality, with great applicants clearly at the top, and less-attractive ones down the line (when that happens, it's easy to see which ones to pursue). If you're lucky, you will get that curve, with two or three that are great, but other mediocre submissions. You may want to advance only the top few, banking on the survival of at least one or two as you put them through your next screening stage. Or you may have a rather flat group, without great differences between, say, the first and the fourth. In that event, it makes sense to advance a greater number, in hopes that you'll learn enough at the next stage to more clearly differentiate the applications (that is, create a steep curve).

- **Advance enough to account for washouts at the credit- and reference-checking stages.** You may learn things from the credit report and landlords or employers that will disqualify an applicant whose self-report looked great. Advance enough applications to account for a few who will fail at the next stage, so that you'll have a few left from which to pick.

- **If there are applications at the top that require further investigation (such as a request that a student supply a cosigner or a school transcript), deal with that right away.** This applicant's place depends on satisfactory alternate proof of good-tenant potential, and you'll want to nail it down right away.

- **Did you get a miserable turnout?** Your choices may be very disappointing. Though these applicants have made it past the minimum criteria, you may not be very excited about any of them. You may want to hold off, readvertise, and try again (see "What to do when you have no qualified applicants," in Chapter 15).

As you can see, the number of applications that you advance to the next stage is completely dependent on what you're working with, and under what market conditions. You could advertise this unit next month, get lucky with a couple of great prospects, and never

proceed with the very candidates who, this time, have ended up near the top of your list. Further, you don't know what the next screening stage will reveal— your top picks may drop out or be eliminated by a credit report that doesn't match the self-reported information or a poor recommendation from a current or past landlord. For that reason, keep your ranked applications handy—you may have to reach for the next ones up if your first batch disappoints.

When you've decided whom to advance, make a note on the Application Review, using the "Proceed, reasons," "Reject, reasons," or "Hold pending further inquiry, reasons" lines. Your entries might look something like this:

- Proceed: "Excellent income, reasonable debt, no red flags at Open House"
- Reject: "Proposes too many occupants (4)"
- Hold: "Long-time self-employed— call asap and ask for letter from commercial landlord and one vendor."

Don't reject your runners-up right away. If you get washouts at the credit check or reference check stage, you may need to go back and advance them. Work quickly—you won't want to leave these applicants in limbo (they'll drop out soon enough on their own, anyway).

Take Ten Minutes

Spend a moment reflecting on how well your application and its supporting documents—your rental kit—have worked for you. Ask yourself:

- Did applicants follow my directions? If you see mistakes from more than a few applicants, perhaps you need to clarify your Rental Application Instructions.

- Am I rejecting applicants on an issue that isn't on my Rental Policies handout? Your handout should cover the basic traits you're looking for in a tenant and will help prospects decide whether to submit the application. If you find yourself rejecting over an issue that should be on your sheet—for example, your policy to require pet references—add it to your policies sheet for next time.

- Do I have completed Credit Check Payment forms from those whom I've advanced to the next stage? If you find that this credit card method is not working, consider asking for a cash or check payment of the fee when you collect the application.

- Did I get applications from unqualified applicants because my ad, open house, or tour was insufficiently specific and informative? You may need to make certain issues very clear, such as your policy on cosigners (guarantors). Failing to do so will result in a lot of time reviewing applications that you reject.

- Go to the Marketing Worksheet for this property ("Post-rental results") and make a check mark opposite the advertising medium where each applicant found out about your rental (the applicant should have supplied that information at the end of the application). When you have rented this unit, you'll see how many applicants came via each advertising avenue, and which avenue produced your selected tenant.

Information about a potential tenant's financial health and bill-paying history is a critical component of your screening efforts. Looking at a credit report (and knowing what to look for) will tell you not only whether the tenant can afford the rent (in light of other ongoing debts), but whether the applicant has a history of paying bills on time. Credit reports also contain information that should confirm applicants' answers to questions in your rental application, such as employers' names. When you study the applicant's credit report, you're on the third step of the five-step screening process described in Chapter 1.

This chapter gives you some basic tools for ordering and reading credit reports, including:

- an explanation of what's in a credit report
- advice on how to evaluate what you see and what constitutes a red flag

- understanding an applicant's credit score, which is a common add-on for credit reports, and
- how to follow federal guidelines on safeguarding and disposing of credit reports and similar sensitive applicant information.

Be sure to order a credit report for everyone—including all roommates—whom you've advanced past your second-level screening (your review of the information reported on the Rental Application). As important as credit reports are, they shouldn't be the end of your screening, because they're not going to give you reference confirmations or neat predictions on whether applicants will be stable tenants. In addition:

- If you want criminal conviction histories, you'll need to order a criminal background report, or work with a tenant-screening agency, which you can do online from

Decide Early Whether to Use a Screening Firm

It's wise to decide early in your screening efforts whether you're going to hire a resident-screening firm. If you want to order a credit report yourself, do a Megan's Law check yourself, and contact references on your own—but would really like to see an applicant's "risk score" and know whether someone is on the FBI terrorist list—look for the few screening services that will unbundle their products. If you don't find one, don't hire a screening firm unless you're prepared to pay them to duplicate your earlier efforts.

several outfits. These services are described in Chapters 13 and 14.

- If you want others to contact references and provide conclusions, you'll need to hire a property management company or a local real estate office to handle these screening tasks.

When you're done reviewing the credit reports for the applications that you advanced to this stage, you'll rerank the pile, based on what you learned. Perhaps the person who provided great answers on your application turns out to be someone who didn't tell the truth about an eviction, bankruptcy, recent tenancy, or amount of debt. You may want to reject that one outright. As for the others, perhaps you found only confirming information on the credit report—great, move them on to the next stage without reshuffling. Or, you may want to rerank based on new information the credit report revealed, such as a poor bill-paying history.

After you've contacted employers and past or current landlords, again noting where you learn of disturbing facts, you'll rerank again (you might advance the third-place holder based on rave reviews, for example). Then, you'll have your top pick. So you see, you're almost there.

Before You Order an Applicant's Credit Report

☑ Make sure prospective tenants have submitted complete Rental Applications that pass your initial screening, given you written authorization to check their credit report, paid the credit check fee for running the report, and provided a Credit Check Payment form if paying by credit card (Chapter 10).

☑ Review your Rental Policies, such as income requirements and debt level maximums, so that you know how to evaluate what the report will show (Chapter 7).

☑ Consider joining a landlord's association for better deals if you run lots of credit reports.

☑ Hold off on ordering a report if you suspect that references (an employer or current landlord) won't be supportive. You may want to call them first.

Make sure that you are truly interested in renting to applicants before pulling their reports. Never keep a credit check fee when you haven't pulled the report.

Sources of Credit Information

The words and phrases used to describe services offered by third parties can get confusing. Here's the range. Chapter 15 explains how to prepare and send an adverse action letter.

Type of company	What do they provide?	What's in it?	Must you use an adverse action letter when rejecting?
Credit-reporting agency	Credit report	Personal history, accounts reported monthly and those in default, public records information (evictions, civil lawsuits), inquiries from other creditors, consumer's personal statements, credit score (additional feature)	Yes
Multistate Megan's Law searching company	A report that allegedly tells you whether an applicant is on any state's Megan's Law database	A list of matches, which purportedly are the same person as your applicant	Yes
Online back-ground-reporting service	Investigative back-ground report	Criminal conviction history, property ownership, licenses, much more	Yes
Investigative background service	Criminal background report (typically promised instantly)	Criminal conviction history, property ownership, licenses, much more	Yes
Tenant-screening or resident-screening service (most are online)	Credit report and investigative report of their own	Everything in a credit report and most elements of an investigative background report; some will contact references, some will recommend or pick a tenant	Yes
Brick-and-mortar real estate office or property management firm	They do the screening for you, using their own methods or your rental application (you work it out)	They may recommend a tenant, choose a tenant, or just turn over the results of their search for you to make the decision	Yes, if their screening methods involved any of the above that require such letters

What If the Credit Report Is Empty or Slim?

Some credit reports will be pages long, and others will fit on one sheet. The lengthy ones usually indicate a mottled credit history, and often give you reasons to reject. But a practically empty report—one with little or no credit use information—isn't necessarily the kiss of death. Reports may be meager if they're for recent immigrants, first-time, young renters, or the occasional throwback who doesn't have a credit card and pays by check or cash. Ironically, a consumer who doesn't buy a lot of merchandise using credit cards or store credit, and whose job and housing situation are long-standing and stable, is likely to have a practically empty report. You may also see a slim report for a recently divorced applicant (usually a woman whose ex-spouse had all accounts in his name).

Be flexible if the lack of a credit history is the only issue preventing this applicant from advancing to the next stage (checking references). In fact, you may have to speak with references in order to get information you'd normally find in a credit report. For example, a conversation with an employer, current landlord, college counselor, or teacher may assure you that a young, first-time renter honors his or her obligations.

Use equal care when dealing with a recently divorced spouse. Perhaps the couple's financial habits were excellent, and unfortunately in the name of the ex only. On the other hand, the relationship may have foundered precisely because of your applicant's irresponsible behavior—and conveniently, credit was in the ex's name. You may need to ask some questions to correctly interpret the empty credit report.

Landlord's Forms Library

Credit Report Evaluation. This is a worksheet used to record how an applicant meets your screening criteria in areas such as debt level and bill-paying history.

File the credit report with the applicant's rental application, but be sure to keep the file secure. (Secure handling is explained in "Handle credit reports, criminal background reports, and tenant-screening reports carefully," below.) You may want to keep the report for several years, for use as evidence should you be challenged in a fair housing claim. In that event, use a black felt pen to obliterate identifying information, such as all but the last four numbers of Social Security and account numbers.

How to get a credit report

Credit reports are created by credit bureaus or agencies. These are profit-making companies that gather and sell information about a person's credit history. There are three major credit bureaus: Equifax (www.equifax.com), Experian (www.experian.com), and TransUnion (www.transunion.com).

There are also thousands of smaller credit bureaus, known as affiliates. The affiliated companies get their information from Equifax, Experian, and TransUnion.

It's very easy to get a credit report for your applicants. Unfortunately, you cannot easily order one directly from the four main credit bureaus mentioned above. Instead, you need to work through a smaller credit-reporting agency (or tenant-screening service, if you want more than a simple credit report). You can set up an account with these intermediaries for yourself, or you may decide to join a state or local apartment association, which may have a group deal for its members.

If you type "credit report and landlord" into your Internet search engine, you'll get loads of results. Visits to the websites reveal hard-sell advertising that often borders on the sleazy. Each site promises immediate, accurate, in-depth reports, and they all want to sell you more than just a credit report.

Choosing one agency among the welter of possibilities is a bit intimidating. Spend some time on the companies' websites. Do you see a clear explanation of their services, prices, and procedures? Look for a company that has been in business for a while, and provides you with a sample report that's clear and informative. If you're interested in paying for more than a simple credit report, look for an outfit that operates in your area or state—if your applicants are local, a local company will have more information on them than one situated far away. Chapter 14 covers what to look for in a screening service.

Proving your right to pull a report

Strictly speaking, you don't need a consumer's written okay as long as you're pulling the report for a legally recognized reason (which you have, since the applicant knows you'll be looking at the credit report and wants you to do so). But because many consumers and businesses believe that written permission is necessary, it's a good idea to obtain written permission. Requiring written permission may help stop identity theft, too.

Some credit-reporting agencies will tell you that you must have a legally recognized reason to pull a report, and leave it at that. Others will state that you must have the consumer's written permission, but not ask for proof; and others will insist that you supply this permission on a form of their own. If you can, avoid agencies that require use of their form, since it's one more piece of paper to deal with, and a duplicative one at that. Choose an agency that will take you on your word (that you're pulling the report for a legal purpose). You'll usually see this question on the order form, or may be asked to fax the applicant's signed consent form.

The Law You Need to Know

The Fair Credit Reporting Act (FCRA), 15 U.S. Code §§ 1681 and following, governs credit reports. Among other things, it requires you to have a valid business purpose before pulling a report, and it dictates the way you must notify applicants if you reject them based on information you learn in a credit report.

The "Disposal Rule" of the Fair and Accurate Credit Transactions Act of 2003, known as the FACT Act, 69 Fed. Reg. 68690, requires that you keep confidential information in a safe place and dispose of it when you no longer need it.

Identifying information and costs

Some agencies require a Social Security number (SSN) and date of birth (DOB). The rental application in this book does not call for a DOB, on the grounds that it will easily enable a disappointed, older applicant to accuse you of familial (age) discrimination should you reject them at an early stage of the application process (that is, before seeing the credit report, which will typically include the DOB). You should be able to get a credit report using an SSN or ITIN, as explained in Chapter 6. Agencies that require a DOB are asking for too much information, though you may find it difficult to obtain a report without one.

With most credit-reporting services, you can obtain a credit report the same day it's requested. Fees usually run $10–$20 per credit report, depending on how many reports you order each month and the features you order (such as a credit score, which is a standard add-on). More expensive packages will include a report from more than just one of the major reporting bureaus.

Charging your applicant for the report

When you're ready to order the report, you may process the applicant's credit card number or deposit the cash, check, or money order.

- **Credit card payments.** For applicants who gave you a Credit Check Payment form with their credit card information, run the number according to the instructions from the bank that you're doing business with. Note on the bottom of the form, under "Transaction run for credit report," the date you ran the card, the credit-reporting agency you used, your name, and the amount.
- **Cash, check, or money order payments.** On your copy of the Receipt for Credit Check Fee, under "Office use" at the bottom, note when you ordered the report, the name of the credit-reporting agency, your name, and the cost of the report.

What's in a credit report?

A credit report contains a goldmine of information on a prospective tenant's financial health and history, including:

- personal information about the applicant, such as employment history
- accounts reported monthly, such as department store credit cards
- accounts reported in default, showing whether the applicant has been late or delinquent in paying rent or bills, including student or car loans, or whether the account has been discharged in bankruptcy
- public records, such as evictions and civil lawsuits, and
- inquiries from other creditors, such as car dealers.

Many credit reports also contain a credit score, a numerical rating of the likelihood that this person will not default on the rent (credit scores are explained in detail below). Finally, some special credit reports, called investigative reports, contain even more information, based on personal interviews with neighbors, landlords, and others. You'll get such a report if you work with a tenant-screening service, explained in Chapter 14.

The limits of credit reports

While it's important to get a credit report for every applicant at this stage of your screening, you should be aware that these reports are not easy to read and they are not necessarily accurate or up to date (no matter what hype you read on the credit-reporting agencies' websites). Let's look at these issues a bit.

Credit reports are hard to read

The credit report is generated by a computer, with lots of shorthand and abbreviations. To shorten the printout, the type will be tiny and the layout cramped. You'll see different designs and features, depending on which of the three major bureaus generated the report. The bureaus often change the way their reports look.

If you're unfamiliar with credit reports, take a few minutes to go online to the three main bureaus and look for a sample report. Your experiences online will educate you more than looking at a sample report here—by the time you

---

How Are Credit Reports Compiled?

Credit bureaus mainly depend on others to tell them about consumers' buying and payment histories. The bureaus depend on monthly reports from the following sources:

- banks, savings and loans, credit unions, finance companies, and other commercial lenders that issue credit cards and make mortgage, personal, car, and student loans
- non-bank credit and charge card issuers (such as American Express, Discover, and Diner's Club), and
- large department stores, oil and gas companies, and other creditors receiving regular monthly installments.

Job histories come mainly from credit applications prepared by consumers when they apply for credit.

The credit report also reflects public records that are maintained by government agencies and are accessible to anyone. Local, state, and federal court filings are public records, as are the data kept at land records offices. Credit bureaus hire private companies to search public records for information such as lawsuits (including evictions and divorces), court judgments and judgment liens, foreclosures, bankruptcy filings, tax liens, mechanic's liens, and criminal arrests and convictions. In addition, federal law requires child support enforcement agencies to report child support delinquencies to credit bureaus.

read this, the look and feel of the reports may have changed, so you may as well look online at the most current versions you can find.

Credit reports can be outdated

The credit report is not infallible. Ironically, people who have the least to do with the credit industry—those with few credit cards, no installment purchases, few job changes, and no creditors at their heels—are the ones most apt to have an outdated report. The reason is simple—the bureaus depend on reported incidents of credit activity, and without activity, the report will be blank. Steady and modest consumers are largely below the radar. For example, the credit report for one such consumer, someone who's worked at Nolo for 15 years, shows her latest job as the one she left 20 years ago!

Credit reports can be inaccurate

Not only can a report be outdated and incomplete, it can be just plain wrong. Mistakes are rampant, especially among reports for consumers with common names. Irony is at work here, too—concerned over identity theft, businesses now ask consumers for the minimum of identifying information. The unintended consequence of not putting a full SSN or a date of birth next to a reported consumer transaction or delinquency is that it's easier than ever for a bureau to confuse one consumer for another. It's

also very common for bureaus to fail to note accounts whose delinquencies have been remedied.

Consumers can get one free copy of their report every year, and people who are looking for rentals are well advised to get the report and check it for accuracy and completeness (your Rental Policies advised them to do just that). If your applicants have followed directions, their reports should be accurate or at least contain their statements with their own versions of disputed issues. Since you've asked applicants to check and correct their reports, you can assume that the report and any statements are accurate and you can deny an application based on what you see. In reality, you may want to at least give the applicant a chance to explain and respond, however, since it's always possible that an error has crept in since the applicant last checked.

The usefulness of the credit report may be questionable

In the end, you must have a realistic understanding of the limitations of the credit report, and you should consider listening to applicants who react in amazement when you tell them what you've read. The report is not going to tell you much about applicants whose involvement with credit (credit cards and installment purchases) and the court system is low to begin with. Applicants at the other end of the scale—those with tons of debts, lawsuits, or evictions—will generate a more useful report, and it's probably accurate (the chance that there's a mistake of identity goes down as the number of entries go up).

How to evaluate an applicant's credit report

The following sections explain what you'll find in a credit report, covering what each entry means and what kinds of entries constitute red flags. Unfortunately, the credit bureaus all arrange their reports differently, so that the look and feel of each is quite different. But they all include the elements discussed here.

There are several specific ways that the credit report will help your screening efforts. If it's complete and accurate, it will:

- corroborate identifying information reported on the rental application, such as the applicant's name, SSN, and other information
- corroborate the applicant's job and salary
- confirm any reported evictions, bankruptcies, and other lawsuits, and confirm credit accounts, installment purchases, and loans, and
- provide additional information, such as any wage garnishments or tax liens.

As you go through the sections below, you'll see a Warning discussion after each explanation. These highlight red flags that may crop up in two general ways:

- **When information on the credit report doesn't square with answers on the rental application.** For example, you'll want to reject an applicant (or contact him or her and inquire) if the SSN varies from the one listed on the rental application.
- **When additional information in the credit report shows that the applicant may be a poor risk.** For example, you'll see more details on bill-paying history in the credit report than in answers on the rental application.

Use the second column of the Credit Report Evaluation worksheet, entitled Red Flags, to note when you find something worrisome on any element from the credit report. Before starting, be sure to fill in the applicant's name, where and when you got the report, your name, and the date you're evaluating the report. Having one sheet of paper that sums up what you've learned from the credit report will help you as you discard the clear rejects and rerank this pile of applications before advancing to the next screening stage (calling references). For more information on when to reject or be flexible on specific issues, look back at Chapter 10, which explained how to evaluate answers on the rental application (you'll be looking at the same information in the context of the credit report).

You'll find the Credit Report Evaluation on the CD-ROM that accompanies this book. A sample is shown below.

Personal information about the applicant

A credit file usually includes the subject's name and any former names, past and present addresses, Social Security number, and employment history (including salary).

Whether an applicant is married, separated, divorced, or single, his or her credit file should contain information about the applicant only. Information about both spouses should appear in both files only if both spouses are permitted to use or are obligated to pay an account. For example, information about joint accounts should appear on both spouses' credit reports, though the name of the spouse may not appear (a mortgage, for example, may be described as a "joint contractual responsibility").

Make sure that the name, current address, employment, and Social Security numbers match. If you've recorded the date of birth, check this too. Mismatches may indicate identity theft; they could also be mistakes on the part of the reporting bureau.

Compare the date of birth shown on the report with the date that the applicant first used credit (for example, when the applicant got a credit card or purchased an item in an installment sale). If the gap is 30 or more years, the information in the report may not belong to this applicant (most people engage in credit transactions before the age of 30). Large gaps may also indicate that this person was incarcerated, or was married and the credit was in the spouse's name (if the latter, you may want to question the applicant).

Accounts reported monthly

Most information in a credit file covers credit history. Certain creditors (see "How Are Credit Reports Compiled?" above) provide monthly reports to credit bureaus showing the status of the applicant's account with them. The credit report will contain the name of the creditor, type of account, account number, when the account was opened, maximum credit allowed, and the applicant's payment history—that is, whether this person takes 30, 60, 90, or 120 days to pay. You'll also see whether the account has been turned over to a collection agency, whether the account has been discharged in bankruptcy, or whether the applicant is disputing any charges. If the applicant has outstanding loans, you'll see the applicant's credit limit or the original amount of a loan and the current balance.

As you review the credit card accounts your applicant uses, note how close he or she gets to each card's limit. Will this applicant be able to handle a sudden expense by putting it on a credit

Credit Report Evaluation

Applicant: _____Maureen Jones_____

Report received from: _____ScreeningService.com_____ Date: __July 2, 20xx__

Evaluated by: __Katie Smith_____ Date: __July 3, 20xx__

Factor	Red Flags
Personal information	OK
Accounts reported monthly	a few late phone bills (last late payment was 2 years ago)
Accounts reported when in default	OK
Public records	OK
Bankruptcies	none
Evictions	none
Inquiries	OK
Personal statements	none
Credit score	700

Conclusions

No discrepancies between rental app. and credit report. Credit score is OK—
advance this applicant.

_____

_____

_____

_____

card—or is he or she close to being maxed out? If the applicant is spending (and charging) up to the limit, your rent bill might be the one that suffers if an unexpected expense hits.

⚠️ **An applicant who has many credit accounts that are paid later than 30 days may have a hard time paying your rent (it's due in 30 days, too).** If collection agencies are in the picture, you know that money management has been a problem for this applicant. Applicants who have maxed out their limit have no cushion, and may have a harder time paying the rent than those who can shift sudden expenses to a credit account. If there are accounts that were discharged in bankruptcies, the date of the discharge should correspond to the applicant's self-report of the bankruptcy on the rental application (analyzing a bankruptcy is covered below).

Accounts reported when in default

Many businesses provide information to credit bureaus only when an account is past due or the creditor has taken collection action against the holder. In these situations, the credit report will generally include the name of the creditor, type of account, account number, and the delinquency status— whether the debtor is 60, 90, or 120 days late; whether the account has been turned over to a collection agency or

the debtor has been sued; or whether the account has been discharged in bankruptcy.

Creditors who generally report accounts only when they are past due or in collection include landlords and property managers, utility companies, local retailers, insurance companies, magazines and newspapers, doctors and hospitals, and lawyers and other professionals.

While creditors tend to report these accounts only when they are past due, credit bureaus increasingly gather monthly information from utility companies, phone companies, and local retailers to add to credit reports. The goal is to increase the data contained in files of people who don't have much traditional credit history, such as young people and immigrants.

⚠️ **If you see unpaid rent reported by a landlord, you should inquire further.** At least call this landlord or question the applicant. Many landlords view utility bill-paying behavior as a reliable indicator of rent-paying behavior, and they will view unpaid phone, gas, electricity, and other routine bills as a big red flag.

You should also be wary of what you *don't* see. Any applicant with a serious dispute with a landlord, hospital, insurance company, or doctor or other professional has been hounded for payment and been told that the past-due account will be noted on the applicant's credit report (and that the applicant has a right to add his or her own 100-word statement disputing the debt). If you don't see any statements, you can assume the debt is legit and the consumer just hasn't dealt with it.

Public records

This portion of the report includes debts that have been turned over to a collection agency, tax liens, wage garnishments, foreclosures, lawsuits that resulted in judgments against the consumer (but not criminal convictions), as well as bankruptcies and evictions (covered separately below). You may also see information regarding divorces and annulments.

⚠️ **Wage garnishments are a serious matter, indicating that the applicant has refused to pay a debt that's been adjudicated by a court.** Pay some attention to debts that your rental application didn't ask about, such as tax liens. When you add up the total debt load, the applicant's ability to shoulder your rent may be in doubt.

Bankruptcies

The report should note (perhaps in the public records section) any bankruptcies that were discharged within the past ten years. If a bankruptcy is an automatic disqualifier for you, this will be the first you've learned of it (since you asked about bankruptcies on the rental application). You may want to reject now, on the added grounds of an inaccurate application.

If your applicant did report the bankruptcy, and you've advanced the application to this stage, you're obviously willing to look beyond the filing to the applicant's post-bankruptcy financial behavior. You recognize that filing for bankruptcy and being financially successful and responsible afterwards may be indicators of very responsible behavior, especially when the bankruptcy was caused not by wanton spending, but by job loss, medical expenses, or other unavoidable disasters (you may see a 100-word explanation from your applicant explaining the cause, as suggested in Chapter 6). Here's how to use the credit report to confirm what you know and give you important additional information:

- If the applicant's written explanation pointed to medical expenses, look for evidence of doctors' and hospital bills in the report.
- If the applicant described a job loss, make sure it's reflected in the report. Steady employment before and during the bankruptcy tells you something is fishy.
- What kind of bill-paying behavior do you see after the discharge? A return to high spending and late payments tells you that the unwise spendthrift habits may repeat.

⚠ **If you see a pattern of big credit card debt both before and after a bankruptcy, you can conclude that the applicant is following a ruinous pattern.** This bodes ill for you as the next in a long line of creditors. When the applicant's explanation for the cause of the bankruptcy doesn't square with entries on the report, you've probably been told a tale, and can reject (or at least inquire further).

⚠ **Reject if you have a no-evictions policy and the applicant lied on the application.** If you're willing to evaluate the eviction in the context of the overall picture, look for unpaid accounts, frequent job changes or other legal entanglements. Reject if the picture that emerges is one of a rule-breaking individual. Most landlords will reject if they see more than one eviction.

Evictions

Some credit reports will give you eviction information (usually in the section on court judgments or public records). Resist drawing conclusions based on who won an eviction lawsuit. If the tenant won, he or she might have had a righteous case—or just a sympathetic judge. On the other hand, perhaps a victorious landlord was justified—or maybe he or she just outgunned the tenant. You will never know.

For most landlords, an eviction record is the kiss of death. If you're willing to look further, however, consider any eviction in the context of the applicant's overall application. Some landlords, like some employers, doctors, and lawyers, are unscrupulous and take advantage of tenants. Most tenants will leave as soon as possible, but some will stay and fight. If you see an eviction, consider its age and what's happened since.

Inquiries

The final section in a credit report is called "inquiries." These are the names of creditors and others who requested a copy of this person's report during the previous year or two. There are two kinds of inquiries, and you should be concerned only with the first:

- **Hard inquiries** come from sources that consumers ask to look at their reports, such as potential employers, landlords, and merchants.

- **Soft inquiries** can come from someone offering a consumer unasked-for credit (such as a credit card company), a merchant (such as a used car dealer) who gets a window-shopping customer to sign a form allowing the merchant to pull a report, a current creditor performing a review of a consumer's file, or the credit bureau itself (in response to the consumer's request for a copy of his or her report or complaint that the file is inaccurate).

Lots of hard inquiries indicate that this applicant is actively looking for work, housing, or credit. There's nothing inherently wrong with this—unless you see something that doesn't mesh with information you already have. If the applicant listed his or her last residence as a five-year tenancy, but you see two periods of inquiry within that time (and can conclude they're for housing, based on the report seeker's name, such as "Shady Oaks"), you may suspect that there was a tenancy or two within that period that the applicant didn't report—and perhaps all was not smooth sailing. Pay attention to these hard inquiries, too:

- **Applicant's request for credit.** If you already know that the applicant is maxed out on credit cards and see that he or she is looking for more, beware—this person is not attempting to live within his or her means.

- **Inquiries from government agencies, particularly district attorney and human services offices.** These offices are in charge of enforcing child support orders, which are a debt like any other. While you shouldn't automatically think less of someone with child support, you're entitled to worry if that person is the subject of an enforcement agency's repeated inquiries.

- **Inquiries from collection agencies.** These outfits don't bother going after someone unless there's

something to collect—so they run a credit check. If you rent to this person, the current address will be picked up by the agency, which may find and garnish your tenant's wages (thus imperiling his or her ability to pay the rent).

Be careful not to draw negative conclusions based on many landlord inquiries, as long as they match the applicant's rental history. Remember, if every landlord insists on pulling a credit report for him- or herself, there will be many entries if this applicant is casting a wide search, and particularly if the market is tight.

Personal statements

People who believe that their credit report contains incomplete or inaccurate information may dispute its inclusion in the report. For example, it's not uncommon for consumers to pay a disputed debt but find that the merchant has failed to remove the unpaid account from the report. When the consumer complains, the credit bureau is obliged to investigate, and if the bureau doesn't come to a resolution that's acceptable to the consumer, the individual can write a "personal statement." The statement (or a summary of it) must be included in any credit report. The statement needn't be included if the consumer is explaining extenuating circumstances or other reasons why the debt couldn't be paid.

Credit score

The credit score is a number that is *supposed* to indicate the risk that an individual will default on payments (like rent). The credit score is sometimes known as a "FICO" score (named for the biggest credit-scoring company, Fair Isaac Corporation). Only Equifax uses the "real" FICO score; TransUnion and Experian use their own, similar scoring methods. A bare-bones credit report won't include a credit score, but you can order one for a little bit extra (with some reporting agencies, you'll have no choice but to pay for one). The true value of a FICO score is debatable, as explained below in "What does the score really tell you?"

Fair Isaac uses several factors when generating credit scores—but interestingly, income is not a factor. The issue is how people manage what they have, as evidenced by:

- the individual's on-time bill-paying history (about 35% of the score)
- amounts owed on credit accounts (about 30% of the score). Fair Isaac looks at the amount owed on all accounts and whether there is a balance. They are looking to see whether the consumer manages credit responsibly. It may view a large number of accounts with high balances as a sign that the person is over-extended.
- length of credit history (about 15% of the score). In general, a longer credit history increases the score.

- any new credit (about 10% of the score). Fair Isaac likes to see an established credit history without too many new accounts. Opening several accounts in a short period of time can represent greater risk.
- types of credit (about 10% of the score). Fair Isaac is looking for a healthy mix of different types of credit. This factor is usually important only if there is not a lot of other information upon which to base a score.

What's an acceptable range?

FICO scores range from lows of 300 to 400 to highs of 800 to 900. High credit scores indicate less risk, and low scores indicate potential problems. Fair Isaac estimates that about 40% of Americans have scores over 750. Anything over 750 is considered to be a very good score by most lenders and should be sufficient for your purposes, too (see more about evaluating the score below). Most landlords will sign on to the following guide:

Credit Score Ranges	
Score	**Risk**
340 to 500	worst risk
501 to 550	high risk
551 to 600	medium to high risk
601 to 650	medium risk
651 to 700	medium to low risk
701 to 820	low risk

Ironically, a score of 700 or above may indicate that this person won't remain your tenant for long, since someone with a score like this can probably get a loan to buy a house or secure a mortgage! Still, many people are choosing to remain tenants, for perfectly good reasons.

⚠️ **Credit scores can vary according to who supplies the information and when.** Fair Isaac calculates a FICO score based on the data provided by each credit bureau. It's common to see up to a 50-point difference among ratings. A bureau may have inaccurate information, and bureaus collect data at different times of the month.

A new credit-scoring player appeared on the scene in 2006. VantageScore creates a risk score ranging from 501 to 990 (higher numbers mean less risk), and is used by all three major credit bureaus. VantageScore is supposedly superior to FICO and other scoring methods because it can more readily create a report for consumers with limited credit histories.

What does the score really tell you?

A low FICO score does not necessarily tell you that this person will be a poor rent-paying tenant. Look at the score in the context of the entire credit report. In particular, look for:

- **High and one-time medical bills, student loans.** High medical bills, including co-pays, can lower a score and paint an unfavorable picture of even the best tenant. The same is true for student loans. These persons may still be steady rent- and bill-paying individuals— look at the rest of their payment histories to find out.

- **Divorce.** Check the date of the divorce and look at payment history before and after. If you see positive credit history before, but evidence of struggles after (thus causing the low score), take that into account. Your applicant may need some time to recover, and he or she may not necessarily be an irresponsible tenant.

- **Utility bills.** FICO scores are affected if these are delinquent. Here, you should be concerned—a tenant who can't pay for this basic necessity is very close to not paying other housing costs, too, such as the rent.

- **Maxed-out credit cards.** A consumer with one maxed-out card will score lower than someone with the same amount of debt that's spread over several cards, each of which is utilized no more than 30%. How fair is this? Someone who pays one maxed-out card on time is not necessarily a worse risk than someone who has spread his or her debt load around, right? Well, yes, except in this respect: If there's a sudden expense, the multiple-card holder will be in a better position to pay for it by charging it to one of several cards (thus leaving some money available to pay your rent).

- **Inquiries.** The credit score will go down if there are lots of recent inquiries. Take a look at who the inquiring parties are, as explained above, and discount the value of the credit score if there are lots of soft inquiries.

⚠ **There's some evidence that card companies are underreporting credit levels, which hurts a credit score.** Keep this in mind when looking at credit limits and the utilization score.

To sum up, if you get a credit score, evaluate it in light of the entire picture presented by this applicant. If it corresponds to what you've learned thus far, by showing that this person is not seriously spending beyond his or her means and disregarding current bills, that's all you need to know. But if it doesn't fit the picture that's emerged thus far, spend some time taking it apart along the lines suggested above. You may find that a low score reflects events or issues (such as a medical emergency that generated huge bills) that are not likely to recur.

💡 **To keep up on credit-scoring develop- ments,** visit www.creditscoring.com, a private website devoted to credit scoring.

Rerank your applications

If you're fortunate, the entries you saw on applicants' credit reports simply confirmed their own reporting as contained in the Rental Application. In that event, you can take this pile to the next stage, calling references. You may, however, need to rethink the rankings, by:

- rejecting those who lied to you on the rental application (see Chapter 15 for how to legally communicate that rejection), or
- moving some applications up or down in the standings based on additional information you gained from the report.

Take a look at the notes you made in the Red Flags column on your Credit Report Evaluation. If you noted some worrisome aspect of the financial picture—say, a poor bill-paying history—you may want to drop this applicant behind someone else who doesn't have this or any other negative mark. Or, you may want to consider accepting this applicant but only if he or she can supply an acceptable cosigner. Or, you may want to make some follow-up calls if the red flag is so out of whack with what you've seen so far that you suspect it's a mistake and something your applicant can easily clear up.

It's up to you to weight what you noted in the Red Flags column and take action accordingly, and there's no reasonable way to ascribe points or grades to what you've entered. You'll simply need to look at the entries, consult your common and business sense, and decide whether the entry merits an upward or downward move for this applicant, or further investigation. As long as you can give a solid business reason for your decisions, you will be on legally safe grounds. Record your decision in the Conclusions section at the end of the Credit Report Evaluation worksheet.

Before moving on, take a moment to go back to the Tenant Information Sheet for each applicant. Enter your findings and conclusions in the section titled "Credit report." Your entries there might look something like the ones below.

! **If you reject based on what you learned in the credit report, you *must* follow specific procedures to communicate that rejection.** Don't just pick up the phone—send the required letter. Chapter 16 shows you how to do it.

Handle credit reports, criminal background reports, and tenant-screening reports carefully

Under federal law, you must take special care that credit reports (and any information stored elsewhere that is derived from credit reports), tenant-screening reports, and criminal background reports are stored in a secure place where no one but those who "need to know" has access. ("Disposal Rule" of the Fair and Accurate Credit Transactions Act of 2003, known as the FACT Act, 69 Fed. Reg. 68690.) In addition, you must dispose of such records when you're done with them, by burning them or using a shredder. This portion of the FACT Act was passed in order to combat the increasing instances of identity theft. It applies to every landlord who pulls one of these reports, no matter how small your operation. The Federal Trade Commission, which interprets the Act, encourages you to similarly safeguard and dispose of *any* record that contains a tenant's or applicant's personal or

---

Tenant Information Sheet (excerpt)

Credit report

Looks fine—plenty of available credit. Information consistent with rental application.

Summing Up the Credit Report

After reviewing the credit report, note your conclusions on the Tenant Information Sheet.

Negative findings	Positive findings
Several credit cards, each maxed out—no cushion	No late payments, credit cards not used to the limit
Employment information differs from application, could not verify application entries	Employment and residence information matches application
Charge-offs by two department stores	Department store balances are zero, "never late"
Recent bankruptcy, followed by new credit cards (high balances)	No bankruptcies; no negative results of lawsuits
Unexplained gaps in residences, employment history (see application)	No residence or employment gaps
Low credit score	High credit score
Collection actions by electric company and phone company	Few hard inquiries for credit
Many maxed-out credit cards, wages garnished, several collection agencies in the picture—drop to bottom of ranked pile, consider requiring cosigner	

financial information. This means that you should handle rental applications in the same manner.

Implementing the Disposal Rule will require some effort and follow-through, though it need not be a burdensome chore. Follow these suggestions:

- **Maintain applicant, tenant, and employee files in a locked cabinet.** This is a good practice for many reasons. Only you and your manager should have access to these files.

- **Determine when you no longer have a legitimate business reason to keep an applicant's credit or other report.** The Act requires you to dispose of credit reports or any information taken from them when you no longer need them. Unfortunately, you may need these reports long after you've rejected or accepted an applicant—for example, they may be essential in refuting a fair housing claim. Under federal law, such claims must be filed within two years of the claimed discrimination, but some states set longer periods. Keep the records at least two years and longer if your state gives people extra time to file a fair housing claim.

- **Establish a system for purging old reports.** Don't rely on haphazard file purges to keep you legal when it comes to destroying old reports. Establish a purge date for every applicant for whom you pull a report and use a tickle system.

- **Choose an effective purging method.** The Disposal Rule requires you to choose a level of document destruction that is reasonable in the context of your business. For example, a landlord with a few rentals would do just fine with an inexpensive shredder, but a multiproperty operation might want to contract with a shredding service.

- **Don't forget computer files.** Reports stored on your computer or PDA (such as a BlackBerry), or information derived from them, must also be kept secure and deleted when no longer needed. Purchase a utility that will "wipe" the data completely—that is, a program that will delete not only the directory, but the text as well.

The Disposal Rule comes with teeth for those who willfully disregard it—that is, for those who know about the law and how to comply but who deliberately refuse to do so. You could be liable for a tenant's actual damages (say, the cost of covering a portion of a credit card's unauthorized use), or damages per violation of between $100 and $1,000, plus the tenant's attorney fees and costs of suit, plus punitive damages. The FTC and state counterparts enforce the Act and impose fines. For more information on the Rule, go to the FTC website at www.ftc.gov and type Disposal Rule in the search box on the home page.

Take Ten Minutes

Now that you've finished reviewing credit reports, make sure your ranked set of acceptable applications is ready for the next step:

- You may have decided that some discrepancies between a rental application and credit report merit a follow-up. Settle these issues before advancing the applicant to the reference check stage.
- If you rejected some applicants outright, consider the number of applicants left in your ranked pile. Do you have enough, in view of the market and the attractiveness of your place? If necessary, go back to the runners-up from the rental application rankings and run credit checks on the highest two or three.
- Enter your conclusions at the credit check phase on each applicant's Tenant Information Sheet—even those you don't advance. If you are later challenged on the reasons for not advancing an applicant, you may need to point to your notes as evidence that you applied sound business judgment at this step.

Checking Landlord, Employer, and Personal References

An applicant's current and previous landlords and boss can be extremely helpful in your tenant screening. By now you should have gone through the first three steps of the five-step screening process described in Chapter 1:

- prescreened applicants on the phone or at an open house
- reviewed the completed Rental Applications (eliminating the clear rejects, ranking the others), and
- done a credit check (sending rejection letters and reranking, if necessary).

You're now ready for the fourth step—calling references to see if the top candidates will be good tenants who will pay the rent, be considerate of your property, and be good neighbors. This chapter explains how to interview past landlords, employers, and personal references and maximize the results you get from these efforts. This chapter assumes you will be doing the calls yourself. If you do not want to make these calls, consider hiring a property management firm or engaging the services of a local real estate office—but don't skip this step.

⚠ Call references for all proposed tenants. Just as you know to pull a credit report for all proposed cotenants, be sure to contact references for all roommates, too. Even if you have written letters of recommendation, follow up with a phone call to confirm that the letter is legit.

✔ Before You Call References

☑ Be sure you have applicants' written authorization to contact references. You may need to fax this authorization, so get a signed copy of the applicant's Consent to Contact References and Perform Credit Check form.

☑ Have your schedule handy, in case it's inconvenient when you call and you need to make a separate appointment to talk.

☑ Print out a copy of the Tenant References form (or open the file on your computer), enter the name of the applicant, the rental property address, and each reference's contact information. If you call more than one employer or landlord, use your word processor to copy and paste needed sections to the form.

☑ Contact any applicant whose reference names and contact information didn't match up with what you found on the credit report, and clear up the discrepancy.

Landlord's Forms Library

Tenant References. This is a Worksheet to keep track of your conversations with an applicant's current and previous landlords, employers, and personal references. It consists of key questions, such as whether a tenant paid the rent on time.

Be sure to keep notes of all your conversations with references and keep them on file. You'll especially want to keep a record of negative information—such as a description of damaged property from a previous landlord—so that you can survive a fair housing challenge if a rejected applicant claims your rejection had discriminatory motives.

Contact past and current landlords

A frank conversation with a fellow landlord can be the best source of information on any applicant. This person has had the same business relationship with the applicant as you will have, understands your business, and can tell you specifically how this person measures up as a tenant.

Your best bet is a conversation with your applicant's *past* landlord. Not the current landlord—the one before, or before that. Why? Because if, for example, this person is a problem tenant, his current landlord has every reason to sing his praises in order to get rid of him. He'll become your problem tenant. For that reason, call a prior landlord before you contact the current one, if possible (your Rental Application has space for applicants to list a prior landlord). When you're dealing with someone who's been renting from the same landlord for ten years, however, don't bother looking for the prior landlord—you can assume that a ten-year tenancy is a good one (but do call to confirm!).

Occasionally, a group of roommates will move together to a new place. When you call that current landlord, you can ask about the behavior and rent-paying histories of each tenant. Make sure you have a Tenant References form for each roommate, and enter the landlord's remarks on each roommate's form.

Questions to ask previous landlords

You'll want to learn as much as possible about the tenant's behavior from other landlords. The Tenant References form guides you through the key questions to ask them (you'll see that the questions for the current landlord are slightly different than those for prior landlords). Simply jot down the answers you get to the questions on the form (adding a sheet if necessary), which should cover:

- **Move-in and move-out dates, reason for leaving, and whether the tenant gave proper notice.** First, make sure that the tenant's rental application information matches what the landlord tells you. Any discrepancies should raise a red flag. Be concerned if the tenant left with inadequate notice.

- **Rent and payment history.** You'll want to make sure that the tenant has a history of paying rent on time. If there were one or two late rent payments, was there a good reason and did the tenant work it out with the landlord?

- **Security deposit history.** You'll want to know if the prior landlord used the deposit to cover any damage during the tenancy, or if the current landlord expects to do so when this tenant moves out. If so, the tenant's finances may be significantly depleted, imperiling his or her ability to pay your rent.

- **Relationships with neighbors.** Ask if the applicant got along with neighbors and was considerate of their needs and space.

- **Landlord's own experiences.** What was it like to deal with this tenant— did the tenant cause damage to the property, make bogus complaints, act unreasonably when the landlord needed to enter to do repairs?

- **Was the tenant a good pet caregiver?** If you allow pets, ask if the tenant had a pet in the former living

situation too, and if so, did he take good care of the pet and clean up after it? Were there any complaints from neighbors about the pet, such as excessive barking or threatening behavior? (Don't stop here—be sure you meet the pet! See suggestions for evaluating pets in Chapters 6 and 10.)

If your policies disallow pets, ask current landlords if the tenant has a pet. People have a tough time giving up their pets—this person may plan on bringing his or her dog with him or her, despite your policy. (Remember, of course, that you must allow service or companion animals needed by disabled persons.)

Ask any other questions that will shed light on the applicant's ability to meet specific rental terms. For example, if yours is a smoke-free property, ask if the applicant is a smoker, and compare the response to the answer on the rental application. If you are concerned about home businesses, ask whether the applicant ran one and whether there were problems. If you have a garden, and the tenant's prior or current situation includes a garden, too, ask how well the tenant tended it.

Suppose your applicant has indicated that he or she has a criminal record, and you're willing to look at the whole picture rather than rejecting outright (Chapter 10 covers how to evaluate the relevance of a criminal background).

Naturally, you'd want to ask the current and prior landlord or employer whether they've found this part of the applicant's past to be a problem. Don't do it unless you are positive that the reference already knows about the conviction. As relevant as you think the answer may be, understand that your applicant has shared this information with you, not them. Revealing this aspect of your applicant's past could have serious consequences for the applicant, and could land you in a lawsuit for invasion of privacy. If someone with a past conviction is still acting illegally or otherwise creating problems, you'll learn the truth by methodically going through the multiple screening steps outlined in this book (you can get a thorough criminal background check if you wish, as explained in Chapter 13).

If your applicant is a family, question the current landlord as to the number of residents this applicant currently lives with. Are there minor children living with the applicant now but not mentioned in your application? It's best to double check with applicants when you suspect that there may be more to the family than initially reported—but if you learn that more people will be living in the rental than you were told, you may reject as long as your occupancy policy is legal.

How did the current and prior landlords screen this tenant?

You might also ask a current or prior landlord what kind of screening they used when choosing this tenant. The answer can help you. For example, suppose the landlord tells you he screened extremely closely, and was well satisfied with the tenant's performance. That should reassure you. On the other hand, if the outcome was not so rosy despite careful vetting, perhaps this applicant misrepresented key information to the prior landlord—and may be doing the same with you.

If the landlord used a tenant-screening company (covered in Chapter 14), ask if you can have a copy of the report. Although the report will be dated, it could be useful to you, for corroboration purposes if nothing else. If you reject based on what you read in that report, you'll need to send the applicant an adverse action letter, described in Chapter 16.

You'll find a file for Tenant References on the CD-ROM that accompanies this book. A sample appears below.

Start your conversation by making sure it's a good time to talk. Explain the purpose of your call and that you only need 10–15 minutes to ask a few questions about the prospective applicant. If it's not convenient, make an appointment to talk at a later time.

When you call, you may find that the landlord will talk freely, without need of the applicant's written consent. If someone asks for proof that the applicant has given permission for the

Tenant References

Name of applicant: __Barry Moran__

Address of rental unit: __1185 "D" Street, Collegetown, CA__

Current Landlord or Manager

Current (name, property owner or manager, address of rental unit): __Doris Wong__
__Oaks Apartments, 38 10th Avenue, Collegetown, CA__

Date: __July 10, 20xx__

Questions

When did tenant rent from you (move-in and move-out dates)? __June 30, 20xx–__
__July 1, 20xx__

Was this tenancy ☑ Month-to-month ☐ One-year lease ☐ Other, specify:
_____

What was the monthly rent? __$1,000__

Did tenant pay rent on time? ☑ Yes ☐ No   Notes: _____

Did you have to give tenant a legal notice demanding the rent? ☐ Yes ☑ No
Notes: _____

Did you have to give tenant notice of any lease violation other than nonpayment
of rent? ☐ Yes ☑ No   Notes: _____

Was tenant considerate of neighbors—that is, no loud parties and fair, careful use
of common areas? ☑ Yes ☐ No   Notes: __Pretty good—other than one loud__
__party__

Were there problems with unauthorized roommates or excessive number of guests?
☑ Yes ☐ No   Notes: __One unauthorized roommate (became a tenant)__

Did tenant have any pets? ☐ Yes ☑ No   Notes: _____

If so, were there any problems? ☐ Yes ☐ No   Notes: _____

Did tenant make any unreasonable demands or complaints? ☐ Yes ☑ No

Notes: _____

[Tenant References, page 1 of 5]

Why is the tenant leaving? _Says he wants a bigger place_

Has tenant given notice? ☑Yes ☐No   Notes: _____

Do you think you'll need to use the security deposit to cover damage or uncleanliness? ☐Yes ☐No _____ _don't know_ _____

What screening tools did you use when choosing this tenant? _he was_
recommended by another tenant—checked employment + prior landlord

Any particular problems you'd like to mention? ☐Yes ☑No   Notes: _____

Would you rent to this person again? ☑Yes ☐No   Notes: _____

Other comments:
Landlord seems to be forthright.

_____

_____

_____

_____

· ·

Prior Landlord or Manager

Current (name, property owner or manager, address of rental unit): _Tamara Wise,_
Resident Assistant, Blake House (University)

Date: _July 9, 20xx_

Questions

When did tenant rent from you (move-in and move-out dates)? _his sophomore_
year in college (Fall 20xx–Summer 20xx)

What was the monthly rent? _____ _n/a (part of university fees)_

Did tenant pay rent on time? ☑Yes ☐No   Notes: _n/a_

_____

[Tenant References, page 2 of 5]

Did you have to give tenant a legal notice demanding the rent? ☐ Yes ☐ No
Notes: _____ n/a _____

Did you have to give tenant notice of any lease violation other than nonpayment of rent? ☐ Yes ☐ No   Notes: _____ n/a _____

_____

Was tenant considerate of neighbors—that is, no loud parties and fair, careful use of common areas? ☐ Yes ☐ No   Notes: _ as much as any other student ... _

Were there problems with unauthorized roommates or excessive number of guests?
☐ Yes ☑ No   Notes: _____

Did tenant have any pets? ☐ Yes ☑ No   Notes: _____

If so, were there any problems? ☐ Yes ☐ No   Notes: _____

Did tenant make any unreasonable demands or complaints? ☐ Yes ☑ No
Notes: _____

Why did the tenant leave? _ semester ended _____

_____

Did tenant give you the proper amount of notice? ☐ Yes ☐ No   Notes: _ n/a _

_____

Did you have to use the security deposit to cover damage or uncleanliness?
☐ Yes ☑ No _____ his room checked out okay _____

What screening tools did you use when choosing this tenant? _ n/a _____

_____

Any particular problems you'd like to mention? ☐ Yes ☑ No   Notes: _____

_____

Would you rent to this person again? ☑ Yes ☐ No   Notes: _ Resident _
   Assistant says he was an OK kid _____

Other comments:

_____

_____

_____

_____

conversation, immediately offer to fax the applicant's consent form, and set up a time to call back and resume the conversation after the fax has arrived.

Don't draw immediate conclusions about landlords who don't call back. This person may not be willing to take the time to talk to you, or may have lost your phone number. Or, he or she may have nothing but bad things to say and is fearful of sharing them. Make one more attempt to talk and then move on, and consider asking for another reference to make sure you develop a full picture of this applicant.

References you're asked not to call

Don't be surprised if applicants ask you not to contact current landlords. Like job-seekers who ask that their current employer not be alerted to their job search, so, too, applicants may not want their landlords to know they're planning on moving. Applicants make this request for one of three reasons:

- **Fear of preemptive termination.** This applicant hasn't told his landlord that he's looking, and worries that when the landlord finds out, she will deliver a preemptive termination notice. Suppose, for example, a month-to-month tenant is looking in the summer and hopes to move to a new place in the fall. He's searching at a time of year when there are lots of rentals available

(and lots of tenants searching), but when he gives notice to his current landlord (perhaps in September), that landlord will begin advertising at the worst time of year (close to the holidays). Knowing this, the current landlord may deliver a 30-day notice when he learns of his resident's plans in August, so that she, too, can advertise during the high season.

- **Fear of a poor (but unjustified) reference from a bad landlord.** Applicants may also tell you that their current landlord is a jerk and will give an undeservedly bad recommendation.

- **Fear of a poor (but justified) reference from a landlord.** It's also possible that you're dealing with a problem tenant who doesn't want his or her current landlord to share the truth with you.

How should you handle applicant requests not to call their landlords? First and foremost, you must not let the applicant dictate your screening decisions, and you must talk to the current landlord before making an offer.

Here's how to proceed:

- **Applicants who have not given notice.** Tell your applicant that you will respect his request not to contact his current landlord—initially. If he progresses through your screening, by remaining in the running after you've reviewed his Rental Application, credit report review, and employer and personal references, you will need to talk to the current landlord. In the meantime, make sure you talk to a past landlord or two; or ask whether there is anyone at this rental address (perhaps a sympathetic neighbor or employee) who will talk to you and keep the matter confidential.

- **Applicants who tell you that the current landlord is a jerk and will unfairly criticize them.** These applicants are alerting you to a bad rental situation and you must check it out. You may want to initially defer (and rely on alternate sources, as suggested above), but do make the call. Beware the landlord who says, "Oh, no problems at all! They're wonderful residents!" This landlord really does have a problem with your applicants and is praying that you'll take them off his or her hands. In that event, you'll need to rely on other sources of information to decide whether the problem at this site is landlord driven (as your applicants claim) or tenant driven. Applicants' true colors will consistently emerge as you gather information from multiple sources.

How to get information from reluctant landlord references

In an ideal situation, the landlord reference will be willing to talk and have a lot to say about the applicant. In some cases,

landlords are friendly but terse, and you may need to draw them out on things like long-term guests, problems with noisy parties, or an unreasonably demanding tenant.

If you encounter a landlord or manager who isn't forthcoming with answers to your questions, consider the circumstances. A current landlord may feel caught between a desire to get rid of a troublemaker and not wanting to lie—in this event, silence probably indicates a negative recommendation. Some landlords are excessively worried about lawsuits, and will answer with "name, dates (of the tenancy), and monthly rent" only, even for residents who were okay. To smoke out some information, try these questions (enter the answers in the "Other comments" section of the Tenant References form):

- "Do you have a policy against giving references?" A landlord who says yes may just want to get off the phone; one who says no may be signaling to you that you need to read between the lines (since he can't say anything nice, he's choosing to say nothing at all).
- [For prior landlords] "Is your current tenant an improvement over this tenant?" If your applicant was a problem, the answer will be a hearty "Yes!" If the current resident is a step down, you'll probably learn about your applicant by way of comparison. Either way, the answer will be revealing.

- "Would it help if I faxed you a more complete release form?" If the prior landlord's hesitation is due to fear of a lawsuit, your offer to send a more effective shield (though our consent form is perfectly adequate) should reveal it. Take heed—if a fellow landlord is worried about lawsuits filed by this person, perhaps you should be, too.

- "Were you able to advertise the unit right away?" This question seeks information on how the applicant left the rental. Landlords who tell you that they had to completely refurbish a unit after a year's tenancy may be saying, "This tenant left the place a mess." Get some details if you can.

How to uncover false landlords

Some applicants will give you a list of "past landlords" who are simply friends willing to front for the applicant. It's hard to expose these imposters because, unlike employers, small-scale landlords don't have to perform the verifiable tasks (such as filing a "dba" or "doing business as" statement) that employers must accomplish. (You can check up on supposed employers that way, as explained below.) Obvious tip-offs that you're dealing with a fake include:

- an unusually gushing recommen-dation (a businessperson normally doesn't feel so moved)

- vague answers to detailed questions that a real landlord would remember about this applicant or the property (this landlord should know whether the applicant asked to do some painting or other alterations during his or her tenancy), and

- inability to understand common landlording lingo. For example, if you make "small talk" and mention "Schedule E," a fumbled answer or silence at the other end suggests you're dealing with someone who's not in the business of residential renting.

The above tip-offs are simply that—they aren't proof that you're talking to a pretend landlord. Here are some additional ways to unmask an imposter:

- **Check out the supposed rental address at your county recorder's office.** People who offer false prior landlords may make up an address—but if it doesn't exist, you won't find a match in the local land title office. Many counties have their records online and have made them searchable.

- **Use a mapping program on the Internet.** A mapping program will point to made-up addresses on real streets, but not fake streets. If the applicant lists a street that doesn't exist, the program (such as *MapQuest*) won't be able to find it (or will tell you it's only been able to find something similar).

- **Drive by.** If the prior rental is within reasonable driving distance, just drive by. You may find that the address doesn't exist or is a single-family home lived in by the same family for decades.
- **If the address is in a multifamily building, find the owner or manager yourself.** A made-up address that includes "Apartment 10" tells you that this is a large complex with multiple units. Find it in the phone book and determine the contact information yourself. If it's different than the name and phone number on the application, you know that you've been given a real address but a fake landlord.
- **Give some incorrect information and see if the reference verifies it.** Here are a few examples:
  - **Rent.** Include in your conversation: "The monthly rent was [state an amount that's different from the one reported on the application] and the security deposit was [state a similarly different amount], right?" Unless the friend was extremely well coached, you'll hear a stumble or an assent.
  - **Length of stay.** Or you might say: "I understand [the applicant] lived at your property from [incorrect start date] to [incorrect ending date]." Again, the false landlord will usually go along with your statements.
  - **Personal information.** Intentionally misstate the applicant's number of children, spouse's name, or the make and year of the applicant's vehicle. If you're dealing with a real landlord, he or she will correct you on at least one of these. A pretender is more likely to go along, thinking that his or her role is to mollify you, not set you straight.
  - **Say something about the rental.** Refer to a make-believe event, neighbor's name, or feature of the property. A real landlord will correct you ("No, actually the neighbor's name was Jim," or "We don't have high-speed Internet— are you sure you're calling the right property?"). A pretend landlord will usually agree with you.

Alternate sources of information for first-time renters

If your applicant is a first-time renter, such as a student, you won't be able to talk with current or past landlords. Having a cosigner will help you secure a source of rent (see the discussion and sample agreement in Chapter 15). Chapter 10, "Step 2: Rental History, When to be flexible," suggests contacting employers, teachers, counselors, or community or youth group leaders for alternate sources of solid information on a young person's character.

Recording your conclusions on the Tenant Information Sheet

After your conversation, sum up what you've learned and write your conclusions on the applicant's Tenant Information Sheet discussed in Chapter 7, in the "Current and past landlord references" section. Your conclusions may look like the sample, below.

Stop when you've heard enough. No law requires you to call additional references when you learn something that puts this applicant out of the running, such as a thoroughly awful report from a prior landlord. There's no reason to call the employer.

Contact current employer

The next step in your evaluation process is to contact the applicant's current employer to find out whether the person would make a good tenant—for example, that he or she is reliable and gets along well with others. First, you'll verify that the applicant actually works there and earns the amount entered on the application (remember, the rental application asked for pay stubs, so you should have this information already). Jot down your answers in the Employment Verification section of the Tenant References form.

You may well find that employers (or their human resources departments) will not talk with you without written consent from your applicant. If you encounter such a request, offer to send the separate form your applicant signed (the Consent to Contact References and Perform Credit Check), and set up a time to resume your conversation.

Employers you're asked not to call

You may occasionally hear an applicant tell you that he has a horrible boss and wants you to check with a coworker or someone else at the company. You have less reason to defer to this request than when an applicant asks you to skip his current landlord, because whether someone moves has little to do with job

Tenant Information Sheet (excerpt)

Current and past landlord references

Both landlords would do business w/ him again—no serious issues

security—in other words, an employer has little reason to retaliate when hearing that an employee is changing apartments.

It's a different situation when your applicant is moving from another city or state and will be leaving a job where he or she hasn't yet given notice. Like the applicant who fears a preemptive termination from a landlord, this applicant may be worried that his or her employer will fire him or her immediately. Here, too, you can be flexible but not give up this important source of information. Explain that you will eventually need to talk to this employer if the applicant makes it through the initial stages of your review. Check to see whether the applicant has a job lined up in your city—someone who is moving to a new city without a firm job offer will be a poor risk for you and someone you might eliminate early on anyway.

Questions to ask employers

Since there are many qualities in a good employee that also make a good tenant— such as punctuality, ability to get along with others, respect for others' property, and honesty—you'll want to discuss these issues with the applicant's employer or supervisor. This won't always be possible—see the next section, which addresses what to do when an employer will give only employment dates and salary—but if you encounter an employer who's willing to have a conversation, take

advantage of it. Here are questions you'll see on the Tenant References form:

- "Does the applicant come to work on time? Meet deadlines?" These types of questions may tell you about whether you can expect the rent on time, too.
- "Does the applicant get along with coworkers?" Hopefully, friendly relations with coworkers spell neighborliness, too.
- "Have you had occasion to reprimand the employee within the past 12 months? What for?" Someone who breaks the rules at work may not respect your boundaries, either.
- "Is the employee's work station or office neat and clean?" An employee who takes care of his or her work space may also take similar care of your property.
- "Has the employee made unreasonable demands of coworkers or management?" Someone who's a prima donna or shirks work may become an equally demanding tenant.

Listen carefully as you talk with employers—you may hear some very important information, delivered inadvertently. For example, do you hear anything that suggests that this person is on the cusp of a promotion—to another work site, perhaps? You may be dealing with someone who will have to break her lease to take her new position.

What doesn't the employer tell you?

Finally, listen to what the employer does *not* tell you when you ask specific questions, and read between the lines. Often, an employer will not want to give negative information, but won't want to lie, either. One way out is to not answer a clear question directly, but instead to talk about something that is innocuous but true—for example,

- You, "Has the applicant made unreasonable demands at work?" The employer, "We run a pretty smooth operation here."
- You, "Does the applicant get along with others?" The employer, "I don't see any written record of complaints."
- You, "Does the applicant come to work on time and meet deadlines?" The employer, "You'd need to speak with [another person] about that—unfortunately, he's not here at the moment."

Whether you want to press on when an employer stonewalls you is a matter of how persistent you're willing to be. Often a follow-up question will tell you all you need to know—this person is not going to be helpful. For example, in the third example above, if you ask when you might speak with the relevant employee and are told, "Well, actually, that person doesn't work here anymore," give up and concentrate on other sources.

How to get information from reluctant employers

Alas, in this day of heightened awareness of employees' privacy, many employers won't give you more than name, rank, and serial number, even when you've sent them a broad release like the one in this book, and even when they would have nothing but good things to say about the applicant. If you run up against a stickler like this, there may not be much you can do.

On the other hand, you may be able to get some information around the edges that will prove useful. Try asking the question, "Does your company have a policy against giving information beyond an employee's date of hire and salary?" Here's what you may get in response, and what that response may signal:

- **If the employer reluctantly says yes**—especially if he adds that it's been foisted on him by higher-ups or the lawyers—you may be getting a signal that, except for this restriction, the speaker would like to give some positive information. Follow up with a question about the speaker's view of the policy. If you continue to hear resigned and sympathetic remarks (such as, "I know it's hard to get information—I run into the same problem when hiring employees—and this rule hurts the good employees, too. But my hands are tied"), you may be getting an indirect recommendation.

....

Employment Verification

Contact (name, company, position): _Dave Ho, Linkso Corp, Database Team_
Supervisor

Date: _July 12, 20xx_   Salary: _$40,000/year_

Dates of employment: _March 20xx–present_

Does the employee come to work on time and meet deadlines? ☑Yes ☐No
Notes: _____

Does the employee get along with coworkers? ☑Yes ☐No   Notes: _____
_____

Have you had occasion to reprimand the employee within the past 12 months?
☐Yes ☑No   Notes: _____

Is the employee's work station or office neat and clean?   ☑Yes ☐No

Notes: _____

Has the employee made unreasonable demands of coworkers or management?
☐Yes ☑No   Notes: _____ He's got good ideas, but is sometimes pushy. ____
_____

Would you recommend this person as a prospective tenant?   ☑Yes ☐No
Notes: _____

Other comments:
"He's a nice guy." _____

_____

_____

_____

_____

_____

_____

_____

_____

_____

_____

[Tenant References, page 4 of 5]

- **If you hear a curt, "Yes, that's the rule,"** you may be able to conclude that the speaker is grateful that he doesn't have to give you unflattering details about his employee. Of course, it is possible that you're simply dealing with a harried worker who doesn't want to give you any more time. In large companies especially, when human resources departments may be overloaded and not have much personal contact with workers, this "party line" could be just that, and it would be unfair to jump to conclusions.

- **If you hear "No, we have no such policy,"** take heed. Individuals who choose not to give information beyond the basics are almost always doing so because they would have negative things to say.

How to uncover false employers

Now and then, you'll encounter an applicant who lists a made-up employer— a friend willing to fill the role. Or, the applicant will list a real job but give you the name and phone number of a friend who plays the part of the employer. The pay stubs you've required as part of the application packet can also be faked. Like false prior landlords, these pretenders can be unmasked with a few well-placed questions and legwork on your part. If you're tipped-off by an "employer" who sounds too gushy or too vague, consider these steps:

- **Look up the company in the phone book or online.** If the company exists but the number you've been given doesn't correspond to the number you find, call the public number and ask to be connected to the person your applicant listed. It's possible that your applicant gave you a direct number—but it's also possible that no one by that name works at this company. You'll find out.

- **If the employer is a corporation or limited liability company or limited liability partnership (LLC or LLP), look on your state's website for evidence of these business entities.** (These types of business entities must file papers with their home state.) Your state's official site is www.[state postal code].gov, and registration information is often found on the secretary of state's site. Most states have a query system that enables you to search for a name and see whether the entity has an active registration.

- **If the employer is a partnership or is a sole proprietor (someone doing business by him- or herself), the business must file a "dba," or "doing business as" statement with the county of residence.** Again, many counties have online databases that are searchable by name.

- **Ask "the employer" to follow through with a written document.** Now and then, you may suspect that an applicant has listed a real company and given you the real owner—but you suspect that the applicant doesn't work there and the owner is a willing friend. Perhaps your suspicions were aroused because the applicant hasn't attached any pay stubs (conveniently explaining that the job is brand new). To uncover this ploy, ask the "employer" whether he or she would be willing to fill out *and sign* a description of the applicant's job and pay. Many will get nervous and say no. Be sure to follow up and ask the applicant to provide employment information for his or her *previous* job. Applicants who are pulling this ruse are usually ones without jobs, having been fired from their last. You may reject applicants in this situation.

Alternate sources of information for self-employed or unemployed applicants

Like first-time renters, self-employed applicants present you with a challenge.

You need alternate sources of information to determine whether this person has the financial and behavioral good tenant traits you're looking for. Chapter 10, "Step 2: Evaluating the application answers, Employment history" suggests what to ask for when dealing with a self-employed person (tax returns, references from vendors and commercial landlords). An unemployed applicant can be similarly checked out—with students, require a cosigner and references from school.

Recording your conclusions on the Tenant Information Sheet

As you did when you finished talking to current or past landlords, go back to the applicant's Tenant Information Sheet and turn now to the "Employment references" section. Looking again at the notes you made on the Tenant References form, summarize your findings and write the summary on the information sheet. The "Employment references" entry might resemble something like the one below.

Tenant Information Sheet (excerpt)

Employment references

Boss says no problems. Salary confirmed. "Nice guy."

Contact personal references

The application provides a place for applicants to list personal references—names of friends, relatives, teachers, or anyone whom the applicant believes will give them high marks. By definition, these references are there to serve the interests of the applicant, and the information they give you ("Gee, he's a great guy!") is impossible to verify. But they still provide useful information, particularly for someone you're on the fence about or a first-time renter who does not have landlord references.

When you call personal references, try to determine whether the speaker has enough experience with the applicant to form the glowing opinion you'll surely hear. This is also an opportunity to check on the truthfulness of certain statements on the application. Here are a few sample questions; jot your answers down on the "Personal Reference" section of the Tenant References form:

- "How long have you known the applicant?" Enthusiastic descriptions of your applicant carry more weight the longer the reference has known the applicant (but you also want current experience—the friend who hasn't seen your applicant for a few years may be quite out of touch with what he or she is like now).
- "In what capacity (friend, employer, teacher, relative) have you known the applicant?" Generally, a reference from someone who

has dealt with the applicant on a business level will be more relevant than a friend or relative.

- "Have you ever been in a business relationship with the applicant?" If yes, ask how this worked out. If not, ask whether this person would consider entering into any type of business venture with the applicant. Remember, you are about to begin a business relationship with this person. If you hear, "I don't think it would be a good idea…" ask further. You may hear that the applicant is a nice person but impossible with money—not a good quality in a tenant.
- "Have you ever lived with the applicant?" If this question is appropriate to ask, the answer will tell you a lot about the applicant's ability to be considerate of others and take good care of your property.
- "Can you give specific examples of the qualities you've just mentioned?" If the reference can give you a detailed and believable context for his or her opinion, it will be more persuasive than a generalized, "She's a wonderful person, I'm sure you'll be satisfied." You may also learn that the reference's standards aren't worth much (you can discount the reference who enthusiastically praises your applicant's partying style, and not much more).

Personal Reference

Contact (name): ___Mary McShane___

Date: ___July 10, 20xx___

How long have you known the applicant? ___Since he was a little boy___

In what capacity have you known the applicant?

☑friend   ☐roommate   ☐coworker   ☑Other _neighbor_

Have you ever been in a business relationship with the applicant?   ☐Yes ☑No

Notes:___

Have you ever lived with the applicant?   ☐Yes ☑No

Do you think the applicant will be a stable tenant?   ☑Yes ☐No   Notes: _____

"I've always thought he was responsible—he used to walk my dog and do my

yard, and did a good job."

Have you been asked by the applicant to serve as a reference before?

☑Yes ☐No   Notes: ___to get a summer job___

Would you recommend this person as a prospective tenant?   ☑Yes ☐No

Notes: ___

Other comments:

[Tenant References page 5 of 5]

- "Have you been asked by the applicant to serve as a reference before? For what purpose?" You might learn some interesting things here, including information that will either corroborate or contradict statements on the application or information you received from other sources. For example, if the personal reference says, "I was called by the fellow who runs the restaurant where Joe works," ask when that happened and for the name of the restaurant. The reply should correspond to the employment information on Joe's application. If it doesn't, that's a red flag.

After speaking with the personal reference, evaluate the results with a grain of salt. You should have heard the same things you did when speaking with prior landlords and employers—descriptions of the applicant's reliability and consideration for others. If you hear otherwise—or are tipped-off to possible false statements on the application—this step will have been well worth your time.

Now, turn once again to this applicant's Tenant Information Sheet and write down what you learned from the personal references in the "Personal references" section.

Reranking and rejecting applicants after talking with references

Now it's time to take another look at applicants' rankings. First, pull out any applications that you will clearly reject (such as the one whose employer told you that the applicant no longer worked there as of last week). See Chapter 16 for information on how to communicate the rejection.

Next, rerank the resulting group if the information you learned from references changes the standings. Did one applicant shine above the others, with detailed, believable reports from current and past landlords and employers? These qualities may be better indicators of a probable good tenant than so-so reports on someone who makes more money or

---

Tenant Information Sheet (excerpt)

Personal references

Thesis advisor thinks v. highly of him. Lacrosse coach says he's a team player, v. responsible.

has a lower debt load. Or, did you hear worrisome things from someone who impressed you with their professional assessment of the rental and apparent steadiness (maybe the current landlord refused to talk to you, the employer was not forthcoming, and the past landlord told you he or she would not rent again to this applicant).

Some of you will want to take the added step of checking to see if your top-ranked applicants have a criminal record. Read Chapter 13 for information on the pros and cons of such a decision, and how to go about getting a report. If you are not going to do a criminal background check, you're done! The applicant at the top of your ranked pile is the best bet for you. Skip to Chapter 15 for information on how to accept tenants (including those whom you'll accept subject to an acceptable cosigner).

■

Checking Applicants' Criminal Backgrounds

Your nightmare tenant is a drug dealer, deadbeat con artist, child or spouse abuser, or opportunistic thief. Visions of late-night police raids and ribbons of caution tape surrounding a crime scene are enough to make you wonder why you don't invest in stocks instead of residential rental property. How likely is it that these fears will become reality? To a large degree, you can protect yourself, your tenants, and your property by thorough screening and questioning. This book shows how conventional methods, such as setting rental policies that signal your intent to run a tight ship, and contacting landlord and employer references, will identify and weed out applicants with relevant criminal backgrounds. This chapter covers additional tools—checking Megan's Law databases and hiring a firm to perform a criminal background check—and the legal and practical issues involved with using them.

Your qualified legal right to reject tenants with criminal backgrounds

With a few exceptions, you are legally free to reject someone with a criminal background. Ex-convicts are not a protected category under state or federal antidiscrimination laws, with the exception of applicants who have convictions for past drug use. As explained in Chapter 2, the Fair Housing Amendments Act classifies past drug addiction as a disability, even when that addiction resulted in a criminal conviction. Persons with convictions for drug sale or manufacture, however, are not protected, nor are people who currently use illegal substances.

Well, that's clear enough, you say—I'll have no legal worries if I reject applicants with records, as long as they aren't for drug use, right? Not quite. Here are a couple of restraints on that position:

- If your state or local laws prohibit "arbitrary" discrimination—that is, discrimination on the basis of one's personal characteristic or trait, such as body size, occupation, or style of dress—you might find a judge who will rule that having a criminal record constitutes a personal characteristic. In California, for example, the statewide ban on arbitrary discrimination has been applied to people of unusual dress or appearance. See Chapter 2 for more on this issue.

- If your property is in California or New Jersey (or in Madison, Wisconsin), you cannot access Megan's Law databases to deny rental housing. See "How to do a Megan's Law search on your own," below, for more on this topic.

If these limitations don't apply to you, don't jump to the conclusion that you can reject ex-cons at will, past drug users excepted. Lawyers for released felons have formulated several ways of

The Law You Need to Know

Many state and federal laws are involved in criminal background checking. They don't add up to a consistent message, as you'll see from the list below. This chapter tries to help you navigate the law with a minimum of confusion and risk.

- The federal fair housing laws give you clear permission to deny housing to persons with drug manufacture or sale convictions. They also *forbid* you from denying housing to persons solely because of their drug use convictions. With every other conviction, it's not so clear.
- State law in California and cities in some states forbid arbitrary discrimination. Landlords subject to these laws may find that courts consider it "arbitrary" to reject applicants solely on the basis of a criminal record.
- California and New Jersey (and Madison, Wisconsin) landlords cannot use their state's Megan's Law databases for the purpose of denying housing.
- In multifamily rentals, you have a legal duty to protect, or at least warn, tenants about known dangers. That's why you must reject someone whom you know poses a current, direct threat to safety.
- In many states, privacy rights are sacrosanct. You may be civilly liable if you reveal an applicant's or tenant's past to your other residents.
- If you pay a criminal background search firm to do a background search, you must inform applicants no more than three days before ordering the report, according to the Fair Credit Reporting Act.
- If you reject an applicant because of information contained in a background report, you must send an adverse action letter as your rejection (see Chapter 16).

challenging this position, and lawyers for landlords are taking them seriously. (In the section below, "The risks of running a criminal background check," you'll see a few of them.) In fact, rather than advising their clients not to worry about blanket rejections of all but past drug users, some legal experts have changed the conversation. They've counseled their clients to ask of every applicant with a record, "Does this person currently pose a direct threat to me or other tenants or to the property?" Only when landlords can say "Yes" to the latter question will they be on safe legal footing when rejecting on the basis of a criminal record.

✓ Before You Run a Criminal Background Check

☑ Perform conventional screening, such as check credit reports and references, so that any information you learn can be measured against what you already know.

☑ Understand the risks of ordering a background check, and evaluate whether the gain is worth the risk.

☑ Check your state's restrictions, if any, on accessing Megan's Law databases.

☑ Get signed permission from your applicants before ordering a criminal background report.

How to avoid renting to people with dangerous criminal backgrounds

The screening process recommended in this book will help you find and choose tenants who pay the rent on time, take good care of your property, and are considerate neighbors. It's designed to screen out people who are not only likely to cause you relatively minor problems, such as late rent payments and spats with neighbors, but it will expose those who are likely to be more of a threat, whether they have a criminal background or not. In other words, in the course of your normal screening, you may have exposed the bad guys already (or they may have dropped out voluntarily, sensing that they were about to be found out). Here's a summary of how this works:

- **Announce a rental policy of renting only to applicants who demonstrate a history of honest, nonviolent behavior and inform applicants of this policy.** Chapter 6 advised you make this part of the Rental Policies handout you provide applicants. Some applicants with recent, unsavory convictions may drop out at this point, and never even bother to complete an application. Others, with old and arguably irrelevant convictions, may decide to proceed. If someone's record is indeed old and superseded by many years of lawful living, you may decide that they're not a current, direct threat, and that you won't reject simply on the basis of their criminal past. (Chapter 10 has more information on how to make this decision.)

If you're bound and determined to smoke out applicants with criminal histories, announce that you will run a criminal background check on every applicant to whom you make an offer—but don't run checks on anyone. Applicants won't know you're bluffing and they may drop out if they think that you'll be taking this extra step. Be sure to always ignore your policy, to avoid fair housing issues—that is, don't run criminal background checks on anyone. But beware—suppose a tenant (for whom you didn't order a report) turns out to be an ex-convict with a past that should have disqualified him. If he commits a crime on your property, you may face legal trouble from any victim-tenants (they'll argue that you all but guaranteed a crime-free property).

- **Ask about criminal convictions on the rental application.** The rental application included on the CD-ROM asks applicants if they've been convicted of any crimes and, if so, to provide details. See Chapter 10 for advice on evaluating what the applicant's answers tell you about whether this person is likely to pose a risk to other tenants or to property. You may eliminate applicants who report a criminal background on their application

that leads you to conclude that they pose a direct threat to other tenants or property.

- **Run a credit check on all applicants whose rental applications pass muster and compare it to information entered on the rental application.** If you see discrepancies—a job listed on the application that's not on the report, or claimed employment without mention of the employer on the report—you may be dealing with someone who was in prison for a period of time and trying to fill in the gaps. This is one way you'll catch those who have not answered truthfully on the application.

- **Interview past landlords, employers, and personal references.** As you've probably gathered by now, interviewing past landlords, employers, and references requires you to be a bit of an investigator. If you're looking to expose those who have falsely answered, "None" to your rental application question on criminal convictions, you'll want to probe and compare—where are the discrepancies, the gaps, the stumbled responses? If you get an inconsistent picture about where the applicant was living and where he or she was working, you may be dealing with someone who is concocting a past.

Despite your careful screening thus far, you may still be hesitant to make an offer to someone who has made it to the top of your ranked list but who, you fear, may have lied on the rental application and escaped your detection thus far. If you want the assurance of extra screening (though its value is debatable, as shown below), it's time to go to the next level by paying an online criminal-background-checking service to canvass criminal conviction databases, or checking some of them yourself. There's no reason to take this step before you've exhausted your conventional screening, because those methods will normally expose most bad risks. At the end of this chapter, you'll see some advice on whether the expense and risks are worth this extra step, in view of your situation and your rental property.

The basics of criminal background checks

Beyond asking an applicant directly and learning indirectly through references and possibly a credit report, there are three ways to get information on a prospective tenant's criminal background:

1. **Check your state's Megan's Law database of crimes against children and sexually violent crimes against adults.** This is something most landlords can do themselves, as described later in this chapter.

2. **Pay an online background-checking service to examine national data-bases of convicted persons.** These firms will also check Megan's Law databases and reveal civil lawsuit judgments (including evictions) marriages, licenses, unclaimed money, death records, and lots of other information that's available in databases that the firms pay to access. The prices vary widely, from less than $10 to $200 or more, depending on the number of reports.

3. **Hire a tenant-screening firm, which will canvass conviction databases.** These firms (also known as resident-screening firms) will also deliver credit reports and verify bank account information, employment history and income, rental and eviction history, and Social Security number, and will sometimes recommend a tenant as a good risk. Chapter 14 discusses these firms in detail.

Since background-reporting services access public records, why do you need their services for a criminal conviction search—can't you do it yourself? It's a matter of access—these firms tap into electronic databases that are public knowledge but not available in their online form to the public. Some screening services even claim to have access to the FBI's Terrorism Watch List, which is off-limits to individuals.

The risks of running a criminal background check

When you decide to run a credit report, you ask one of three national organizations to furnish the report, whose contents are accurate in most cases. Unfortunately, no such simplicity and reliability exists with criminal background reports. Here are some of the problems.

Risk #1: You won't get reliable information

Criminal background screening is notoriously unreliable. The information just isn't complete or accurate, for these reasons:

- Reporting agencies rely on public records that have been automated and posted to an accessible database. But not all courts are automated (especially those in less-populated or less-affluent areas). And not all of them post information to the databases used by the screening services.
- The Fair Credit Reporting Act prohibits agencies from reporting information that is more than seven years old (other than bankruptcies, which can be reported for ten years).
- Accurate matches are very difficult, because people can be convicted under multiple names and files may lack corroborating information such as Social Security numbers.

- Inaccurate matches are common, because many people share the same names.
- Megan's Law databases, in particular, are infamously out of date and incomplete, as described below.

The upshot is that a search may miss your applicants entirely, confuse them with other people, or give you a "false pass" by failing to find some convictions. The result is that you may end up offering a rental to someone who does indeed have an unsavory past; and you may deny someone who had the misfortune to have a name that sounded similar to a convicted felon's.

Risk #2: A thorough search is costly and time-consuming

A criminal background search will cost at least $40 and often more (the packages offered by these services sometimes resemble fly-by-night tour operations). State laws that allow landlords to charge for running a credit report do not include permission to charge for a criminal background check, so you'll be footing the bill yourself.

To be completely thorough, you'll have to search everywhere the applicant has lived (because not every state or city will post their records to an online database). But a nationwide search is unrealistic— only a few states have records that a searching firm can access online. The rest of the country will have to be searched by hand—a process that could take weeks and cost thousands. No landlord (or set of applicants) will wait that long (let alone pay that much).

Risk #3: You won't get relevant information

Not only is it unrealistic to believe that you'll get reliable, quick results from a criminal records searching firm, but you won't necessarily get information that is relevant to whether the applicant is currently a direct threat to others' health or safety, or to property. Here's why:

- **The actual crime the person was convicted of may be the result of a plea bargain, bearing little resemblance to the crime that was charged.** For example, drunk driving is often pled down to "unsafe driving." The plea may have everything to do with the prosecutor's inability to prove the original charge (maybe the defendant is, in fact, innocent of the original charge)—or it may be the result of a heavy court calendar, a missing witness, or over busy prosecutor. The point is, you'll never know how that "unsafe driving" conviction started out, and why it ended as it did.
- **Some crimes that show up on your report shouldn't form the basis of a rejection, unless you know more.** For example, a conviction for embezzlement, tax evasion, or another white-collar crime,

tells you nothing about whether the applicant is a threat to your property or other people.

Risk #4: You may be sued by a rejected applicant

No one with a criminal record (other than for use of illegal drugs) who has been rejected by a landlord has successfully sued the landlord over that rejection. However, only one case has squarely held that landlords are at liberty to consider an applicant's criminal past, and it's binding only in Wisconsin, Indiana, and Illinois (*Talley v. Lane*, 13 F.3d 1031 (1994)). In other states it's an open question. Lawyers who represent tenants have all sorts of theories to support a case against landlords who have blanket policies against renting to those with any criminal past. They include:

- **Denying housing equals double punishment.** This person already paid for the crime with time in jail; inability to rent a home is added punishment.
- **Fair housing laws impliedly protect past offenders.** The federal law gives landlords clear permission to reject only those convicted of drug manufacture or distribution. By implication, other offenders may not be so summarily rejected.
- **Denying housing amounts to racial discrimination.** More minorities than nonminorities are convicted of crimes, so when landlords

deny housing to ex-offenders, more minorities are affected than nonminorities. When a practice has the effect of discriminating against a minority, a judge may call it discriminatory even when the landlord intended to avoid ex-offenders, not discriminate against a minority. Discrimination like this is called "disparate impact" discrimination.

- **Denying housing may amount to sex discrimination.** This theory is like the one mentioned just above—those convicted of crimes are overwhelmingly male, so when you reject based on a criminal background, you'll be rejecting more men than women.

Taken together, these theories present a worrisome front. Landlords' lawyers take them very seriously, and they account for the conservative advice ("Don't do a background check") that many give their clients.

Risk #5: An offender will slip through your screening, commit a crime, and you'll get sued

Finally, the cruelest cut of all: You do your best to screen out offenders, but fail to learn of someone with a bad past (Risk #1). He or she becomes your tenant and commits a crime on your property—and you get sued by the victim. How can this happen? When you screen and announce it as a policy (which you'd be wise to do, in order to let some applicants opt out), a court might decide that you sent the message to tenants that no one with a criminal record will end up residing on your property. As a result, the theory goes, tenants will feel safe, will stay, and perhaps not take adequate safety precautions. If victims can convince a judge or jury that your representations lulled them into a false sense of security, you may become liable.

Criminals Don't Soil Their Nests

A study of crime at apartment complexes showed that 93% of all crimes on the property were committed by strangers, 2%–3% by employees of the owner or management company, 2%–3% by residents' guests, and only 1%–2% by residents themselves. Arguably, you have more to fear from strangers than from residents. (Source: National Apartment Association *Legal Symposium*, November 16, 2005.)

Risk #6: You decide to rent to someone with a nondangerous criminal past, don't tell your other tenants, and this person commits a crime on your property

Suppose you run a background check and come up with convictions that reasonably appear to be benign—they don't tell you that this person currently poses a direct threat to other tenants or your property. For example, you may uncover an old conviction for a white-collar crime or even a violent crime that was followed by years of law-abiding behavior. You rent to this individual and, alas, he commits a crime on your property. If the victim of this crime learns that you knew of the perpetrator's past, the victim may sue you. The theory is that once you learned of the past conviction, however irrelevant you thought it was, you had a duty to warn your tenants of the possible danger living among them. If a tenant can show that a warning might have resulted in the victim taking precautions or in any way avoiding the incident, a judge or jury might find that you're in some degree responsible for the consequences.

Risk #7: You decide to rent to someone with a nondangerous criminal past and you tell your other tenants

Finally, consider the fact pattern in Risk #6, but suppose that you decide to inform other tenants of your new tenant's past. Now you potentially face two unpleasant results:

- **Your new tenant sues you for invasion of his or her privacy.** In some states, especially California, courts take invasion of privacy claims very seriously.
- **Your tenants disagree with your assessment of the risk and decide that they don't want to take a chance—they leave.** To make matters worse, tenants with leases claim that the new tenant's presence posed such a serious threat that they are legally excused from honoring their leases (in legalese, the theory is that you have "constructively evicted" them). If a judge buys their theory, you won't be able to hold them financially responsible for the balance of the lease, as you could with any other lease-breaking tenant (subject to any state-imposed duty to re-rent, of course).

The risks of not running a criminal background check

Now let's look at the flip side—what risks do you take if you do *not* check Megan's Law databases yourself or hire a background reporting firm to check criminal conviction databases?

Risk #1: Other tenants will learn about a tenant's criminal past and leave in droves

If you rent to a person who has registered as a convicted sex offender, it's quite likely that your other tenants will find out about this person's past before you do. (All they have to do is visit their state's website and enter his or her name, as discussed below). Then, you'll be faced with a building full of anxious residents, many of whom will move at the first opportunity if their own circumstances permit it.

Risk #2: You may not be able to evict a person whom you learn has a criminal past

Suppose you learn from other tenants that you've rented to someone with criminal convictions, particularly someone on a Megan's Law list. You may be genuinely afraid for your other tenants' safety, or maybe you just want to stem the tide of good tenants leaving (Risk #1). Can you get that person off your property, when he or she hasn't committed any crimes there or otherwise been a problem tenant?

- **Month-to-month tenants.** If your tenant rents month-to-month, and your property is not in a city with rent control that requires just cause to evict, you can give a no-fault termination notice, which typically gives the tenant 30 days to leave. Your tenant could fight it by claiming that you're discriminating (see Risk #4, above, in the discussion of risks of running criminal background checks). If you want this person gone sooner, you'll have a hard time (see the next bullet point).
- **Tenants with leases or "for cause" terminations for month-to-month tenants.** You can't terminate a tenant's lease unless he or she has done something wrong (such as nonpayment of rent or other serious lease violations); and you can't terminate a month-to-month tenant in anything less than the usual 30 days unless he or she, too, has done something wrong. So, with a tenant who has not reoffended yet, where's the "bad act" that you need to support your termination? There isn't one.

You might be successful with a three- (or five-) day notice if your Rental Application, like the one in this book, specifies that material misrepresentations are grounds for termination. You run the risk that a judge might find that, since the tenant hasn't done anything wrong on your property yet, the tenant's failure to disclose was not material. In short, until the tenant does something that will clearly support a termination, you may have to make do with a no-cause termination (for month-to-month tenants) or wait until a leaseholding tenant's lease is up.

Risk #3: An offender will commit a crime on your property

Naturally, if someone is hurt, you will feel horrible. If there's property damage, your insurance company might reassess the risk of insuring your property and increase your premiums. The consequences will continue into the future, too, because now you'll have to answer in the affirmative if a prospective tenant asks you whether you've had any crimes on the property. No amount of "but it will never happen again because now I...." will erase the fact that crimes have happened on your watch. Worried prospects will look elsewhere.

Risk #4: An offender will commit a crime on your property and you'll be sued for not conducting a search

Finally, you must consider the possibility that you'll be sued because you *didn't* get a background report on someone who committed a crime against one of your other tenants. Although no court has yet to make background searching a landlord's duty (as it is with some kinds of employment), there's always a chance

that a judge somewhere will do so. Your chances for getting nailed on this one go up if you did not do thorough reference checking on your own. On the other hand, landlords who conscientiously screen in every respect other than running a background check are less likely to be held responsible when a criminal nevertheless slips through their net.

How to decide whether to do a criminal background check

If you thoroughly screen tenants as recommended in this book, you may feel that it's not necessary to do additional screening for criminal background, especially because of the risks involved. Or, you may be inclined to do a criminal background check because you don't trust applicants to accurately or completely self-report. And you may think it's a no-brainer, in view of the apparent accessibility of such information on the Internet. Unfortunately, the decision is not so cut and dried.

Unlike many other aspects of renting out residential property, there is no consensus among experts (lawyers, property managers, and owners) on the right decision. In years to come, court decisions, legislation, and technological advances (presumably resulting in more complete and accurate databases) will undoubtedly give you some guidance, but for now, it's quite unclear. In the end, the decision is going to be an individual one, which you'll reach by weighing the risks for and against the search in the context of your rental property situation. The chart "Criminal Background Searching: Should You Do It?" below, provides some guidance.

⚠️ **Don't make the mistake of running a criminal background check on only certain top applicants—for example, only men or only people of a certain ethnicity.** If you're going to run a check like this for the one or two who have made it to the top of your ranked list, you must run it for all who reach that point. Otherwise, you're inviting a charge of discrimination based on sex, age, ethnicity, or national origin.

If you've decided to check an applicant's criminal record, either by yourself (checking online databases or local court records) or by hiring an online firm, read on. If you're *not* going to undertake these steps, but will engage a tenant-screening firm (that will check criminal background, pull a credit report and more), go to Chapter 14. Those of you who are satisfied with your screening should go to Chapters 15 and 16, regarding choosing and rejecting tenants.

Inform prospective tenants of your policy and get consent

Your first step towards implementing a background-checking policy is to inform every applicant who gets a rental application from you, by including your policy in your Rental Policy handout, and obtaining applicants' consent (Chapter 6 has a form for that, too). The Fair Credit Reporting Act does not require disclosure or consent if you do the looking yourself, but it does require it when you pay an online service, so you should play it safe and get permission. But practically speaking, even if you're doing the checking yourself, it's a good idea to always

---

California Leads the Way

The California Apartment Association (CAA) advises their members not to do a Megan's Law search, period. The stand of the CAA may affect landlords in an unexpected way—when an industry leader with the stature of the CAA announces a policy, it can become, in a court's mind, the "industry standard" and the measure of reasonable behavior for all landlords.

Criminal Background Searching: Should You Do It?

There are many pros and cons to ordering a criminal background report for your applicants. The right answer for you and your property depends on many factors. This chart summarizes some of them.

Factors that suggest you might want to do a background check	Factors that point away from doing a background check
You have a multi-tenant building, which means you have a legal duty to protect your other tenants.	You are renting a single-family residence or a duplex and you live in the other half (you're comfortable with the screening you've done and are confident that you can uncover an unsavory past short of background searching).
Your other screening efforts are less than thorough—though this is hardly a legal excuse, if you're sued.	You will thoroughly screen tenants using the methods described in this book.
The rent is low—something a newly released offender could expect to pay.	Your rent is relatively high, which means that newly-released offenders, at least, won't qualify on income grounds alone. Of course, this will not exclude offenders who have secured good-paying jobs.
Your state or local law does not constrain you from using Megan's Law information to deny housing.	Your property is in California, New Jersey, or Madison, Wisconsin, which means you cannot use the state Megan's Law database for the purpose of denying housing. (You are, nevertheless, free to do other background searching.)
Your local or state antidiscrimination laws do not prohibit arbitrary discrimination (refusing to rent to ex-offenders might constitute arbitrary discrimination).	Your local or state antidiscrimination laws prohibit arbitrary discrimination.
Your local or state apartment association has not recommended against doing background searches.	Your local or state apartment association has recommended against doing a background search.
Your lawyer has advised you that you may safely do a background search, and you have this opinion in writing (if you're later sued, you may have recourse against this lawyer based on the advice).	Your lawyer has cautioned you against doing background searches for your applicants.

disclose and obtain consent, since many people *think* you must do both (just as they think they must give consent for you to pull a credit report). There are other sound reasons for disclosure and obtaining consent:

- **Disclosure may protect you from an invasion of privacy lawsuit.** An applicant who learns later that you canvassed online databases or ordered a criminal record search could sue you for invasion of privacy. By disclosing your intentions, you're giving the applicant an opportunity to opt out.
- **Self-screening.** When prospects learn that you'll do a background search, some with unsavory pasts will opt out of the selection process right there. That's a good thing for you—having them drop out before you order a report will save you time, money, and exposure to the risk of a lawsuit.
- **Discrimination protection.** If you follow the advice in this book, you'll order a report on every applicant who makes it to the top of your ranked pile of applications, after you've checked credit and references. Telling applicants that this will happen gives you some measure of defense if you're hit with a "disparate impact" lawsuit later (see Risk #4 in "The risks of running a criminal background check," above). For the same reason, you will always tell applicants that you

do not discriminate on the basis of race, religion, and so on.

The Rental Policies document you gave every applicant when handing out applications includes an optional statement on running a background check. Include the statement or modify it to suit your needs. You should also obtain applicants' consent to perform the search (use the form, Consent to Criminal and Background Check). See Chapter 6 for details on these forms.

How to do a Megan's Law search on your own

Megan's Law is the name given to laws in every state that require persons convicted of violent sexual offenses and sexual offenses against children to register with law enforcement wherever they live. Law enforcement uses the information to keep track of the registrants and to alert the community when they feel notification is warranted. Most states have posted their databases on the Internet, where anyone can search for a name and get information on that person's record and whereabouts, and sometimes see a photo.

Every risk identified above in "The risks of running a criminal background check" applies to your own use of a Megan's Law database. Knowing the problems, should you decide to go ahead, here's how to make the best of your search with the least amount of risk.

Observe state law restrictions on landlords' use of Megan's Law databases

Though every state maintains a database, not every state clearly allows the public to use the information for the purpose of denying housing. Restrictions are either in the statute or on the state websites, as shown below in "Restricting Your Use of Megan's Law." If you are subject to restrictions like these, you'll have to get your background information through another source, such as a background-reporting firm.

How to find your state's Megan's Law database

There is no official Megan's Law website. Instead, almost every state maintains a website with information on its Megan's Law database and instructions on how to access it. Simply type "Megan's Law [your state's postal code]" into a search engine. Or, go to www.klaaskids.org and choose

Restricting Your Use of Megan's Law

The following states and city limit landlord's use of Megan's Law database information. Other states and cities may follow suit in the future.

State or city	Rule
California	Database users may use the information to protect a person "at risk," but may not otherwise use it to deny housing. The California Apartment Association advises landlords in California to steer clear of Megan's Law searches.
Madison, WI	Landlords may not, in general, discriminate against anyone on the basis of an arrest or conviction record.
Massachusetts	Database users cannot use the database to illegally discriminate—though past offenders are not clearly protected by state antidiscrimination laws.
Nevada	The state's website indicates that users cannot use the information to discriminate.
New Jersey	Users can't use sex offender information to deny housing unless the denial promotes public safety (statute does not define what information, in what context, would promote public safety).

the Megan's Law link. You'll be taken to a page with links to every state. The site has summarized each state's provisions and provides a link to the state's search page and local links when they exist.

You may also want to try the numerous online services that purport to search a number of sex offender databases. If you do that, you're in effect ordering a criminal background search—whether the search is limited to Megan's Law databases or not is immaterial. The point is, now you're dealing with a criminal background report, covered below.

How to get a criminal background report

If you want the added assistance of nationwide checking for all criminal convictions (including Megan's Law offenses) and you don't want to search multiple Megan's Law sites yourself, you'll need to order a criminal background check on your applicants, using one of the ubiquitous online services. Here are some suggestions on how to maximize the value of the information you get, and minimize the chances that you'll encounter one of the risks discussed above. (You'll get such a report if you hire a tenant-screening firm, too, as described in Chapter 14.)

Make background checking part of a very thorough screening process

Don't make the easy mistake of thinking that a criminal background report will give you all you need to know about a particular applicant. In fact, for the reasons explained above, it may tell you relatively little (and it may be wrong). If you act on what the report tells you (whether you reject or accept) without also obtaining information from references and a credit report as suggested in this book, you may be setting yourself up for these scenarios:

- **The report misses a conviction that shows this applicant is a current danger to other residents or property—information that you could have used to reject.** You rent to this person, who commits a crime on your property. Had you done your own conventional screening (such as talking to prior landlords or employers), you may have discovered the facts. If you're sued by a victim, you may have a hard time defending your failure to double check a reporting system that you know is flawed.

- **You reject an applicant based on a criminal background report that has mistaken your applicant for someone else.** The applicant, who happens to be a member of a minority, sues you. Even if you win, you could have saved yourself a lot of grief by doing corroborative screening, which would have alerted you to the report's inaccuracies.

The lesson here is simple: Never order a background report unless you're prepared to use conventional methods to corroborate its information.

Choose a reputable criminal-background-reporting firm

Type "criminal background report" into your Internet search engine, and you'll get plenty of results. How to distinguish them? It's not easy. But a few minutes spent logging onto their websites will give you an idea of the scope of their searches, the extent to which they stand behind their results, and the general attitude of the operation. Let's look at some of these factors:

- **Scope.** There's no way that any search service can canvass every criminal court record, for the reasons explained above. If the website acknowledges that it's operating under these limitations, that's good; a blustery promise to search everywhere is bad. A firm that represents that it searches "on site" is puffing—they're not sending investigators to every courthouse in America. A site that promises access to "billions" of entries is exaggerating.

- **Coverage within a state.** Some firms claim they search huge numbers of records, but when you look at a state or two, the coverage is quite limited. For example, Sentrylink. com boasts 170 million records at its disposal, yet it covers only eighteen of California's 58 counties. Check the coverage for your state—aware, of course, that your applicants may have lived in any state.

- **Accuracy.** Most sites admit that they will not guarantee results, but some inspire downright fear. Here's a favorite: "This information is provided as reference material only, the information although obtained from official records CANNOT and should NOT be assumed to be accurate." Look for an outfit that aims lower (in terms of scope) and thus needs to disclaim less.

- **Turnaround time.** Instant searching will generally produce poorer results than searches that take a few days, because an instant search may miss databases that have to be specifically accessed for your report.

- **Sample report.** Take a look at the report layout and language. Choose an outfit that delivers easily read, jargon-free reports. Look also for help in deciphering the reports, perhaps on an FAQ page on the website.

- **Website appearance.** There's no excuse for a sleazy look. If you see handcuffs adorning every page, a promise to check up on your Friday night date for no extra charge, and text that reads like it was penned by a gangster, look elsewhere.

In the end, when picking such a service there's no substitute for references from other landlords whose judgment you respect, and some trial and error on your own part.

Enter your findings on the Tenant Information Sheet

If you've performed or ordered a background or Megan's Law search and report on your applicant, enter the results of the search in the "Additional screening tools" section of the Tenant Information Sheet. Hopefully, you can just say, "no convictions reported," as shown in the sample below.

How to reject following a Megan's Law or criminal background check

Very occasionally, you'll discover through a Megan's Law search or criminal background check done by a firm you hire that your top candidate has a conviction that eluded you during your own thorough screening. If you can reasonably say, "This person poses a current, direct threat to other tenants or the rental property," you'll be on safe legal ground to reject. But first, consider contacting the applicant to confirm the truth of the report, since it's very common for these reports to include mistaken information.

If you're convinced of the accuracy and relevance of the conviction information, the way you reject will depend on who has done the verifying or checking of the self-reported answers. When you or your employee does the checking, you may reject any way you wish. But when you're basing your decision even in small part on a credit report, criminal background report, or tenant-screening report, you have to follow the FCRA rules, which are explained in Chapter 16, Rejecting Applicants.

Tenant Information Sheet (excerpt)

Additional screening tools

Criminal background check (MegaSearch, 7/15/xx), shows no record.

Take Ten Minutes

Reading through this chapter has led you to adopt criminal background checking as your last step before making an offer—or not. If you *are* going to adopt this step:

- Make sure your Rental Policies sheet clearly states your intentions and that you give applicants your Consent to Criminal and Background Check form.
- Begin evaluating criminal-background-checking services before you get to the end of your own screening, so you can make the request without losing time.
- Talk with other landlords or landlord associations on the industry practice in your area—are landlords regularly ordering criminal conviction reports, and with what companies?

If you are *not* going to screen your top picks, look back through your notes for any indication of unexplained gaps in their rental or employment history. Check your notes from conversations with references for bits and pieces that may add up to grounds for concern. Now is the time to chase down lingering questions about this applicant's history and character.

How to Choose and Work With a Tenant-Screening Agency

At some point in your tenant selection process, you may be tempted to call in reinforcements. You may be out of time, tired of talking to prospects, or anxious to get the selection process over and done with; or you may not feel comfortable with the prospect of calling prior landlords, employers, and personal references, and you're wondering—isn't there another way to do this? There are lots of companies ready to take your business. They're called tenant-screening services or resident-screening firms.

You can think of credit-reporting agencies, criminal-background-searching firms, and tenant-screening firms as services that give you increasing amounts of information about your applicants:

- A credit-reporting agency gathers financial and other history and produces a credit report. (Chapter 11)
- A criminal background search firm canvasses multiple state conviction databases and gives you a report telling you whether your applicant matches names on the databases, and for what convictions. (Chapter 13)
- A resident- (or tenant-) screening service typically provides you with a credit report, checks criminal conviction databases, confirms employment and past residences, and more. Most will issue a risk score and may include a recommendation on whether to rent to the applicant.

At the outset, it's important to understand what a screening service will *not* do:

- As a rule, tenant-screening services will not call or otherwise contact references—if you want the personal scoop from these sources, you'll have to do it yourself or hire a management company or local real estate office to screen per your instructions.
- Screening firms don't advertise for you.
- Screening services won't have much to say about people who live "off the grid" or otherwise don't engage in regular consumer transactions with banks and stores, nor will they provide much information for people who are here illegally and live on a cash basis and are otherwise below the radar.
- These services will not accept your application and analyze it. Typically, you furnish basic information (name, SSN, sometimes a date of birth) and that's it.
- Most tenant-screening services don't offer their services "by the drink." They have a basic package, which includes a credit report and criminal background check, plus confirmation of employment and residential information supplied by the applicant. The extras may include a risk score, which purports to rate the applicant, and other database checks.

How useful are tenant-screening services?

Tenant-screening services are a relatively recent industry, appearing about twelve years ago and really taking off when the Internet became widespread and easy to use. Here's how tenant-screening services characterize their business; it's their appeal (and their limitation).

Consistent decisions

Big residential property owners employ leasing agents who sign up tenants. One of the biggest challenges faced by big apartment owners is properly training agents to screen carefully and legally. Owners worry that every agent will not adhere to the good-tenant criteria set by the owners. In particular, they fear fair housing lawsuits resulting from careless or even rogue agents.

- **The appeal of screening services.** When the whole process is sent off-site, to a company that relies only on "objective" data when reaching its recommendation, the owners no longer have to worry about inconsistent, poor decisions from on-site personnel.
- **Do you need this feature?** If you handle your vacancies yourself, or employ one or two employees whom you carefully supervise, you have little reason to worry about inconsistent decisions or risky leasing agents. You're it!

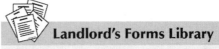

Landlord's Forms Library

Tenant-Screening Firms Comparison. A worksheet to use as you shop for a screening service. It will prompt you to look for or ask about particular services, such as eviction reports, terrorism watch list reports, and so on.

The worksheet you use to investigate different tenant-screening outfits need not be part of your applicants' files, since you're simply choosing a firm to screen them. But if you later want to switch firms, you'll find it handy to have the results of your first review at hand. You may be able to eliminate certain firms or go right away to the runner-up who might turn out to be the best one.

Decisions based on objective facts, not subjective conclusions

As landlords strive to fairly evaluate applicants, they wrestle with the soft information that can be so important, yet hard to quantify. How do you measure the value of a past landlord's review, and how should you factor in your impressions of an applicant you met briefly at a property showing? A required income-to-rent ratio is easy to understand and apply; evaluating what you hear from references is harder to reduce to measurable terms.

- **The appeal of screening services.** Screening firms deal with the challenge of soft information by simply not considering any—they don't interview references, and they never meet the applicants. Their scores and approval recommendations are based purely on credit reports and whether the applicant shows up on various databases.

- **Do you need this feature?** Though soft information is hard to quantify, you don't need to shy away from it. As the lessons of Chapter 12 teach, you can ask relevant questions of past landlords, employers, and personal references and end up with insights into an applicant that you can put into the mix. As long as you apply sound business judgment, and do so consistently, there's no reason to deprive yourself of these crucial sources of information.

Access to enhanced databases

The large screening firms all have access to databases that credit bureaus will not use, such as specialized eviction databases and criminal conviction lists. In fact, some of the databases are proprietary—that is, the firms themselves maintain them. Importantly, they may license them to the smaller, regional companies—the ones you're likely to deal with.

- **The appeal of screening services.** There's no getting around the appeal of checking your applicant

---

The Law You Need to Know

- You need your applicants' consent before submitting their names to tenant-screening companies, according to the Fair Credit Reporting Act. You can use the Consent to Criminal and Background Check form in Chapter 6 for that purpose.

- If you reject an applicant based on what you learn in a report issued by a tenant-screening service, you must send an adverse action letter. See Chapter 16.

- The contract you sign with a tenant-screening company will relieve it, in advance, of any damages you might suffer as a result of its mistakes or negligence.

---

against a nationwide database of convicted felons, or government-maintained watch lists. How useful these databases are, however, is debatable (see the discussions of several of them, below).

- **Do you need this feature?** As you'll see when going through the features offered by many firms, some of the database search results you'll see are simply pulled out of the credit report by the screening firms. If you follow the thorough screening process this book recommends, you may not need the added search capabilities of a screening firm.

Obtain written consent from applicants

Under the Fair Credit Reporting Act (15 U.S. Code §§ 1681 and following), a screening report is an "investigative consumer report," which means you must tell the applicant (within three days of requesting the report) that you'll order a report that will concern character, reputation, personal characteristics, and criminal history. You must also tell the applicant that more information about the nature and scope of the report will be provided upon request (if asked, you have to provide this information within five days). The Consent to Criminal and Background Check form that you gave applicants with the rental application (see Chapter 6) meets these disclosure requirements.

Do you need to reinform applicants that you'll be conducting a screening search? Take a look at the signature date on the consent form. If you're ordering the report more than three days later, you have to inform the applicant again. You can do this by faxing the original to your applicant and asking for a signature on the reauthorization line (then have the applicant fax the form back to you). You might be okay if you simply call, ask for phone authorization, and make a note of the call and the authorization on the form.

Before You Submit an Applicant's Name to a Tenant-Screening Service

☑ Identify what services you want, following our advice in this chapter and earlier ones on credit reports (Chapters 10 and 11), landlord, employer, and other references (Chapter 12), and criminal background searches (Chapter 13).

☑ Understand the limitations inherent in the information you'll get from tenant-screening services, especially concerning criminal background checks. These services don't necessarily have any more access to conviction records than the firms that search criminal records only.

☑ Make sure prospective tenants have given you written authorization to perform a background check.

☑ Be certain that your bottom line can handle the expense of hiring a resident-screening firm. Unlike the cost of a plain credit report, which you can pass on to the applicant, you cannot confidently make the applicant pay for resident screening (a court might consider this practice illegal).

How to find a tenant-screening service (and how much they cost)

The best way to find a tenant-screening service is to ask other landlords for recommendations. If you are a member of a local or state apartment association, see what services they recommend and if members are entitled to bulk deals with a resident-screening firm.

Most tenant-screening outfits operate only online—you generally won't find "resident screening" or "tenant screening" in the yellow pages. In fact, part of their appeal is the convenience of being able to transact business via the Internet. If you don't have a recommendation for a particular firm, simply type "tenant screening [your state]" into your Internet browser's search box. You'll get dozens of results, including lots of sponsored links high on the results list that have paid for this premium placement (their high placement does not mean that they're any better than those further down the list).

You'll see promises of instant reports for as little as $9.95, although most charge from $15 to $35, depending on the services you want. The most complete package of information (one that includes credit reports, SSN fraud checks, eviction searches, employment verification, and a recommendation based on a risk score) will cost more. Many operations give no pricing information on their websites—you have to contact a sales representative, whose job is to not only give you the information but sign you up.

A good service will offer pricing options to independent owners as well as big operators and apartment associations that

---

Tenant Screening: Who Are the Main Players?

Four large companies dominate the scene when it comes to servicing landlords with more than 100 properties:

- ChoicePoint, Inc. (www.choicepoint.com)
- First Advantage SafeRent (www.residentscreening.net)
- RealPage, Inc. (www.realpage.com), and
- TransUnion (www.creditretriever.com).

Chances are you won't be doing business with these outfits, but you'll find it instructive to visit their websites and see what they offer the big property owners. ChoicePoint, in particular, has an informative website. Use what you learn to measure any regional screening firm you investigate (the comparison worksheet in this book lists many of the features offered by the big four).

may be able to secure bulk deals. If you have multiple rentals, look for a service that gives discounts for repeated use.

You'll find the Tenant-Screening Firms Comparison worksheet on the CD-ROM that accompanies this book. Use it to organize your evaluations of the screening firms you consider.

How to evaluate services provided by tenant-screening firms

The sheer number of resident-screening firms operating nationwide is daunting. Take some time to look carefully at several firms' websites. You'll quickly find that some rise way above the others in terms of clarity and willingness to explain exactly what they do. Others simply promise reliable results and leave it at that. As you go through the sites, use the comparison form to guide your evaluation. The sections below track the form.

What's the look and feel of the screening service?

Your report won't be very helpful if it's confusing or full of jargon. A good service should provide an online demo that shows you just what you'll get. If a company's demo is hard to follow or looks skimpy, look elsewhere.

A good service should also present an FAQ page, along with an opportunity for you to ask questions directly by calling a customer service phone number. This feature tells you a lot about the customer care this service is willing to support—and customer care may become important to you if you sign up with a particular firm. If the answers make

---

Who Takes Responsibility for Mistakes?

It shouldn't surprise you that part of your contract with any screening firm includes an agreement that you won't hold them responsible for any mistakes they make concerning your applicants. This means that if you rent to someone who has a relevant criminal background that was missed by the service, you won't be able to sue them if that mistake causes you any monetary damages. For example, if that tenant attacks another resident, who sues you for carelessly allowing a dangerous person to live on your property, you'll have no legal recourse against the screening company.

sense and don't overhype the product, that's reassuring. On the other hand, if you encounter a hard sell, beware—it's usually a sign that the underlying product is weak.

Who sets the application criteria?

If you've stayed with us throughout this book, you understand that your tenant selection criteria are relative—that is, they depend on the market, the attractiveness of your property, and your willingness to hold out for a while until the right applicant comes along. A year from now, if market conditions have changed, or if you've refurbished your rental, you may find that your standards have changed. In short, you're making decisions based on what you have to work with at the time.

Resident-screening companies that give you a score or recommendation will not know what your rental standards and criteria are unless they're willing to ask you and apply them. In other words, unless you can set the acceptance criteria (such as rent-to-income ratio or an acceptable interval since any prior eviction), you'll be stuck with the company's tenant selection criteria. So, the first question to ask of any screening firm is: Can I set the acceptance criteria that you will apply? These firms will charge more than those who don't customize their analysis for individual clients.

Does someone review the report before it's sent to you?

As you know now, it's quite possible for credit reports, and particularly criminal background reports, to have errors. Many such errors are evident in the report itself (when different names appear); others become known when you compare entries in the reports to other information you have, such as entries in a Rental Application or information from a reference.

Screening firms that promise instant results cannot have anyone reviewing the reports. Look for a firm that takes this extra step. Without it, the basis for the report's conclusion may be faulty and the report may be worthless.

Will the service screen groups of applicants who intend to live in the same rental?

When you rent to more than one applicant, you know that you're entitled to insist that everyone meet your criteria, including rent-to-income ratio. The legal basis for this requirement is the "joint and several" responsibility of each roommate to cover the rent. In reality, however, you will often rent to applicants who could not handle the entire rent on their own, but whose combined income meets your standards. Look for a screening firm that will evaluate the creditworthiness and income of the group as a whole—this will give you the picture you need, and save you the expense of paying for multiple reviews.

Does the service maintain a "skip watch"?

Some of the larger resident-screening firms invite their client landlords to report "skips," or tenants who leave owing rent. These firms maintain a database of such tenants, and will check an applicant name you supply against their list. The value of this service depends on the likelihood that the deadbeat's prior landlord(s) also used this screening service, which is impossible to assess. You may pick up this information from a credit report if the wronged landlord also reports the bad debt to the credit bureaus. The worth of this feature is debatable.

Does the service give you a "landlord debt" report?

Some firms promise to tell you whether the applicant owes money to prior land-lords. This feature is presumably different from a skip watch, in that it does not rely on a landlord reporting to the screening firm. The landlord debt portion of the firm's report may be nothing more than entries from landlords taken out of the bad debt section of the credit report and presented in their own section. You'll want to know more about this feature if you sign up with a firm that offers it.

Will you get separate check-writing and utility payment histories?

Some firms will show you the applicant's check-writing history and utility payment history as separately listed entries. If the banks and utilities have reported the bad debts to a credit bureau, you should see these events in a regular credit report. However, the screening firm may be looking at other databases of check-writing behavior, such as: ChexSystems, a nationwide specialty consumer-reporting agency that collects and maintains information from member financial institutions such as banks and credit unions; Shared Check Authorization Network (SCAN), which maintains a database of returned checks and instances of fraud; and TeleCheck, a company with a database of returned checks and instances of fraud.

Does the service pick up evictions?

A credit report may not include evictions. For a complete picture, you'll need to check court records that have been posted online. All screening services promise a thorough check; some even vow to look at courthouse records in person, if necessary. Whether even the most powerful searching tool will uncover every eviction is another matter, since these searches depend on eviction information being posted online by the courts that handle them. Not every court in the United States posts such information; and the frequency of their postings can vary widely (if you're worried about an eviction in the recent past, you may not see it if the court posts new information every six months). You may see promises of searches "through 33 million records," but it's hard to evaluate what that means unless you know what percent of the total number of eviction records are available online (and how far back the search will reach).

Ask a screening company to give you a record of evictions you've filed at your own property. Or, have a friend ask the screening company to confirm a pretend eviction suffered by you (using yourself as the ruse will avoid any privacy concerns associated with using someone else's name). If you get an incomplete or inaccurate record on the evictions you've filed, or if the service fakes it and confirms your nonexistent eviction, look elsewhere.

Do you get credit reports from more than one bureau, and do you get a copy?

Every screening company should pull a credit report, and careful screening services will contact more than one of the three main companies (Experian, Equifax, and TransUnion) to make sure there are no discrepancies. A good company will have contracts with all three. Some companies will give you the credit report (looking just like it would if you were to order it); others will incorporate the information into their own report.

Do you get a "risk score"?

Some firms will generate a "risk score" for every applicant. By looking at the applicant's financial and rental background (including income, debt load, bill-paying history, bankruptcies, and evictions), the score tells you what the chances are that this applicant will end the tenancy not owing rent. The score does not consider whether the tenant was a pain in the neck, harassed his or her neighbors to the point of driving them away, or caused prior landlords any number of problems that didn't rise to the level of evictable offenses. Since the score doesn't capture these human factors, whether such a score is truly useful is debatable. A careful landlord will call references before relying on the risk score.

Does the service run a Social Security number (SSN) fraud check?

You don't want a tenant who may be concealing negative information by using someone else's identity. A screening firm should search the database of SSN records and alert you if an applicant's SSN is invalid or belongs to someone who is deceased. This is a valuable tool and not a search that individuals can perform on their own.

How extensive is the criminal background check?

Online screening firms will be as wildly reassuring as their simpler brethren, criminal-background-checking operations, when it comes to describing the millions of records they'll review to see if your applicant's name matches a name on a Megan's Law registry or other conviction database. Individuals don't have access to the non-Megan's-Law databases, so if you're concerned about criminal background and haven't ordered a criminal background report, you'll want the results of this search. Chapter 13 describes in detail the value (or lack thereof) of these criminal background searches.

You'll want a screening firm that has access to federal databases and the highest number of state databases (at least 40). You should look for depth, as well (do they look at county-maintained databases, or state-maintained?), and you'll want to know how frequently these lists are updated.

Does the firm search government "watch lists"?

The FBI maintains a "terrorism watch list," as well as a "most wanted list." Various other federal agencies maintain

similar lists. These databases are not available to the public. A decent screening firm will have access to many such databases.

Will the service check references?

Most screening firms will not contact references (their promise to "confirm employment" may involve simply looking for employment information on the credit report). That's because talking to humans (and reaching subjective conclusions about what they have to say) has no place in the screening firms' business model, which depends on factual, verifiable data that's fed into mathematical models, which predict rent-paying behavior. In addition, the firms can't check references and still remain competitive in price, since these interviews take so much time; nor could they interview and still deliver the instantaneous results they promise.

If you encounter a screening firm that promises to contact references or verify employment and past residences, do some investigation *before* you sign up. Will they do more than simply verify that the applicant works here or lived there? What questions will the firm ask? Will they ask questions you provide? Do they attempt to confirm answers? If you're not satisfied with the answers, you're probably better off calling references yourself. (And if that is something you don't want to do, consider hiring a local management company or real estate office to do it for you.)

Does the service recommend the tenant?

Finally, does the screening service approve your tenant? And will they do so with qualifications (such as recommending a cosigner)? At first blush, this might seem attractive, and you'll probably see a reassuring promise that by using this feature you'll be insulated from fair housing claims (the theory is that since the screening service cannot meet the applicants and has no knowledge of their ethnic or racial background, it can't discriminate). But this feature is over-hyped. True, a once-removed screener might have some theoretical advantages, but if you're prepared to follow fair housing laws, you shouldn't be afraid to use and trust your skills to legally evaluate applicants. If you allow a third party to choose applicants whom they have never met, you're giving up on the personal screening that every landlord can and should do.

If you use screening reports that score or approve your applicants, it's very important that you understand the company's insistence (in the service contract with you) that they will not bear any liability for their negligent or wrongful acts (see "Who Takes Responsibility for Mistakes?" above). For example, suppose you reject an applicant based on the company's recommendation (they mistakenly match him with a name on a terrorist list), and that applicant later files a lawsuit against you. You won't be able to bring in the screening company as the real culprit (and source of any settlement or award).

Does the service send adverse action letters?

When you reject an applicant based on information that you receive from a resident-screening company, you must send the applicant an "adverse action letter," according to the Fair Credit Reporting Act. A few companies will send the letter on your behalf, thus saving you this step. Keep in mind that the letter is simply a form that you fill out (there's one in this book). Chapter 16 covers adverse action letters in detail.

Does the screening firm also handle debt collections?

Larger firms will offer you not only a report on your current applicant, but a debt collection service if tenants leave you with unpaid rent. You shouldn't need this service if you've chosen carefully— still, now and then you'll get stung. This service should be unbundled from the regular tenant screening. Whether it's a reason to choose one firm over others depends on how much the firm will keep versus the deal you'd get from a regular debt collection agency.

What was your overall experience working with this company?

The last line on the Tenant-Screening Firms Comparison worksheet is a place for you to record your experiences with the firm you chose. Use this to note any communication problems ("never got through the phone tree"), turnaround time ("report took two days"), ease of use once you got the report ("confusing" or "clear and easy to read") and the name of anyone in customer service who helped you with your order or any problems. You may want to refer to these notes next time you consider hiring a firm (though you would be well advised to do another Internet search, since this industry is quite volatile).

How to use the screening report

To keep costs down, most landlords who sign up with screening services will do so after they've reviewed and ranked several rental applications. They'll submit names of the top few applicants, or maybe just the highest-ranking one. The screening report will include a credit report, an eviction history, criminal background report, and possibly more, as explained above. Some screening firms will give you an "approved" stamp; others will supply a risk score. Now, what should you do with this information? That depends on how "deconstructed" the credit information is—whether you get just the facts or a recommendation or credit score. Let's look at the possibilities.

Screening reports that give you "just the facts"

The simplest (and least expensive) tenant-screening reports will deliver undigested information that you'll need to evaluate. For example, you may get a conventional credit report, plus a background report listing convictions and arrests; and you may get more information (such as eviction and utility-paying histories). To make sense of the credit report, you'll need to look at Chapter 11, which explains how to evaluate credit reports,

---

Handle and Dispose of Screening Reports Carefully

A report from a tenant-screening company is subject to the federal Disposal Rule, which governs how to safeguard documents that contain sensitive personal information that could be exploited by an identity thief. See "Handle credit reports, criminal background reports, and tenant-screening reports carefully," in Chapter 11.

Tenant-Screening Firms Comparison

Name of company				
Product demo (is it impressive?)				
How long has the service been in business?				
FAQs and ability to ask questions directly?				
Customer service, hours				
Individual landlords set tenant selection criteria?				
Does a human review any results before the report is sent to you?				
Report for groups of tenants living together?				
Skip watch included?				
Landlord debt report?				
Check-writing history?				
Utility debt?				

Name of company				
Eviction checks?				
Separate credit report supplied?				
Credit report from multiple agencies?				
Do you get a risk score?				
SSN fraud report?				
Criminal background checks?				
Government watch lists (Terrorism Watch and Most Wanted)?				
Verifies references? Contacts references?				
Does the service approve the tenant?				
Adverse action letter sent?				
Debt collection services?				
Overall experience with this company				

and you'll want to look at Chapter 13 for criminal background reports. Similarly, if you receive an eviction history report, you'll need to decide whether any entries are relevant and would affect this applicant's standing in your ranked pile of applicants. After you've evaluated the screening report's entire contents, you'll be able to slot an applicant into the right place in your ranked list.

Are you ready to make an offer? Not quite. Screening companies rarely contact references, and when they do, you can be sure they won't be asking the kind of in-depth questions suggested in this book. (They definitely won't contact the functional equivalents for past landlords and employers that we suggest for first-time renters and self-employed applicants.) You'd be foolish to conclude your screening without a conversation with these sources. As mentioned earlier, the most-solvent and financially responsible tenant can be a royal pain in the neck, and you won't know what it's like to do business with this person unless you talk to someone who has.

So, one more task awaits the conscientious landlord—call those references, using Chapter 12 as your guide. If you're loath to do so, try to find a local property management company or real estate office that will do it for you. But beware—these companies typically want the entire job, and may not be interested in selling their services piecemeal. On the other hand, if business is slow, you might be able to make a deal.

Double check information in the screening report against answers on the rental application. If you find serious discrepancies between self-reported information and the report, inquire further (the report may be wrong, or the applicant's answers may be untrue).

Screening reports that give you a score or an "approved" stamp

More elaborate reports will generate a risk score, which purports to tell you the likelihood that a tenant will leave without owing rent. A service that allows you to set the acceptance parameters may go further and tell you whether an applicant is approved or not per your specifications. Great, you say—there's my ranking order and my top pick! Not so fast. Like the landlord who received an unanalyzed screening report, you, too, have not spoken with references. Call them and then rerank, if necessary.

When you use a tenant-screening report that includes a score or recommendation that you do *not* follow, understand that your contrary decision has some risks— you guessed it, they're fair housing risks. They can come up like this: Suppose the company approves an applicant but doesn't call references. As a conscientious landlord, you make the calls, and learn from prior landlords and employers that this person is demanding, hard to get along with, messy, and often breaks the rules. But since none of this behavior

Resident-Screening Services: Will They Work for You?

Paying a resident-screening service isn't necessarily the best way for you to screen your applicants. But, in some situations and for some landlords, it's a good idea. Use this table to guide you towards the right decision for you.

Hiring a resident-screening service is a good idea when...	Hiring a screening service isn't necessary when...
You believe that a mathematical model, analyzing past payment history and more, will be a worthwhile indicator of a good tenant.	You believe that you can use a variety of tools, including conversations with prior landlords and employers, to predict who will be a stable tenant.
You're really busy and haven't much time to devote to screening.	You have enough time to handle by yourself the tasks a screening agency will do.
You want a criminal background check and credit report, combined in one report.	You've decided to forego a criminal background check and rely on applicants' answers on the Rental Application and your own corroborative checks (such as looking for employment gaps on the credit report).
You want a Megan's Law database check but you live in California, New Jersey or Madison, WI, and realize you can't use the databases yourself.	You live in a state and locality that doesn't restrict your use of Megan's Law databases, and you're willing to check yourself.
You are so concerned about fair housing claims that you want a service to pick the tenant for you.	You are confident that you understand how to follow fair housing laws.
You don't have much faith in your ability to evaluate the information on a credit report and Rental Application, and would like someone else to make the call.	You are reasonably confident that you can gather and evaluate evidence on each applicant and make an informed selection.
You want a multistate eviction history search.	You are willing to critically accept the applicant's answers on your Rental Application, which you'll corroborate using the tools in this book (such as checking with references).
You want to screen for placement on government watch lists.	You are confident that your own screening methods will uncover worrisome details.
You want added services that some screening firms offer, such as skip reports and bad debt collection.	You're confident you will pick up deadbeat tenants using conventional screening that you can do yourself; you're willing to engage collection agencies when you need them.

resulted in an eviction or firing, the screening model didn't pick it up. You're on sound footing to conclude that renting to this individual will be a bad risk, and you can safely drop that applicant in the rankings or choose someone else. But if the rejected applicant is a member of a protected group, you might find yourself accused of discrimination since you didn't follow the screening company's recommendation (the applicant can get a copy of the report, and will argue that you must have rejected him because you wanted to discriminate). Unless the negative reports from references are quite strong, you may have a hard time defeating a claim that discrimination, not business sense, motivated the rejection. (Be sure you keep good notes on your Tenant References worksheet, in case you need them later.) The lesson here: If you're going to use a tenant-screening firm, call references yourself, first—you may save yourself the cost of a report.

Transfer your conclusions to the applicant's Tenant Information Sheet

You'll want to note what you learned from the tenant-screening report on your applicant's Tenant Information Sheet, the master document for all the screening information you're gathering for each applicant. Go to the section called "Additional screening tools," and note the upshot of the report. Your notes may look like the sample from the Tenant Information Sheet shown below.

Accepting and rejecting applicants based on screening reports

With your rental applications in their final ranked order, you're ready to make an offer! There's nothing special about how to communicate a straightforward offer, though there are some practical tips that will make for smooth sailing (see Chapter 15). But if you accept an applicant contingent on certain conditions—such as supplying a cosigner, paying a higher deposit, or signing a longer lease—you have to follow legally prescribed ways to communicate that qualified acceptance. Chapter 15 covers conditional acceptances.

As for the rejects, they must be informed according to legal procedures, which are explained in Chapter 16.

Tenant Information Sheet (excerpt)

Additional screening tools

Used DataSure. Report is consistent w/ rental App.

Take Ten Minutes

If you used an online tenant-screening service, take a minute to reflect on your experience:

- Could you understand their report? If it was confusing, don't use this service again.
- If you had questions, were they answered quickly and thoroughly? Could you talk with a human—or did you have the feeling that you were dealing with a machine?
- Did your own initial screening corroborate the service's results (and recommendation, if there was one)? If not, think about why. Were your efforts lacking, or was the mathematical modeling used by the service apparently way out of whack? You may not know until the tenant recommended by the service has lived for a while at your property.

Congratulations! You're finally at the end of the screening process. You've shown the rental, talked with prospective tenants, reviewed rental applications, run credit reports, and checked landlord, employer, and personal references. In some cases, you've even done criminal background checks or used a tenant-screening firm. You're now ready to make a decision and offer the rental to someone who meets your criteria (or comes as close as you're going to get). This chapter helps you pull together all you've learned about the applicants and make your final choice. The next chapter guides you through the steps you'll take to communicate rejections to the other applicants.

Keep your options open until you've got a commitment. Don't reject runners-up until your first choice has signed a lease or rental agreement or given you a holding deposit.

What to do when you have no qualified applicants

If you've found a great tenant, you can skip this section. But what if you end your screening process with no applications that meet your basic rental terms? For example, despite your top pick's good credit and a solid job, you heard from a former landlord that he was the source of many neighbors' complaints and the landlord was glad to see him go. The next

candidate has worrisome credit card debt, the next one is between jobs, and the next one wants to bring a dog that you've met and don't trust. What to do?

You have a choice: Readvertise and hope that the next pool of interested renters will yield better candidates, or compromise on your basic rental terms and choose the best candidate in the current batch. With either choice, you risk losing money:

- **Start over.** If you readvertise, your unit will remain vacant during the next screening process, you'll incur advertising and miscellaneous showing expenses, and you'll spend more of your own time on re-renting efforts. You can estimate the cost by adding together the month(s) of lost rent you can expect, the cost to go through the entire process again, and the value of your time.

- **Compromise.** If you lower your basic rental criteria and choose the top candidate, you'll have a tenant whom good business sense has already told you may give you problems, by not paying the rent, being inconsiderate of neighbors or property, and so on. Unless you decide to lower the rent, the monetary size of this risk is impossible to calculate. For example, the person with too much debt may default on the rent, but will he leave quietly and quickly when you terminate? If not, you're looking at an eviction lawsuit, plus months of unpaid rent if the tenant fights back. You'll also have re-renting costs much sooner than planned (say, at the end of a few months instead of the end of a year's lease). What about the chap with a dog who looks like the hound from hell? You may be looking at something as minor as torn up tulip beds, or as major as the exodus of frightened tenants or an expensive lawsuit by a tenant attacked by the dog. The financial consequences of choosing a bad tenant could end your business right there.

Common sense tells you to make the less risky choice—that is, to start over. This option will be easier for owners who have a cushion—who do not depend on their rental income for basic living expenses, or whose mortgage is not dependent on the monthly rent check. These owners can more readily afford to keep a unit vacant while they look for an acceptable tenant. Those whose businesses run hand-to-mouth, so to speak, may be tempted to grab the best applicant and hope for the best. But if things go awry, they will be the least able to weather the storm and stay in business.

If you find yourself in this predicament on a regular basis, there's something wrong—why aren't you able to attract a stable, rent-paying tenant? Perhaps one of the issues in "What's the Problem, and What Can You Do About It?" below, explains why good tenants avoid your rental and iffy sorts are all you're left with.

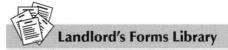

Landlord's Forms Library

This chapter includes letters and notices that you'll need when it's time to accept your tenant:

- **Acceptance Letter.** This letter spells out the basic terms of the rental, which you will have already covered when you called your successful applicant. It will minimize any chance that later the applicant will claim that you negotiated at the last minute.

- **Notice of Conditional Acceptance Based on Credit Report or Other Information.** This letter satisfies the Fair Credit Reporting Act's requirement (in some situations) that you impart specific information to applicants when you accept with conditions (such as requiring a higher security deposit).

- **Notice of Conditional Acceptance, Cosigner Required.** This letter satisfies the same requirement as that mentioned just above and applies specifically when you require a cosigner.

- **Cosigner Agreement.** This is a contract signed by you, your tenant, and the cosigner. It makes the cosigner's willingness to stand behind the tenant legally enforceable.

- **Holding Deposit Agreement and Receipt.** Use this form if you decide to ask for a holding deposit.

What's the Problem and What Can You Do About It?

The problem	Examples of the problem	Can you fix it?
Something in the rental is a universal turnoff.	The paint is awful, the appliances are ancient, the place is dirty.	You bet. Spend some money now to avoid losing more money as your property stays vacant (see Chapter 8 for advice).
Something about the neighbors discourages good tenants.	Applicants ask around and learn that the upstairs tenant is loud and obnoxious.	You're legally required to preserve every tenant's "quiet enjoyment" of his or her rental. When one tenant makes this impossible, you may terminate that tenancy.
The neighborhood is scary.	Street lighting is poor, surrounding businesses attract low-lifes and denizens of the night.	Work with other property owners and local police to cleanup your neighborhood— insist on regular patrols and better street lighting.
People don't want to have you as a landlord (sorry, but we have to face every possibility).	You're too enthusiastic and applicants think you're going to be an obnoxious landlord; or, you're so detached that they fear you won't take care of your property or consider their reasonable requests.	Absolutely. Find out what you're doing wrong (talk to other landlords or even current tenants) and shape up.

✓ Before You Choose Your New Tenant

☑ Look again at the Tenant Information Sheets and worksheets for the top pick and make sure that you've properly ranked the applicants. Was there something worrisome that you noted and meant to follow up on, but didn't? Take care of loose ends now.

☑ Make sure you've checked out all roommates or adults who will be living together.

☑ Confirm that the current tenants, if any, will be out as scheduled and you can move in your new batch on the date you promised.

☑ Talk to contractors who are working on repairs or refurbishing to confirm their expected finish date.

☑ Look again at your lease or rental agreement and make sure it reflects every key term you and the top applicant agreed to. If you negotiated and changed any term, the rental document must reflect these changes.

If you think you've done everything possible to attract good tenants but are still coming up with unacceptable applicants, think long and hard about your business model. The good-tenant criteria explained in this book are industry standards that have proven successful—that is, they result in the choice of stable, rent-paying tenants who make your business profitable. If you're asking market rents and have a decent property, but you're consistently taking big risks by disregarding these standards, it may be time to sell and invest in something else.

💡 **Consider offering a conditional acceptance in lieu of a rejection.** You may be able to reduce the risk of problems by requiring a higher deposit, insisting on a cosigner, or offering the rental on a month-to-month basis instead of a year's lease. See "Conditional acceptances," below.

How to choose among qualified applicants

If you're lucky, you'll have several tenants who have successfully advanced through all levels of your screening process and who meet your basic rental terms—rent, security deposit, length of rental term, number of occupants, pets, and so on. In some cases (discussed in Chapters 9 and 10), you may have decided to negotiate on some issues, such as the move-in date. But at this point, you're done negotiating and ready to choose. Many times, the best applicant will become readily apparent. These people are almost always the ones with consistently superior rental and credit histories and references. They have also given you no reason to think that they will become demanding, unreasonable tenants.

Pull out the Tenant Information Sheets for all of your applicants who made it through your screening stages. They should already be arranged from most qualified to least, since you ranked and reranked them every time you moved to the next screening level. If there is one applicant who is far and away the best candidate, you can move on to "How to communicate an acceptance," below.

If you're in a hot market, or have an attractive rental at a competitive price, you may find that more than one set of applicants are clustered at the top and would be acceptable tenants. In that event, rerank. You may find that although they are all acceptable, one person or group of tenants, in particular, appears to be more stable, financially secure, or comes with exceptionally glowing references. If you still have a few candidates who are very close, look again at the notes you made on their Tenant Information Sheets to see if you missed a detail that is telling, one way or another. For example, do one applicant's frequent job changes and apartment moves make sense, given his occupation—or are these indicators of someone who just won't stay, even though he might be a fine tenant for the short time he's with you? Knowing that low turnover is the key to profitability, you may want to choose instead the equally qualified Steady Eddy who will stay with you for a nice long time.

The Law You Need to Know

- If you accept an applicant conditioned on additional requirements (such as providing a cosigner), the Fair Credit Reporting Act requires you to send an adverse action letter as part of your acceptance, described below.
- You can significantly enhance the value of a cosigner by including terms in the agreement concerning notice of tenant defaults, service of legal papers, responsibility for subtenant and assignee defaults, and others (see the Cosigner Agreement in this chapter).
- Holding deposits are attractive but tricky. Under legal principles in all states, you can't simply pocket the whole thing as a penalty if the tenant doesn't take the rental. You can keep only what will compensate you for your losses. See the discussion on holding deposits below.

Resist the temptation to initiate a bidding war. When you have closely matched applicants in tight competition for your rental, a natural next step might be to say, "But if you can commit to a longer lease… or a higher rent …." This is very risky and could land you in legal hot water. If applicants offer more, that's another matter (see Chapter 9).

If you still have a tie, the only safe course is to offer the rental to the applicant whose completed application you received first. (Check your Application Review form, if you used it; or the Tenant Information Sheet, if you transferred the submission date and time there.) If you extend an offer to a latecomer, you're risking a fair housing claim if an applicant who applied earlier is a member of a legally protected group.

How to communicate an acceptance

Now for the best part! After deciding that you'll make an offer to an applicant, note this on the Tenant Information Sheet and decide how you'll send the news. Unlike a rejection (which you are wise to communicate in writing), an acceptance is always happily received by phone or email, though you'll want to follow up with a letter, as explained below.

Make the call

Most prospects are anxious to hear from you. The sooner you communicate an offer, the better off you'll be, especially if the market is soft and you know that tenants have ample choices. A phone call during the day or early evening is always acceptable.

Calling an applicant with an offer to rent your property also gives you one last chance to confirm that the applicant will meet your rental terms. It's not unreasonable to go over them again, just to make sure that everyone is on the same page. Before placing the call, take out the applicant's Tenant Information Sheet, and go to the section at the bottom titled "Straight Acceptance" ("straight" means that you're not attaching any conditions, such as the need for a cosigner). The form prompts you to cover the basics of the rental, and you can confirm the answers (number of occupants and so on) as you mention them. For example, you might say:

I'm so glad you'll be moving here. Let's just double check the details:

You'll be coming to my office on Thursday of this week to sign a year's lease and moving in on September 1.

There will be three occupants: you, Jane Larabee, and Hannah Silver, and you have no pets, right?

The monthly rent is $1,000 with a deposit of $1,500. First month's rent and the deposit are due before you move in on September 1.

Anything else we need to discuss?

Use the Straight Acceptance section of the Tenant Information Sheet to check off the applicant's responses to your review of the rental terms. Your sheet may look like the sample below. Don't get off the phone without setting up a time for the new tenant to sign the lease or rental agreement—see "Signing the lease or rental agreement," at the end of the chapter.

Now and then, someone you've accepted will attempt to bargain with you, either over the rent or some other term that you made clear long ago. Should you negotiate now? As ever, you must be realistic. If the market is soft, and you doubt you'll be able to secure a better tenant, you may decide to negotiate. See Chapter 9 for tips on whether to negotiate.

In some cases, you'll want to make your offer conditional—for example, you'll want the applicant to provide a cosigner, or you may require a holding deposit to seal the deal. See "Conditional acceptances," and "Holding deposits," below, for more on these subjects.

Follow up with an acceptance letter

It's a good business practice to confirm your acceptance conversation with a letter. Applicants will appreciate the peace of mind it gives them (especially those who don't give you a holding deposit). It will also prevent a tenant from claiming that you agreed in the acceptance conversation to lower the rent, accept two dogs instead of one, and so on. The last thing you want is to get into a "but I thought you said" argument when the applicant comes to sign the rental documents. Use the Acceptance Letter to confirm your offer (fill in the relevant information as to rent, deposit, and so on for your rental, and delete the "Holding deposit" paragraph if you do not require one).

You'll find the Acceptance Letter on the CD-ROM that accompanies this book. An example is shown below.

Tenant Information Sheet (excerpt)

Straight Acceptance

Communicated on <u>May 10, 20xx</u> (date) via ☑ phone ☐ email ☐ mail

Accept with holding deposit, if any, amount: <u>not needed</u>

Rental terms confirmed: ☑ rent   ☑ deposit   ☑ starting date
                          ☑ rental te rm ☑ occupants   ☑ pets

Total of first month's rent and deposits <u>$1,800</u>

due on <u>June 1, 20xx</u> .   Method of payment <u>personal check</u>

Response: <u>eager acceptance</u>

Acceptance Letter

[*Date*]

[*Tenant*]
[*Street Address*]
[*City, State, and ZIP*]

This letter confirms our conversation on [*date*] at [*time*], in which you accepted my offer to rent the property at [*rental property address*]. As we discussed, these are the rental terms:

Rent: _____ Deposit: _____ Rental start date: _____

Rental term: ☐ Month-to-month
              ☐ Lease, ending on: _____

Number of occupants: _____ Pets: _____

Deposit and first month's rent total [*amount*] to be paid by [*method of payment*] on or before _____ at this address _____
_____ .

Holding deposit of [*amount*] to be paid by [*date*] at this address _____
_____ .

We will sign the rental documents on [*date*] at [*time*] at [*address*].

Thank you for deciding to live here. I look forward to working with you to ensure that your move in and tenancy are smooth and enjoyable. If you have any questions, please don't hesitate to call me.

Yours truly,

_____
Landlord/manager

Conditional acceptances and adverse action letters

Now and then, you may want to offer your rental on slightly different terms than advertised. For example, you might decide that you will rent to this applicant but only if he can pay a slightly higher deposit or provide a cosigner. Or, if even your best applicant has slightly worrisome finances, you may want the first month's rent and the deposit to be paid in cash or a cashier's check (requiring cash rent is not legal in California unless the tenant has given you bounced rent checks, however). Occasionally, you'll ask for a different rental term than advertised, to address a concern you might have (if you're worried about this tenant's behavior, you might insist on a month-to-month arrangement instead of a lease, because you can terminate easily and without cause with a monthly term). When your offer includes conditions like these that

are different than the advertised terms you've been applying as a rule, you're making a conditional offer (that is, you'll accept the applicant conditioned on his or her complying with your new requirements).

Offering a conditional acceptance may mean that, pursuant to the Fair Credit Reporting Act (FCRA), you must send the applicant an adverse action letter. This letter is not an outright rejection—which may also require an adverse action letter (as discussed in Chapter 16). Here are the rules:

- You must send an adverse action letter if the *source* of the information that prompted your conditional offer was a report issued by a credit-reporting agency, criminal background search firm, or a tenant-screening firm, even if other factors also influenced your decision.
- You do not need to send an adverse action letter if the applicant him- or herself supplied the information,

Accepting Multiple Tenants

When you're accepting more than one applicant to live in a rental, it's a good idea to send acceptance letters to every roommate (you may, however, make the acceptance call to just one member of the group, if the roommates have designated that person as the contact). Sending letters to everyone ensures that they all know that the offer has been made, and on what terms. Remember, because you can theoretically demand the entire rent from each roommate, it's important that every resident have a clear sense of what the rental entails. You probably don't have to send duplicate letters to married couples.

Do You Need to Send an Adverse Action Letter?

Your conditional offer will be based on information you may have received from any number of sources. Depending on the source, you may or may not have to send the federally required adverse action letter. Follow this guide.

You *don't* have to send a formal adverse action letter if the following describes your decision.	You *must* send an adverse action letter if the following describes your decision (even if other factors played a part, too).
After reviewing the applicant's self-reported financial information on the application, you conclude a cosigner is needed.	You decide to require a cosigner after studying the applicant's credit report.
The applicant proposed a cosigner him- or herself.	You decide you need a cosigner when you learn from the credit report that the applicant has a lot of debt.
Based on your conversations with prior landlords, you offer a month-to-month rental instead of a lease.	Notations in the credit report of unpaid utility bills prompt your decision to offer a month-to-month rental instead of a lease.
You accept on a month-to-month basis, not a lease, after running a Megan's Law check yourself and discovering an old conviction.	You increase the deposit (to within legal limits) after reading a tenant-screening firm's report showing a lawsuit filed by a prior landlord.
You increase the security deposit (to within legal limits) after you or your manager speaks with a past landlord, who tells you that the applicant threw wild parties.	You increase the security deposit (to within legal limits) after the property management company or real estate office that you contract with speaks with a past landlord, who told them that the applicant threw wild parties.
You ask for a holding deposit when you see, on the Rental Application, that the applicant is a student who doesn't plan to begin school until the fall, several months away.	You ask for a holding deposit when the rental history on the credit report shows many short-term rentals and frequent interstate moves.

through conversations with you, by providing his or her tax returns, or by entering information on the rental application. You also do not have to send the letter if your decision was based on the results of a criminal background check *done by you or your employee* (by checking Megan's Law databases).

You'll always want to send your own acceptance letter, as explained in the section just above. But, in the situations described, you'll need to send an adverse action letter, too.

You'll want to communicate your conditional acceptance by phone, before sending your acceptance letter and adverse action letter. Use the "Qualified Acceptance" section at the end of the Tenant Information Sheet to record the conversation. Convey the basic rental terms as you would if making a straight offer, but include the special or different terms you're suggesting. Don't forget to arrange for a time for the applicant to come in and sign the lease or rental agreement (see "Signing the lease or rental agreement," below). The Qualified Acceptance section may look like the sample below.

Assuming the conversation goes smoothly, you can use the conditional acceptance template in this book when sending a conditional acceptance. The letter, shown below, gives you a place to describe your added requirement, and it tells the applicant his or her rights under the FCRA.

You'll find an adverse action letter, Notice of Conditional Acceptance Based on Credit Report or Other Information on the CD-ROM that accompanies this book. A sample appears below.

The adverse action letter is not difficult to fill out. First, enter the name and address of the applicant and the rental property address. Then check the box(es) that describe the basis of your decision:

☐ **Insufficient information in the credit report provided by….** Check this box when the credit or background report

Tenant Information Sheet (excerpt)

Qualified Acceptance

Offer conditioned on __acceptable cosigner__

Communicated on ___March 17, 20xx___ (date) via ☑phone ☐email ☐mail

☑ Adverse action letter required, sent ___March 17, 20xx___ (date)

cannot verify income, employment, or other important issues. Be sure to include the name, address, phone number, and website address (URL) of the credit-reporting or other agency.

☐ **Negative information in the credit report provided by....** Use this box when the credit or other report reveals facts that make this applicant a poor risk, and

☐ **The consumer-credit-reporting agency noted above....** Check this box if you checked *either* of the previous two boxes.

☐ **Information by a third party....** Check this box if you've used any third party, such as a real estate office, property management firm, or another independent contractor that interviewed an applicant's current or past employer, landlord, neighbors, or any other personal contacts.

The letter advises the applicant of his or her rights under the law, including the right to obtain copies of credit, criminal background, or screening reports and dispute their contents; and to get more information from you if your decision was from a third party. See Chapter 16, "Adverse action letters," for guidance on how to respond to requests for more information.

How to deal with cosigners

If you're flush with acceptable tenants, you may not have to bother with cosigners. Most of the time, you won't be so lucky; and many times, the best applicant (such as a young renter) will need a cosigner to qualify. It would be a mistake to automatically rule these applicants out. And remember, despite your feelings about cosigners, you must consider them if disabled applicants who are otherwise qualified present you with a cosigner in order to meet your financial requirements. So take a few minutes to read this section.

Applicants who know they need a cosigner's help may have approached you already with a prospect (your Rental Policies may have alerted the applicant of the need to provide this extra assurance). Hopefully, you've secured the suggested cosigner's consent to run a credit check and verify employment, and assessed the person's suitability at the same time that you evaluated the applicant. But suppose you're the one who's asking for a cosigner? Even though it's late in the game, you can still impose this condition, but you'll have to work quickly to make sure you don't lose other qualified applicants if the cosigner turns out to be unacceptable.

The cosigner signs an agreement that makes him or her "jointly and severally" responsible, with the tenant, for the tenant's financial obligations under the lease or rental agreement. This means

Notice of Conditional Acceptance Based on Credit Report or Other Information

To: [*Applicant*]

[*Street Address*]

[*City, State, and Zip*]

Your application to rent the property at [*rental property address*] has been accepted, conditioned on your willingness and ability to:

_____

_____

Your rights under the Fair Credit Reporting Act and Fair and Accurate Credit Transactions (FACT) Act of 2003. (15 U.S.C. §§ 1681 and following.)

Source of information prompting conditional acceptance

My decision to conditionally accept your application was prompted in whole or in part by:

☐ Insufficient information in the credit report provided by:

[*Credit-reporting agency*]

[*Address, phone number, URL*]

☐ Negative information in the credit report provided by:

[*Credit-reporting agency*]

[*Address, phone number, URL*]

☐ The consumer-credit-reporting agency noted above did not make the decision to offer you this conditional acceptance. It only provided information about your credit history. You have the right to obtain a free copy of your credit report from the consumer-credit-reporting agency named above, if your request is made within 60 days of this notice or if you have not requested a free copy within the past year. You also have the right to dispute the accuracy or completeness of your credit report. The agency must reinvestigate within a reasonable time, free of charge, and remove or modify inaccurate information. If the reinvestigation does not resolve the dispute to your satisfaction, you may add your own "consumer statement" (up to 100 words) to the report, which must be included (or a clear summary) in future reports.

☐ Information supplied by a third party other than a credit-reporting agency or you. You have the right to learn of the nature of the information if you ask me in writing within 60 days of learning of this decision. This information was gathered by someone other than myself or any employee.

_____   _____

Landlord/Manager   Date

that you can ask the cosigner to make good on the rent, deposit, or any other financial obligation that stems from the rental, including damage costs that you assess at the end of the rental term.

Cosigners (other than parents) rarely become a constant source of rent funds. Most of the time, the cosigner supplies one or two months' rent, then tells the tenant that "enough is enough." The tenant moves, or you serve the tenant with a pay or quit notice when the cosigner's check fails to arrive.

How to ask for a cosigner

Most of the time, you'll be the one asking for a cosigner. Use this book's form, Notice of Conditional Acceptance, Cosigner Required, which is specifically tailored to this situation. Follow the instructions above for filling out the conditional acceptance letter.

As you'll see when reading this form, it tells your applicant that you will measure any proposed cosigner against the same financial standards that you used when evaluating tenants. A cosigner must have:

- a monthly income of at least three times the sum of the rent plus the cosigner's own rent or mortgage (for example, if the cosigner's mortgage is $2,500 and the applicant's rent is $900, the cosigner's monthly income must be three times $3,400, or $10,200)

- positive references from an employer, and

- an acceptable credit profile.

When you send the conditional acceptance, attach the Consent to Contact References and Perform Credit Check and a Credit Check Payment form (discussed in Chapter 6), and ask the cosigner to complete them as soon as possible. When you receive these back, run the credit check and contact the proposed cosigner's employer to verify employment and income. Unless the cosigner is as financially stable as your applicant, he or she is not likely to be of much use should you call upon him or her to cover for the tenant.

You'll find the Notice of Conditional Acceptance, Cosigner Required form on the CD-ROM that accompanies this book. An example appears below.

When the applicant proposes the cosigner, you need not send an adverse action letter. Similarly, if the Rental Application shows that this person is a first-time renter, or a student from out of state, and you have an announced policy of regularly requiring cosigners in such situations, you can skip the letter (though you should still require a credit check and completed application from the cosigner). Remember, facts that the applicant brings to your attention do not trigger your duty to send adverse action letters.

Notice of Conditional Acceptance, Cosigner Required

To: [*Applicant*]

  [*Street Address*]

  [*City, State, and Zip*]

Your application to rent the property at [*rental property address*] has been accepted, conditioned on your willingness and ability to supply a cosigner.

Your rights under the Fair Credit Reporting Act and Fair and Accurate Credit Transactions (FACT) Act of 2003. (15 U.S.C. §§ 1681 and following.)

Source of information prompting conditional acceptance

My decision to conditionally accept your application was prompted in whole or in part by:

☐ Insufficient information in the credit report provided by:

  [*Credit-reporting agency*]

  [*Address, phone number, URL]*

☐ Negative information in the credit report provided by:

  [*Credit-reporting agency*]

  [*Address, phone number, URL]*

☐ The consumer-credit-reporting agency noted above did not make the decision to offer you this conditional acceptance. It only provided information about your credit history. You have the right to obtain a free copy of your credit report from the consumer-credit-reporting agency named above, if your request is made within 60 days of this notice or if you have not requested a free copy within the past year. You also have the right to dispute the accuracy or completeness of your credit report. The agency must reinvestigate within a reasonable time, free of charge, and remove or modify inaccurate information. If the reinvestigation does not resolve the dispute to your satisfaction, you may add your own "consumer statement" (up to 100 words) to the report, which must be included (or a clear summary) in future reports.

☐   Information supplied by a third party other than a credit-reporting agency or you. You have the right to learn of the nature of the information if you ask me in writing within 60 days of learning of this decision. This information was gathered by someone other than myself or any employee.

Procedure for evaluating cosigner

Attached to this notice, please find the:

- Consent to Perform Credit Check and Contact References, and

- Credit Check Payment forms.

Please give these items to your proposed cosigner and return them to me, with payment, by [*date you set for returning the forms*]. I will evaluate your cosigner using the same financial criteria I apply to all applicants. I will tell you whether your proposed cosigner is acceptable as soon as possible.

_____   _____

Landlord/Manager   Date

What to look for in a cosigner

A cosigner who has shaky or insufficient finances won't be worth anything. Before accepting a cosigner, you'll need to know that this person can shoulder the burden of a month's rent or more. As you review the cosigner's credit report, look for evidence of the following:

- **Available funds.** Does the cosigner have enough liquid resources to regularly cover a month's rent or other obligations of the tenant if, for example, the tenant leaves with a few thousand dollars' worth of damage? If the cosigner is a renter, add the applicant's rent to his—can he handle this for a month or more? If he has a mortgage, add the rent to this, too.
- **Stability.** This cosigner won't do you much good if you can't find him. Someone with ties to the community, such as a long-term job or property ownership, is less likely to be gone when you need him than a 20-year-old student friend of your applicant.
- **Location of the cosigner.** A cosigner who lives out of state is less attractive than a local person, and you can reject a cosigner on this basis if you don't want to take the chance that he will count on distance and inconvenience to avoid his obligations.

How to contract with a cosigner

Once the cosigner's credit checks out and you agree that he or she will be part of the picture, use the Cosigner Agreement on the CD-ROM that accompanies this book. The idea is to make the lease or rental agreement dependent on a committed cosigner who has signed on the dotted line. To make sure everything falls into place, follow these steps:

1. Prepare your lease or rental agreement and include a clause that provides that it is contingent (it depends) on the signed agreement of your cosigner. Attach a blank version of the Cosigner Agreement, and refer to it. Your clause might read something like this: "This rental document is contingent on the signed agreement of Mark Smith, 1234 Shadow Lane, Anytown, TX, to serve as a cosigner."

2. You and your tenant should sign the lease or rental agreement and send a copy, plus a blank copy of the Cosigner Agreement, to the proposed cosigner. The cosigner will keep the lease or rental agreement copy and sign and mail back the Cosigner Agreement.

3. When you receive the signed Cosigner Agreement, your lease or rental agreement will become legally enforceable. Keep the Cosigner Agreement in a safe place, attached to the original rental document.

Your Cosigner Agreement will impress upon both tenant and cosigner that the obligation is serious, and it points out the consequences to the cosigner if he or she is called upon to cover the tenant's financial responsibilities. Consider the following points in the cosigner agreement:

- **You have no obligation to give the cosigner notice of the tenant's rent default (Clause 3).** Cosigners may expect that you'll warn them of the tenant's failure to pay rent before you make a demand for rent from the cosigner. The Cosigner Agreement makes it clear that you aren't obligated to do so, and can contact the cosigner right away.

- **You have no obligation to use the security deposit first to cover the tenant's rent shortfall (Clause 3).** This part of the Cosigner Agreement is very important. You need not exhaust the security deposit before turning to the cosigner.

- **The cosigner's obligations extend to sublessees and assignees (Clause 4).** If the tenant assigns or subleases, the cosigner is still obligated. This may help prevent rogue sublets (sublets without your permission).

- **The tenant is the cosigner's agent for service of process (Clause 5).** In this clause, the cosigner agrees that any legal papers intended for him may be served on the tenant instead. This means that if the cosigner is far away and you decide to sue him, you won't have to hire a process server to find him. Serving the papers on the tenant will mean that the cosigner will be legally served and expected to answer your lawsuit. If the cosigner doesn't respond to the lawsuit, you can get a default judgment against him. You still have to collect, but you can always hire a collection agency and get something back at least.

- **If the landlord and cosigner end up in a lawsuit over the agreement, the loser will pay the winner's costs and attorney fees, plus the costs to collect these (Clause 6).** This attorney fees and costs clause is standard in many contracts. It discourages frivolous lawsuits.

You'll find the Cosigner Agreement on the CD-ROM that accompanies this book. A sample is shown below.

Holding deposits

Some landlords remain nervous about the seriousness of their applicant's acceptance, particularly if the market is soft or the tenancy will begin a significant time in the future and the two of you haven't signed a lease or rental agreement. One way to make it clear to your new tenant that the shopping days are over is to ask for a holding deposit. It's not a good idea to ask for the security deposit or the rent until the tenant signs the lease or rental agreement. Use the

Cosigner Agreement

1. This Cosigner Agreement [Agreement] is entered into on _____ , ____ ,
   between _____ (Tenant),
   _____ (Landlord),
   and _____(Cosigner).

2. Tenant has leased from Landlord the premises located at _____
   _____ [the Premises]. Landlord and Tenant signed a lease or rental
   agreement specifying the terms and conditions of this rental on _____ ,
   _____ . A copy of the lease or rental agreement is attached to this Agreement.

3. Cosigner agrees to be jointly and severally liable with Tenant for Tenant's
   obligations arising out of the lease or rental agreement described in Paragraph 2,
   including but not limited to unpaid rent, property damage, and cleaning and
   repair costs. Cosigner further agrees that Landlord will have no obligation to
   give notice to Cosigner should Tenant fail to fulfill Tenant's financial obligations. Landlord may demand that Cosigner perform as promised under this
   Agreement without first using Tenant's security deposit.

4. If Tenant assigns or subleases the Premises, Cosigner will remain liable under
   the terms of this Agreement for the performance of the assignee or sublessee,
   unless Landlord relieves Cosigner by written termination of this Agreement.

5. Cosigner appoints Tenant as Cosigner's agent for service of process in the
   event of any lawsuit arising out of this Agreement.

6. If Landlord and Cosigner are involved in any legal proceeding arising out of
   this Agreement, the prevailing party will recover reasonable attorney fees,
   court costs, and any costs reasonably necessary to collect a judgment.

Landlord: _____ Date: _____

Print name: _____

Tenant: _____ Date: _____

Print name: _____

Cosigner: _____ Date: _____

Print name: _____

Holding Deposit Agreement and Receipt form, shown below.

The holding deposit should be large enough to make it difficult for the tenant to walk away from the deal, but not so big as to be impossible to meet. Be sure that your Rental Policies have announced your intention to ask for this deposit (see the optional clause in Chapter 6). If the policies didn't mention it, and you decide to ask for a holding deposit based on information in the applicant's credit report or from a prior landlord or employer, you'll have to send an adverse action letter, described in "Conditional acceptances," above. On the other hand, if you're asking for a deposit based on an external event, such as the unexpected softening of the market, you won't have to send the letter.

Use the holding deposit fairly—when your tenant moves in, apply it in full to the first month's rent. If the applicant fails to sign a lease or otherwise doesn't show up, understand that you can't automatically keep the entire amount. Under the contract laws of every state, you can keep as much as will cover your damages, but not more (you cannot use the holding deposit as a penalty). Here's what that means:

- **Lost rent.** You can keep as much of the holding deposit as will compensate you for lost rent. This is calculated as per diem rate (monthly rent ÷ 30). Use 30 days

regardless of the number of days in the actual month, times the days of lost rent.

Suppose your first choice for your $900 per month rental doesn't show up, and you end up renting to your runner-up. That applicant moves in a week after the original applicant was supposed to begin renting. Calculate the amount of the deposit that you can keep as follows:

Per diem rate ($900 ÷ 30)	$ 30
No. days rent missed ×	7
Amount you can keep	$ 210

- **Re-renting expenses.** In the worst case scenario, none of your other applicants will qualify or be available to take your rental. In that event, you'll have to begin the whole search process again. Calculate your costs to re-advertise, show the unit, and check references, and deduct that cost from the deposit. If the holding deposit doesn't cover it, you can sue in small claims court for the excess, but consider first whether the amount is worth your time and trouble.

You'll find a Holding Deposit Agreement and Receipt on the CD-ROM that accompanies this book. A sample appears below.

Holding Deposit Agreement and Receipt

1. This will acknowledge receipt of the sum of $[*holding deposit*] by [*Landlord*] from [*Applicant*] as a holding deposit to hold vacant the rental property at [*rental property address*], until [*date*] at [*time*].

2. The property will be rented to Applicant on a [*month-to-month* or *lease*] basis at a rent of $_____ per month, if Applicant signs Landlord's [*lease or rental agreement*] and pays Landlord the first month's rent and $[*security deposit*] security deposit on or before that date, in which event the holding deposit will be applied to the first month's rent.

3. Landlord and Applicant agree that if Applicant fails to sign a lease or rental agreement and pay the remaining rent and security deposit, Landlord may retain of this holding deposit either or both of the following:

   a. a sum equal to the prorated daily rent of $[*rent per diem*] per day, until a new tenant begins paying rent, and/or

   b. a sum equal to any actual damages Landlord suffers, such as the costs of rerenting.

_____   _____
Applicant   Date

_____   _____
Landlord/Manager   Date

Signing the lease or rental agreement

When you hear your applicant's enthusiastic "Yes! I'll take it!" be sure to set up a time when the two of you can meet to sign the rental documents (and note this in the acceptance letter you send the tenant and under "Appointment to sign rental documents" on the Tenant Information Sheet). This meeting should take place as soon as possible. From your point of view, it will commit your applicant to this rental, which should discourage him or her from continuing to shop for an apartment. Applicants, too, often want the assurance that you are bound to the deal, especially when the market is tight and they fear you may find another applicant willing to pay more.

When signing a lease or rental agreement, be sure to date the signature as of the date you really sign it. Don't use the date when the tenancy will begin (the tenancy start date should be stated in the text of the document). That way, your tenant (and you, too) are legally bound to the deal right away, even if the tenant won't move in for many months.

Tenant Information Sheet (excerpt)

Appointment to sign rental documents

Date to sign rental documents ___ May 25, 20xx ___

Confirming letter sent ___ May 15, 20xx ___ (date)

Begin the New Tenancy Right: Ten Tips for a Successful Start

Having identified and secured your next new tenant, you're no doubt feeling relieved and eager to think of something other than credit reports, calls to landlords, and the often difficult attempt to make value judgments, however business driven and valid they are. So, let's concentrate on some nuts and bolts—how can you shift the methodical and careful approach that's worked so far to the next stage, that of welcoming your successful applicant and doing all you can to ensure a successful move in? Here are some tips:

1. **Pull your ads.** You'd be surprised at how easy it is to lose track of where you've placed your ads. Discontinue them and check to see if you can get a refund from newspapers or online services if you cancel early.

2. **Send new tenants a move-in letter.** Lots of details won't make it into your lease or rental agreement, but they are very important, such as the manager's phone number, where to report maintenance problems, details on garbage and recycling, and use of laundry rooms.

3. **Make sure you've wrapped up any loose ends with other applicants.** Read Chapter 16 on how to communicate rejections.

4. **Double check with current residents regarding their moving plans.** Make sure that everyone is on track to leave as expected.

5. **Confirm any planned work and schedules with contractors during "turnover time."** Be sure that all will be ready for the next occupants.

6. **Inspect the rental unit.** Make sure it's up to snuff, especially if it's been vacant.

7. **Prepare a landlord-tenant checklist for move-in day.** Your new tenants will be responsible only for damage they cause. Walk through the unit together when they arrive to assess the condition, so you can fairly measure what they're responsible for when they leave.

8. **Set up a file for this tenancy, beginning with the lease or rental agreement.** Keep all of the application materials, too, in case you need them later.

9. **Make sure you're ready to track income and expenses, such as rent and repairs.** Set up a spreadsheet or use a computer program to make it easier to fill out your Schedule E at the end of the year.

10. **Keep up-to-date with the ever-changing field of landlord-tenant law.** Make sure you're in the loop. Purchase new editions of Nolo's books for landlords (see order information at the end of this book).

Take Ten Minutes

You're done! Well, almost. Take a lesson from the military or big business and hold a little debriefing session with yourself. Like the Army and General Motors, you stand to learn a lot by a candid assessment of what worked and what didn't.

- **Review the Marketing Worksheet for this rental.** You may have already entered information on how applicants learned of your rental; if not, go back through your applications and record the data. Now, where did your most qualified applicants come from? If one marketing avenue (say, the college newspaper or a local online service) produced most of the applicants who ended high on your ranked list of applicants, concentrate on these methods next time.

- **Reflect on current tenants' role in your screening efforts.** For those of you who were working around current residents, think back on how you juggled the legitimate (and legally required) privacy needs of current tenants with your marketing and screening efforts. Was it ultimately counterproductive to try to rent this place while people lived there? If so, is that because your current tenants weren't fairly prepared (and compensated) for the inevitable intrusions that attend any vigorous marketing effort? Or did you make some mistakes—by promising showings that didn't correspond with legal notice laws?

- **Assess the time you've spent screening tenants—and the cost.** This book was designed for rental property owners who want to handle the selection process themselves—but was it worth it? Did you spend inordinate amounts of time at the expense of your regular job or your family or personal life? If so, think about the balance: If you were uncomfortable or at sea when interviewing applicants, speaking to references, or deconstructing a credit report, consider the alternatives (hiring a property manager, using an outside screening service, or investing elsewhere).

- **Sometime down the line, talk to your (hopefully stable) not-so-new tenants.** Over a cup of coffee or a quick chat at the mailbox, ask about their experience as they went through your screening and selection process. What did they find impressive, professional, reassuring … and what seemed excessive, irrelevant, or just plain silly? Think about the answers—maybe you need to explain your reasons behind certain questions, or perhaps there are practical issues that you didn't investigate ("Hey, I couldn't believe you didn't ask about…!") that will give you valuable tips for future screening (just be sure the suggestions are legally safe).

How to Reject—What to Say, What to Write

One of the toughest parts of being a landlord is rejecting tenants who haven't made the cut. Depending on how far along an applicant has progressed in your screening process, you will communicate and document the rejection in one or more ways:

- in a conversation, either on the phone or face to face
- in notes on the applicant's Tenant Information Sheet, where you'll enter the reason this person was rejected
- in a formal, legally required adverse action letter, which you must send under certain circumstances
- in a response to an adverse action letter, in which you must explain the information that caused your rejection, or
- in a less formal letter or email, which you may choose to send to those who aren't entitled to the formal letter.

On a personal level, it's not pleasant to say no, especially if the applicant is appealing in some ways but just doesn't meet your acceptance criteria or isn't the best of the bunch. On a legal level, it's very important to reject the right way. Sometimes it's just a matter of a word or a phrase that will make or break a fair housing complaint.

The chapter begins with ten tips on conveying a rejection, then goes on to explain the adverse action letter, which you must send when you reject based on information you receive from credit or background reports. It also explains how to communicate a rejection depending on the reason, such as insufficient income or too many occupants. For each particular reason we offer:

- suggested language for the conversation (be it on the phone, during a tour or open house, or at a later stage of screening), and
- wording you can use on your Tenant Information Sheet, to document the rejection, and in your response to a request for more information (following your sending of an adverse action letter).

The Law You Need to Know

The advice in this book has guided you towards legal reasons for rejecting applicants. This chapter tells you how to do it, and explains the legal rules that underlie those steps. In particular, the Fair Credit Reporting Act and Fair and Accurate Credit Transactions (FACT) Act of 2003 (15 U.S.C. §§ 1681 and following) specifies certain types of written notification you must send (called adverse action letters), depending on the circumstances of your rejection and whether the rejected applicant asks for more information.

✓ Before You Pick up the Phone, Jot a Note, or Write a Letter

It's always a good idea to pause for a moment before saying "No" to a caller, visitor, and anyone who has submitted a rental application. Ask yourself:

- Am I rejecting for sound, business-related reasons? (See Chapter 2 for details on discrimination.)
- Have I applied my selection criteria consistently, yet flexibly, with respect to first-time renters and self-employed applicants?
- Am I being too choosy? Should I lower the rent in order to capture otherwise-qualified tenants?
- What does my radar tell me about this applicant—should I tread with special caution, after hearing someone lecture me on the fine points of landlord/tenant law?
- Do my notes on the Tenant Information Sheet and any conversations I've had with an applicant's references clearly support the reason for my rejection?

Ten tips on how to reject

The following tips are the operating principles behind the conversations and written phrases for the rejection issues covered in this chapter. They are designed to help you legally reject an applicant with the minimum of fuss and the lowest chance that this person will take offense, visit a lawyer, and file a complaint. If you think that some of these tips are overly solicitous, get over it. Successful landlords know how to handle people, and if that means bending over backwards to soften a blow, do it. You don't have to be obsequious, but you do have to be tactful and willing to use a kind word rather than a harsh one, an artfully phrased sentence rather than one filled with legal landmines.

1 Don't hide behind "you were qualified, but applied too late"

The timid landlord's first refuge when rejecting applicants is to assure them that they were qualified, but someone equally qualified applied first. This is a comfortable dodge because you don't have to get into the truth behind the rejection, which can be hard to phrase and hard to hear. Now and then, this will be a truthful explanation, but most of the time renters hear it from landlords who are really rejecting for cause (because of negative information) but don't want to say so. These owners don't understand the risks they're taking by this seemingly safe approach.

Here's the difficulty: People with a problematic rental, employment, or credit history know who they are. They're hoping that you will not discover a particular problem (or problems), will listen to their explanations of why the skeleton isn't relevant, or will be so eager to fill your vacancy that you'll disregard it. When someone hears that you found them qualified, they'll know it isn't true, and may question your real reasons for rejection—were they based on that recent eviction, or the fact that the applicant has a family with two young children? You get the picture—by telling a lie, you've given applicants who are members of a protected class an opening to challenge you and argue that your real motives were illegal discrimination. You'll be better off stating the true reasons (and be darn sure they're based on sound business principles).

② Be consistent

Depending on why you reject and at what point during your screening procedure, you may be conveying a rejection in a conversation, making a note on the applicant's Tenant Information Sheet (perhaps with no communication with the tenant), and sending a formal, adverse action letter. In all cases, but especially when rejecting farther down

Landlord's Forms Library

This chapter contains letters you can use to communicate rejections:

- **Notice of Denial Based on Credit Report or Other Information.** A letter that contains the legally required information you must send to applicants whom you reject based on information from third parties, such as credit-reporting agencies, criminal background search firms, or tenant-screening agencies.
- **Response to Request for Further Information.** A letter you can send when rejected applicants request more information, after receiving your adverse action letter.
- **Denial of Request for Further Information.** Send this letter when you may legally decline to furnish more information, and
- **Rejection Letter.** A letter you can send to applicants who aren't entitled to an adverse action letter.

Rejection letters are among the most important documents in an applicant's file. You must be able to prove that you sent required adverse action letters, if challenged. Keep all correspondence related to rejections in the applicant's file, which you should store for at least three years.

the line—after a phone screening, property visit, and credit report review—be sure that your documentation is consistent. Every notation should support the next. If your notes are all over the place, a clever fair housing lawyer may seize on the inconsistency as evidence of a sinister, discriminatory motive. Don't create that chink in your armor.

③ Make it about the property or you—not the applicant

No one likes to be told that they don't have the right stuff—that they make too little money, plan to live with too many people, have an employer who won't vouch for them, or have spending habits that aren't honorable. Still, if this is what you learn, it may be the reason you're saying, "No." It's possible that the applicant is, in fact, a steady, though modest, wage-earner; the family may be big, but supportive and wonderful; the employer is a jerk who wouldn't recognize, let alone recommend, the best of workers; and the applicant got into financial trouble because he or she was gullible but honest (and has since learned a lesson). You'll never know the real story, and unless you're desperate for tenants (or really want this particular applicant), you can't take the time to investigate.

So here's the key to using your system, but breaking the news gently: Put the onus on you or the property, not on the applicant. The more you can cast the

rejection as a failure of something or someone other than the applicant or his or her history, the easier it will be for the disappointed applicant to hear your news.

You'll see lots of examples of this principle in the specific "How Not to Do It" conversations below. For example, don't say that the caller doesn't meet your rule that the tenant's income must be three times the rent. Instead, explain that the income requirement for this rental doesn't correspond to the caller's situation. Or, if the applicant wants to live in your two-bedroom flat with his immediate family, cousin, and aunt, don't say his family is too big. Simply say that the size of the unit will not accommodate his needs. Responses like these suggest to your caller that it's you or your property that haven't been able to deliver, not him.

④ Suggest an alternative

If you can, suggest other rental options. You may be familiar with properties in the neighborhood or city that the prospect is more likely to qualify for. For instance, you might mention that the apartment complex down the street does take pets, or you might suggest other places to look for advertisements. ("Have you checked out the bulletin board at the Community Center? There are often ads that you won't find in the paper.") Be careful, however, that you don't steer applicants (see Chapter 2) or convey a message that the caller belongs "on the other side of the tracks." Be very sure you're not sending callers to areas of town that are, for all intents and purposes, segregated.

5 Use the passive voice

When you phrase something in the passive voice, you're eliminating the subject in the subject-verb duo. If the verb is, or points to, something uncomfortable, it's nice to be able to hide the subject. For example, if you're too embarrassed to write, "I made some mistakes," you'd say, "Mistakes were made." As you can see, the passive voice is rather slippery and dishonest, and all good writers avoid it (but politicians love it).

Whether you want to lower yourself in this manner is, truly, a matter for you and your grammar conscience. However smarmy, the passive voice will come in handy when you want to duck. It's also a good way to deflect attention from an applicant whose shortcomings have prompted the rejection. For example:

- "The application was denied." You denied it but would like to leave the impression that someone else may have done the deed.
- "Income minimum was not met." This is another way of saying that the applicant doesn't make enough money for your rental.
- "References for pet were insufficient." You've contacted the current

landlord, who reports that the dog barks all day, but here, you're focusing on the reference, not the dog.

6 Don't argue

If you've decided to hold firm on a particular rental term, stick to your guns and don't get sucked into an argument. You'll simply waste time and introduce the possibility that you'll get mad or exasperated and say something unwise. The best approach when you encounter a persistent applicant is to acknowledge that you understand what the person is saying and understand that the issue is important, but you aren't able to accommodate the request. If necessary, repeat it. Once you begin justifying your position, you're in for a debate.

7 Respect the confidentiality of applicant references

Whenever possible, protect the source of negative information. For example, if you learn from the current employer that this applicant is on probation, you don't have to share the source and details of your rejection right away with your applicant. You can simply say, "I did not get a positive picture from your references," and you may want to mention the promise you made to references that you would protect their confidentiality. The applicant does not know which reference supplied the negative information. You would be wise, however, to note the details on the applicant's Tenant Information Sheet.

8 Know when to shut up

Knowing when to say nothing is a very hard skill to learn and apply. Most of us naturally want to explain and justify our position, and convince the other side that we're right. But once you begin explaining, justifying, or apologizing, you're inviting a debate or argument that you don't want.

Some applicants hope that their silence in the face of your "No" (whether on the phone or face to face) will trigger an explanation, justification, or apology. They'll deliberately not respond to your message, hoping that you'll feel uncomfortable or guilty and will reopen the issue with a restatement of your decision or a defense of it. This will give your prospect an opening to try to talk you out if it. Don't fall for this common trap. If there's silence at the other end of the line or from your prospect, try to fill it with some innocuous remark, such as, "I'm sure you'll find a rental that suits you," or "These times are really tough for lots of renters." If you need the erstwhile excuse, "My other line is ringing," use it. And if you're talking in person at the rental or in the office, you can always stand and move toward the exit, saying graciously, "Let me see you to the door."

9 Always say thank you and wish the prospect good luck

It never hurts to be mannerly. Always thank callers and visitors for their interest and wish them good luck. You never know what may result from your good manners—these prospects may not qualify, but they may recommend your property to a friend or acquaintance, if they've had a good experience dealing with you.

10 Don't give them something to talk about

Just as you must respect the privacy of your residents, you should also respect the privacy and feelings of those who *don't* become your tenants. Refrain from sharing the details of rejected applicants' work and personal lives with the successful applicant or anyone else. You never know where your gossip might end up—it might land on a lawyer's desk.

Adverse action letters

Your decision to reject an applicant will be based on information you received from any number of sources. Depending on the source, you may need to send a federally required adverse action letter that describes the basis of your decision and explains the applicant's rights to more information as to the rejection.

Situations that do not require an adverse action letter

You may communicate your rejection in a conversation alone (or in a letter or email, as explained below in "Communicate post-application rejections by mail or email") if the basis of your rejection is one of the following sources:

- information supplied by applicants themselves, in conversations with you or on your Rental Application
- information you learn by contacting an applicant's reference (the Fair Credit Reporting Act is a bit unclear on this point, but the Federal Trade Commission seems to have interpreted the law this way), or
- information you learned about an applicant when you or your employee accessed a Megan's Law database and saw the applicant's name in it.

"Do You Need to Send an Adverse Action Letter?" below, provides examples of situations when you don't need to send an adverse action letter.

Situations that require an adverse action letter

You *must* send an adverse action letter if your decision to reject an applicant was based in whole or in part on the following sources of information:

- a credit report
- a criminal background report, or

- a tenant-screening company, management company, or any other third party who is not your employee.

Even if information from the credit or background report or third party played a small part in your decision to reject someone (perhaps a negative landlord reference also was a factor), you must still send the adverse action letter. In practical terms, this means that most of the time, you'll need to send a notice like this if you hire a tenant-screening company or even look at a credit report.

You'll find an adverse action letter, Notice of Denial Based on Credit Report or Other Information, on the CD-ROM that accompanies this book. A sample appears below.

How to prepare an adverse action letter

The notice of denial letter is not difficult to fill out. First, enter the name and address of the applicant and the rental property address. Then check the box(es) that describe the basis of your decision:

☐ **Insufficient information in the credit report provided by ....** Check this box when the credit report, criminal background report, or screening report cannot verify income, employment, or other important issues

Notice of Denial Based on Credit Report or Other Information

To: [*Applicant*]

[*Street Address*]

[*City, State, and Zip*]

Your rights under the Fair Credit Reporting Act and Fair and Accurate Credit Transactions (FACT) Act of 2003. (15 U.S.C. §§ 1681 and following.)

THIS NOTICE is to inform you that your application to rent the property at [*rental property address*] has been denied because of [check all that apply]:

☐ Insufficient information in the credit report provided by:
[*Credit-reporting agency*]
[*Address, phone number, URL*]

☐ Negative information in the credit report provided by:
[*Credit-reporting agency*]
[*Address, phone number, URL*]

☐ The consumer-credit-reporting agency noted above did not make the decision not to offer you this rental. It only provided information about your credit history. You have the right to obtain a free copy of your credit report from the consumer-credit-reporting agency named above, if your request is made within 60 days of this notice or if you have not requested a free copy within the past year. You also have the right to dispute the accuracy or completeness of your credit report. The agency must reinvestigate within a reasonable time, free of charge, and remove or modify inaccurate information. If the reinvestigation does not resolve the dispute to your satisfaction, you may add your own "consumer statement" (up to 100 words) to the report, which must be included (or a clear summary) in future reports.

☐ Information supplied by a third party other than a credit-reporting agency or you. You have the right to learn of the nature of the information if you ask me in writing within 60 days of learning of this decision. This information was gathered by someone other than myself or any employee.

_____   _____

Landlord/Manager   Date

Do You Need to Send an Adverse Action Letter?

This guide will help you figure out whether you need to send a rejected applicant an adverse action letter.

You *don't* have to send a formal adverse action letter if the following describes your decision.	You *must* send an adverse action letter if the following describes your decision (even if other factors played a part, too).
You reject because you won't vary a basic rental term, such as the rent or deposit amount, your pet policy, or your occupancy limit, when asked by the applicant.	You hire a tenant-screening company, which gives you a report that includes negative information (such as a recent out-of-state burglary) leading you to reject this applicant.
Information supplied by the applicant on the rental application shows that he or she cannot meet your criteria (no current income or source of support, for example).	You pay an online criminal-background search firm for a nationwide search and report, which tells you that the applicant has a recent conviction that you conclude makes him or her a poor risk.
In conversation with the applicant, you learn he's being evicted and you decide he's a poor risk for that reason.	You sign up with a consumer-screening agency that supplies only a credit report, and decide to reject on the basis of what's in the report.
A self-employed applicant provides tax returns that show an income below your "three times the rent" standard.	Your local apartment owners' association has an arrangement with a tenant-screening company that gives you a report that leads you to conclude that an applicant is a poor risk.
You, your manager, or other employee calls a current or past landlord, employer, or personal reference and learns information that leads you to conclude that this person should be rejected.	You pay someone on a contractual basis to do your tenant-screening (this person is an independent contractor, not your employee). The report this individual gives you leads you to conclude that you won't rent to an applicant.
An employed applicant supplies pay stubs that are significantly below the monthly earnings reported on the application, and you reject for this discrepancy.	You contract with a local real estate office to investigate potential renters and decide against an applicant based on what they tell you.
You require every applicant to show proof of legal immigration status, and the applicant has not supplied adequate proof.	

For more information, see the Federal Trade Commission's advice, "Using Consumer Reports: What Landlords Need to Know." Go to the FTC website at www.ftc.gov, and enter the title in the home page search box.

☐ **Negative information in the credit report provided by ...** when the afore-mentioned reports reveal facts that make this applicant a poor risk

☐ **The consumer credit-reporting agency noted above ....** Check this box if you checked *either* of the previous two boxes.

☐ **Information supplied by a third party ....** Check this box if you've used any third party, such as a real estate office, property management firm, or another independent contractor that interviewed an applicant's current or past employer, landlord, neighbors, or any other personal contacts.

The letter advises the applicant of his or her rights under the law, including the right to obtain a copy of the relevant report from the firm that issued it, to dispute its contents, and to get more information from you should your decision be the last one explained above.

How to send the adverse action letter

It's a good idea to mail the adverse action letter to your applicant—emailing the letter does not give you the paper trail you'll need if the applicant claims he or she never received it. If you want to be extremely cautious, send the letter return receipt requested. This will give you proof that the applicant received your letter on a certain date. That date may become important: If your denial was based on information from a third party other than a credit or other reporting agency (the fourth box on the form), the applicant may request an explanation within 60 days of learning of your denial. Knowing for certain when the 60 days begins to run will allow you to calculate the time without having to estimate how long the letter remained in transit.

How to respond to requests for more details

As you saw on the adverse action letter, you must tell rejected applicants that if you rejected them based on information gathered by a third party, they have the right to ask you for information concerning "the nature of the information." Just as you were mindful of the need to express yourself sparingly and legally when prescreening tenants, here, too, you must choose your words with caution (unfortunately, there are no legal guide-lines on what the fuzzy phrase, "the nature of the information" means). Using this book's Response to Request for Further Information letter as your template, give the applicant a truthful explanation, but one that will not invite an angry phone call or support a lawsuit. Refer to the section, "Rejections: How to say them, how to write them" for suggested ways to convey the nature of the information.

Response to Request for Further Information

To: [*Applicant*]
    [*Street Address*]
    [*City, State, and Zip*]

This notice complies with the Fair Credit Reporting Act and Fair and Accurate Credit Transactions (FACT) Act of 2003. (15 U.S.C. §§ 1681 and following.)

On [*date*], I sent you a letter notifying you that your application to rent the residential property at [*property address*] had been denied. The letter advised you of your rights under the Fair Credit Reporting Act (15 U.S. Code Sections 1681 and following). It explained that if you are rejected due in whole or in part to information gathered by third parties other than a credit-reporting agency, background-reporting firm, or tenant-screening firm), you have the right to learn of "the nature of the information" if you so request in writing within 60 days of learning of the denial. This right to further information does not apply to information gathered directly by the landlord or landlord's employee.

I received your written request on [*date you received applicant's request*]. Your application was denied based in whole or in part on _____
_____ .

Yours truly,

_____   _____
Landlord/Manager   Date

You'll find the Response to Request for Further Information letter on the CD-ROM that accompanies this book. The text appears below.

How to deny a rejected applicant's request for further information

Now and then, you'll receive requests for further information that arrive too late—that is, you'll get them more than 60 days after the applicant learned of your adverse action. Strictly speaking, you don't have to respond. But think twice before choosing to ignore the request, especially if:

- **The request is only a few days late.** Applicants may argue that they received your letter several days after it should have been delivered. Everyone has had exasperating experiences with the postal service, and it's not impossible for a letter to get waylaid. Unless you sent the adverse action letter return receipt requested, you have no proof that it got there earlier. It's easier to send the response letter than get embroiled in an argument like this.
- **You fear that a fair housing claim is just around the corner.** Refusing to respond to the request may serve to further inflame the applicant. Send it, but be aware—if you're being set up, choose your words with utmost care.

If you receive such a request quite a bit after the fact, especially if you want to cut off communications with an applicant whom you suspect will never go away, send the Denial of Request for Further Information letter, which is simple to fill out (just enter the applicant's information and the relevant dates). Check the first box when the request is too late and fill in details as requested.

You may also receive a request from applicants who don't understand (or accept) that they aren't entitled to further information if you, or your employee, gathered the information (by speaking with references, for example). If this explains what happened—you did the work yourself and didn't use a screening service or otherwise contract out the screening—check the second box in the letter.

You'll find the Denial of Request for Further Information letter on the CD-ROM that accompanies this book. A sample appears below.

Denial of Request for Further Information

To: [*Applicant*]
    [*Street Address*]
    [*City, State, and Zip*]

On [*date*], I sent you a letter notifying you that your application to rent the residential property at [*property address*] had been denied. The letter advised you of your rights under the Fair Credit Reporting Act (15 U.S. Code Sections 1681 and following). It explained that if you are rejected in whole or in part due to information from third parties (sources other than yourself or a credit report), you have the right to learn of "the nature of the information" if you so request in writing within 60 days learning of the denial. It advised you that this right to further information does not apply to information gathered directly by the landlord or landlord's employee.

☐ I received your written request on [*date you received the letter*]. This was [*number of days between the date the applicant learned of the adverse action and your receipt of the request*] days after your receipt of the denial letter. Therefore, I do not have a duty to disclose to you the nature of the information that supported my decision. (15 U.S. Code Section 1681m(b)(1).)

☐ The information was gathered by myself or my employee.

Yours truly,

_____   _____
Landlord/Manager   Date

Rejections: How to say them, how to write them

Here are some common reasons landlords reject tenants, along with suggested ways to break the bad news, how to document rejections in your records, and how to phrase the rejection in a letter (in response to a request for more information, following an adverse action letter). Following each set of oral and written suggestions, you'll also see a section on how *not* to say it or write it.

Applicant's income is insufficient to pay the rent

It's very common to encounter applicants whose gross income is less than three times the monthly rent, which is the standard ratio required by most land-lords. You will discover whether a prospect meets this requirement early on, perhaps in the phone screening (should you choose this level of screening) and certainly when you review the Rental Application. Now and then, you might want to be flexible on this point (see Chapter 10), but most of the time you'll stand firm.

 "I'm sorry, but I won't be able to consider your application. I use the industry standard that calls for the rent being no more than one third of the tenant's gross monthly income. You sound like a great renter otherwise and I'm sure you'll soon be successful in finding a rental."

"Gross income is less than three times the rent."

Rejecting Because of Insufficient Income: How *Not* to Do It	
Poor choice of words	**What's the problem?**
"You don't make enough."	Don't focus on the applicant's earning capacity (you'll just embarrass him).
"With your job, you don't make enough to qualify."	How the applicant makes his income, as long as it's legal, is of no concern to you.
"Bus driver, doesn't make enough."	In cities that give protected status to persons on the basis of their personal characteristics, such as occupation, this could invite a lawsuit.

Applicant proposes too many occupants for the unit's size

The maximum number of occupants you'll allow in the rental is one of your most important rental policies. This number must at least be in keeping with the federal standard of two per bedroom, and if your state or locality has legislated a more generous standard, you must follow that. See Chapter 2 for more information on occupancy standards.

If you've set an occupancy standard that allows fewer occupants than the relevant legal standard and are challenged by, say, a large family, you'll survive the challenge only if you can convince a judge that sound business reasons underlie your policy (such as physical limitations of your property). On the applicant's Tenant Information Sheet, in the "Rental application, notes" or "Interview conclusions" sections, be sure to reference the basis for your lower number (and you'd better have a good, objectively-verifiable basis for your standard!).

"In keeping with [*federal, state or local*] law, the maximum number of occupants for this rental is [*X*]. I'm afraid this rental is too small for your needs." If your standard is lower than the relevant legal standard, just refer to "the occupancy policy for this unit."

"Exceeds occupancy standard." If you're using a standard that permits fewer occupants than the relevant legal standard, be more specific when making notes on the Tenant Information Sheet, such as, "Exceeds property's occupancy standard of [*X*] residents, based on flow restrictions of water well."

Rejecting Because of Too Many Occupants: How *Not* to Do It	
Poor choice of words	**What's the problem?**
"Your family is too big." "You've got too many kids." "There are too many unrelated adults for the number of bedrooms."	Remember, it's the sheer number of occupants, not their ages, sex, or relation to each other, that matters. This landlord is inviting a claim of discrimination against families and, in some states and cities, against unmarried adults.

Applicant wants a pet in a no-pets rental

Despite a clear ad that says "No pets," you're bound to encounter callers and visitors who have a dog or cat and apply anyway. They may be certain that they can talk you into accepting their darling puppy, kitten, or pet pig; or, in a soft market, they may be banking on your being less choosy. And, indeed, you may want to rethink your policy, if the market and/or a personal meeting with the applicant and his or her pet convinces you that it would be a good business decision to take this applicant, pet included (see Chapter 10 for advice on situations that warrant flexibility). Of course, if your applicant is legally disabled and asks to bring a service animal, you must bend your no-pets policy when you obtain verification that the owner needs the animal to live comfortably and safely on your property (see Chapter 2 for details on this).

In multi-family rentals: "Your [_pet_] sounds like a well-behaved animal, but I must apply my policy consistently—there are many tenants in the building who have rented with the understanding that this is a no-pets building, and I have a legal duty to honor that expectation."

In single-family rentals: "I've found that my overall costs are lower when there aren't animals in the rental. I know you have a well-behaved pet, but I've decided to follow this policy."

"Has a pet, no-pets policy." You may also want to write, "Has a pet, no request for accommodation."

Rejecting When the Applicant Wants to Bring a Pet: How _Not_ to Do It	
Poor choice of words	**What's the problem?**
"I can't accept you with that [_pet_]."	This suggests that there's something wrong with the owner and/or the pet. You might as well diss the applicant's child—you're asking for hurt feelings or an argument.
"The last dog made a mess. I've had it with dogs."	You're inviting a discussion of the last tenant's dog and how the applicant's dog is superior. It's an impossible discussion because you're each in the dark—you don't know the applicant's dog, and the applicant doesn't know what you just went through.

Applicant wants renovations or other policy changes

If you've been in the rental property business for very long, you've doubtless encountered tenants who consider the landlord their protector and provider. Your job, they feel, is to make the rental nice for them, whatever their needs (or whatever the costs). They have lists of requests, usually starting with a lower rent or security deposit, and including repaint-ing, new appliances or carpet, a month of free rent, and so on. Experienced land-lords can spot these difficult types a mile away, and resist renting to them if at all possible, seeing only aggravation ahead.

How do you reject someone you know will nickel-and-dime you forever? This person may well meet your standard criteria concerning income and credit.

Though you can hardly have an announced policy of "No whiners," you can turn these folks away by putting the request or complaint in the context of your rental policies, instead of reacting personally—and then saying "No." Often, you'll employ Tip #8 ("Know when to shut up") and simply refuse to engage. This shift will make it clear that you're not going to play the role of landlord-as-parent. You'll see examples below.

"I understand that new window coverings are important to you, but this rental will not be refurbished at this time." "I'm afraid I'm going to have to stick with the advertised terms."

"Applicant wants [*requested amenity or policy variation*], which is not part of the advertised package."

Rejecting Because of Excessive Demands: How *Not* to Do It	
Poor choice of words	**What's the problem?**
"Demanding, wants better terms." "Whiner, will be nothing but trouble."	Though this description may be accurate, it's fodder in the hands of a tenant's lawyer because it suggests that there's something personally wrong with the applicant. If this person happens to be a member of a protected class, the lawyer will argue that your personal aversion had less to do with the applicant's demands and more to do with illegal discrimination.

Applicant does not have sufficient identification or proof of right to be in the United States

Your rental policies will advise all applicants that you'll need photo identification and an ID that will enable you to order a credit report, such as a Social Security number (SSN) or Individual Taxpayer's Identification Number (ITIN) (see Chapter 6). You may reject applicants who cannot supply this information, as long as you follow this policy consistently. You'll need to be careful, however, that your rejection doesn't suggest that you're excluding certain types of people, as shown below.

Except in California, you may also want to require all applicants to provide proof that they are legally in the United States. Chapter 6 explains how applicants can satisfy this rental term. If your applicant cannot furnish adequate proof, you can reject using a clear statement that this requirement was not fulfilled.

I'M SORRY, BUT... "I require a photo ID and Social Security number or ITIN from everyone. I cannot process your application without them." "I cannot advance your application without sufficient proof that you are legally in the United States."

✎ "Did not supply required photo ID [and SSN or ITIN]." "Did not provide proof of right to be in the United States."

Rejecting Because of Missing or Insufficient ID or Proof of Legal Status: How *Not* to Do It	
Poor choice of words	**What's the problem?**
"Doesn't have an SSN."	Immigrants who are legally in this country may not have an SSN. If you reject applicants without SSNs, you may face a claim of discrimination on the basis of national origin.
"No driver's license."	You may be rejecting on the basis of no photo ID, but if you phrase it as "no driver's license," you exclude those who might have other forms of ID, such as immigration cards.
"Foreigner, no ID." "From [*country*], no papers."	You might as well say, "I'm discriminating on the basis of national origin" and invite a HUD inspector to come on over.

Applicant's references are not supportive

Calling landlords and employers listed on the rental application will give you a chance to learn from another person what it's like to do business with this applicant. These conversations are essential. Someone can look great on paper, but in fact be an unpleasant, rule-breaking neighbor or employee—a poor risk for you.

When communicating a rejection on this basis, you'll have to be quite careful. If you're delivering the rejection orally, you should do your best to protect the source, especially if you've promised to do so, as explained in Tip #7. A description of "no positive references" might suffice, and mentioning that you promised to not divulge details might satisfy some rejected applicants.

Be especially careful when rejecting on the basis of what an employer tells you, unless it's other than, "He doesn't work here!" (that's a pretty obvious basis for rejection). As explained in Chapter 10, you're looking for information that's relevant to this person's likely behavior as a tenant and should ignore other remarks (an employee might be unskilled at work but a perfectly hassle-free tenant, for example).

"I'm sorry, but I didn't receive sufficient positive recommendations from your references."

"Landlord did not recommend."
"Employer could not recommend."

Rejecting Because of Negative References: How *Not* to Do It	
Poor choice of words	**What's the problem?**
"Your landlord said you were a bad tenant." "You've caused lots of problems at your current complex." "Your employer says you're often late and are a so-so employee."	Too vague and personal.
"Your boss says you haven't met your production goals."	This quality may have nothing to do with whether this person will be a good tenant.

Applicant has a relevant criminal history

The rental application in this book includes a space for applicants to list any criminal convictions. You may see a conviction that reasonably leads you to conclude that this person poses a current, direct threat to your property or other tenants. You'll want to reject this applicant, and can do so orally if you wish and leave it at that (since the information came from the applicant, not a third party). You should enter the reason on the Tenant Information Sheet, too. (See Chapter 13 for guidance on evaluating criminal history.)

Some of you may have decided to investigate your applicant's criminal background further, either by hiring a tenant-screening service that will include a search of various conviction databases, or by doing a Megan's Law search yourself. Chapter 13 explains the pros and cons of this decision. Suppose you obtain a background report and learn of a conviction that wasn't listed, and you conclude that the applicant poses a current, direct threat. You can convey your rejection orally, and should also make a note on the Tenant Information Sheet (in the "Additional screening tools" section), but you must also send an adverse action letter. You may have to send a response if the applicant requests more information. (You don't have to send the letter if you or your employee accessed your state's Megan's Law database on your own.)

Rejecting Because of Criminal Background: How *Not* to Do It	
Poor choice of words	**What's the problem?**
"We don't rent to people with a record."	You know that some convictions aren't relevant, and you shouldn't be using them as a reason for denial, but this explanation suggests that you reject for any record. Don't give applicants an opening to challenge you.
"You aren't the kind of tenant we want around here."	If the applicant is a member of a legally protected group, regardless of his status as a convicted person, you've handed him a basis for filing a complaint.

When you discover that the applicant did not list convictions that you later discover, you have the first grounds for denial—an inaccuracy on the rental application concerning an important issue. Be sure to mention and list that as the first grounds for denial, and then support your conclusion (that the inaccuracy is material) by specifying the conviction. As explained in Chapter 13, you'll be on thin ice if you mention a 20-year old conviction for driving under the influence when the rest of the record and personal history is clean.

> "I'm denying your application because important information you reported on your Rental Application was not accurate. In addition, I'm denying based on your conviction for [*name the conviction*] in [*year*]."

> "Inaccurate rental application answers; relevant criminal conviction ([*name the conviction and the year*])."

Information from the credit or other report is negative

The credit report should hold no surprises for you if the applicant has been truthful on your rental application. Still, it will happen, and you'll learn of unreported debts, see a series of charge backs, or discover that there's a recent bankruptcy. When your rejection depends even a little bit on what you learn from the credit report, you must send an adverse action letter. Here's what to say (and write, on the Tenant Information Sheet and in response to any request for further information):

> "I can't advance your application after reviewing your credit report." "The denial is based on your credit score, which does not meet our minimum requirements."

> "The credit report shows a financial picture that does not meet our minimum requirements."

Rejecting Because of Negative Credit Report: How *Not* to Do It	
Poor choice of words	**What's the problem?**
"The denial is based on your poor credit history/low credit score."	You're making it personal, by emphasizing the applicant's "poor" showing.
"The credit report is bad."	Invites the applicant to challenge the accuracy of the credit report. You can assume it's valid unless the applicant can convince you to the contrary.

Applicant is qualified, but the early bird got the rental

If you're lucky, you'll end up with more than one qualified applicant for your rental. When you really can't rank one above the other—this is not, after all, a science—the only safe tiebreaker is to offer the rental to the applicant whose completed application you received first. You don't have to send an adverse action letter (since negative information from a third party gathered by someone other than your or an employee did not cause the rejection).

It's a good idea to take the time to communicate the bad news (though you could say nothing and hope the applicant figures things out). You'll invite an angry response if you turn away, without explanation, people who know they have good credit, a fine reference from their landlord and employer, and enough income. Besides, these conversations aren't as tough as the ones that are outright rejections, since you're simply saying, "Someone equally qualified beat you to the punch."

"I'm sorry, I can't offer you this rental. You were qualified and I would have rented to you, but another applicant who was equally qualified submitted a completed application ahead of yours. When there's a tie, I find that the fair thing to do is to rent to the person who turned in the application first."

"Qualified, but application received after that of [*applicant you have chosen*]."

Rejecting When Applicant is Qualified, But Too Late: How *Not* to Do It	
Poor choice of words	**What's the problem?**
"You gave me your application too late."	This suggests that the applicant failed by delivering the application late. Unless you did impose a deadline, don't confuse matters.
"Another applicant got here first."	This is imprecise and may be inaccurate (an earlier caller or visitor may not have delivered a *completed* application before the person you're rejecting). Accurately describe your deadline (day and time you received the completed application).

Communicate post-application rejections by mail or email

When you reject an applicant at an early stage, such as over the phone, there's no need to follow up with a confirming letter. At the other end of the process, as we've seen in this chapter, you *must* send a letter when your denial is based on information in a credit or background report, or collected by other third parties. And as you read just above, it's good manners to communicate with those who *were* qualified, but gave you their application after an equally qualified candidate.

Now, what about those applicants whom you reject for cause (because of negative information), but who aren't legally entitled to an adverse action letter—should they get a written rejection? For example, when you review the self-reported information in the rental application and conclude that this applicant is not a good risk, should you call, send an email or letter, or just let the application lapse and hope the applicant gets the hint?

Many successful landlords will tell you that the less said, the better. They point to the time it takes to call and write and add that these actions are apt to invite arguments. Who has the time, anyway? Others will say that good manners teach that if an applicant has filled out your lengthy application and paid for a credit report, the least you can do is send a form letter. Besides, there are two sound legal reasons for communicating a rejection in writing at this stage:

- **A written rejection documents your reasons for turning this applicant down.** You'll cite insufficient income, poor references, a low credit score, or any of the other legal reasons that will support a rejection. Should you be challenged later, you'll want this written evidence of your law-abiding motives.

- **A letter in place of a phone call may avoid what could be an unpleasant conversation.** Delivering a rejection is never fun, and if your applicant is angry or pushy, you could be in for an uncomfortable exchange. Worse, in the course of the conversation you may say things that you'll regret, including explanations that can be twisted and used against you. You might want to use the letter or email as the sole means of delivering the bad news. This is not to say that you'll never end up in a conversation with a persistent applicant (someone who really wants the place may call you before you've even written the letter), but if your letter gets there first, at least you can say, "As I said in my letter…" and repeat this as long as it takes to get off the phone.

If you side with the say-it-in-writing group, keep it short and sweet, with a minimum of explanation. If you do

Rejection Letter

To: [_Applicant_]

    [_Street Address_]

    [_City, State, and Zip_]

Thank you for applying to rent the property at [_rental property address_]. I have carefully considered your Rental Application, but I will not be able to make an offer to you, due to [_reason for denial_].

Yours truly,

_____   _____

Landlord/Manager   Date

communicate your denial in person or on the phone, you can also follow up with a written rejection, using a letter or a similar email.

 The Rejection Letter is on the CD-ROM that accompanies this book. A sample appears above.

Don't send the Rejection Letter if your situation requires an adverse action letter. If your decision was prompted in whole or in part by information on the applicant's credit report or information you received that was gathered by other third parties, such as property management companies or tenant-screening firms, you must send an adverse action letter. The Rejection Letter is not appropriate in these situations.

Take Ten Minutes

You've learned how, and in what manner, to convey a rejection. Now, look back on the process that led to the applicants' unsuccessful bids for your rental.

- Did you reject for the same reason, over and over? Maybe you need to make your rental criteria more explicit.
- Pull out your Marketing Worksheet and enter the number of rejects that came from each advertising medium you chose. Did one avenue produce a lot of unsuitable applicants? Drop that one next time, or improve your ad.
- Did you skip phone screening, but end up rejecting a large number of applicants at the very end of your labor-intensive screening process? Maybe you should consider phone screening, to get to the issues that might eliminate unsuitable candidates early on.

Appendix:
How to Use the CD-ROM

The CD-ROM included with this book can be used with Windows computers. It installs files that use software programs that need to be on your computer already. It is not a standalone software program.

In accordance with U.S. copyright laws, the CD-ROM and its files are for your personal use only.

Please read this appendix and the "Readme.htm" file included on the CD-ROM for instructions on using the CD-ROM. For a list of files and their file names, see the end of this appendix.

Note to Macintosh users: This CD-ROM and its files should also work on Macintosh computers. Please note, however, that Nolo cannot provide technical support for non-Windows users.

Note to eBook users: You can access the CD-ROM files mentioned here from the bookmarked section of the eBook, located on the left hand side.

Installing the Files Onto Your Computer

To work with the files on the CD-ROM, you first need to install them onto your hard disk. Here's how:

Windows 2000, XP, and Vista

Follow the CD-ROM's instructions that appear on the screen.

If nothing happens when you insert the CD-ROM, then:

How to View the README File

To view the "Readme.htm" file, insert the CD-ROM into your computer's CD-ROM drive and follow these instructions:

Windows 2000, XP, and Vista

1. On your PC's desktop, double-click the **My Computer** icon.
2. Double-click the icon for the CD-ROM drive into which the CD-ROM was inserted.
3. Double-click the file "Readme.htm."

Macintosh

1. On your Mac desktop, double-click the icon for the CD-ROM that you inserted.
2. Double-click the file "Readme.htm."

1. Double-click the **My Computer** icon.
2. Double-click the icon for the CD-ROM drive into which the CD-ROM was inserted.
3. Double-click the file "Welcome. exe."

Macintosh

If the **Nolo's Landlord Resources CD** window is not open, double-click the **Nolo's Landlord Resources CD** icon. Then:

1. Select the **Landlord Resources** folder icon.
2. Drag and drop the folder icon onto your computer.

Using the Word Processing Files to Create Documents

The CD-ROM includes word processing files that you can open, complete, print, and save with your word processing program. All word processing files come in rich text format and have the extension ".rtf." For example, the file for the Move Out Letter discussed in Chapter 3 is on the file "MoveOut.rtf." RTF files can be read by most recent word processing programs including MS *Word*, Windows *WordPad*, and recent versions of *WordPerfect*.

The following are general instructions. Because each word processor uses different commands to open, format, save, and print documents, refer to your word processor's help file for specific instructions.

Do not call Nolo's technical support if you have questions on how to use your word processor or your computer.

Opening a File

You can open word processing files with any of the three following ways:

1. Windows users can open a file by selecting its "shortcut."
   i. Click the Windows **Start** button.
   ii. Open the **Programs** folder.
   iii. Open the **Landlord Resources** folder.
   iv. Click the shortcut to the file you want to work with.

Where Are the Files Installed?

Windows: By default, all the files are installed to the **Landlord Resources** folder in the **Program Files** folder of your computer. A folder called **Landlord Resources** is added to the **Programs** folder of the **Start** menu.

Macintosh: All the files are located in the **Landlord Resources** folder.

2. Both Windows and Macintosh users can open a file by double-clicking it.

   i.   Use **My Computer** or **Windows Explorer** (Windows 2000, XP, or Vista) or the **Finder** (Macintosh) to go to the **Landlord Resources** folder.

   ii.   Double-click the file you want to open.

3. Windows and Macintosh users can open a file from within their word processor.

   i.   Open your word processor.

   ii.   Go to the **File** menu and choose the **Open** command. This opens a dialog box.

   iii.   Select the location and name of the file. (You will navigate to the version of the **Landlord Resources** folder that you've installed on your computer.)

Editing Your Document

Here are tips for working on your document.

Refer to the book's instructions and sample agreements for help.

Underlines indicate where to enter information, frequently including bracketed instructions. Delete the underlines and instructions before finishing your document.

Signature lines should appear on a page with at least some text from the document itself.

Printing Out the Document

Use your word processor's or text editor's **Print** command to print out your document.

Editing Files That Have Optional or Alternative Text

Some files have optional or alternate text:

- With optional text, you choose whether to include or exclude the given text.
- With alternative text, you select one alternative to include and exclude the other alternatives.

When editing these files, we suggest you do the following:

Optional text

Delete optional text you do not want to include and keep that which you do. In either case, delete the italicized instructions. If you choose to delete an optional numbered clause, renumber the subsequent clauses after deleting it.

Alternative text

Delete all the alternatives that you do not want to include first. Then delete the italicized instructions.

Saving Your Document

Use the **Save As** command to save and rename your document. You will be unable to use the **Save** command because the files are "read-only." If you save the file without renaming it, the underlines that indicate where you need to enter your information will be lost, and you will be unable to create a new document with this file without recopying the original file from the CD-ROM.

Listening to the Audio Files

This section explains how to play the audio files using your computer. All audio files are in MP3 format. For example, "Interview with Attorney Janet Portman" is on the file "Interview.mp3."

Most computers come with a media player that plays MP3 files. You can listen to files that you have installed on your computer or directly from the CD-ROM. See below for further information on both.

The following are general instructions. Because every media player is different, refer to your media player's help files for more specific instructions. Please do not contact Nolo's technical support if you are having difficulty using your media player.

Playing the Audio Files Without Installing

If you don't want to copy 22 MB of audio files to your computer, you can play the CD-ROM on your computer. Here's how:

Windows

1. Insert the CD-ROM to view the **Welcome to Landlord Resources CD** window.
2. Click **Listen to Audio**.

If nothing happens when you insert the CD-ROM,

1. Double-click the **My Computer** icon.
2. Double-click the icon for the CD-ROM drive you inserted the CD-ROM into.
3. Double-click the file "Welcome. exe."

Macintosh

1. Insert the CD-ROM. (If the **Landlord Resources CD** window does not open, double-click the **Landlord Resources CD** icon).
2. Double-click the **Landlord Resources** folder.
3. Double-click the **Audio Resources** folder.
4. Double-click the audio file you want to hear.

Listening to Audio Files You've Installed on Your Computer

1. Windows users can open a file by selecting its "shortcut."
    i. Click the Windows **Start** button.
    ii. Open the **Programs** folder.
    iii. Open the **Landlord Resources** folder.
    iv. Open the **Audio Resources** folder.
    v. Click the shortcut to the file you want to work with.
2. Both Windows and Macintosh users can open a file by double-clicking it.
    i. Use **My Computer** or **Windows Explorer** (Windows 2000, XP, or Vista) or the **Finder** (Macintosh) to go to the **Landlord Resources** folder.
    ii. Double-click the file you want to open.

3. Windows and Macintosh users can open a file from within their word processor.
    i. Open your word processor.
    ii. Go to the **File** menu and choose the **Open** command. This opens a dialog box.
    iii. Select the location and name of the file. (You will navigate to the version of the **Landlord Resources** folder that you've installed on your computer.)

Files on the CD-ROM

The following form files are in rich text format (RTF):

Form Title	File Name
Acceptance Letter	Acceptance.rtf
Notice of Denial Based on Credit Report or Other Information	DenialNotice.rtf
Application Review	ApplicationReview.rtf
Checklist for Repairs or Refurbishing	ChecklistRepairs.rtf
Consent to Contact References and Perform Credit Check	ConsentCredit.rtf
Consent to Criminal and Background Check	ConsentBackground.rtf
Cosigner Agreement	CosignerAgreement.rtf
Credit Check Payment	CreditCheckPayment.rtf
Credit Report Evaluation	CreditEvaluation.rtf
Denial of Request for Further Information	DenialInformation.rtf
Departing Tenant's Questionnaire	DepartingTenant.rtf
Employer Referral Amendment	EmployerAmendment.rtf
Holding Deposit Agreement and Receipt	HoldingDeposit.rtf
How to Show This Rental Worksheet	ShowRental.rtf
Landlord's Plans to Advertise and Show Rental	LandlordsPlans.rtf
Legal Status in the United States	LegalStatus.rtf
Letter of Recommendation	Recommendation.rtf
Marketing Worksheet	Marketing.rtf
Move-Out Letter	MoveOut.rtf
Notice of Conditional Acceptance Based on Credit Report or Other Information	AcceptanceCredit.rtf
Notice of Conditional Acceptance, Cosigner Required	AcceptanceCosigner.rtf
Pre- and Post-Tour Survey with Current Tenants	TourSurvey.rtf
Pre-Move-Out Inspection Report	InspectionReport.rtf

Form Title	File Name
Pre-Move-Out Inspection Request	InspectionRequest.rtf
Pre-Move-Out Inspection Request, California	InspectionCalifornia.rtf
Receipt for Credit Check Fee	ReceiptCreditCheck.rtf
Rejection Letter	RejectionLetter.rtf
Rental Application Instructions	Instructions.rtf
Rental Application	Application.rtf
Rental Policies	RentalPolicies.rtf
Rental Property Comparison Chart	PropertyComparison.rtf
Rental Property Fact Sheet	FactSheet.rtf
Response to Request for Further Information	Response.rtf
Showing Checklist	ShowingChecklist.rtf
Tenant Information Sheet	TenantSheet.rtf
Tenant References	TenantReferences.rtf
Tenant Referral Program	ReferralProgram.rtf
Tenant-Screening Firms Comparison	FirmsComparison.rtf
Visitor Information	VisitorInformation.rtf
Visitor Log for Open House	VisitorLog.rtf

The following audio files are in audio (mp3) format:	
Segment One: Complaints and Concerns	Segment1-Complaints.mp3
Segment Two: Discrimination	Segment2-Discrimination.mp3
Segment Three: Challenging Perks from the Competition	Segment3-Challenges.mp3
Segment Four: Occupancy Issues	Segment4-Occupancy.mp3
Segment Five: The Mistake of Puffing	Segment5-Puffing.mp3
Interview with Attorney Janet Portman	Interview.mp3

Index

NOLO Keep Up to Date

 Go to **Nolo.com/newsletter** to sign up for free newsletters and discounts on Nolo products.

- **Nolo Briefs.** Our monthly email newsletter with great deals and free information.

- **Nolo's Special Offer.** A monthly newsletter with the biggest Nolo discounts around.

- **BizBriefs.** Tips and discounts on Nolo products for business owners and managers.

- **Landlord's Quarterly.** Deals and free tips just for landlords and property managers, too.

 And don't forget to check **Nolo.com/updates** to find free legal updates to this book.

Let Us Hear From You

 Comments on this book? We want to hear 'em. Email us at feedback@nolo.com.

FIND2

NOLO Catalog

BUSINESS	PRICE	CODE
Business Buyout Agreements (Book w/CD-ROM)	$49.99	BSAG
The California Nonprofit Corporation Kit (Binder w/CD-ROM)	$69.99	CNP
California Workers' Comp	$34.99	WORK
The Complete Guide to Buying a Business (Book w/CD-ROM)	$24.99	BUYBU
The Complete Guide to Selling a Business (Book w/CD-ROM)	$34.99	SELBU
Consultant & Independent Contractor Agreements (Book w/CD-ROM)	$34.99	CICA
The Corporate Records Handbook (Book w/CD-ROM)	$69.99	CORMI
Create Your Own Employee Handbook (Book w/CD-ROM)	$49.99	EMHA
Dealing With Problem Employees	$44.99	PROBM
Deduct It! Lower Your Small Business Taxes	$34.99	DEDU
The eBay Business Start-Up Kit (Book w/CD-ROM)	$24.99	EBIZ
Effective Fundraising for Nonprofits	$24.99	EFFN
The Employer's Legal Handbook	$49.99	EMPL
The Essential Guide to Family & Medical Leave (Book w/CD-ROM)	$49.99	FMLA
The Essential Guide to Federal Employment Laws	$44.99	FEMP
The Essential Guide to Workplace Investigations (Book w/CD-ROM)	$39.99	NVST
Every Nonprofit's Guide to Publishing	$29.99	EPNO
Form a Partnership(Book w/CD-ROM)	$39.99	PART
Hiring Your First Employee: A Step-by-Step Guide	$24.99	HEMP
Form Your Own Limited Liability Company (Book w/CD-ROM)	$44.99	LIAB
Home Business Tax Deductions: Keep What You Earn	$34.99	DEHB
How to Form a Nonprofit Corporation (Book w/CD-ROM)—National Edition	$49.99	NNP
How to Form a Nonprofit Corporation in California (Book w/CD-ROM)	$49.99	NON
How to Form Your Own California Corporation (Binder w/CD-ROM)	$59.99	CACI
How to Form Your Own California Corporation (Book w/CD-ROM)	$39.99	CCOR
How to Run a Thriving Business: Strategies for Success & Satisfaction	$19.99	THRV
How to Write a Business Plan (Book w/CD-ROM)	$34.99	SBS
Incorporate Your Business (Book w/CD-ROM)—National Edition	$49.99	NIBS
Investors in Your Backyard (Book w/CD-ROM)	$24.99	FINBUS
The Job Description Handbook (Book w/CD-ROM)	$29.99	JOB
Legal Guide for Starting & Running a Small Business	$34.99	RUNS
Legal Forms for Starting & Running a Small Business (Book w/CD-ROM)	$29.99	RUNSF
LLC or Corporation?	$24.99	CHENT
The Manager's Legal Handbook	$39.99	ELBA
Marketing Without Advertising	$20.00	MWAD
Music Law: How to Run Your Band's Business (Book w/CD-ROM)	$39.99	ML
Negotiate the Best Lease for Your Business	$24.99	LESP

Order anytime at WWW.NOLO.COM
Call 800-728-3555 • Mail or fax the order form in this book

Prices subject to change.

Nolo's Crash Course in Small Business Basics (Audiobook on 5 CDs) .... $34.99 ABBIZ
Nolo's Quick LLC .... $29.99 LLCQ
Nonprofit Meetings, Minutes & Records (Book w/CD-ROM) .... $39.99 NORM
The Performance Appraisal Handbook (Book w/CD-ROM) .... $29.99 PERF
The Progressive Discipline Handbook (Book w/CD-ROM) .... $34.99 SDHB
Retire—And Start Your Own Business (Book w/CD-ROM) .... $34.99 BOSS
Small Business in Paradise: Working for Yourself in a Place You Love .... $19.99 SPAR
The Small Business Start-Up Kit (Book w/CD-ROM)—National Edition .... $29.99 SMBU
The Small Business Start-Up Kit for California (Book w/CD-ROM) .... $29.99 OPEN
Smart Policies for Workplace Technologies: Email, Blogs,
   Cell Phones & More (Book w/CD-ROM) .... $29.99 TECH
Starting & Building a Nonprofit: A Practical Guide (Book w/CD-ROM) .... $29.99 SNON
Starting & Running a Successful Newsletter or Magazine .... $29.99 MAG
Tax Deductions for Professionals .... $34.99 DEPO
Tax Savvy for Small Business .... $36.99 SAVVY
The Work From Home Handbook .... $19.99 USHOM
Wow! I'm in Business .... $21.99 WHOO
Working for Yourself: Law & Taxes for Independent Contractors,
   Freelancers & Consultants .... $39.99 WAGE
Working With Independent Contractors (Book w/CD-ROM) .... $34.99 HICI
Your Limited Liability Company (Book w/CD-ROM) .... $49.99 LOP
Your Rights in the Workplace .... $29.99 YRW

CONSUMER

How to Win Your Personal Injury Claim .... $34.99 PICL
Nolo's Encyclopedia of Everyday Law .... $29.99 EVL
Nolo's Guide to California Law .... $34.99 CLAW
Your Little Legal Companion (Hardcover) .... $9.95 ANNIS

ESTATE PLANNING & PROBATE

8 Ways to Avoid Probate .... $21.99 PRAV
The Busy Family's Guide to Estate Planning (Book w/CD) .... $24.99 FAM
Estate Planning Basics .... $21.99 ESPN
Estate Planning for Blended Families: Providing for Your Spouse & Children in a
   Second Marriage .... $34.99 SMAR
The Executor's Guide: Settling a Loved One's Estate or Trust .... $39.99 EXEC
Get It Together: Organize Your Records (Book w/CD-ROM) .... $21.99 GET
How to Probate an Estate in California .... $49.99 PAE
Make Your Own Living Trust (Book w/CD-ROM) .... $39.99 LITR
Nolo's Simple Will Book (Book w/CD-ROM) .... $36.99 SWIL
Plan Your Estate .... $44.99 NEST
Quick & Legal Will Book (Book w/CD-ROM) .... $21.99 QUIC
Special Needs Trusts: Protect Your Child's Financial Future (Book w/CD-ROM) .... $34.99 SPNT

FAMILY MATTERS

GOING TO COURT

HOMEOWNERS, LANDLORDS & TENANTS

First-Time Landlord: Your Guide to Renting Out a Single-Family Home.......................... $19.99 USFTL
For Sale by Owner in California (Book w/CD-ROM).. $29.99 FSBO
How to Buy a House in California .... $34.99 BHCA
Leases & Rental Agreements (Book w/CD-ROM) .... $29.99 LEAR
Neighbor Law: Fences, Trees, Boundaries & Noise.. $29.99 NEI
Nolo's Essential Guide to Buying Your First Home (Book w/CD-ROM) .... $24.99 HTBH
Renters' Rights: The Basics .... $24.99 RENT
Saving the Family Cottage: A Guide to Succession Planning for Your
    Cottage, Cabin, Camp or Vacation Home.. $29.99 COTT
Selling Your House in a Tough Market: 10 Strategies That Work.................................... $24.99 DOWN

IMMIGRATION

Becoming a U.S. Citizen: A Guide to the Law, Exam & Interview .... $24.99 USCIT
Fiancé & Marriage Visas.. $34.99 IMAR
How to Get a Green Card .... $29.99 GRN
Student & Tourist Visas.. $29.99 ISTU
U.S. Immigration Made Easy .... $39.99 IMEZ

MONEY MATTERS

101 Law Forms for Personal Use (Book w/CD-ROM) .... $29.99 SPOT
The Busy Family's Guide to Money .... $19.99 USMONY
Chapter 13 Bankruptcy: Keep Your Property & Repay Debts Over Time........................ $39.99 CHB
Credit Repair (Book w/CD-ROM) .... $24.99 CREP
Easy Ways to Lower Your Taxes .... $19.99 USLOT
The Foreclosure Survival Guide .... $21.99 FIFO
How to File for Chapter 7 Bankruptcy... $29.99 HFB
The New Bankruptcy: Will It Work for You?... $24.99 FIBA
Nolo's Guide to Social Security Disability (Book w/CD-ROM) .... $29.99 QSS
The Sharing Solution: How to Prosper by Sharing Resources, Simplifying Your Life &
    Building Community.. $24.99 SHAR
Solve Your Money Troubles: Debt, Credit & Bankruptcy .... $24.99 MT
Stand Up to the IRS... $29.99 SIRS
Stopping Identity Theft: 10 Easy Steps to Security .... $19.99 USID
Surviving an IRS Tax Audit .... $24.95 SAUD

RETIREMENT & SENIORS

Get a Life: You Don't Need a Million to Retire Well.. $24.99 LIFE
IRAs, 401(k)s & Other Retirement Plans: Taking Your Money Out............................... $34.99 RET
Long-Term Care: How to Plan & Pay for It .... $24.99 ELD
Nolo's Essential Retirement Tax Guide .... $24.99 RTAX
Retire Happy: What You Can Do Now to Guarantee a Great Retirement .... $19.99 USRICH
Social Security, Medicare & Goverment Pensions... $29.99 SOA
Work Less, Live More: The Way to Semi-Retirement .... $17.99 RECL
The Work Less, Live More Workbook (Book w/CD).. $19.99 RECW

PATENTS AND COPYRIGHTS

SOFTWARE

Call or check our website at www.nolo.com for special discounts on Software!

Special Upgrade Offer

Save 35% on the latest edition of your Nolo book

Because laws and legal procedures change often, we update our books regularly. To help keep you up-to-date, we are extending this special upgrade offer. Cut out and mail the title portion of the cover of your old Nolo book and we'll give you 35% off the retail price of the New Edition of that book when you purchase directly from Nolo. This offer is to individuals only. Prices and offer subject to change without notice.

Order Form

Name	
Address	
City	
State, Zip	
Daytime Phone	
E-mail	

Our "No-Hassle" Guarantee

Return anything you buy directly from Nolo for any reason and we'll cheerfully refund your purchase price. No ifs, ands or buts.

☐ Check here if you do not wish to receive mailings from other companies

Item Code	Quantity	Item	Unit Price	Total Price

Method of payment

☐ Check   ☐ VISA
☐ American Express
☐ MasterCard
☐ Discover Card

Subtotal	
Add your local sales tax (California only)	
Shipping: RUSH $12, Basic $6 (See below)	
"I bought 2, ship it to me FREE!" (Ground shipping only)	
TOTAL	

Account Number .

Expiration Date

Signature

Shipping and Handling

Rush Delivery—Only $12

We'll ship any order to any street address in the U.S. by UPS 2nd Day Air* for only $12!

* Order by 9:30 AM Pacific Time and get your order in 2 business days. Orders placed after 9:30 AM Pacific Time will arrive in 3 business days. P.O. boxes and S.F. Bay Area use basic shipping. Alaska and Hawaii use 2nd Day Air or Priority Mail.

Basic Shipping—$6

Use for P.O. Boxes, Northern California and Ground Service.

Allow 1-2 weeks for delivery.

U.S. addresses only.

For faster service, use your credit card and our toll-free numbers

Call our customer service group Monday thru Friday 7am to 6pm PST

 Phone
1-800-728-3555

 Fax
1-800-645-0895

 Mail
Nolo
950 Parker St.
Berkeley, CA 94710

NOLO

Order 24 hours a day @ www.nolo.com